Praise for *The Spy Who Loved*

"Admirable and overdue."
—Ben Macintyre,
The New York Times Book Review

"Well written and thoroughly researched . . . One British functionary described her dispatches from the field as 'good reading.' The same can be said of Ms. Mulley's biography of this extraordinary woman."
—*The Wall Street Journal*

"This summer's most spellbinding saga of espionage and adventure."
—*Vogue.com*

"A stunning biographical achievement."
—Alison Weir,
New York Times bestselling author of
Innocent Traitor and *The Lady Elizabeth*

"While a few books about Christine have emerged in the intervening decades, only now, with the publication of Clare Mulley's scrupulously researched and expertly rendered biography, do we have a multi-dimensional, uncensored, impartial portrait of the legendary spy—said to be Churchill's favorite—whose forty-four-year existence was filled with more eye-popping adventures than we'd find plausible in any novel or movie. . . . Outstanding."
—*The Daily Beast*

"Better than any James Bond novel . . . The most frank and comprehensive tribute yet to Christine . . . A thrilling account."
—Laura Miller, *Salon*

"Impressively researched, and absolutely fascinating. Christine Granville is one of those women you can't help wishing you'd met in real life."
—Jojo Moyes, *New York Times* bestselling
author of *Me Before You*

"Excellent. . . . A romping adventure of international espionage, grand plots and sex, with the fate of the world hanging in the balance. . . .

Careful research has created sustained tension, vitality, and immediacy which are truly page-turning."

—Gordon Thomas, bestselling author of
The Pope's Jews and *Gideon's Spies*

"Brings alive a glamorous, swashbuckling heroine."

—*The Sunday Times* (UK)

"Engrossing biography details the high-voltage life of one of Britain's most remarkable female spies . . . Fascinating."

—*Mail on Sunday* (UK)

"An astonishing story, brilliantly told. If a Hollywood movie isn't made about Christine Granville's remarkable life, I'd be amazed."

—Charles Cumming, award-winning author of
A Foreign Country

"[A] splendid book . . . Christine Granville remains as alive, well, and compelling as ever: a figure of radiant magnetism, ruthless determination and a courage that—as several of them attested—could make a strong man shudder." —*The Telegraph* (UK), Five Stars (out of five)

"I enjoyed and admired *The Spy Who Loved*. . . . A really gripping account of the remarkable Christine Granville." —Simon Mawer, bestselling author of *Trapeze* and *The Glass Room*

"Assiduously researched, passionately written and highly atmospheric biography . . . Not just the story of a uniquely brave and complicated patriot, but also a scholarly and tautly written account of secret operations in occupied Europe." —*The Economist*

ALSO BY CLARE MULLEY

The Woman Who Saved the Children

CLARE MULLEY

THE SPY WHO LOVED

The Secrets and Lives of Christine Granville

ST. MARTIN'S GRIFFIN ☙ NEW YORK

THE SPY WHO LOVED. Copyright © 2012 by Clare Mulley. All rights reserved.
Printed in the United States of America. For information, address St. Martin's Press,
175 Fifth Avenue, New York, N.Y. 10010.

The picture acknowledgments on p. 412 constitute an extension of this copyright page.

www.stmartins.com

The Library of Congress has cataloged the hardcover edition as follows:

Mulley, Clare.
 The spy who loved : the secrets and lives of Christine Granville / Clare Mulley.—1st
U.S. edition.
 p. cm.
 Includes bibliographical references and index.
 ISBN 978-1-250-03032-0 (hardcover)
 ISBN 978-1-250-03033-7 (e-book)
 1. Skarbek, Krystyna, 1908–1952. 2. Women spies—Great Britain—Biography.
3. Spies—Great Britain—Biography. 4. World War, 1939–1945—Secret service—
Great Britain. I. Title.
 D810.S8G727 2013
 940.54'8641092—dc23
 [B]
 2013010210

ISBN 978-1-250-04976-6 (trade paperback)

St. Martin's Griffin books may be purchased for educational, business,
or promotional use. For information on bulk purchases, please contact
Macmillan Corporate and Premium Sales Department at 1-800-221-7945,
extension 5442, or write specialmarkets@macmillan.com.

First published in Great Britain by Pan Books, an imprint of Pan Macmillan,
a division of Macmillan Publishers Ltd

10 9 8 7 6 5 4 3 2

To my parents, Gill and Derek Mulley,
who watched the sky turn red over London during the Blitz, and have
reached out for better international relations ever since.

'A few rare people, who live for action,
are never in any doubt what they should do.
For them capture is always unbearable and escape
their only interest from the start.'

AIDAN CRAWLEY[1]

'In the high ranges of Secret Service work
the actual facts in many cases were in every respect
equal to the most fantastic inventions of
romance and melodrama.'

WINSTON CHURCHILL[2]

Contents

Thank you Ian, for your kindness and cleverness, and the wonderful Kate, Gill and Derek Mulley, Michelle Wheeler and George Morley, for all their excellent editing. Thanks also to my agent, Andrew Lownie, who first introduced me to Christine.

This book could not have been written without the generous support of many people who knew Christine and her circle, and their relatives, including Countess Maryś Skarbek and Count Andrew Skarbek, Elizabeth Skarbek, Maria Pienkowska, Count Jan Ledóchowski, Christine Isabelle Cole, Suzanna Gayford, Christopher Kasparek, Jane Bigman-Hartley, Ann Bonsor, Julian de Boscari, Tim Buckmaster, Harriet Crawley, Diana Hall, Eva Hryniewicz, Daniel Huillier, Princess Renata Lubomirski, Zbigniew Mieczkowski, Steven Muldowney, Izabela Muszkowska, Countess Jolanta Mycielska, Maria Nurowska, Ann O'Regan, Margaret Pawley, Julian Pope, Ivor Porter, Noreen Riols, Teresa Robinska, Krystyna Sass, Matt Smolenski, Tom Sweet-Escott, Ada Tarnowska, Andrew Tarnowski, Dorothy Wakely, Michael Ward, Joanna Cammaerts-Wey, Katharine Whitehorn, Sarah Willert and Virginia Worsley. Thank you all for taking the time to share your memories and family stories.

My very sincere thanks are also due to the very knowledgeable and generous Dr Jeffrey Bines, oral historian Martyn Cox, the late SOE historian M. R. D. Foot, former coder Maureen Gadd, Nicholas Gibbs, Maciek and Iwona Helfer, Major Chris Hunter, Krystyna Kaplan, SOE historian Steven Kippax, Michal Komar, Captain Kozac, Christine's Polish biographer Colonel Jan Larecki, Warsaw genealogist Tomasz Lenczewski, Eugenia Maresch, Dr Michael Peske, Monika Plichta, Dominik Rettinger-Wieczorkowski, Ian Sayer, Albertine Sharples, Dr David Stafford, Dr Penny Starns, Benita Stoney, Bęczkowice parish priest Henryk Szymanski, Anna Teicher, and film director Mieczysława Wazacz, as well as the archivists and historians at the British Library; the Imperial War Museum; the Liddell Hart Centre for Military Archives, King's College London; Le Musée de la Résistance de Vassieux-en-Vercors, France; the Museum of Pawiak Prison; the National Archives, Kew; the Polish Underground Movement Study Trust, London; the Warsaw Royal Castle archive; the Warsaw Uprising Museum; and specifically to Susan Tomkins, archivist at Beaulieu; Duncan Stuart, former chairman of the Special Forces Club's Historical Sub-Committee; Dr Władysław Bułhak and Natalia Jarska at the Institute of National Remembrance, Warsaw; and Krzysztof Barbarski and Dr Andrzej Suchcitz at the Polish Institute and Sikorski Museum, London.

Legend:

- Territories incorporated into the Reich
- General Government
- Soviet Occupation
- To Lithuania

- Pre-war Poland
- Post-war Poland
- Pre-war country boundaries
- Other boundaries

Baltic Sea

Königsberg

Danzig

EAST PRUSSIA

Vistula

POLA

Berlin

GERMANY

Warsaw

Łódź

Trzepnica

Breslau

Częstochowa

Kraków

Vistula

Prague

CZECHOSLOVAKIA

Zakopané

AUSTRIA

Vienna

HUNGARY

POLAND, BEFORE AND AFTER WWII

LITHUANIA

Kaunas•

•Katyn

•Vilnius

SOVIET UNION

N D

Bug

San

•Lwów

TRANSCARPATHIA
annexed by the
Soviet Union, 1945

ROMANIA

N

120 kilometres

75 miles

THE ROUTE OF THE OPEL, 1941

FINLAND

Helsinki
Leningrad
Stockholm

SOVIET UNION

Moscow

REICHSKOMMISSARIAT OSTLAND

Warsaw

REICHSKOMMISSARIAT UKRAINE

Stalingrad

EMPIRE

Zakopane

SLOVAKIA

HUNGARY
Budapest

ROMANIA

Belgrade

SERBIA

M.

BULGARIA

ALB.
Tirana

Sofia

Black Sea

Istanbul

Ankara

TURKEY

GREECE
Athens

Aleppo

SYRIA

CYPRUS

LEBANON
Beirut

Damascas

Mediterranean Sea

Haifa

PALESTINE
Jerusalem

Amman

IRAQ

JORDON

EGYPT
Cairo

Legend

☐ Allied countries

☐ Occupied Allied Countries

☐ Axis Countries

☐ Axis held territories

☐ Neutral countries

╍╍╍ Route of the Opel

━·━·━ Country boundaries

Preface: Stories of Trust and Betrayal

In 1973, twenty-one years after Christine Granville's tragic death, two of her lovers entered into a studiously polite, and short-lived, correspondence. The Polish count Wladimir Ledóchowski thanked his compatriot and former fellow special agent Andrzej Kowerski for his 'willingness to cooperate' in a book about Christine. Ledóchowski wrote optimistically that he took Kowerski's cautious promise of help 'as a token of your trust'.[1] But there was little real trust between these old rivals, and the rest of the letter was set out in neat points, clarifying their agreed approval process for any manuscript to be written about Christine.

Ledóchowski had suggested that he and Kowerski set up what he called a 'Club of the Saved', composed exclusively of those men whose lives had been saved by Christine, several of whom, he had added 'with a twinkle in his eye', had been saved in more ways than one.[2] By his tally there were six potential members who had 'jumped . . . into Christine's life, like parachuters into unknown territory', including himself and Kowerski representing Poland, three British agents including the decorated hero Francis Cammaerts, and a French officer.[3] Ledóchowski conceded that there was little hope of weaving their experiences into a 'logical whole', since: 'I doubt you should look to logic to explain any girl, particularly one like Christine.'[4] But perhaps, from their collective memories, Christine might emerge 'not as a performer of illustrious feats' but, he hoped, 'just as a person'.[5]

Ledóchowski was now surprised to learn that there was already a Christine-focused gentlemen's club in place, with a slightly different remit, and that membership had not been extended to him. Kowerski and four wartime friends, Cammaerts, John Roper,

Patrick Howarth and Michal Gradowski (aka Michael Lis), had set up the 'Panel to Protect the Memory of Christine Granville' soon after her death in 1952.[6] Ledóchowski felt that his life had been irreconcilably intertwined with Christine's, but he had always known that he was not the only person to claim a special relationship with her, nor even the first to hope to write about her. Kowerski's 'panel' had come together when the newspapers were having a field day with stories about the Polish beauty queen who had served as a British special agent. 'We, her friends, did not want her to become a press sensation,' Cammaerts later explained. 'We tried to defend her reputation.'[7] Yet, as Ledóchowski's son later wrote, 'the death of heroes is not usually followed by panels to protect their memories and stop books about them'.[8] Several articles and biographies were quashed but, within months, another of Christine's former friends and colleagues, Bill Stanley Moss, whose daughter had been named in Christine's honour, had serialized her life for the news weekly *Picture Post*, under the title 'Christine the Brave'.[9]

Moss, who had already published an account of one of his own wartime SOE missions in the book *Ill Met By Moonlight*, recognized a good story and was planning a full biography and screenplay for a biopic to star Winston Churchill's actress daughter Sarah.* Asked why she had chosen the role, Churchill replied it was because Christine was her father's favourite spy, further stoking the burgeoning legend.† During his research in 1953, the year after Christine died, Moss had got in touch with Ledóchowski. 'It is probably impossible,' Ledóchowski had written back, 'if Christine's remark-

* Bill Stanley Moss's book *Ill Met By Moonlight* was published in 1950. The Pinewood Studio film based on it, starring Dirk Bogarde, was released in 1957. *Odette*, a biopic of Odette Sansom, had been released in 1950, and *Carve Her Name with Pride*, based on R. J. Minney's book of the same title about Violette Szabo, came out in 1958.

† Zofia Tarnowska, Bill Stanley Moss's wife and a good friend of Christine's, told this story in 2001. As no direct pronouncements by Churchill on Christine are known, this seems to be the source of the much-disputed line that Christine was Churchill's 'favourite spy'. However, Kurt D. Singer, who claimed he knew Christine, also recorded that 'Winston Churchill personally praised her and thanked her'. See his *Spies and Traitors* (1953), p. 201.

able character is to be properly depicted, to picture her as an angel of virtue, to desexualise her. On the other hand this rather embarrassing *for Andrew* situation can, in my opinion, not be reflected in your book'.[10] Moss never resolved the issues and the project was shelved.

Twenty years later Ledóchowski decided to pick up the torch and was seeking Kowerski's support for his own biographical project. The last clause in the agreement between them specified that, 'in case of condemnation of the manuscript', the book was not to be published.[11] Although Moss's widow, Christine's friend Zofia Tarnowska Moss, felt that Ledóchowski's manuscript was written 'very tenderly', she was not in the club, and four of the five members of Kowerski's all-male panel rejected the draft out of hand.[12] 'So outraged' were they, that they even appointed a lawyer ready to start a lawsuit.[13] Ledóchowski honoured his word, however, and his manuscript was never completed or published.

1: BORDERLANDS

Perhaps appropriately for a secret agent, the deceptions and confusions that surround Christine's life start with her birth.* One story has it that Christine was born at the Skarbek family estate on a stormy spring evening in 1915, and that her arrival coincided with the appearance of Venus, the evening star, in the sky. As a result she was nicknamed 'Vesperale'. In an even more romantic version of events, she was born 'in the wild borderlands between Poland and Russia', to a family that was noble, 'tough, used to invasions, warfare, Cossacks, bandits and wolves'.[1] In fact Christine arrived in the world on Friday 1 May 1908. One of her father's childhood nicknames for her was 'little star', but she was born at her mother's family house on Zielna Street, in central Warsaw, now the capital of Poland. Then, however, Warsaw was technically in Russia. Poland as we know it today was not a recognized country: apart from a brief reappearance, courtesy of Napoleon, for more than a century Poland had been partitioned into three sections, each of them subsumed into the empires of Russia, Austro-Hungary and Prussia. Christine was born into a family of aristocratic patriots, loyal to a country that would not officially exist again until she was ten years old.

She was a small and seemingly frail baby, so frail in fact that her parents feared for her life, and she was hastily baptized Maria Krystyna Janina Skarbek by a local priest less than two weeks after her birth. Five years later, Christine would go through the rite a second time in Bęczkowice, where her parents had moved in 1913.

* Although she was 'Krystyna' until 1941, to prevent confusion I consistently use her adopted name, 'Christine', of which, she later wrote, she was so proud.

The record of this second event has somehow survived in the local parish archive despite a series of wars and regime changes. Written in Russian, it was dated with the Russian Julian and Polish Gregorian calendars, as both the 17 and 30 November 1913.[2] The Church does not officially sanction second baptisms, but Christine's parents, one a rather lapsed Roman Catholic, the other a non-practising Jew, had long wanted a more elaborate celebration of their daughter's arrival than had been possible at her birth. Their move out of Warsaw had conveniently provided a new local parish priest with whom to make arrangements.

Two certificates of baptism, five years apart and showing three different dates, serve as notice for Christine's birth. But she has a single death certificate, part typed, part closely penned into the printed boxes of a Royal Borough of Kensington register office form. Here her given name is 'Christine Granville', her occupation is listed as 'former wife', and although the certificate is dated 1952, her age is recorded as just thirty-seven. Somewhere between 1908 and 1952, Warsaw and London, life and death, she had changed name and nationality, left two husbands and numerous lovers, won international honours but buried her career, and cut seven years from her life.

Christine's father, Count Jerzy Skarbek, was a charming man. Described by his cousins as darkly attractive with 'a seductive little moustache', and by his nieces as 'a very handsome man of patrician beauty', he had that enviable ability to be at once hugely popular among his male friends, and almost irresistibly attractive to women, who seemed to constantly surround him.[3] But the Count's dark good looks were matched by his dark intentions. He was the archetypal aristocratic cad and bounder.

Jerzy Skarbek led a privileged life, typical of the landed gentry and very far from the struggle for existence faced by much of the Polish population in the late nineteenth century. The Count had been a 'master' since childhood, accustomed to having a valet and a groom. It was part of the innate order of the world. And yet, arguably, Jerzy Skarbek was not a Count at all.

With the exception of some Lithuanian princely families, histor-

ically Poland's large enfranchised class, or 'szlachta', did not hold aristocratic titles. It was traditional for them to regard each other as equals, to be addressed as 'dear brother', and even – when Poland was still an independent country – to elect the Polish king. But many of the ancient nobility became so impoverished that they were effectively peasants with coats-of-arms. And many families who sported illustrious titles, as opposed to simply having noble names, owed these to their imperial overlords, who were, as a rule, buying favours. It was the Russian tsar Nicholas I who granted the Skarbeks' title in the mid-nineteenth century. The fact that Jerzy Skarbek was not descended from this branch of the family made little difference to his social status. He was known to be a member of one of the oldest families in Poland, and was certainly accepted as an aristocrat in the circles that he believed mattered.*

Jerzy Skarbek certainly felt the honour of his family keenly, and any perceived slight rankled. As a child Christine remembered him rising from the table when a guest claimed descent from the last Polish king, Stanisław August Poniatowski. '[And I am] descended from a cobbler!' Jerzy responded with some style, referring to the medieval Kraków cobbler who had killed the fabled Wawel dragon by enticing it to devour a sheepskin stuffed with sulphur, and from whom he claimed descent.[4] Few families boast a dragon-killer among their ancestors, let alone one who then married a king's daughter. There were plenty more such stories in which the Skarbeks' history was intertwined with Polish legends, and these would later fuel Christine's own deeply held sense of personal, family and national pride. The one piece of jewellery that she wore throughout her life was not a wedding ring, but a Skarbek signet ring. This was designed with a slice of iron embedded in its face to commemorate the defiant eleventh-century Skarbek who would not bow to a German emperor for all his war chests of gold. Instead the proud

* Jerzy Skarbek referred to himself as Count, and was named as such in his press obituary and on his tombstone. Christine listed her parents as Count and Countess Skarbek on her British Certificate of Naturalisation, dated December 1946, and elsewhere. For Polish genealogy and titles see Tomasz Lenczewski, 'The Marriage of Coats of Arms and Accounts', *Rzeczpospolita*, 22 VII (2008).

Pole defiantly tossed his gold ring into the German coffers, shouting, 'Let gold eat gold, we Poles love iron!' The insulted emperor was later routed in a great battle when Polish swords indeed proved their might over the mercenary imperial German forces.

Not all notable Skarbeks had been so warlike, however. The nineteenth-century count Fryderyck Florian Skarbek was a highly respected economist, historian, author and social and political activist who, as president of the Charities Council, had introduced many important social reforms. Count Fryderyck had grown up on the family estate of Zelazowa Wola in the flat but not particularly productive plains west of Warsaw, where he was tutored by a distant relative called Nicholas Chopin. The estate was not hugely rich, and the house itself was quite modest, with the traditional long stretch of low rooms flanking a four-column portico entrance with balcony above. Despite the grand piano in the drawing room, it was essentially a comfortable family home, with geese and ducks free to wander on the porch. When the tutor's son was born in 1810, he was named after the count, who had sensibly been invited to be the boy's godfather. Fryderyck Chopin's first printed work, a polonaise, would be dedicated 'to Her Excellency Countess Victoria Skarbek, composed by Fryderyck Chopin, a musician aged eight'.[5] Count Fryderyck probably paid for the piece to be published, which would account for its dedication to his sister, and he went on to be one of Chopin's earliest and most ardent supporters. The Skarbek family remained immensely proud of the connection, especially when, after Chopin's death in 1849, he was widely regarded as the embodiment of Poland's nationalist politics and poetic spirit.

Jerzy Skarbek had inherited a noble name, a rich family history, and little sense of restraint. The Skarbeks owned acres of land, an assortment of houses, a collection of farms, and stables full of thoroughbred horses, but by his mid-twenties Jerzy's indulgence in wine and women, roulette and racing had quickly diminished his income. In 1898 his family arranged for him to marry an exceedingly wealthy, clever and 'absolutely beautiful' Jewish banking heiress.[6] In December that year, Stefania Goldfeder, newly baptized, was delighted to be embraced into the fold of one of Poland's oldest

families. The marriage was solemnized in the rites of the Helvetic Reform Church, apparently acceptable to both the Roman Catholic Skarbeks and the Goldfeders, who were non-observant Jews.

The wedding caused a scandal, albeit a minor one. No one in Warsaw had any doubts about the bridegroom's motives, and there were some knowing smiles when the society pages chose to celebrate the Goldfeder family as belonging to 'a class of financiers actively involved in the task of the material reconstruction of our martyred nation'.[7] Jews, once sheltered by the Polish Commonwealth, had been heavily discriminated against by the Russian occupiers, and although there was a small assimilated Jewish intelligentsia, most Polish Jews spoke a different language, ate different food and wore different clothes. They were a source of curiosity, to be patronized or avoided. Even assimilated Jewish families were still subject to social ostracism, and if Jewish doctors and lawyers were popular it was partly because they brought with them a certain sort of professional distance. Once Jerzy and Stefania's wedding ceremony was over, the members of the nobility and those of 'the financial circles' went their own ways, each with good reason to frown upon the motives of the other in this union. But while it was said that Jerzy did not marry Stefania, but rather he married her money, it is perhaps equally true that Stefania married the noble Skarbek name. The following year Jerzy bought a grand country estate at Mlodzieszyn, in what is now eastern-central Poland, which he felt both befitted a married man of his station, and was far enough removed to soften some of the noisier Warsaw gossip.*[8]

The Goldfeders were not without their own conceits and connections, however, mostly among rich merchant bankers and industrialists. Christine would later laugh that while her Skarbek cousins had names reminiscent of the marble plaques adorning Warsaw's churches, the Goldfeder relatives were even better known, displayed as they were among the shop signs in Warsaw's most fashionable

* Jerzy Skarbek is listed as the landowner of the Wechadlow estate, in the Pinczo district, where Christine probably lived until she was three years old, when they moved to Trzepnica.

streets. The Goldfeder bank itself was a beautiful three-storey building, with French windows on the upper floors leading to balconies overlooking the broad streets in the centre of the city.* But the Goldfeders also had respectably cultured connections. Stefania had two younger brothers. One married the sister of André Citroën, the motor magnate; the other became the Polish honorary consul for Japan. Their mother, Roza Goldfeder, the unchallenged matriarch of the family, lived in considerable style between her houses in Warsaw and the country – a style that Stefania was keen to maintain. Stefania's furs and dresses were imported from Paul Poiret in Paris, her pleated negligees from Mario Fortuny in Venice. Guerlain supplied her perfume, as they had Queen Victoria's. Her eau de toilette came from Lubin, historic Paris perfumiers to the Empress Josephine, and to supplement her heirlooms, Stefania's jewels were created for her by Bulgari in Rome. All of this show Jerzy Skarbek understood. He too liked the fine things in life: his Bunting riding boots, 'for the hunt, polo and the park', were imported from London and Paris, and his bay rum hair tonic came from Vienna. Together Jerzy and Stefania toured Europe with a large retinue of servants, collecting small business cards and paying large bills.

However, beyond their love of luxury and deep respect for social status, the newly-weds had little in common. Not only was Stefania Jewish, she was also intelligent and well educated, having been immersed in European culture, and she was essentially kind-hearted and 'much respected and liked by everyone'.[9] One story has her arranging for the daughter of the family's cook to have a prosthetic leg fitted after discovering that the girl had been hidden away for fear that her parents might lose their jobs. She then employed the girl for many years. Once the newly-weds had returned to Poland, Stefania yearned for the peace in which to read literature and poetry, and the time to listen to music. She did not mind the country-house hunts and shooting parties, or even Jerzy's visits to

* The Warsaw address of the Goldfeder bank was ul. Zielna 45. It formed part of the ghetto border before it was destroyed during the war.

the casino, but she could not find lasting happiness with a husband who fundamentally did not respect her, and who refused to curb his womanizing upon marriage. But, so long as appearances were maintained and funds were available, Jerzy saw no reason to change his lifestyle to suit anyone other than himself.

Stefania, at least, was fulfilling her side of the marriage bargain. Having restored the family fortune, in 1900 she completed her duties by producing a Skarbek heir. But Jerzy was disappointed in his son, Andrzej, who seemed to lack his own robust constitution and lust for life. Perhaps most damningly, Andrzej was not keen on riding, and would shelter behind his mother's skirts at the very sound of approaching horses; whether it was the arrival of the horse or the rider that caused him most anxiety is not recorded. It would be another eight years before Stefania safely delivered Christine. Although slight enough to cause concern at her birth, and staying slender as she grew, Christine soon proved herself to be tough and strong-willed and was drawn at once to her powerful, charismatic father. Jerzy meanwhile liked to think that Christine, unlike his son, had inherited his Skarbek good looks. Delighted to see his reflection in his daughter, he gave her his almost exclusive affection, calling her his 'Happiness' and his 'Star'.

At the beginning of 1912, when Christine was three, Jerzy bought another manor house, this time at Trzepnica in the Łódź uplands whose rivers run into the Vistula. As Stefania was named joint owner in the deeds it is likely that the 200,000 roubles it took to buy the estate from a famous Polish opera singer came from the Goldfeder fortune. The Trzepnica house followed the traditional style, built in rendered brick, long and low, and given distinction by a colonnaded portico, under which the family's dogs would greet arriving guests, 'their eager paws leaving sandy imprints on their clothes'.[10]

The formal family rooms, with their polished parquet floors, ornate stucco ceilings and French windows, were heated by a huge and beautifully painted porcelain wood-burning stove. Family portraits in gilded frames, some adorned with heraldic coronets, covered the walls. It was all very fine, but Christine rarely gazed into her ancestors' eyes or sat in the Biedermeier chairs, and she learnt early

on not to risk setting even a vase of flowers on the rosewood-inlaid table from Zelazowa Wola, upon which her great-grandfather was said to have held the infant Chopin to be baptized. These rooms, filled in summer with a soft green light filtered through the maples beyond the windows, and in winter with 'the shadowless reflection of snow on the lawn', were Stefania's sanctuary, and held little appeal for her energetic daughter.[11] More fun were the annexes for guests, tutors and nurses, and the numerous kitchens and larders that kept the estate pretty much self-sufficient.

The house was surrounded by acres of beautiful gardens, the more formal lawns bordered by roses, flowering cherries, maples, and ancient oaks so large that four men clasping hands could not reach around them. Beyond, a meadow led to a series of paddocks, woods and farm fields, all with their own outbuildings, and all belonging to the manor. In fact the estate was so large that it contained three small villages: Trzepnica, Jelica, and, two kilometres away, Bęczkowice, the steeple of whose parish church could be seen, rising above the flat horizon, from the porch of the house.

For a few years Jerzy revelled in the role of local landowner, holding grand house parties, hunts, dinners and receptions for his two brothers and his sister, his distant but wealthy Skarbek cousins from Lwów, and his society friends. He would show Christine off at these occasions, at first proudly lifting his pretty dark-haired daughter high to the ceiling, or standing her on a table and asking her to sing to them. Later he enjoyed watching his guests choke back their often coarse vocabulary to fit the sudden presence of the young lady now curtsying before them, her almond-shaped eyes demurely lowered but still taking it all in. Their 'cogs were visibly screeching', Christine would later laugh.[12]

Despite such distractions, Jerzy quickly grew bored with his country seclusion, and was already tired of his socially questionable wife. Much as he loved his fiery young daughter, even Christine did not suffice to keep him home for long, and his visits to friends' estates and to Warsaw were ever extended. Even there he could not entirely disassociate himself from his wife. A scurrilous song popular in Warsaw at the time ran: 'Listen Count and take heed, not to step

into debt. It may land you in a stew, having as a wife, the daughter of a Jew.'[15] His response was to drink hard, and laugh harder. As a child Christine could never understand why people would laugh at her father's jokes recalling family stories about Chopin and causing hilarity with his imitations of Polish Jews speaking Polish, and yet when her grandparents spoke with the same accent it wasn't funny. And when his friends praised Jerzy as a master at 'little Jewish jokes', he would only reply darkly that he had paid dearly for the knowledge. Stefania responded by retreating increasingly to the sanctuary of her upstairs room, laid low with migraines.

Too young to understand the dynamic between her parents, Christine felt more and more irritated, and slightly embarrassed, by her mother and her constant indisposition. Her father, conversely, seemed strong, handsome and obviously wonderful. Widely adored but unconstrained by those around him, delighting in life and yet wearing it lightly, to Christine her father embodied the romantic, courageous and fiercely independent spirit of Poland. Spending time with Jerzy was exciting and challenging and yet, unlike Stefania, he never had quite enough time for his daughter. Christine was already developing deeply divided feelings towards her parents, and forming a complex picture of love, loyalty and courage.

When Jerzy was at Trzepnica, Christine led a charmed, and very privileged, childhood, basking in her father's attention, and supported behind the scenes by her mother's love and money. Bright, adventurous and supremely self-confident, she had quickly eclipsed the older but more gentle Andrzej in Jerzy's affections, and as a child she was indulged with every opportunity and freedom. In summer she roamed the estate from sunrise until dusk, spending hours trying to spot deer or buck, searching for wild strawberries or climbing the great oaks. In winter she would be ferried between the snow-covered trees in a sledge drawn by horses straining at their bits, the coachmen holding the reins taut and standing erect, or she would seek out warmth and stories in the stables or servants' quarters. Sometimes, for instance after the leatherworkers' annual call to carry out repairs to the harnesses, she might even receive a present, such as a whip or a riding crop.

Ignoring Stefania's protests, Jerzy mounted Christine on a pony almost before she could walk, teaching her to ride confidently astride a horse like a man. She also learnt to hold a gun, use a knife, and tend to the estate animals. Alike in many ways, father and daughter loved nature, above all sharing a passion for dogs and horses, with whom they seemed to have a deep natural connection. Christine was rarely without a hound at her heels, even – to her mother's chagrin – inside the house.

The first races Christine watched were dachshund 'steeplechases', set up among the topiary hedges on her aunt's sweeping lawns. But Jerzy was an enthusiastic horse-breeder whose colts ran on Warsaw's racetracks, and it was not long before Christine was racing first ponies, then her saddle-mare, Liza. She loved pleasing her father with each new achievement and soon learned to take pride in them herself. At one house party Jerzy walked his guests over the field to the stables, only to find that his fierce black stallion, Satan, who had thrown his last rider and broken the man's legs, was missing. The groom feared the horse must have been stolen, but after a while they noticed that Christine was missing too. Aged only twelve, she had saddled up the forbidden horse and was finally seen riding him back. Clearly, for Christine, there were already worse things than the risk of serious injury, such as being bored or perhaps being ignored. Later she would ride competitively with such success that one of Jerzy's younger friends, Colonel Bobinski, was reduced to unscrupulous tricks like distracting her horse by bringing out its stable-mate, to try to protect his bets. Christine just laughed at him. When she came in first her father would tell her not to take credit for her horse's victory, from which she understood that he was proud of her, but that she should also wear her pleasure as lightly as she took her knocks.

Christine always loved the exhilaration of competition, but she was equally happy riding out to inspect the Trzepnica fields with her father, and occasionally with her brother. She had quickly realized that with charm she could coax whatever she wanted from people. Animals responded to her. Land demanded greater respect. Like her father, she grew up to believe herself to be the lord, and

protector, of all she surveyed. But it was still the stables where she
felt most at ease. One afternoon in 1919 she showed off the Skarbek
stud to the young son of one of her father's friends, whom she had
been left to entertain while the adults talked horses, business and
politics. It was then, in the immediate aftermath of the First World
War, that a precocious eleven-year-old Christine first met Andrzej
Kowerski, a boy of seven, who had also been riding since the age
of three. Although not particularly notable at the time, it was a
meeting that they would later recall quite differently: she with some
amusement, he with a sense of the prophetic.

Two million Polish troops had fought with the various armies
of their three occupying powers in the First World War, sometimes
in opposing forces. Over half a million died. By then in his forties,
Jerzy Skarbek was too old to have been called up, but he celebrated
in style as the Russians were finally driven out of Warsaw in 1915,
when Christine was seven years old, and three years later when the
defeated Germans were also forced to withdraw. But although the
capital was quickly festooned in red and white flags, and Poland was
a nation once more, the end of the Great War did not mean the
end of the conflict.

In the winter of 1919 the Bolsheviks prepared to export their
revolution through Poland to Germany. By August the following
year, the Red Army had reached Warsaw's defences and defeat
seemed inevitable. But the Russian front collapsed in the face of a
daring assault led by the country's newly appointed regent, Józef
Piłsudski. In the 1880s Piłsudski had spent five years in Siberia
supplying Lenin's brother with explosives to throw at the tsar, but
he wasn't about to support Communism above the independence
of his own nation. His brilliant attack on the Red Army outside
Warsaw, which became known as the 'Miracle at the Vistula',
crippled the Russian forces and brought an unexpected and decisive
Polish victory. In Lenin's own words, the Bolsheviks 'suffered an
enormous defeat' which effectively ended Soviet hopes for a cascade
of Communist revolutions in Poland, Germany and other countries
economically devastated by the First World War. Piłsudski was,
in the words of one Polish historian, 'a national hero, embalmed in

the legend of a life of struggle for the freedom of Poland, embody-
ing rebellion as well as authority'.[14] This celebration of the Marshal,
as he became known, and all he stood for, made a deep impression
on Christine.

Despite the inevitable years of political instability and econ-
omic depression that followed as war-torn Poland rebuilt itself as
a cohesive nation, Warsaw quickly became one of the liveliest cities
in Europe. Music, film and theatre flourished. The aristocracy
might have lost many of their ranks and much of their property,
but in Warsaw they continued to live in high style, Jerzy among
them. One warm evening in 1920, he was distracted from a pro-
duction of *Tosca* by the stench emanating from a soldier in some
nearby seats. This young man was still in his uniform, with the
heavy leather boots that were worn not with socks but strips of
cloth, or webbing, wound round the feet. On his chest he wore
the Virtuti Militari, Poland's highest military honour. Noticing
that all the ladies nearby were turning their heads and covering
their noses, Jerzy stood up and announced that the smell of a
national hero was a perfume. He then invited the soldier to join
him for vodka after the performance. The young man's name was
Stanisław Rudziejewski and, only eight years older than Christine,
he was soon a firm favourite of both father and daughter, and
a regular at the Warsaw races and Trzepnica house parties. He
also became an early confidant of Christine's, and someone to
whom she would later turn in one of her greatest moments of
need.[15]

Jerzy Skarbek was not known for his piety, so when, in 1920, he
took Christine, then aged twelve, to Częstochowa at Jasna Gora,
the Polish equivalent of Lourdes, it was as much a statement of
patriotism as a journey of pilgrimage. Like thousands of others,
Jerzy was giving thanks for the 'Miracle at the Vistula'. Whatever
his motives, on arrival father and daughter did what every pilgrim
did: offered a bow to the icon of Our Lady of Czestochowa and a
nod to the priest, who then gave Christine a medal of the Madonna,
believed to protect worthy bearers from misfortune. The famous
Black Madonna of Częstochowa, 'Queen and Protector of Poland',

was brought to Poland from Jerusalem in 1382. According to legend, when it was stolen by Hussite plunderers just fifty years later, the horse carrying the icon refused to move. One of the thieves threw the painting to the ground, slashing it with his sword until it bled, whereupon he died in agony on the ground beside the bleeding image. Terrified, the other Hussites retreated. Christine treasured the medal, revealing perhaps a faith, or an inner vulnerability, that she otherwise chose to keep well hidden.

In 1921 Poland signed a peace treaty with Russia and the Ukraine, defining her eastern boundaries. Anticipating a period of stability, Jerzy and Stefania sent Christine hundreds of miles away to a well-known convent boarding school in Jazłowiec, a town that had been won for Poland with, it was believed, the help of the Blessed Virgin, after a long and bloody battle between Poland and the Ukraine.* Christine was fourteen, but as she was starting school two years later than most of her peers she was put into a class of twelve-year-olds. It was an inauspicious start. She was clever. She quickly excelled in French, the language in which the nuns took classes and corresponded with parents, and which well-educated Poles spoke amongst themselves when hoping to prevent their children from eavesdropping. She also enjoyed Latin, maths, drawing and singing, and was often top of her class in history, geography, nature studies and sport – all subjects that would stand her in good stead later in life. However, not used to having to toe the line, follow routines, or take instruction, Christine was naturally indisciplined, fractious and often bored. The school did not cater for this type of clever but 'difficult' child.

Established for the daughters of the Polish aristocracy, while their brothers were tutored at home or educated at militaristic boys' academies, the school aimed to turn out young women who were the embodiment of discipline and decorum. The girls were unquestioning thoroughbreds, privileged from birth and socially conservative, and although they formed a close-knit group, there

* The region around Jazłowiec fell under Soviet control with the outbreak of the Second World War. The town is now in the Ukraine.

was a clear hierarchy. Christine did not at first understand why, but it quickly grew obvious that she did not entirely fit in: something about her was embarrassing. The truth was that the girls of the 'best' families looked down on her for having a Jewish mother. However, it was also the case that few spirited girls were happy at the school. One of Christine's friends was expelled for imitating a dog barking during lessons, another first for standing on a pudding to prove it was inedible, and then refusing to wear her modesty-saving nightdress while having her bath.[16] A third was removed for climbing the trees in the grounds – not an offence in itself, but made so when done without knickers.

Perhaps Christine saw these examples as a challenge. Early every morning before breakfast, the girls had to attend mass. Almost all of them saw this as an ordeal. One dark winter morning Christine decided to test the priest's faith by setting light to his cassock. This was fairly easy to achieve as all the girls carried candles at mass. Would he stop his catechism, she wondered, or would he be saintly and keep going? Realizing – with unwarranted surprise – that he was on fire, she quickly helped to beat out the flames. The priest chose to be kind about the incident, even laughing with her about it. The Mother Superior, however, was not amused. Christine was expelled for unruly behaviour.[17]

She continued her education at a series of prestigious schools that included the Sacré Coeur at Lwów, in eastern Poland, eventually learning the useful ability to conceal her true feelings, and applying herself sufficiently to leave the system with some dignity when she was eighteen. She never considered submitting herself to any kind of further education, however. For her, real life was at Trzepnica, with or without her increasingly serious and silent older brother, or with her father in Warsaw. As she grew older, Jerzy began to take her to the opera. Once, when she was sixteen, she made him laugh when, after watching *Carmen*, she scrawled rather precociously across her programme, 'Love, it's blood, always blood'.[18] That same summer, on a family outing to pick mushrooms, she worried her mother by writing in the dusty path with a stick, 'I am waiting for you'. When Stefania asked to whom she was

referring, Christine replied she hadn't met him yet, but she was quite sure that the future held adventures.[19]

While Christine was moving from school to school, spending the holidays either at home or staying with her young Skarbek cousins, whom she dressed up as soldiers and enthralled with 'fascinating little stories', mostly about the horses at Trzepnica, Jerzy Skarbek continued to enjoy a lavish lifestyle, and invest in his stud. But the depression that followed the First World War not only made the farm at Trzepnica unprofitable, it also eroded the Goldfeder fortune. In 1926, when Christine was eighteen, the family bank went under and her parents were forced to auction first their furniture, including the Zelazowa Wola rosewood table, then the great oaks in the park, which broke Christine's heart, and finally the land, farms and house itself, all at a considerable loss. Being forced to leave Trzepnica was Christine's first, and perhaps bitterest, experience of exile. By the time that so many other families were uprooted from their ancestral estates during the Second World War, she had already, to some extent, been acclimatized to such upheavals. For her, that later invasion of her country would be an assault on her childhood memory of a perfect Poland, an idealized picture of oak trees, servants and stables and of freedom, that in her heart she knew was already lost to her.

Three years later, Christine, now twenty-one, joined her mother and brother in a small apartment in Warsaw, closely hung with the family portraits.* Jerzy abandoned his wife and retreated to a series of health spas, treating his losses as a temporary inconvenience and openly living with another woman.† By now even Christine had to accept that her once beloved father had slowly descended into little more than an 'anti-Semitic drunk', a pathetic figure without the

* Address unknown. Between 1931 and 1932 they lived at 6 Chocimska Street, Warsaw, and later Stefania moved to 15 Rozbrat Street.

† An undated Skarbek genealogy among Maryś Skarbek's family papers, probably produced by Jan Skarbek, and based on Jerzy Dunin-Borkowski's *Almanach Błękitny* (*Blue Almanac*), mentions a second wife for Jerzy Skarbek, listed simply under her family name: Kresiolowska. Jerzy could not have married Kresiolowska legally, but may have been living with her as his wife in Switzerland.

strength of character to sustain him through the disgrace of the forced sale of Trzepnica.[20] As a child she had adored him; now there was little left to admire. Another great oak had been felled, and try as she might Christine would never be able to replace it. Jerzy spent the next few years at Baden near Vienna where, 'after long and severe suffering', he died of tuberculosis in December 1930.[21] In death as in life, despite his reversal of fortune, no expense was spared for his comfort, and his body was returned to Poland to be buried in the family plot in Warsaw's famous Powązki Cemetery.

Christine's education had left her qualified for little other than being a good society wife. Her family's impoverishment, combined with her Jewish roots, now considerably reduced her chances of making a good marriage. But Christine was defiant, determined, wilfully independent and, though not classically beautiful, very aware of how far her handsome looks, charm and sheer force of personality could take her. The future was a challenge, and that was perhaps its greatest appeal.

2: TWO WEDDINGS AND A WAR

The snow fell softly on Poland's plains and pine forests in the long autumn and winter of 1929, creating the annual hush that was broken only by the muted sounds of hoofs, sleighs and church bells. But Warsaw was immune to the silence. Although the snow fell in the broad streets of the capital, great nets and street sweepers prevented the residents from being snowed into their apartments, and the church bells here competed with more insistent tram-bells, the screeching of wheels, and electric motors. Horse-drawn carriages clattered down the cobbled streets, and there were cars too, mostly luxury models, adding their own distinctly modern noises. As the evenings drew in, lamplighters would come ever earlier to light the street lamps. The summer's soda-water sellers had given way to vendors carrying trays of hot dumplings and roasted chestnuts, the balloons that hung from their poles lending some colour to the streets. Even in winter the city was still full of hawkers, barrel organs with shivering monkeys, kitchen-door callers, and elderly men registered as messengers with the city authorities, displaying their permit numbers on dark red-visored caps, who were willing to take on all types of tasks from delivering flowers or love letters to collecting parcels or buying theatre tickets.[1]

Christine was twenty-one years old, and ready for Warsaw's winter season. Being a Skarbek, she was invited to all the society parties, like those at the Wilanów Palace, where balls always started with a polonaise, debutantes wore floor-length white dresses, and all the ladies would be gloved. But for Christine, these evenings were often uncomfortable, as she was well aware that the older women were gossiping behind their fans about her family's recent misfortune and her Jewish blood. She soon preferred spending her

evenings in Warsaw's cinemas, smoky restaurants, pavement bars
and poets' cafés, places called Piccadilly, Picador and, more tell-
ingly, Oasis, Bacchus and Mirage. Polish society dictated that ladies
should be chaperoned in such places, but Christine – shockingly –
chose to go alone or accompanied by a variety of young men. Her
long hair was soon briskly bobbed and set in precise waves to frame
her heart-shaped face. Her lips were painted, and above her dark
almond eyes her brows were plucked and brushed into pencil-thin
strokes. Her high cheekbones and strong features carried the style
remarkably well: at once modern, boyish above her slender frame,
and yet sexy, it was a look that could have been tailor-made for her.

Life in Poland was changing, and where success had once been
measured in immutability, it was now marked in the pace of
transformation. The old Polish order, dressed in stiff collars, frock-
coats and patent-leather shoes, was giving way to a new, more
relaxed, generation, arriving at the theatre on bicycle rather than by
horse-drawn cab, skiing, and taking tennis with their house parties.
As women's knees appeared from under their skirts, men's faces
also braved the new dawn, clean-shaven after generations of beards.
And yet certain manners and social etiquettes were maintained. At
large social gatherings men could be seen planting one kiss after
another as the ladies remained seated in rows, the backs of their
hands raised expectantly. The great Polish novelist Witold Gom-
browicz, who was only four years older than Christine and moved
in the same circles, remembered a rowdy friend once 'sprawling on
the sofa' with her and her friends at one such house party, before
teasing them with a twinkle in his eye, 'You are not really fit for
anything. It is not clear what you should be used for . . . we could
tie you to the end of a rope for when furniture's being hoisted to
an upper floor . . . or perhaps you ought to be planted, like a radish.'
Sadly Gombrowicz did not record Christine's reaction to this
banter, but it is unlikely that she found his friend as 'charming' and
'entrancing' as he did.[2]

While still enjoying her new-found freedom, but determined
not to be a burden to her mother, Christine took an office job at

the capital's impressive Fiat dealership – a workplace that could hardly have been better chosen for meeting wealthy young men hoping to pick up a status symbol. Still, spending days being nice to potential clients and watching the city's street life through the huge display windows would have been dull for any girl who loved to be in the middle of the action, let alone a snobbish member of the once landed gentry with no experience of earning her living. What made it considerably worse was that Christine was slowly being poisoned by the exhaust fumes that rose up from the garage below. They left a permanent shadow on her lungs along with a lifelong aversion to office admin.

But it was at the Fiat offices that Christine first met Gustav Gettlich, a short but wealthy businessman of German origin, who was soon distracted from the Italian cars by the Polish receptionist. Four years older than Christine, Gustav was a very respectable director of a curtain company, who lived with his widowed mother. His father had been a Lieutenant Colonel and successful business-man from Pabianice, in central Poland. Gustav was now looking for the perfect '*pani domu*', a wife who would be an elegant hostess, entertain his clients, cook his meals, and provide him with children. Then he met Christine, who, over a series of evenings watching Garbo films in smoky cinemas before dining in Warsaw's finest restaurants, swept him off his sensible feet.

Soon after they met, her doctors advised Christine to spend time at the fashionable skiing town of Zakopane, high in the Carpathian mountains, whose clear air might help offset the damage caused to her lungs in the Fiat offices. Zakopane was a popular rendezvous for the wealthier Polish intelligentsia and Gustav now regularly checked into the exclusive Hotel Bristol there, before joining Christine on her guesthouse veranda. There they would relax in deckchairs, wrapped up in furs to watch the sun set after a long day in the mountains on heavy wooden skis. Then they went on together to the resort's many restaurants and bars, where they drank vodka and listened to live jazz late into the night. Christine's guesthouse was run by nuns, for girls from good families, and she

must have given them plenty to talk about as well-heeled young businessmen, officers and poets swarmed around her. She was 'absolutely beautiful', one writer recorded in his memoirs.[3]

But the close-knit Zakopane scene was not as anonymous as the bars of Warsaw. Christine's acquaintance Witold Gombrowicz later wrote – in rather patronizing terms – about 'the unfortunate creatures', as he called them, born of aristocratic marriages with Jews, who 'were never fully accepted in the salons'. Christine was 'a lovely young woman', he wrote, but 'in her presence Jewish topics were shunned . . . just as one never speaks of the gallows in the house of a hanged man'. One evening, when Gombrowicz and various young aristocrats had joined Christine on her Zakopane veranda, an older woman in traditional Jewish dress walked past. Seeing Christine she called out to her, 'Krysia, Krysia!' 'The company was immobilized with fear', Gombrowicz recalled. Ashamed of herself in more ways than one, Christine pretended not to hear until the woman shouted, 'Krysia Skarbek!' Sadly we don't know if Christine overcame her social paralysis: Gombrowicz leaves her there, staring at the ground.[4]

When Gustav and Christine got back to Warsaw, Gustav happily returned to soft furnishings. His business gave him all the stability and financial security he needed. When he was not at work he was out with Christine. If anything he was even more entranced by the apparent vulnerability he had seen beneath her usual show of confidence. She, though, was more unsettled than ever. To reassert some personal pride, in 1930 Christine entered the 'Miss Polonia' contest, which had been established the previous year. The prestige accorded to the competition, open only to unmarried ladies of 'good conduct' between the ages of eighteen and twenty-five, was helped by the endorsement of the well-known poet and society figure Tadeusz 'Boy' Zelenski. Its popularity was guaranteed by extensive coverage in the *Express Poranny* (*Morning Express*) newspaper, whose readers were entitled to vote. The number of entries exceeded all expectations, with seventy candidates reaching the final gala. Christine sent in a glamorous photograph taken at one of the capital's most fashionable photographic studios. In it her dark eyes

challenge the viewer with a steady gaze, proud, knowing, and coolly seductive. Four weeks later she learned that she was on the short-list. In the event a rival beat her to the crown, but Christine was declared a national 'Star of Beauty', which was quite enough to confirm her to Gustav as a thoroughly desirable catch.*

Two months later their marriage banns were announced at their local churches. No objections were received, and Christine and Gustav were married on 21 April 1930 at the Spiritual Seminary Church of Warsaw. Christine signed the register 'Marja Krystyna Skarbek'. Her brother Andrzej served as her witness.†5 It was not a large society wedding, but Christine wore an elegant white gown and carried the traditional bouquet of orange blossom with some satisfaction. Gustav was twenty-five, considerably shorter than her, infatuated, untitled but hugely wealthy. Christine was twenty-one, an aristocrat, albeit marginalized, officially beautiful, and rather relieved at how things had turned out.

But while Christine now had the financial security that her mother, in particular, had been desperate to secure for her, Gustav was quickly realizing that his own prospects were not at all as he had imagined. Inexplicably to him, after their marriage Christine continued to prefer nightclubs to cooking, and showed no interest at all in starting a family. She was not, after all, an elegant society hostess-in-the-making; indeed, she was mostly absent. Over the next year, Gustav began to understand that though Christine's compulsive desire for amusement stemmed from insecurity, it was not something he could change, and his infatuation began to cool. Christine, too, faced a bitter realization. The security that Gustav offered did not make her happy in the way she had thought it would. Her marriage had not restored the freedom of her child-hood; it had brought new and unwanted obligations. Feeling unloved and increasingly ignored by her husband, whom she con-sidered to be obsessed by his work, Christine spent more and more

* Miss Polonia 1930 was Zofia Batycka from Lwów, a young actress who went on to represent Poland at Miss Europe 1930, before trying to carve out a Hollywood career.

† Gustav's witness was Andrew Szarski, later a famous war hero.

time in the picturesque mountains of Zakopane. She could already ski better than Gustav and most of her friends. Now she satisfied her need for excitement by dodging the border patrols to smuggle cigarettes across the frontier peaks into Poland, so coming to know a number of the mountain highlanders, or gorals, who would later set up the mountain soldiers' unit during the war.

In 1931 Christine was crowned 'Miss Ski' in a Zakopane version of the Miss Polonia contest. Perhaps sensing that the circle had closed, Gustav decided that they were incompatible and their marriage a mistake that needed to be rectified. They divorced in 1932, travelling to Wilno in Polish Lithuania where, having converted to Protestantism, they could obtain their legal freedom.[6] Christine kept both her married surname of Gettlich and a postal savings account into which her former husband paid a monthly deposit. Although Gustav remarried in 1938 and enjoyed the respectable family life he craved, he never quite forgave Christine for not being the woman of his dreams. Over twenty years later, when pushed, he would describe Christine only as being 'dotty, romantic and forever craving change'.[7]

Christine's brother, Andrzej, seemed to be having better luck. In 1930 he had married and, just as Christine's divorce came through, he and his wife Irena gave Stefania some good news: on 3 August 1932 Irena gave birth to their daughter, Teresa Krystyna. As it is customary in Poland for a child's second name to reflect their godparent, it seems likely that Andrzej invited Christine to act as his daughter's godmother. If so it was not a role she undertook with any great enthusiasm; if anything her first experience of the ties and responsibilities of motherhood put her even more firmly off the idea of having children of her own.*

Half-Jewish, impoverished and now divorced, Christine had little social status left to lose. In some ways this meant that she had more freedom than ever. With Gustav's settlement to pay her rent

* There are unconfirmed rumours that Christine had an abortion in pre-war Warsaw, and stories of other abortions or miscarriages later. If true, this might be one explanation as to why she never had children, even when contraception was hard to come by.

and keep her in silk stockings, she moved to a small but central apartment and threw herself into Poland's more bohemian scene.* Champagne-fuelled evenings were now spent flirting with writers and artists across Warsaw and Zakopane. Christine was 'exceptionally charming', one young journalist remembered, but even to the party crowd it was obvious that she 'was full of odd issues of self-esteem relating to her family'.[8] Things came to a head when she fell passionately in love with a handsome, charming, well-born but equally impoverished bachelor called Adam. 'Love will forgive you everything' ran the theme tune of the Polish blockbuster film *Spy in a Mask*, released in 1933. It must have seemed a good soundtrack for Christine's own life as she and Adam broke with convention yet again by publicly flaunting their romance. Reasoning that Christine made a perfectly good mistress, Adam's worldly mother turned a blind eye to the affair, but when the relationship deepened she invited Christine round to meet her. Her words were as clear and scalding as the lemon tea she served: as a penniless divorcée Christine had no hope whatever of marrying her son. Despite her recent personal history Christine was stunned. It would be a difficult, rather character-building, few years before someone with an independent fortune and absolutely no regard for the social niceties would step into her life. . .

As a teenager, the well-born, brilliant and unpredictable Jerzy Mikolaj Ordon Gizycki had been put off school after witnessing a fellow student being shot and stabbed by Cossack guards after testing home-made bombs in the woods outside their town. Jerzy grew up to be a moody and temperamental young man, given to violent fits of rage. Prevented by his wealthy father from studying art in Paris, he flunked an engineering course and boarded a steamer for America. There, travelling from state to state, he found work as a cowboy, trapper, gold-prospector and chauffeur for J. D.

* Christine lived at Filtreowa 25, Warsaw, a small flat in a good part of town. Stanisław Rudziejewski remembered her passion for silk stockings with the seam up the back.

Rockefeller, and, until his patience wore out, even aspired to be a Hollywood film extra. Although he had plenty of personal vanity, Jerzy did not have the onerous sense of family heritage that plagued Christine. At one point he happily sold his gold signet ring with its family crest to pay for a friend's rail ticket. He was driven above all by his appetite for adventure and self-improvement.

A talented linguist and socially adept, by the 1920s, when he was in his thirties, Jerzy was established as a secretary in the newly opened Polish Legation in Washington, developing a new interest in intrigue. 'The activities of our legation had no secrets for me,' he later boasted, 'I was the only one . . . who had the key to the safe where we kept our codebook.'[9] Jerzy would always maintain warm links with Polish diplomatic circles, but after a few years of conspiracy, and regular tennis matches with the Ambassador, Prince Kazimierz Lubomirski, he left the service to visit New York and London. There he joined the team preparing for Poland's first national participation in the Olympics. In 1924, carrying a huge Polish flag, he led the athletes into the Paris Olympic stadium. The following year he took part in an expedition to West Africa, acting as secretary and photographer to the Polish explorer Anton Ossendowski. It was a trip that instilled a deep love of Africa in him, and that led to the first of a series of books. Having done his part to contain the local elephant population, and contracted malaria, Jerzy felt he could tick off the main safari activities, and returned to Poland in 1932.

But Poland disappointed him. It was ten years since the heroic war with Russia that had followed the First World War, but Marshal Piłsudski's peace had not brought the economic stability or social improvements that Jerzy, like so many Poles, had expected. A natural enemy of conformity, he began to criticize the country's leaders and formed a brief friendship with General Sikorski, who, since Piłsudski's coup in May 1926, had been unpopular among the political elite and who Jerzy felt had been particularly 'shabbily treated'.[10] In between games of tennis, and escorting Sikorski's daughter, Zofia, to her riding lessons, the two men discussed the future of their country, and the roles that each might play in it. But despite this friendship, Jerzy found Warsaw life 'normal, uneventful

... and devoid of excitement and emotional elements'. He soon moved on again, to Zakopane and what he called his 'beloved Tatra Mountains'.[11]

Jerzy knew the Carpathian mountain range well, having spent some months skiing them with his mother and three sisters when he should have been studying engineering. He now settled down to ski some more, hike, write, and socialize with the great and the good who came to stay in Zakopane. Although independently wealthy, Jerzy was unable to resist the call of the Polish Foreign Office, and at one point he spent ten months in Ethiopia ostensibly as consul, but secretly to report back on the possibilities for Polish colonialism on the basis of the Italian experience.* After a brief stop in Rome, where he added another language to his collection while fraternizing with the local business, diplomatic and intelligence communities, Jerzy returned to Poland.[12] While he was never entirely settled, Zakopane would remain his base until the Second World War.

'My constant companion there was Countess Krystyna Skarbek', Jerzy later wrote in his memoirs. 'Excellent horse-woman, fair skier, and the most intrepid human being I have ever met – man or woman.'[13] In those days the wooden skis, buckled on with leather straps, weighed a ton, and without steel edges they would slide almost uncontrollably across ice. Story has it that Christine lost control of her skis during a perilous descent in a blizzard so fierce that the forest trees 'rose and bowed in waves as though a field of wheat'.[14] Jerzy, who, though approaching fifty, was nearly six foot tall and as strong as an ox, reached out and literally grabbed hold of her. One account even has him saving her with a lasso, catching her like a heifer on the American plain, before whisking her off for some vodka to steady her nerves.[15] However he did it, and despite

* In 1935 Italy had claimed Ethiopia for the Italian empire, having invaded with the support of Nazi Germany. Despite the Ethiopian emperor Haile Selassie's impassioned pleas to the League of Nations, within a few years Japan, France and Britain all recognized Italian control in Ethiopia. Unimpressed by arguments of empire, and unconvinced by the likely ability of Polish smallholders to settle effectively in Africa, Jerzy argued strongly against Polish colonial ambitions, but was ignored. Poland bought territory in Liberia, but those Polish immigrants who survived the colonial experiment were quickly repatriated.

being nearly twenty years her senior, once Jerzy had caught Christine he refused to let her go.

Intelligent, financially and emotionally secure, well connected and patriotic but not hugely political, Jerzy neither needed nor wished for anything in life except to satisfy his appetite for freedom and adventure. He had spent half a century avoiding commitments of any kind: study, work, political party membership, alcohol except in moderation, and relationships. 'Fortunately there were no women on the ranch,' he had pronounced as a young cowboy, 'so we lived peacefully and harmoniously.'[16] But Christine was not only young, sporty and very attractive, with good legs, bone structure, posture and deportment: she was also possibly the only person in Poland less domesticated than Jerzy. He was sunk. Theirs was not a one-sided affair though. Jerzy was the only man other than her father who ever dominated Christine, and she would later refer to him as her 'Svengali'.[17] Like Count Skarbek, Jerzy was a handsome, powerful and popular figure, larger than life and not a man to be easily contained, but unlike the count he was intellectually rigorous and had no regard for convention, or prejudice, of any kind. 'We liked each other, and despite some considerable difference in our ages, we became lovers', Jerzy recorded simply. 'Then we got married.'[18] In fact Christine did not marry Jerzy until November 1938, at Warsaw's Evangelical Reformed Church, by which time their relationship was well established.*

Christine and Jerzy made a charismatic couple, and both before and after their marriage were regular guests at Zakopane's many parties, which were attended by a wide circle – including well-brought-up young women from 'good homes' who enjoyed the thrill of mingling with authors, journalists and politicians. With Jerzy in a good humour, Christine's confidence sailed high, and she enjoyed winning over any audience. And if his mood grew dark or bullying, or simply when she got bored, Christine could just as

* Jerzy and Christine's wedding took place on 2 November 1938, at the Evangelical Reformed Church in the Leszno area of Warsaw. The church archives were destroyed during the Second World War.

effectively withdraw, in time developing the useful ability to blend into a room that she had captivated only moments before.

Both essentially restless, when they tired of Zakopane, Jerzy and Christine travelled through Poland, calling in at parties and press clubs in Warsaw, Kraków and Cieszyn, where Jerzy introduced her to writers, painters, and the Diplomatic Corps. It was about this time that the first rumours began to surface that the unfathomable Christine was working for British intelligence. Then they headed to Europe, Christine finding a use for her most sultry Miss Polonia photograph in her new passport. Long months were spent in Paris, then they travelled across France to Switzerland where, having broken his collarbone in an accident, Jerzy wrote books and visited clubs, while Christine improved her skiing, perfected her French, and played at being a journalist. The peripatetic but moneyed lifestyle suited her, and she wallowed in the freedom she now enjoyed. Routine domesticity would never have suited her. She was happy, and despite the pleasure she got from mixing in a more intellectual and international set, she gave little impression of paying any attention to Jerzy's heated arguments about the rise of fascism, the pros and cons of Poland's various international alliances, or the developing crisis in Europe in general.

Towards the end of 1938, the Polish Foreign Office once again called on Jerzy's services, this time to open a consulate in Kenya with responsibility for Kenya, Uganda, Tanganyika and Zanzibar (now Tanzania), and Nyassa (now a province of Mozambique), which together formed a territory about the size of Western Europe. Jerzy was to serve his country as a senior diplomat in a colonial state full of European émigrés and upper-class British officers, lending an aristocratic tone to the white settlements flourishing on the revenue from tea and coffee plantations. Christine was not perfect diplomatic-wife material: she was too edgy and unpredictable for that; but, determined, attractive and increasingly socially adroit, she was definitely an asset in the male world of diplomacy. Despite Jerzy's concerns about colonialism, with his love of Africa and Christine's love of luxurious adventure it must have seemed an ideal future for them.

Their first stop was London, where, while waiting for the official formalities to be concluded, they spent some weeks accepting Embassy invitations and catching up with friends from across Europe. But while Jerzy was in his element, Christine began to feel claustrophobic – their relationship was increasingly intense and demanding. She started to spend more time with friends of her own such as Florian Sokolow, the London correspondent of the Warsaw Press, and son of the Zionist leader Nahoum Sokolow, who had been 'very fond' of Christine.[19] As Florian had his hands full, being attached to the BBC, the Warsaw Press, and also contributing to Zionist papers, Christine even overrode her dislike of office work to offer him some secretarial support while she was in London.[20] As a result, and perhaps for the first time, she began to consider the alternatives open to Polish Jews, the growing anti-Semitism that faced them across Europe, and the attractions of Palestine.

After some weeks in London, Jerzy and Christine finally boarded a steamship to South Africa, Jerzy overseeing the safe stowing of the British estate car, fitted with extra petrol tanks, that was to take them the 2,500 miles from Cape Town to Nairobi. On arrival in South Africa they spent some time with the Polish consul general before heading north. Like Jerzy before her, Christine now found that the wide horizons of South Africa quickly got into her blood. As winter faded into spring, the countryside came into its own. Once across the mountains north of Cape Town they were in the Karroo, 'the land of great thirst'. These usually dry rolling plains would just have been bursting into flower as Christine and Jerzy drove between the few ranches in the shallow valleys. At one point some ranchers used their mules to pull the car through a river, swollen by the last of the winter season's heavy rains. Some of the baggage got soaked but Christine just laughed, stretching her legs out to dry with their clothing in the sun as Jerzy tended to the car. They were making slow but mainly very pleasant progress.*

* This is the route outlined by Jerzy Gizycki in his memoir. Other accounts, including those by Masson and Ledóchowski – both indirectly informed by Christine,

Having driven nearly 900 miles they reached Johannesburg, a city 'full of Polish Jews', Jerzy recorded, at the end of August 1939. On 1 September Hitler invaded Poland, without a declaration of war, on three different fronts, and with one and a half million troops. Two days later Britain, quickly followed by France, declared war on Germany, the only nations to take the initiative and not wait for a direct attack.

Although in 1934, the year before he died, Poland's Marshal Piłsudski had signed a pact of mutual non-aggression with Hitler, within five years it had become clear that Germany coveted both Gdansk and Poland's prosperous western territories. In March 1939 Britain gave Poland an assurance of support should their independence be threatened, and the two countries signed a treaty of mutual assistance in August that year. Unknown to them, that same month Germany and Russia signed a secret non-aggression pact detailing a new partition of Poland, and this now spurred Hitler into action.

In Poland the summer of 1939 had been long and hot, a last glorious hurrah before the country descended into a war for which they were ill prepared. The first reserves only began to receive their army summons towards the end of August, when call-ups started to arrive daily. One of Christine's friends later remembered a romantic last view of 'unploughed stubble in the fields, [which] shone in the golden sunlight', before reporting for duty.[21] This sense of nostalgia was percipient: they were leaving behind a young nation but one still proudly steeped in the traditions of centuries. The German invasion ended nearly twenty years of freedom and independence for Poland, but also a social structure that, for better or worse, would be completely destroyed.

Having received no instructions from the Polish Foreign Office after the German invasion, Jerzy and Christine turned their estate car round and headed back for Cape Town. Any dreams they might

and by Larecki, present routes through Rhodesia or by steamship to Mombasa and then train to Nairobi. Neither Christine nor Jerzy is a reliable witness, but in this case Jerzy's account carries more weight.

have had of a diplomatic role in the sunshine, and perhaps of land, freedom and horses, disappeared overnight. Despite their connections, like most Poles they were stunned by news of the German invasion, but unlike most they were over 5,000 miles from home and unable to play any role in the defence of their country. The return drive was miserable. Hot, exhausted, shocked, terrified for his country, and in a rage at his own impotence, the worst side of Jerzy's domineering character came to the fore, and Christine, who could be equally fierce in her own distress, was no longer in a mood to humour him.

In Cape Town they sold the car and, after a frustrating wait, managed to buy passage on a mail steamship bound for Southampton.* It was, in Jerzy's words, 'the most nightmarish trip'.[22] German submarines had been sighted along the western coast of Africa, so they were forced to travel in convoy, their speed set by the slowest cargo boat, and they stopped for days in different ports on the way. Every morning, news of the latest Polish defeats, and the rapid advance of the German Wehrmacht into Polish territory, was posted up on the ship's bulletin board.

Germany had gained air supremacy within twenty-four hours of invading Poland, bombing both the Polish air force on the ground and targeted sites within Warsaw later the same day. Working through a well-prepared plan, key bridges were then destroyed, trains derailed and refugee columns strafed from the air. Polish troops mounted a constant attack, with some incredible acts of heroism such as the famous cavalry charge against German armoured tanks, but the wonderful Indian summer worked against them. 'Hitler's weather' they called it, while praying bitterly for rain to fill the marshes and hold up the German tanks.[23] But the clear skies held, and by 6 September the Polish Command was forced to abandon its courageous defence of their frontiers. With a huge advantage in both numbers and technology, and few natural

* Christine and Jerzy travelled on the *Cape Town Castle*, arriving in Southampton on 6 October 1939. Jerzy was listed as being with the Polish consulate, Christine as 'housewife'. See TNA, BT26/1186, UK incoming passenger lists 1878–1960.

defences to impede their progress, Hitler's Panzer divisions now rolled with relative ease across Poland's plains.

Warsaw was surrounded within a fortnight. Under the terms of their agreement with Britain, Poland had been asked to hold out for two weeks before the Allies would launch a major offensive. Instead Britain's only action was an air campaign that dropped thousands of 'perfectly useless' propaganda leaflets on German cities, and which as even the head of the British Mission to Poland, Sir Adrian Carton de Wiart, raged, 'had no physical effect on the Germans, and no moral effect' on the Poles.[24] Then, on 17 September, just as Poland was beginning to show signs of withstanding the German assault, the Soviet army crossed Poland's eastern frontier 'uninvited and unannounced', and the Polish president, government and commander-in-chief were forced to cross the border into Romania to evade capture.[25] Vyacheslav Molotov, the Soviet foreign minister, claimed to be taking measures to protect the Polish population, with the result that many Polish regiments welcomed Red Army troops only to be marched into Russia as prisoners: 181,000 in all. It was Poland, not Germany, that now faced a war on two fronts. Within a week of entering Warsaw, at the end of September, Wehrmacht troops were the victorious occupiers. Poland had been crushed between two invading armies, both better equipped and prepared for war than herself.

On 28 September, the day that the Polish capital fell after a brave defence mounted by both the military and civilians, the bulletin board on Jerzy and Christine's ship announced: '*Lost* – a pair of lady's pink panties. *Lost* – Warsaw'. 'A sample', Jerzy wrote bitterly, 'of the famous British sense of humour.'[26] Poland had lost at least 60,000 troops in the September battles, and many more civilians both in the fighting and in the campaign of terror that the SS Death's Head Division now unleashed on the population while hunting down Jews and other 'suspicious elements'. In the industrial town of Bydgoszcz, 800 individuals were immediately arrested and shot, the first victims a group of boy scouts aged twelve to sixteen.[27] The figures were even more terrible in Warsaw. Jerzy had no idea what had happened to his mother and sisters, and Christine had

had no news of her young Skarbek cousins, let alone her mother, who she could only hope had found shelter when needed in the basement of the nearby Prudential Building, or her brother Andrzej, who would certainly have joined the defence of his country.

By the time that Jerzy and Christine reached Britain, on 6 October 1939, Polish casualties were estimated at 200,000. Christine felt the humiliation of her country deeply, but although Poland was being brutally occupied, the Poles had never officially surrendered to the Nazis. The words of the national anthem, 'Poland has not yet perished, so long as we still live', must have been ringing in her head. There were no instructions waiting at the Polish Embassy in London, but sitting out the rest of the war in Britain was not an option that either Christine or Jerzy would countenance. It was too late to enlist in the army at home, but they could still offer their services abroad to help defeat a common enemy.

Before 1939 few Poles knew much about Britain except that it had a large fleet and a vast colonial empire. Only the very well-to-do, like Christine and Jerzy, had visited. France, however, had long-standing political and cultural ties with Poland, dating chiefly from the Napoleonic era, and until June 1940 France was widely regarded as the most likely agent of Nazi Germany's defeat. It was there that the Polish army was re-forming under the leadership of Jerzy's old tennis partner General Sikorski, and there too, in Paris, that the fledgling Polish government-in-exile would soon be established. Jerzy travelled to France but, to his disgust, although he was on the reserve list, at over fifty and with several serious ski injuries behind him, he was rejected for military service. He tried to join a Red Cross unit in Paris, but was again rejected.

Christine was just as determined and impatient to help her country, but she too was barred from active service – because she was a woman. It would take her just a few weeks, however, to find a brave and innovative way around this seemingly insurmountable barrier. Unlike Jerzy, Christine would soon be employing her gift for languages, her adroit social skills, formidable courage and lust for life directly against the occupiers of her homeland.

3: HUNGARIAN EMBRACES

In December 1939 a 'flaming Polish patriot . . . expert skier and great adventuress', according to British Secret Service records, submitted a bold plan to ski into Nazi-occupied Poland from Hungary, via the Carpathian mountains. The patriot was Christine and her aim was to take British propaganda into Warsaw to bolster the Polish spirit of resistance at a time when many Poles believed they had been abandoned to their fate, and to return with intelligence on the Nazi occupation. 'She is absolutely fearless,' the report continued, before concluding rather pathetically, 'she says the matter is urgent.'[1]

'I first met T . . .' Christine's own initial report to her new British bosses opened, 'in 1939, in London, on the introduction of Sir Robert Vansittart and Frederick Voigt of the *Manchester Guardian*.'[2] 'T' was George Taylor, who had been recruited to Section D (for 'Destruction') of the British Secret Intelligence Service, or SIS, six months earlier. Taylor's mandate was to investigate the potential of sabotage and subversion in time of war. He was soon running Section D's Balkan network. At first nearly all secret agents recruited to Section D, and its June 1940 successor, the Special Operations Executive, or SOE, of which Taylor became chief of staff, came through the old-boy network. As a result, even the most rigorous systems of code-names and false identities were often compromised by agents recognizing each other from past meetings on a public-school rugby pitch. But despite this reliable route into the service, these men politely waited to be recruited; they did not apply. Christine meanwhile, a foreigner, and, shockingly, a woman, walked off the boat in Southampton, arrived in London the next day, found the right person to approach and demanded to be taken on.

Christine had formed her plan to volunteer for British intelligence well before she arrived from South Africa. They were, after all, heading to Southampton, and there was not, as yet, any Polish government-in-exile in place to which she could offer her services.* Furthermore 'she did not believe in political solutions . . .', a close friend and fellow agent later commented, but 'she housed an ironic respect for the British government . . . For her there were only good people and bad people', and the British, she decided firmly, were good and ready to go.[3] 'Having talked it over with my wife, we came to the conclusion . . .', Jerzy recorded rather patronizingly in his memoirs, that 'she would look for some exciting underground work.'[4] Christine, however, may have had another, supporting, motive for approaching the British. She was 'hugely afraid of accusations of being a coward,' one of her Polish friends in London wrote, 'and therefore demanded more from herself than from anyone around her.'[5] It seems that Christine was more vulnerable to criticism and the opinion of her fellow Poles than she cared to show.

The business of espionage does not encourage openness, and it is impossible to trace entirely the convoluted process that brought Christine so quickly to the door of the British Secret Service. Jerzy claimed that he met the journalist Freddy Voigt, 'one of the most interesting men I have known', through Christine.[6] This is quite possible. She had dabbled in journalism and had long been socializing with a wide group of writers and foreign correspondents, such as her friend Florian Sokolow, who also knew Voigt. Or the introduction might have come through Józef Radziminski, the Balkans representative of the Telegraph Agency Express, which was in fact a cover operation for Polish Intelligence. Radziminski had met Christine at the Brown Deer, an international press club in Cieszyn in Poland, some years before the war, and may have been sharing sensitive information with her since. Another journalist who met Christine at the Brown Deer noticed 'something about her

* In late 1939 many Poles viewed the Polish political leaders who had so quickly left the country as traitors, before they set up government-in-exile.

which put other women in the shade', and asked for her number, but decided against using it when he learnt both that Radziminski was 'madly in love' with her, and that she was already rumoured to be a British agent.[7] As early as 7 December 1939, the day after Christine docked, Section D files certainly recorded that Radziminski 'will do anything for her and with her', so the British clearly knew something about this relationship.[8] Alternatively Christine's introduction to the British could have been through Harold Perkins, later known to Christine as 'Perks', a tough English businessman who could bend a poker with his bare hands, and who had long had close connections with British intelligence.[9] Perkins had an estate and factory near Zakopane and would have been a regular on the slopes and at après-ski parties, giving him plenty of opportunity to mix with both Christine and Jerzy over the years.*

It is equally possible that Jerzy was dissembling, however, and the introduction to Voigt was in fact the other way round. Jerzy almost certainly had unofficial connections with British intelligence before the war. He had been in Rome after Italy invaded Ethiopia, at the same time as Claude Dansey, Britain's greatest spy-master in the mid-1930s, and he had coincided with Dansey again in Switzerland while travelling with Christine. The appropriately hawk-faced Dansey had been asked to set up an independent intelligence network, outside the official British SIS, in 1930. His recruits included diplomats, journalists and businessmen and women all over Europe, many of whom were not English, but all of whom were strongly opposed to Nazism and were willing to give their services freely in the fight against it. Harold Perkins was almost certainly one of Dansey's contacts, and Jerzy also had the perfect profile. Dansey was backed by Robert Vansittart, permanent under-secretary at the Foreign Office and the first cousin of Lawrence of Arabia, and by their mutual friend the MP Winston Churchill, both of whom had taken a consistently hard line against Nazi Germany. Those few

* Perkins's estate was at Bielsko-Biała, close to Zakopane. Larecki, Christine's Polish biographer, and a former intelligence officer, believes that Perkins may have sent Christine to the Brown Deer Club in 1938 on behalf of Claude Dansey. This is possible, but there is no publicly available evidence.

people aware of Dansey's network knew it as 'Vansittart's Private Detection Agency', but it was known even more clandestinely as the 'Z Organisation'.[10]

However they were introduced, and in whatever capacity, by 1939 Freddy Voigt had been moving in the same circles as Jerzy and Christine for several years. Christine adored him, but Jerzy was torn between admiration for this 'extremely intelligent' journalist and apparent disgust at his rosy cheeks, permanent lack of over-coat and hat, and hair worn 'long at the sides and brushed over the bald top – the slightest gust of wind . . . giving him the look of a long-haired Afghan hound'.[11] Born to German parents, but natural-ized as a British citizen, Voigt spoke fluent English, French and German, and had been a European correspondent for the *Man-chester Guardian* since 1920. Although he was based in Berlin, he travelled widely and had developed a particular interest in Poland. In 1935, already convinced that a second war with Germany was 'inevitable', he returned to London to start fortnightly foreign affairs talks for the BBC.*[12] Whether or not Jerzy and Christine knew that Voigt was on Z Organisation books, he was the obvious person for her to get in touch with in London.† Knowing her potential usefulness, Voigt introduced Christine to Vansittart, whose name and details Christine would still have scribbled in her pocket diary ten years later.[13] Vansittart, who held the Poles in high regard and believed they had been foolishly let down by their allies, interviewed Christine, judged her capable, and directed her to George Taylor.‡

* Voigt's BBC radio broadcasts were designed to spread a dismal view of the war inside Germany. In June 1940 he was joined by the *Daily Express* reporter Sefton Delmer, to broadcast from a 'German Soldiers' Radio Station in Calais', in fact operating from a country mansion near London. See Sefton Delmer, *Black Boomerang: An Autobiography*, volume 2 (1962).

† Christine's friendship with Voigt was interrupted by an intriguing episode. All that is known is that in 1942 she wrote 'he is an exceptional being . . . only I am not in a position to write to him as I no longer have the courage to talk of a famous incident, it makes me vomit!!!' See O'Malley papers (28.8.1942).

‡ In his autobiography, *The Mist Procession*, Lord Vansittart records that he wrote a prescient memo in 1934: 'Poland is in no yielding mood . . . Poland will fight but – a

Taylor was a short, dark man of 'enormous capacity', with 'sharp features and methodological habits', and was regularly described as ruthless, or brilliant, or both.[14] By the time that Christine had outlined her plan, including her proposed route and mention of the smuggler friends who she was confident would help her again now, she had, as a special operations friend later wrote, 'quickly established the kind of immediate rapport she often had with people of rare and not publicly recognized distinction'.[15] Taylor was impressed. 'She is a very smart looking girl, simply dressed and aristocratic . . . It appears that she has visited the Polish winter resort of Zakopane for many years and knows every man in the place', his report notes. 'I really believe we have a PRIZE.'[16]

Christine was indeed a gift for the British. Despite their lack of counter-offensive, Britain had every incentive to support her Polish allies. Just five weeks before the outbreak of war, in July 1939, the Polish Cipher Bureau in Warsaw had given Enigma decryption techniques and equipment to British and French military intelligence – cooperation that would be vital to the Allied victory on the Western Front.

But British support was not just motivated by gratitude, or the need to honour promises; they must have hoped that bolstering any underground resistance in Poland might also help create some rearguard action against the Germans. Intelligence was sparse and unreliable. The Polish political leadership had fled their country but not yet set up their government-in-exile. Section D reports show concern that, cut off from the West, Poles might be persuaded they had been deserted and given no option but to cooperate with their occupiers. Christine presented them with their first opportunity to get some counter-propaganda into Poland and, in her words, 'let the Poles know that Britain and the Allies had not forgotten them'.[17] If Christine had any concern that there might be some truth in this allegation, she kept it to herself. Unlike the

few years hence – will thirty million human beings be able to hold sixty? Of course not – alone. But if Poland is destroyed and if it is out of the picture, Germany will be able to do the very thing she could never hope to in 1914 – to fight on one front.'

British, however, she had no fears that the Poles might accept German occupation; rather, she was afraid that Nazi brutality might help spread Polish support for Bolshevism.[18] Either way, as she saw it, Polish and British interests were aligned. 'We have decided to subsidize a certain Madame Gizycka', Section D filed on 20 December 1939. 'In all further correspondence this lady will be referred to as Madame Marchand.'[19] Thus Christine Gizycka, formerly Gettlich, née Skarbek, assumed the first of many false identities.

Christine left for Hungary the next day, flying from London to Paris, where she caught a train to Budapest. Her transfer to the field was so fast that her MI5 clearance only caught up with her in March the following year, meaning that SIS had managed to approve her plan without officially endorsing it. She was put on the books of Department EH, a somewhat shadowy organization, attached to the Foreign Office but based in Electra House on the Thames embankment, which dabbled in subversive propaganda. A six-month trial period had been agreed, along with a cover story as a French journalist, contacts in Budapest, some basic instruction in the use of explosives, and an initial £250 paid via Voigt's bank account (worth at least £10,000 today), which, they felt, she was 'going to earn'.[20] Putting his wife on the bus for the airport, Jerzy was touched when he noticed through the window that 'she was trying to hide the tears running down her cheeks'.[21] Whether Christine's tears were caused by her grief at leaving her husband, or her relief to be finally on her way to serve her homeland, is a matter for speculation.

Christine arrived at a cold and dismal Keleti station in Budapest on 21 December 1939, four days before Christmas and three months after Hitler had invaded Poland. Hearing Polish as well as Hungarian widely spoken on the streets was cheering, but it was one of the coldest winters on record; snow had brought the city almost to a standstill and in some places drifts reached to roof-level. Christine quickly made her way to the address that had been arranged for her in Derék Utca, a steep walk up from the river in the old part of Buda, and just below the famous Naphegy Hill where the city's executions had once taken place. The flat was tiny,

but had its own small bathroom, a kitchenette able to rustle up hot strong coffee or the tea that Christine liked to drink with lemon but would suffer with slices of bitter green apple if there were no lemons to be had, and a decent-sized living room with chintz curtains at the windows and a large sofa that was also to serve as her bed. In the morning a maid would arrive with breakfast; the rest of the time Christine planned to eat out. She hung up her spare dress and put a change of shoes by the door – she was unpacked and ready to go.*

Despite long-standing Hungarian–Polish friendship, at the outbreak of war Hungary was already to a significant extent a political and economic satellite of Germany. Officially the country was an independent monarchy, and British secret service reports state that the country's regent, Admiral Miklos Horthy, 'regarded anything in the nature of democratic progress with abhorrence'.[22] Certainly the Hungarian Secret Police was well established and the opposition press effectively censored. The Horthy regime never seriously doubted a German victory in the early years of the war, and in any case, being only a small country with a modest unmechanized army and borders with both Austria and Czechoslovakia, they could not afford to offend Hitler. But they did at first remain neutral, and hoped for a compromise peace between England and Germany, ideally at the expense of Russia. On this basis, and as a 'matter of Hungarian honour', Horthy had refused to let Wehrmacht troops attack Poland across the 'Carpathian Rus', the much-disputed territory that then formed Hungary's mountainous frontier with Poland.[23]

Section D believed that the situation inside Hungary was 'well nigh hopeless', but felt that they should make an effort to establish a base there even though 'this could not be more than a gesture'.[24] Christine's first point of contact was Hubert Harrison, a correspondent with the *News Chronicle*, who had been working for George

* Christine told a Budapest-based friend, Erica de Bosdari, that 'you don't need more than two dresses and two pairs of shoes . . . you have to travel light in this life . . . you don't need all that luggage and all that clutter.' Mieczysława Wazacz (director), *No Ordinary Countess* (2010).

Taylor since October. Harrison was a short, dark, thickset man, ten years Christine's senior. They fell out from the start. He was meant to provide her with training, contacts and clandestine technical support, in return for which she was to provide a link to the Poles. 'As a result,' she complained, 'my flat in Budapest became a dump for everything being sent to Poland, including high explosive.'[25] Meanwhile Polish intelligence in Budapest, already keeping an eye on Harrison, now added Christine to their surveillance.

Another contact was her old journalist friend and admirer from Poland, Józef Radziminski, who was also now working for Section D. With Radziminski in town, Christine was quickly introduced to a wide circle of journalists and diplomats at a series of drinks parties and open days at Budapest's various legations. Never one to tolerate a chaperone, she soon found his persistent presence irritating; she was quite able to spot the champagne bottle on a window-box that meant there were drinks at an attaché's lodging, or to pick up on a signal from a flower-seller outside a café letting people know that German officers were walking their way. But Radziminski could not take a hint, and soon she had christened him, rather unkindly, her '*pies kulawy*' or 'lame dog'.* He was the first of many such admirers.

Radziminski's presence in Budapest was not so great a coincidence as it seemed. As the free countries closest to the European action, Hungary and Romania were awash with foreign journalists in late 1939. A surprising number of these were women, including the *Daily Telegraph*'s Clare Hollingworth, who had first broken the story of Germany's invasion of Poland, so Christine's cover as a French journalist was utterly credible. At the same time it was an alias that gave her the perfect excuse for running around Budapest at all hours, wrapped up in her duffle-coat with a notebook, various papers and no doubt some Hungarian biros stashed in her bag, as she tried to organize the contacts, plans and papers she would need for her first crossing into Poland.† Meanwhile most of the traffic

* The Polish expression '*pies kulawy*' is more self-deprecatory than its more insulting-sounding translation, 'lame dog', may suggest.

† The Hungarian László Biro had developed the 'biro' pen to prevent his daughter's

across the Hungarian–Polish border was coming the other way, as Hungary kept its frontier open to accept tens of thousands of Polish civilian and military refugees.

Among the 'slowly moving mass of heart-rending humanity, pushing and pedalling . . . clutching their children and their pitiful bundles' were the sorry members of the 1939 British Military Mission to Poland.[26] When Germany invaded, General Sir Adrian Carton de Wiart, the legendary one-eyed, one-armed, but hard-headed leader of the mission, had been hoping to establish contact with the Polish resistance to arrange the supply of heavy weapons and transmitters. His number two was Lieutenant Colonel Colin Gubbins, a wiry Scots Highlander who 'wore the toothbrush moustache that was then almost a part of the Royal Artillery officer's uniform', but who hid behind this formal neatness an original mind and daring spirit that would later take him on to become head of the Special Operations Executive, or SOE, Churchill's later rein-vention of Section D.[27] Gubbins was supported by Peter Wilkinson, who had already witnessed the German invasion of Prague, and Harold Perkins, the Zakopane factory owner who was now officially working for SIS. All three had strong Polish sympathies, and all would go on to become key contacts for Christine. But at this point they were simply trying to make their way out of Poland, caught up in what Wilkinson described as 'the procession of dusty motorcars, mostly driven by women, crammed with personal possessions and with pale, wide-eyed children looking out of the windows'.[28]

No one at the British Mission would be able to forget the scenes they now witnessed. 'A few cars bore bullet marks and many had mattresses strapped to the roof as a vain protection against the German dive-bombers', Wilkinson noted, while in the opposite direction 'there was a procession of horses being driven westward to the battle', among them 'young foals trotting eagerly to the war alongside their mothers'.[29] Gubbins felt that the fierce determination

school class from dipping her long plaits in their open ink-wells. He first presented it at the Budapest International Fair in 1931, and patented it in Paris in 1938. Being Jewish, that year he also wisely fled Hungary for South America, where he survived the war.

of the old men, women and children he saw tearing up paving slabs
to build barricades was typical of the Polish spirit of resistance.
Wilkinson watched a peasant woman in a headscarf carrying a
bucket across the fields to her mare with its foal, like 'something
Breughel might have painted, a scene that time had forgotten . . .'
A few minutes later the farmhouse was in flames, and the mare and
woman lay dead, 'the latter with her skirts blown over her head
leaving her bare thighs obscenely exposed. Only the foal remained
alive, quietly cropping the grass.'[30] As they continued their flight,
stripping off their uniforms and tearing up their passports, Wilkin-
son began to question Britain's moral authority. Then, as he and
Gubbins used what he called 'some intelligent coaxing' to 'sort out'
some army trucks blocking the road, Wilkinson turned to find a
Polish officer pointing a pistol at him.[31] 'Who are you giving orders
to Poles?' the officer shouted. 'What are you doing in Poland?'
Before Wilkinson had time to respond the traffic started moving
again and the officer moved away, but his question stayed hanging
in the air. Walking back to the car Gubbins asked bitterly, 'What
are we doing here? What help have we been able to give the
Poles?'[32]

Among the Polish refugees slipping across the country's borders
at this time were Christine's young cousins Jan and Andrzej
Skarbek, who crossed the border hidden in a sealed compartment
in a Hungarian troop train, with their mother and, for a while,
their father, although he soon pressed on to join the Polish army
in France. It was some months before Christine learned they had
escaped occupied Poland.* But she did meet someone from her
childhood while she was in Budapest – Andrzej Kowerski, now a
dashing lieutenant.

Christine had first met Andrzej in the stables at Trzepnica
when they were children, and had encountered him again in Zak-
opane when he bought a pair of Jerzy's old skis. A bachelor and a

* The boys remained in Hungary, Andrzej studying medicine at Budapest University,
until the Red Army arrived, when they fled to relatives in Austria. Once old enough
they joined the Polish forces in Italy.

ladies' man, Andrzej was tall and well built, with dark blonde hair and intense blue eyes, always smiling and utterly charming. He loved good food, drink, talking late into the night, dancing and – of course – flirting. His round face with its perfect complexion conveyed a certain innocence that Andrzej had long found it convenient to exploit. Always active, he lived life to the full, spending his time riding or skiing while his mother believed he was at a monastic retreat, and as a student in Kraków he claimed to have survived for three years only 'on vodka and raw meat'.[33] It was a lifestyle not without consequence. When he had last met Christine he had just survived an avalanche, intact, against all the odds, but not long afterwards he lost one leg below the knee when a friend accidentally shot him through the foot on a hunting trip. His prosthetic leg, made in Britain from wood with metal clamps, was heavy, but he refused to let it slow him down. No longer able to ride, he simply transferred his passion for horses into a lifelong love of fast cars.*

When the Nazis invaded, Andrzej joined the 'Black Brigade', Poland's only motorized unit. Repeatedly leading near-suicidal attacks on the advancing Wehrmacht, in the aftermath of one skirmish Andrzej was found alive but near bursting with rage, pinned by one leg beneath a bombed-out tank. 'I don't want a doctor, you blithering idiot,' he had shouted at the officer who found him, 'I want a blacksmith.'[34] Other than a crushed prosthesis he was uninjured. Andrzej had reached the rank of Lieutenant, and was awarded the Virtuti Militari, Poland's highest award for valour, before his unit was captured. While Christine was courting the British Secret Services in London, Andrzej somehow managed to steal an Opel, the car of choice for discerning Wehrmacht officers, and lead his brigade's escape. They re-formed, attacked again, and

* The secret services have a distinguished history of one-legged employees. The first head of SIS, Mansfield Smith-Cumming, hacked his own leg off with a penknife to release himself from a car accident. The American WWII agent Virginia Hall had a false leg she called Cuthbert. After she mentioned that Cuthbert was causing her trouble in a few signals home, one of her colleagues replied he wanted to come over and kill that Cuthbert for her.

were finally forced to cross into Hungary, where they were interned under the terms of the Geneva Convention in a huge barbed-wire enclosure, already filled with lorries, cars and men.

Under international law, internment was meant to be for the duration of the war, but as one Polish Home Army officer later wrote, 'the authors of the Convention did not ... take into consideration the Polish temperament, reluctant to submit to the deprivation of freedom, nor the prevailing pro-Polish sentiment among their [Hungarian] jailors.'[35] Two days later Andrzej drove out of the camp in the same Opel, took off his uniform, hid his car, and became a pedestrian civilian in Budapest.[36] Over 35,000 Polish men and officers would 'escape' from internment camps in Hungary, but few stayed long in the capital. At that time men of military age who were not in uniform needed a doctor's certificate to prove they were unfit for service, but if questioned Andrzej would just pull up his trouser leg, rap on his rather worn-looking wooden leg, and ask how he could possibly be an officer.

Christine had not been in Budapest long when she was invited to an evening at the Café Floris, a press and intelligence hangout. Andrzej was holding court in the smoky back room, recounting his war stories to a lively crowd of friends. 'The door opened and a girl walked in', he remembered. 'I stopped and stared at her. She was slim, sunburnt, with brown hair and eyes. A kind of crackling vitality seemed to emanate from her.'[37] After they had been introduced, Christine had to remind Andrzej to resume his story. 'It is not often one has a chance to talk with someone who fought with the Black Brigade', she fawned, not mentioning that she had only arrived from London a few days before.[38] The stories were good that night, and after a while Andrzej was pleased to see that Christine's dark eyes were 'shining with tears'.[39] Later they talked together alone, and when she explained a little about her situation, Andrzej asked why the British had abandoned the Poles, despite their guarantees. Declaring that it was complicated, Christine suggested they discuss it privately the next evening. 'I'm inviting you out to dinner', she laughed, looking up at him.[40]

It was rare enough for a woman to ask a man out in 1940

Budapest, let alone a beautiful and patriotic Pole clearly intent on risking her neck for her country, and equally clearly unsure of the best way to do so. Brave and vulnerable, full of charm and determination, Christine, apart from the fact that she was married, was pretty much Andrzej's perfect woman. Nevertheless, he was forced to miss their date the following evening.

After he had left the internment camp, it had taken Andrzej just a few days to organize the escape of the rest of his unit. His plan had been to travel with them through the Middle East to France, where they could rejoin the Polish army. However, the Black Brigade's commanding officer, General Maczek, ordered Andrzej to stay in Budapest and organize the 'exfiltration' of as many Polish men and officers as possible. It was not long before Andrzej was known as the Scarlet Pimpernel of Poland.*

Andrzej was soon running a hugely efficient escape route with the help of various Polish contacts on both sides of the border. A distant cousin obtained or prepared all the vital paperwork that would be needed by their escapees.† Andrzej and his friends Prince Marcin Lubomirski and the wife of the head of the Cavalry Officers' School at Grudziadz made contacts inside the internment camps, and arranged the routes across the mountains, through Czechoslovakia and Hungary, and southwards to Yugoslavia. The four of them also drove the vehicles that took the men hundreds of miles across the borders. It was exhausting work. Andrzej's big 'escape car', an old Chevrolet, was unheated, and he often had to dig it out of the snow in temperatures of minus 20, or put blankets under the wheels to get them to grip. More than once he had to enlist the help of local villagers with horses to drag the car out of a snowdrift.

* This nickname had the bonus of associating Andrzej with the dashing Leslie Howard, who had depicted the Pimpernel on screen just five years earlier, and who was now filming a WWII version released as *Pimpernel Smith* in 1941. Howard himself was reportedly supplying intelligence to the Allies until he was killed when the plane he was travelling in was shot down in 1943.

† Paddy Leigh Fermor later wrote that Christine and Andrzej belonged to the same Polish class, defined by 'its fluent French and its vast tangle of cousins'. See the *Spectator*, 'The One-Legged Parachutist' (1.1.1989).

Even on a good day, with little farm traffic and no snow, it took at least four hours to reach Belgrade from Budapest; in winter the round trip could easily take a whole day, or night.

At first Andrzej and his cousin ran the operation from the Metropole Hotel, where there would often be at least ten men sleeping on the floor of their room. One night, after returning from a border crossing, Andrzej found the Hungarian police waiting at the hotel to arrest him. Although the Hungarians were sympathetic to the Poles and turned a blind eye to resistance activities where possible, they had no choice but to imprison anyone caught releasing officers from the internment camps. When questioned about his movements, Andrzej unlatched his leg and laid it on a table. Point taken, he was released, but his wooden alibi was beginning to wear a little thin and it was clear that he and the team needed a more secure address. Öröm Utca – Street of Joy – was perfect. Quiet during the day, at night it was in the heart of Budapest's red-light district where the nocturnal comings and goings of one more mud-spattered car would not be much noticed. From here Andrzej organized the safe transit of hundreds of escaping internees, refugees and army stragglers.

On the day he was due to have dinner with Christine, Andrzej was needed to drive a group of men across the border at no notice. A friend rang her with his apologies and when Andrzej got back the next day, cold and frozen, she rang him. They arranged to meet beside the Danube, near the graceful Lánc-Hid, or Chain-Bridge.[41] It was windy and cold, and Christine was wrapped up in her duffle-coat with the hood pulled up over her hair against the drifting snow. In the silvery-blue dusk Andrzej watched her making her way along the cobbled embankment beside the river, 'walking as she did when she was in a good mood . . . in a dancing way, full of grace'.[42] When Christine swung her 'pretty legs' into the car beside him, neither of them knew it was the start of a long relationship, but Andrzej already felt 'a great spark' between them.[43]

That night they ate at the Café Hangli, famous as a romantic refuge for artists and writers and in the middle of a park on the

banks of the Danube, not far from Christine's flat.* Too cold to eat outside under the trees, they sat by the heavily draped windows where Andrzej drank local wine and held forth about the war, politics and the perfidy of the British. Christine poured water into her wine glass and listened. Andrzej seemed to embody the Polish spirit of resistance as she saw it: dashing and courageous, but ill-informed. Towns and villages across Poland were already plastered with Nazi posters showing a mother holding her dead child in her arms, in front of a burning town. Printed below were the words, 'England, this is your work!' Believing such propaganda, Christine argued, was the first step towards accepting occupation.† She then broke all the rules and told Andrzej her mission. He was horrified, but deeply impressed.

After dinner, Christine and Andrzej went back to her tiny flat and only parted company the next morning. 'Everything was magical and wonderful and funny', Andrzej remembered.⁴⁴ The flowery yellow chintz of the curtains, the coffee Christine had made which they promptly left to go cold, the wonderful directness that he found so disarming, even the sofa that was hardly big enough for one. Given the nature of their work, they decided to keep their affair secret, so when the maid arrived with Christine's breakfast tray Andrzej had to hide in the cupboard. It was a comedy romance but all the more poignant for that.

If Christine's once Catholic conscience ever pricked her, she managed to effectively bury any guilt she might have felt about cuckolding her husband. Although Jerzy was still in France trying to find a way to serve his country, she and Andrzej faced arrest every day and, if handed over to the Gestapo, possible execution. More than ever before, Christine realized that life was precious, and she did not intend to waste whatever she might have left. Over

* Café Hangli was owned and run by the father of the Hungarian food critic Egon Ronay.

† In Warsaw, a month after the invasion, two women were shot simply for tearing down an anti-British poster, but such terror failed to cow the resistance in the city. See Terry Charman, 'Hugh Dalton, Poland and SOE, 1940–42', in Mark Seaman (ed.), *Special Operations Executive: A New Instrument of War* (2006), p. 66.

the next few weeks, when Andrzej wasn't working, the two of them scarcely spent a day without seeing each other. If it was biting cold they would hunker down in her flat, emerging only to go to a café, or walk round the glass-roofed central market, filled with winter produce. Later, as spring started to arrive, the first of the season's flowers stood soaking in leaky buckets in the gallery above. But if the winter sun was bright they would walk through the Old Town's narrow streets and courtyards, listening to the song of the golden orioles in the trees on the slope below the Fisherman's Bastion, or looking up at the balconies with their signs for cheap rooms, dressmakers or furriers. If they had petrol, they would cross one of the seven bridges that spanned the river and drive up the Hármash-atár-hegy, the big scrubby hill on the Buda side. At the top they would stop at an inn and look down over the city. Here they could watch as the lights came out along the banks of the Danube before Andrzej ordered coffee and an ice-cold glass of barack, the Hungarian apricot brandy. Later, huddled together in her rooms against the cold, she would call him her '*kot*', her cat, and he in turn would call her his '*kotek*', 'kitten'. Both were strays, but both were also fiercely patriotic, and their passion for each other seemed to reflect their love of their country, a secret source of strength and pride.

By the end of February 1940, to her growing frustration, Christine had still not managed to cross into Poland. The problem came from the least expected quarter. A British report delicately summed up the situation: 'the Poles have been a bit sticky'.[45] The Polish underground was beginning to organize itself, but there were a number of key groups each with different political connections vying for authority, and intelligence bases not only in Warsaw, Budapest, Bucharest and Belgrade, but also in Athens, Istanbul, Cairo and Stockholm. The main resistance group, which was affiliated to the fledgling Polish government-in-exile, had legitimate concerns that Christine, as an amateur, and 'in the pay of the English' as she wrote bitterly, would be a liability.[46] If Christine had believed that by putting her life on the line for her country she would finally be accepted and valued by her compatriots, she was wrong. Instead she found herself in a familiar limbo, halfway

between Polish patriot and alien other, only this time the 'other' was British agent. As the frictions intensified between the different intelligence communities, the clandestine Polish network in Budapest warned her that 'any movement in Poland which is not our movement is an enemy one'.[47] Although Christine tried to play down the tensions in her reports to Section D, for a while their support for her crossing cooled.

Christine was far from idle, however. Sometimes she joined Andrzej on his raids, but mostly she pursued her own plans to disseminate anti-German propaganda throughout Poland. In January 1940 Section D had sent Basil Davidson, a young journalist with the *Economist* and the London *Evening Standard*, to Budapest by train through Yugoslavia, with a large supply of explosives in a blue plastic bag. His job was to set up a legal news agency, providing stories from the Ministry of Information to the local papers, and also to run a clandestine printing press. Unfortunately, as he later admitted bluntly, 'I hadn't the foggiest idea of how to do that.'[48] Seizing the moment, Christine not only stored the explosives at her flat, but now also began to develop plans for a radio 'Freedom Station' to broadcast Allied news and propaganda into Poland from Hungary. 'I find myself becoming a bit of a fan of "Madam Marchand" and would like to see her get her own way', one Section D report enthused, before rather more pragmatically concluding that, should things go wrong, such an initiative might still 'add some, admittedly undeserved, credit to our own activities'.[49]

In February Peter Wilkinson, previously of the British Military Mission to Poland, arrived in Budapest with a consignment of revolvers, which according to Davidson were too heavy and bulky to be of much use, and in any case required ammunition that was impossible to obtain locally. Davidson proposed to drop the guns in the Danube. Wilkinson then turned his attention to the prospects for propaganda work, and was keen to use Christine, but even his presence could not override Polish objections to her radio scheme. This first encounter between Wilkinson and Christine set the tone for their future relationship: short, curt and professionally disappointing. He was one of the few men she failed to impress.

Wilkinson was a shrewd judge of character, and although he recognized Christine's potential as an agent he found her charm disconcerting and rather disapproved of what he considered her personal amorality. With little achieved, and 'the cold Central European wind and flaky snow coming down', Budapest was 'absolutely miserable', Wilkinson summed up before he left.[50]

In mid-March, another unexpected development put further pressure on Christine: 'her attractiveness appeared to be causing some difficulty in Budapest', Section D reported.[51] The problems started when the Polish journalist and intelligence agent Józef Radziminski, still infatuated, threatened to shoot himself at her flat – 'in his genital organs', Wilkinson reported with some disgust – after Christine had rejected his continued advances.[52] Losing his nerve at the last moment, he merely winged himself in the foot, but according to Wilkinson 'this failure made him even more ardent'.[53] Once able to walk again, Radziminski threw himself from the Elizabeth Bridge onto what turned out to be the still half-frozen Danube. As a result, instead of drowning as intended he merely broke his remaining good leg. 'He only succeeded in wounding himself, and was not arrested', British intelligence briskly rounded off their report, before sending Radziminski a telegram pointing out that this incident was a serious breach of security.[54] Christine's summary of Radziminski is perhaps even more damning: 'he proved unsatisfactory and was dismissed' was all the space she gave him.*[55] Such public displays might have enlivened the day-to-day experience of the freezing British intelligence population of Budapest, but

* It is possible that Radziminski had become Christine's lover in early 1940, as he later stayed at her flat and was seen kissing her on the mouth 'as though taking his due', a jealous Polish officer, Wladimir Ledóchowski, later noted. If so perhaps Christine's damning report on Radziminski can be read on two levels. Christine did harbour a sense of responsibility towards Radziminski. However, in July 1940 she offered to put Section D in touch with him in France, where she understood he had decided 'to stay and *vork*'. 'He has certain "defauts"', Christine wrote, 'but is energetic and courageous'. The War Office was not convinced. '[I] cannot conceive of him being the slightest use' one official wrote after interviewing Radziminski. 'On general grounds, I consider him useless and untrustworthy, and suggest that he should be got rid of at once, or at least interned.' TNA, HS9/1224/6 (15.5.1940).

they also drew unwanted attention to the activities of the city's many 'foreign correspondents'. This, combined with growing Polish hostility to the British agents in Hungary, was enough for Section D to finally encourage Christine to press on with her virtually suicidal mission into occupied Poland.[56]

'Well! Your Poles haven't done much!' Thus, General Ironside, then Chief of the General Staff, castigated Adrian Carton de Wiart when he finally arrived back in London after the Nazis had established their occupation of Warsaw. Having witnessed the determined and courageous response of both the Polish military and civilians during the September campaign, Carton de Wiart felt the remark was premature. Not least since the Poles had never officially surrendered. Knowing this, he replied quietly, 'Let us see what others will do, sir.'

4: POLISH RESISTANCE

'The wind swept like a sword across forest, plain and mountain', a close friend and fellow British agent wrote, perhaps a little melodramatically, of the conditions that awaited Christine on her first journey to carry British propaganda into occupied Poland, in February 1940. 'Birds in the trees were frozen to the branches upon which they had slept . . . and there was blood on the snow to mark the passage of starving wolf-packs.'[1] In fact Christine would encounter neither frozen birds nor starving wolves, but something much more disturbing – her first direct experience of the human cost of war.

In Budapest, Christine had introduced Andrzej to journalists, diplomats and, after Radziminski had been dismissed, the British secret service. Andrzej spoke no English but was 'the only person I could trust', Christine told her Section D bosses when they asked whom she would recommend to replace their lovesick agent.[2] In turn Andrzej vouched for Christine to Janek Marusarz, a star of the Polish Olympic skiing team before the war, and now a mountain courier for the exiled Polish Military Attaché.* Christine already knew Jan slightly from her own skiing days. Now she asked him to take her with him on his next journey into Slovakia, over the 2,000-metre-high Tatra Mountains, across the well-guarded Polish border, and down into Zakopane in occupied Poland. At first Jan thought she was joking. Then he thought she was insane. Not only was there a war on, it was the worst winter in living memory, with

* Jan Marusarz was an intrepid mountaineer, but his younger brother, Stanisław, was more famous as Polish skiing champion. See Stanisław Marusarz, *On the Ski-ramps of Poland, and the World* (1974).

temperatures reaching minus 30 in the mountains and snow lying over four metres deep, often burying the few peasants' huts. There were no ski-pistes, or any other kind of road, and the ski down into Poland would follow several days' hike up the mountains on the other side of the border, carrying illicit documents, supplies, including a small primus stove, and skis. The journey was practically impossible even for him, Jan argued, and he seriously doubted it was something that Christine could survive. Andrzej backed him up, telling Christine to at least postpone her plans until the spring, but 'such were her powers of persuasion', he later reported, that within a few hours Jan had agreed to take her on his next trip, when his progress would be anyway slowed by a VIP that he had to escort across the border.[3]

A week later Andrzej drove Jan, his 'VIP' – known only as 'Richard' – and Christine, who was travelling under the name 'Zofia Andrzejewska' in honour of her lover, to Budapest's Keleti station to catch a train to the Polish border. After a night in a safe house, the three travellers caught an early connection into Czechoslovakia, jumping out with their heavy wooden skis and poles just before the train reached the first station. Two days of climbing followed, with Christine at first stumbling along in Jan's tracks, alternately wearing and carrying her skis. Soon she learnt to welcome the deadening monotony of regular movement, a rhythm that set the pace mechanically. Her companions looked somehow diminished, she noticed, huddled into themselves and climbing with minimal energy as if fearing that any more effort might expel the warm film of air from around their skin. It was so cold that Christine's panting breaths hurt her throat and lungs and her fingers were frozen. Ice quickly formed on her clothes, the tendrils of hair that escaped her woollen cap, her eyebrows, eyelashes and even on the almost imperceptible down that grew above her top lip. That night they slept in their clothes, huddled together in a small wooden shelter, and rose early to keep climbing the next day.

Towards the end of the second afternoon they reached Cicha Dolina, the steep valley that, for centuries, traders, hunters and thieves had crossed to reach Zakopane. That evening a blizzard

blew up. Jan led them to a hut where Christine and Richard collapsed at once, exhausted, onto a bed of pine branches, only temporarily surfacing to drink the hot sweet lemon tea that Jan made. A few hours later Christine was woken by the sound not of the gale itself, but of desperate human cries caught on the wind. She shook the men awake, but when they opened the door the gale filled the hut with freezing snow, and it was impossible to see anything or tell where the calls were coming from. Christine could not even hear the sound of her own voice as she shouted out into the dark, screaming that there was shelter, and Jan had to physically stop her from running out into the storm in which she would be lost in a moment. Richard helped to hold her back, terrified that she might alert Wehrmacht patrols to their hiding place.

The blizzard had blown over by morning, and it was so clear and bright that Christine felt that 'the sharp contours of the High Tatras might at any minute leave a white scratch on the blue enamel of the sky'.[4] They left early to make the most of the day, even though the near-perfect visibility made them vulnerable to border patrols. Halfway up the final ascent they found two rucksacks lying in the snow. Christine went through them but did not find any papers. A short distance further on they came across the bodies of a fair-haired girl and a young man. They lay in the lee of a mountain pine, huddled together, and clasping each other's hands as if hoping this gesture of love might somehow protect them from the freezing blizzard. 'Here are your Germans', Christine said acidly. She covered the faces of the dead with pine branches and drew a cross in the snow above their heads. It was scant ceremony but all she could do.[5]

Christine was deeply shaken, and she, Jan and Richard finished their climb in silence. Later they heard that thirty people had died in the mountains that night, trying to cross out of Poland.[6] German patrols would find so many bodies emerging from the thawing snow that spring that they would double their border guards the next winter.[7] And yet, despite heavy losses, Polish couriers, including Christine, continued to carry secret messages sewn into the seams

of their clothes, or parcels of explosives, money, radio transmitter parts or even microfilm across the mountains in both directions, throughout the war.

The sheer ski down to Zakopane provided Christine with some sense of release. Jan's parents welcomed her like a daughter and, after eating, she slept for more than a day. In the morning she sent a postcard to Andrzej, which let him know she had survived the crossing. Then she set to work. As the only sizeable centre in the mountains, Zakopane was full of Wehrmacht officers who, when not patrolling the passes, had entirely taken over the Hotel Bristol where Christine had often dined with her first husband, Gustav Gettlich. Nevertheless she secretly met a number of old friends to secure their support, including several Zakopane highlanders who were already transporting people and money over the mountains.[8] A few days later, dressed in fresh clothes, hair washed, lips painted, rucksack packed with a paper parcel of propaganda material, she was sitting on the train to Warsaw. Jan and 'Richard' had gone on ahead.

When Christine later recounted the story of this adventure, the given route was from Vienna to Kraków, a journey she never undertook during the war. Perhaps she was already being cautious about giving away too much information, but the gist of the tale was always the same. Realizing that armed guards were moving towards her, making spot-checks along the crowded train, she was growing increasingly uneasy about her bundle of papers. She considered her options: get rid of the documents, or jump out of the moving train with them before the next station. Neither seemed possible without drawing far too much attention, and certainly not when the compartment door opened and she was joined by a uniformed Gestapo officer. Christine gave him a quick, flirty, assessing look. Soon they were chatting away, and after a while she asked the officer if he would be kind enough to carry a black-market parcel of tea she was bringing to her sick mother. A parcel of tea might get her shot, but a packet of deeply incriminating papers would mean a brutal interrogation before the firing squad.

Fortunately the officer was a gentleman and very willing to help: he put the parcel in his suitcase until they parted company at Warsaw central station.⁹ Christine, and her documents, had arrived.

The order and activity that met her at the station belied what lay ahead. Warsaw station had been left untouched by the Nazi bombing campaign, and trains still surged east carrying troops and ammunition into Poland, and westwards taking conscripted Polish workers back to Germany. Beyond the station, however, in the space of just six months, Poland's capital had changed almost beyond recognition. On the elegant boulevards in the centre of the city there was now hardly an undamaged building. In several quarters whole streets of proud homes and public buildings had been completely destroyed, and the pavements were strewn with crumbling brickwork, the remnants of broken furniture poking through the snow, and piles of rubble through which paths had been cleared down to cellars used as storerooms or classrooms, to house secret printing presses and, more often, simply as dormitories for Warsaw's inhabitants.

After just twenty years of independence, Poland had again been carved up by Germany to the west and Russia to the east, with a so-called 'General Government' zone, where Warsaw sat, between them. Martial law was enforced throughout, with execution or internment in concentration camps the only penal alternatives. In the German zones citizens were obliged to register with the Nazi authorities, who would rate them as either ethnically German, a German national within three generations, non-German but also non-Jewish, or a Jew. Within these groups people were ranked according to their work capacity and political loyalties, and given identity passes and ration cards that reflected their value to the Nazi regime: a German worker received 4,000 calories a day; a non-productive Jew was entitled to less than 200 or nothing, except starvation in the ghetto, which had been established in the autumn of 1940. There were shortages of petrol, salt, sugar, meat, clothes and fuel. Bread queues formed outside the bakeries long before dawn. Beef was reserved for Germans and any Pole caught with it could be executed. Any sign of resistance, such as sheltering a Jew

or possession of a wireless set, was also punishable by death. Selective executions took place daily. These would later give way to indiscriminate shootings and hangings.

Once she reached Warsaw, Christine was supposed to blend in with the subdued inhabitants of the city, taking care to draw no special attention, before getting in touch with the organized resistance. Instead, shocked at the devastation the new regime had wreaked on the capital, she walked straight to her mother's apartment. The city's Jewish population had been separated from their Aryan neighbours almost immediately, but Stefania was still living in the undamaged suburban house that Christine and her brother had once shared with her, at 15 Rozbrat Street.

Confident in the protection of her aristocratic name, her conversion to Catholicism, and the fact that she spoke fluent German, Stefania had ignored Nazi edicts about the registration of Jews, preferring the risk of denunciation and arrest to life in the ghetto. From her mother, Christine learned that, having fought against the invading troops, her brother Andrzej, along with several of their cousins, had joined one of the clandestine Polish resistance groups that would later come together to form the official 'Home Army'. In return Christine told her mother about her journey across the mountains and the bodies frozen in the snow, but did not speak about why she was back in Poland. She stayed with Stefania for two days, talking, crying, laughing and arguing as she begged her mother to leave the capital. On their third morning, Stefania insisted that they brave the streets together to light candles and pray at St Alexander's Church in Three Crosses Square. Fearing that her continued presence was likely to place her mother in even greater danger, Christine then slipped away into the city.

'Warsaw is the source of all our misfortunes', wrote Hans Frank, the brutal governor general of German-occupied Polish territories. It was 'the focus of all disturbances, the place from which discontent is spread through the whole country.'[10] Frank, Hitler's former legal adviser, had been appointed to his post in October 1939. By early 1940 he was waging a campaign of terror aimed at subduing the burgeoning Polish resistance and the population in general. Accord-

ing to Himmler, Poles were to be taught 'to count to 500, to write their name, and to know that by divine order they owed obedience to the Germans'.[11] The entire population lived in constant fear of arrest, torture, transportation or extermination. They were shot on almost any pretext, not just for hiding arms, defying the curfew or trading on the black market, but for anti-Nazi comments or failing to make way for a Wehrmacht soldier on the pavement. A policy of 'Collective Responsibility' had quickly been introduced, under which random Polish civilians were killed in reprisals for German deaths. The official reprisal rate was one hundred Polish lives for every German killed, but occasionally four times that rule was applied, with the names of the dead then broadcast in the streets.[12] Confiding to a colleague that his 'mission' was to 'finish off the Poles at all costs', Frank boasted that he could not advertise the names of all the Poles he had to shoot because 'the forests of Poland would not be sufficient to manufacture the paper'.[13] But Polish resistance escalated in direct response to Nazi brutality, and soon Poland was statistically the most dangerous part of German-occupied territory, with Third Reich officers dreading postings to Warsaw in particular.[14]

Unlike many occupied countries, Poland would never have a significant collaborationist faction, let alone a Quisling leader. Faced with such brutal repression the Poles had only two options: absolute submission or clandestine resistance. Within a month of the defeat of the Polish army, an underground press had been established and two weekly resistance newspapers began to circulate in the capital.* Third Reich authorities immediately put all printing presses under surveillance, banned the bulk purchase of paper and made the distribution of uncensored publications a crime punishable by death. A daily paper, a digest of BBC reports, and six more periodicals were launched over the next twelve months, all keen for Allied news to fill their pages. By 1941 a highly organized resistance propaganda unit was also producing a range of publications in Polish and

* The first, the *Information Bulletin*, appeared regularly for the next five years with a circulation of over 50,000.

German, designed to demoralize the occupiers. Some were satirical, or simply inserted sections of pornography into official-seeming publications. Others were 'black propaganda' purporting to be produced by dissenting political groups within Germany, and were so well forged that the Gestapo searched for their source within the Reich. Forged maps, identity and ration papers, and even Third Reich proclamations were also produced; one, plastered across the city one morning, ordered all German civilians to evacuate immediately, causing chaos at the railway stations.[15]

An ambitious underground supplies unit was also quickly established. It aimed to provide arms and munitions not just for immediate operations such as rail sabotage and the targeted assassination of Nazi officials, but also to arm a general uprising, to take place, it was hoped, in conjunction with Allied action. Weapons left over from the September campaign were supplemented by a few Allied airdrops coordinated by Colin Gubbins, and those guns that could be captured or bought from individual Wehrmacht officers. But the majority of bombs, timing devices, automatic and close-combat weapons were secretly manufactured in underground workshops, or in the German-managed Polish factories where workers would tack resistance-tailored blueprints over the Nazi ones above their workbenches. The nerve of the Polish defiance was extraordinary. When raw materials or parts became an issue, some of the thousands of workers forcibly recruited and transported to factories in Germany redirected deliveries to Warsaw, which soon began to arrive with, for once, pleasing German efficiency. By early 1944 the Polish 'Home Army' would be sending out bogus orders to all the main factories in Germany. By then virtually the entire population of Warsaw supported the resistance, either passively or actively, and within four years enough arms and explosives had been produced to fuel a major guerrilla war.[16] Despite arrests, transportations and executions, by 1944 Poland boasted the largest resistance movement in occupied Europe, with an army of over 300,000 men and women. In addition, a Polish-Jewish resistance movement was organized in 1942 that would eventually help over 100,000 people evade Hitler's 'final solution'.[17]

In February 1940, however, when Christine first arrived in occupied Warsaw, the city still teemed with a variety of spontaneously established resistance groups, all running their own intelligence, propaganda and sabotage operations. All were keen to establish contact with their émigré government, as much for funding as from political motives, so couriers coming from abroad were in great demand. Christine asked a series of trusted friends to make some introductions. Still new to the game, though, she was not sufficiently discreet. She seems have told the same story of the horror in the mountains to everyone, leaving a clear trail once her more careful contacts started sharing their information.[18] Soon there was a growing discussion among the resistance networks as to whether the British intelligence agent Krsytyna Skarbek-Gizycka, alias Zofia Andrzejewska, should be trusted.

One of these networks, the ZWZ, was run by a group of senior Polish officers loyal to the government-in-exile, and they regarded Christine, as a British agent, with caution.* The Poles would fight hard to maintain a higher degree of independence from their British allies than any other resistance movement in occupied Europe. They not only already had their own intelligence and courier networks, they soon had their own radio codes and frequencies. This desire for autonomy was partly driven by Poland's long history of conspiracy and resistance under occupation, but also by a distrust of British foreign policy that would, in the event, prove justified. The Poles looked to the British to supply arms and money, but the first clandestine British flight to Poland would not take place until February 1941. This operation proved that air links were possible, but 'the real lesson', so Peter Wilkinson, Gubbins's number two, argued, 'was the sheer impracticability of attempting to equip the underground army in Poland by means of air sorties from the UK'.[19] It was a truth that neither Gubbins nor the Polish General Staff could bear to accept, but with limited flights and no air bases

* The ZWZ was the 'Związek Walki Zbrojnej', 'Union of Armed Struggle'. It was not until February 1942 that the official Home Army, the 'Armia Krajowa' or AK, which was also loyal to the Polish government-in-exile, was established from the ZWZ, and went on to absorb most of the other underground Polish forces.

within easy range, the supplies Britain dropped to Poland could never be sufficient.*[20] Meanwhile Polish resistance networks were an essential source of information about the wartime potential of the Third Reich.[21] The ZWZ could see no advantage in working with somebody reporting directly to the British rather than trading intelligence through their own hierarchy. Furthermore Christine had little experience in covert operations and was well known in the Polish capital. She was, the ZWZ decided, a liability.

Unfazed, Christine determined to make contact with some of the more independent resistance groups. First among these was the Musketeers, created and led by the 'eccentric inventor and engineer' Stefan Witkowski.[22] Five years older than Christine, Witkowski had been an ambitious design engineer in the air industry whose confidence and connections had secured him military funding to develop a number of ever more unlikely projects until he destroyed his career, along with part of a Polish castle, while testing his 'death ray' machine.[23] He then moved to France and Switzerland, where he worked on building aircraft engines and formed links with Polish, and probably also British, intelligence, for whom he 'analysed' German industry.† After the defeat of Polish forces in 1939, he used his Swiss-based company as a cover for more clandestine work. Recruiting many former officers from the anti-tank rifle – or 'musket' – unit, with which he had briefly served, he established an intelligence organization known, not very cryptically, as the Musketeers.[24] By 1940 they had intelligence and counterintelligence cells across Poland, and courier networks stretching through Budapest into Switzerland and France.[25] Although respected as a charismatic leader and brilliant organizer, the ZWZ leadership

* Peter Wilkinson later argued that it would have taken an impossible 8,000 sorties to arm Gubbins's initial plans for Poland, Czechoslovakia and France. Eventually 485 successful sorties delivered a total of 600 tons of supplies to Poland. This was one-tenth the amount dropped to Greece, and less than a quarter of that sent to Yugoslavia. Britain was more successful in training Polish troops, agents and pilots in Britain.

† In his history of the Musketeers, Roman Buczek says that Witkowski was recruited for intelligence work by Stefan Mayer, who supervised the pre-war Polish Enigma cipher-breaking operation that led directly to Britain's 'Ultra' Enigma-reading operation, exerting a profound influence on the course of the war.

regarded Witkowski as something of a wild card. Tension grew as it became clear that he had no intention of subordinating the Musketeers to the Polish High Command and was keen to establish his own direct contact with British intelligence. Once word was out that a British agent was seeking contacts in Warsaw, Witkowski quickly arranged a meeting.

Christine met Witkowski at the flat of the aristocratic activist Teresa Łubienska. Having lost her only son in the battle for Warsaw, Łubienska was both helping to fund the Musketeers through the sale of her jewellery and taking an active part in its operations.[26] Although she and Christine were very different sorts of women, from different generations, they would soon come to regard each other with the greatest respect. Christine also quickly gained Witkowski's confidence, and handed over her parcel of papers. Picking up on the vibrant energy of the slight young woman in front of him, he gave her the pseudonym 'Mucha', or 'Fly'.[27] Then, pacing the room, he outlined the Musketeers' objectives, structure, and the type of intelligence he could provide, in the hope that she could secure some British funding. Later he would introduce her to several key people in the organization, including Michal Gradowski, known as 'Lis', 'the Fox', who was also a courier on the Warsaw–Budapest route, and who would soon be passing microfilm to Christine in Hungary.*[28] Witkowski also introduced her to the great Polish hero Kazimierz Leski, then the Musketeers' chief of counterintelligence. Leski clearly remembered the 'lovely, graceful, very intelligent and absolutely charming girl', but later claimed that as he looked at Christine he could not help wondering why he had been invited to meet her.[29] Finally he decided that Witkowski was trying to build his prestige by flaunting his new contact from British intelligence.†

* In fact Christine knew Gradowski from before the war. It was his wife who, years earlier, had been expelled from the same convent school as Christine for climbing trees while not wearing knickers.

† Leski's account is also interesting in that it contains a number of disparities, such as the claim that Christine discussed her experiences in Turkey with Witkowski at this meeting. This is not possible, as Christine's last visit to Poland was in 1940, and she did not reach Turkey until 1941. Either Leski was confused – although other details

Witkowski arranged to meet Christine again the following month, to give her the Musketeers' latest reports to be smuggled out of the country. With a deep bow, he then kissed her hand, and the fly was waved away. It was only once she was back in the street that Christine realized she had made no demands or suggestions of her own. Witkowski had controlled their relationship from the start.

Christine spent three weeks in Warsaw on this, her first visit to occupied Poland. Officially the objects of her mission were 'to counter the anti-British propaganda of the Germans by spreading British propaganda' and 'to collect and transmit intelligence'.[30] She proved highly effective at both. She had already handed over her propaganda reports for reproduction in the underground press, and shared, she wrote rather enigmatically, 'everything Harrison had given me' with the Musketeers.[31] She then assessed the impact of British contact so far. Leaflet drops over Poland had been 'magnificent' she reported diplomatically, but when repeated they should give straight news rather than propaganda. She went on to devise a new scheme for broadcasting special news bulletins at a fixed time and on a fixed wavelength, to be picked up by ordinary radio sets in Poland. These were to supplement the British and Allied broadcasts being subjected to German jamming, and were also to be used as a news agency service, to supply the many small illegal news-sheets across the country. One of her contacts, a well-known left-wing Polish journalist, was so keen about the potential of the plan that he put in a request for £100 a month to fund a new weekly newspaper with a circulation of 10–15,000 copies. British Section D was impressed. But Christine would later report that she also faced serious difficulties owing to the work of some 'Volksdeutsche' (ethnic Germans living in Poland), who claimed to be British agents and started a campaign to discredit her among resistance networks. She was 'in danger of being killed as an agent provocateur', she wrote, and was only cleared by old friends and contacts who vouched for her.[32]

such as Christine's pseudonym, Mucha, are correct – or he had another agenda, perhaps relating to his portrayal of the controversial Witkowski.

Not all of Christine's activities went down well with her British bosses, however. Somehow, almost certainly through the Musketeers, she made contact with General Stanisław Bałachowicz, a renowned champion of Polish liberty prior to 1919. Bałachowicz, whose 'prestige is very great' the British noted, had organized some 500 officers for guerrilla work inside Russia 'when the moment arrives'. Their plan was to start a revolt in Poland and the Ukraine against Russia, and, carefully stressing that the organization was 'purely military and had no political affiliations', Christine wanted to help supply British anti-tank guns, rifles, ammunition and money. 'No! – This on no account', one British Section D officer scribbled in the margins against the suggestion.[33] British and Polish views of the Russians would never be reconciled, and their interests would become diametrically opposed after Russia joined the Allies in 1941.

Christine also told London of her astonishment at 'the terrible disorder of the German administration'.[34] The Gestapo and the Wehrmacht distrusted one another, and as a result new orders were being posted daily, withdrawn, cancelled, contradicted and re-enacted, causing chaos. Christine tried to keep a mental note of everything she witnessed. She watched Warsaw's residents, often dressed in little more than rags, forced to clear snow from the roads and railways lines, before being rebuked for breaking the curfew. She saw children emerging from damaged buildings to take messages and parcels of bread and other goods across the city. She saw groups of Jews, some wrapped in blankets, all with beautifully hand-stitched Star of David armbands sewn on to the sleeves of their shirts or jackets, running together in the middle of the road to conform to recent edicts about their freedom of movement, and then being beaten for being in a group of more than three. Once she witnessed an elderly Jewish gentleman, dressed in a decent overcoat and felt hat, being pushed into the road by a Wehrmacht officer with his hand on the perforated barrel of his sub-machine gun. Having instinctively held out her hand, Christine quickly drew back and a moment later found herself smiling at the officer when he asked for her papers.[35] Momentarily hating herself, she began to understand a little more about the campaign of terror that enabled

the Nazis to control even Warsaw with its huge and passionate underground resistance. Later she would report that 'in Warsaw alone over 100 Poles are shot every night. The terror is indescribable. Yet the spirit of the Poles is magnificent'.[36]

Christine was staying with different close friends who could be trusted not to talk, but one afternoon an old acquaintance recognized her by chance in a crowded café and called out her name across the room, adding loudly, 'What are you doing here? We heard you had gone abroad!'[37] Having denied being Mrs Gizycka, wife of the well-connected diplomat serving overseas, let alone Krystyna Skarbek, well known to be the daughter of a Jew, Christine ordered more coffee, deliberately lingering to show she had nothing to hide. That evening she left Warsaw, spending two weeks crossing Poland mostly by rail, but also by horse and cart, and on foot. She was collecting local information on the continuing industrial production around the country, the transit of German supplies and equipment, and the composition and distribution of large military units both inside the country and along the demarcation lines, noting that many troop transports were leaving Poland, either crossing the Russian frontier, or heading towards Romania and Turkey.

One incident, though, was particularly distressing: the containment and eventual massacre of thousands of Bavarian troops kept in railway coaches for two weeks without food. Poles caught throwing food through the train windows were shot at. 'Finally they were taken out, lined up and shot down', Christine reported. 'It is believed they had tried to revolt.' In the same dispatch, she examined the morale of the German army and their attitude towards the Polish population. As a rule, troops in transit were 'very drunk on vodka', issued, she noted, 'purposely to keep them in good spirits'. All in all she felt that there was significant dissatisfaction, with the occupying troops fearing 'that if Germany loses they will all be massacred'.[38]

Most of Christine's information came from the local resistance groups who had been observing railway stations and the traffic on the major roads since the start of the occupation. Travelling in

winter was cold, dispiriting and tiring. She passed ruined villages, towns full of burned-out houses, and the broken equipment of war: shattered tanks, wrecked gun-carriages and vehicles destroyed in dive-bombing attacks on columns of Polish troops and crowds of refugees just a few months before. In places soldiers' graves lined the roadside, some still marked with makeshift crosses in the snow, and occasionally with the helmets of the fallen. Elsewhere the graves were more recent. But Christine knew her work was valuable, her false papers were good, and despite the ubiquitous – and often random – shootings she felt safer in the country, where there were fewer arbitrary round-ups of civilians than in the capital. She only returned to Warsaw to keep her appointment with Witkowski and collect the small package of 'Foto-Plat' microfilm that had been prepared for her to take out of the country. Then, as Zakopane was now the headquarters for the Gestapo in the Polish highlands, she learned that Witkowski had arranged for her to join a ZWZ courier, operating under the name of 'Jan Grodzicki', taking a different route back to Budapest.

'Grodzicki' was in reality a courageous and intellectual noble-man – Count Wladimir Ledóchowski. Although his family had lost most of their estates in 1920, Wladimir had the natural self-belief of the upper echelons of Polish society. According to one admiring female friend he was also possessed of 'explosive intelligence', along with 'brilliant agate-streaked blue eyes . . . and intense charm, felt by all women'.[39] Having fought heroically with the Polish Horse Artillery Division in the September campaign, Wladimir had been given command of a battery of guns defending Warsaw. The way he told it, it was over a bowl of flamingo soup in the capital's zoo, the night before the Nazis entered Warsaw, that Wladimir secured his colonel's permission to disobey orders to surrender, and instead continue the fight with the resistance. An excellent skier, he was employed by the ZWZ to memorize messages and courier reports from Warsaw to the Polish Embassy in Budapest. On his first crossing, in December 1939, he brought out the first reports of the situation inside occupied Poland. He then put out word that he was being sent on to Paris, but in fact spent a week in Budapest

before he could undertake his clandestine return to Poland in the new year.

One evening he happened to meet Andrzej Kowerski in a Budapest bar where they spent a pleasant evening swapping war stories over bottles of red wine. They seemed set to become great friends, until Andrzej recounted how in September he had led a successful attack against a local German HQ in Krakowiec, wiping out the enemy with the loss of only the elegant country house in which they were based. Wladimir had to choose his words carefully when he explained that Krakowiec was the estate where he was born, and which he had been due to inherit from his grandmother.[40] It would not be the last uncomfortable moment in their friendship.

Back in Poland, in March 1940, buying a ticket for the night train to Nowy Sacz, Wladimir was struck by the girl in the queue behind him, her pretty face half hidden beneath a Tyrolean hat with a snipe's feather stuck in the ribbon. It was Christine, and when she happened to join him in the same second-class carriage he began to wonder where she was going with her jaunty hat, duffle-coat and rucksack, but no skis. Discreetly he watched her yawning like a cat and struggling to find a comfortable position before she finally fell asleep. In the morning Christine cheerfully brandished her third-class ticket, threw him a look and a smile, and disappeared into the crowds. Some hours later, when Wladimir arrived at his ZWZ safe house, there in the front room was Christine, brushing her auburn hair.[41] Not for the first time, he noticed that she was 'remarkably pretty'.[42]

Over breakfast, Christine told Wladimir that she had left Salisbury for London when war broke out and was now returning from her first trip to Poland for the British.[43] She then spoke about her desperate journey across the Tatra mountains, and the bodies of the young couple she had found. Not realizing that she had given away her identity with her story, Christine began to sweat as Wladimir outlined exactly who she had been talking to in Warsaw, before finally confronting her with her real name. It was only after Christine had countered by boasting that her Budapest contacts included not only Andrzej Kowerski but his friend Wladimir

Ledóchowski, currently in Paris, that Wladimir conceded she had the better of him, as according to his information Wladimir Ledóchowski was right here, in his own shoes.[44] He then roared with laughter at his victory, delighted by Christine's frown.*

Christine, Wladimir and their ZWZ guide caught a train bound for the mountains in the late afternoon. Told to try to look like a local, not a tourist, Christine stuffed her hat into her rucksack. It was dusk by the time the train slowed down at the points near the mountain station, and they jumped, three shadows peeling off from the side of the train and disappearing between the goods trucks on the tracks before heading into the woods. Some gendarmes fired a few shots after them, but they were clear.[45]

After several hours hiking along forest tracks and cattle paths, and through deeper and deeper drifts of snow as they climbed higher, they passed the low concrete posts that marked the Slovak border. To mark the moment also, Wladimir pulled Christine over and planted a kiss on her lips. 'She kissed me slowly and passionately, as though she was prepared for it', he wrote in his diary, after which she climbed on to the border post, opened her arms wide and called out 'more, more!'[46] As she shouted her encore over the mountains, it was not just more kisses that she seemed to be demanding, but more freedom and more adventure: more of the very stuff that gave her life meaning. Later, with Christine leaning on his shoulder as they walked through what Wladimir called 'the snowy desert', they talked about their first impressions of each other, and how fortunate they were to have been thrown together in this way. But when Christine thanked the war for liberating her from boredom and routine, enabling her to take risks and experience real danger, Wladimir protested. Christine retorted that Andrzej Kowerski 'blesses the war every day' for giving him an alternative to life as a farmer, and a predictable future as 'an

* Ledóchowski wrote several different accounts of his first meeting with Christine. This version is taken from his journal, later lost in the Polish Embassy in Ankara and only published after his death. Written at the time, and without the intention of publication, it is the most likely to be accurate. His draft biography of Christine has a similar romantic story, set on a train station in the sun.

ordinary man who has children and goes out to drink vodka after the harvest'.[47] Ordinary, Wladimir had to admit, was not a word that sat comfortably with Christine.

It took two days for them to walk through Slovakia, and although they got lost more than once, despite their guide, they were now walking downhill and away from the winter lingering in the mountains. At night they slept together, sharing the warmth of their bodies and satisfying the desire that had grown with the fear of the last few weeks. Christine smiled at finding that Wladimir wore a Madonna medallion under his shirt, and was later woken by his fingers drumming out coded messages on her body as he slept.[48]

Finally they left their guide, and took a taxi through a series of villages until they reached a deserted stretch of road near the last Slovak town before the Hungarian border. That afternoon, Christine's boots got stuck in the mud of a flooded field. Wladimir swung her, 'swearing like crazy', over his shoulder, her feet pummelling his chest until he grabbed her ankles, and carried her to firm ground. 'I wonder', she challenged him on being set down, 'whether you realize that I let you do it to please you?' 'Of course,' he laughed, 'I simply adore being saddled by you. Pity you had no spurs, it could have been so much nicer.'[49] But Christine responded by sulking rather than smiling; even their sparring could not distract her from their imminent return to the comparative safety and routine of Budapest. 'I feel my holiday is over', she sighed.[50] The next day they boarded an express train for the capital. In the carriage Christine brushed her hair, smoothed her eyebrows and painted her lips crimson, but her mood was still morose. It was only when they reached their destination and Wladimir told her he had nowhere to stay that she suddenly brightened.

5: A STRING OF ARRESTS

When Christine and Wladimir arrived at her flat on Budapest's Derék Utca, the door was opened by Józef Radziminski. Christine's hasty explanation that he was simply a journalist colleague using the flat while she was away was somewhat undermined when, having sullenly packed his bags, Radziminski kissed her on the mouth, 'as though taking his due', Wladimir later wrote resentfully.[1] Christine then bundled Radziminski out, pointedly making him promise not to tell *anyone* she was back. Dodging any difficult questions, she then ushered Wladimir into the bath, before taking him out for dinner where, he noted, 'she ordered wine with the assurance of someone who knows best'.[2] Back at the flat she emerged from the bathroom in a lacy negligee and took him to bed. In the middle of the night the phone rang. Wladimir listened as Christine whispered, 'Oh, it's you darling . . .' When he asked what was going on, she only answered angrily, 'Radziminski, the pig. It is all his fault.'[3] Some uneasy months followed.

It did not take long for Wladimir and Andrzej to work out what was going on, but both were keen to make their own excuses. Wladimir respected but also pitied Andrzej, the 'wounded soldier', but he underestimated his bond with Christine.[4] He assumed that her inability to break with Andrzej stemmed from pity. Christine encouraged this belief, once rather cruelly questioning how anyone could make love to a one-legged man. Wladimir refused to have an affair with Christine under Andrzej's nose, but neither could he let her go. He swore he did not love her, but also swore that he would do anything for her. Andrzej, meanwhile, understood the intensity of relationships formed in the face of extreme danger, but he remained confident that his relationship with Christine, based as it

was on more than just a shared taste for risk, would endure. To Andrzej, Wladimir was a pest, deluding himself that the heat of the moment was anything greater. Christine, selfishly abandoning herself to the thrill of living life on the edge, saw Andrzej while he was in Budapest, but when he was smuggling Polish internees to safety in Yugoslavia she would meet Wladimir, 'shut his mouth with kisses', and assure him that they would resume their affair on their next trip to Poland.[5] Often, though, the three of them would go out together, Wladimir burning with jealousy when he saw Christine in Andrzej's arms. 'Red wine covered my eyes', he wrote rather sentimentally in his journal after a long evening that had ended with him ranting impotently at 'the same stars that saw our kisses'.[6]

If this was not enough, Christine's husband, Jerzy Gizycki, who was still in France, writing news and propaganda for the British, now started pressing for news of his wife, in the hope of a reunion. Christine had been keeping in touch with him, both through Section D and directly, but at the start of April 1940 Jerzy was 'seriously worried' that he had not heard from her for some time.[7] Section D replied explaining, with wartime delicacy, that Christine was 'in your own country, visiting her relatives, consequently it is not very easy for her to write to you as you will understand'.[8] Their letter crossed with one from Christine, though it seems that hers was just as delicate, since Jerzy reported that it had put his mind at ease. But soon he grew anxious again. Christine had been recalled to London, and should have been travelling through Paris, where Jerzy hoped to meet her, but by mid-May, France was at imminent risk of military and political collapse, and Christine's plans had to be postponed. She was stuck in Budapest. 'Hard luck for me', Jerzy wrote, seemingly unconcerned about any danger he might be facing; 'I just hope she does not get into any serious trouble.'[9]

In fact Christine was finding it hard to get anywhere near close enough to the danger she craved. She had handed her Musketeers' microfilm over to Section D's Hubert Harrison as soon as she got to Budapest. A few days later she followed this with her own report, which Harrison forwarded to London before he headed to Belgrade,

the capital of Yugoslavia. When he returned, six weeks later, Christine was still waiting to be contacted by his stand-in, but – as ever – she had not been idle. She was now the Musketeers' reception point for couriers like Michal Gradowski, bringing information out of Poland, and with Andrzej she was soon also supporting a secondary courier and escape route across the Tatra mountains, managed by her Zakopane skiing friends.

Christine had never developed a good relationship with Harrison. From the start he had frequently missed their prearranged rendezvous, he was lax in paying her salary and expenses, and was often seen drunk in public with other British officers like Ted Howe, whom she also held in scant regard.[10] Now Christine felt that she had to badger Harrison daily to ensure that he actually read the reports that her contacts were risking their necks to bring out of Poland. Even then, she later reported angrily, often 'he failed to act on it in any way'.[11] Later she received a letter from Witkowski, saying that he thought the British 'seemed very queer people and were acting very strangely'.[12] Christine did not yet know that the Polish government-in-exile was developing serious concerns about the allegiances of both Witkowski and the Musketeers, and that all information provided by them was being treated with extreme caution. 'There has been some disagreement among the Poles themselves as to what they really want', Hugh Dalton, the head of British special operations, reported to Churchill later that year. 'Ways and means to help them have been closely examined but it has not been found possible to do much to date.'[13]

Christine and Andrzej's response to Britain's apparent – and, to them, inexplicable – failure to act on the intelligence provided was to work more broadly with any representative of the Allies in Budapest. A conversation about state-of-the-art Polish high-velocity rifles, designed to pierce the armour of a German tank, had lit up the 'fishy eyes' of the impeccably moustached French military attaché in the city.[14] The speed of the German invasion had been such that the top-secret rifles had never been used in Poland, and as the blueprints had been hastily destroyed any future production would require reverse engineering.[15] When the attaché promised

expenses and French decorations for a sample of the gun, Andrzej arranged for his distant cousin in the resistance, Ludwig Popiel, to collect the rifle he had buried in a sealed box in the forests on his family estate the previous September.

As a major in the Carpathian Lancers, Ludwig would twice be awarded the Virtuti Militari, and later won the British Military Cross for capturing a German machine-gun nest when armed only with a handful of bricks.[16] He now threw himself into resistance work with equal courage. Accompanied by a friend, he took the same treacherous mountain crossing into Poland as Christine had done and retrieved the rifle. Having sawn off the stock and barrel, a few days later the two men smuggled the gun back to Budapest, where they hid it, rather unimaginatively, under Ludwig's bed. They then met Andrzej and Christine in a bar. Before long a loud and heated argument broke out about what to do with the gun. Increasingly irritated, Christine decided to leave the men to it. When Ludwig returned home late that evening, he found that the Hungarian police, now full of pro-Nazi officers, had ransacked his room. Worse still, the rifle was gone. Seeing that he was compromised, Ludwig was about to flee when there was a knock at the door. Christine stood on the threshold, fighting a smile as she looked steadily at him. It was only after Ludwig had stammered out his shameful confession that she put an end to his torment. She had driven over that afternoon, broken into his boarding-house room, collected the rifle, dismantled it, taken it to Derék Utca and sewn it inside the mattress of *her* bed. She had beaten the police to their quarry by an hour, her quick thinking saving both the rifle and Ludwig's neck. That night, she told him, she fully intended to enjoy sleeping on the gun, before delivering it to the French herself in a diplomatic bag.*

* Unfortunately the rifle never saw service with the Allies because reverse engineering was too time-consuming. Meanwhile captured Polish anti-tank rifles were used to great effect by both the Germans and Italians. This account of the rifle-smuggling story comes from Bill Stanley Moss, 'Christine the Brave', *Picture Post*, vol. 56, no. 11 (13.9.1952), p. 14. A different account has Christine and Andrzej taking the rifle from Ludwig, without his approval, so that they could supply it to the British/French rather

Shortly after this, Christine was recalled to London, but the Belgians had surrendered at the end of May, Panzer divisions were fanning out across northern France and the French and British were in flight. With Harrison again away, Christine was temporarily cut off from London, and from her source of income. She applied to Polish intelligence in Budapest but they were still nervous about taking her on.* British policy and Polish interests were aligned for the time being, but the Poles were well aware that there might be some future divergence. One officer summed it up: 'We are the Polish Underground, and we do not wish the British to peek inside our underpants.'[17] Furthermore, believing that as a British agent Christine was likely to be under German surveillance, the Poles also cautioned Wladimir about being seen in public with her.[18] That riled Christine, and her vocal criticism of her Polish counterparts probably did her no further favours.

Once it was clear that there would be no funding for her proposed radio station to broadcast news into Poland, Christine decided instead to take fresh news and propaganda material into Warsaw herself. Sitting in cafés by the Danube, she, Andrzej and Wladimir would scour the *Polish News*, *Paris-Soir* and the evening edition of *Pester Lloyd*, the leading German-language publication outside the Third Reich, and discuss the progress of the war with the friendly Hungarian, British and Polish journalists in the city. One of these was Basil Davidson, the former *Economist* correspondent who was now running a legitimate Budapest-based news agency and, as yet unknown to Christine, serving as a British intelligence officer publishing and circulating large amounts of propaganda. Davidson liked and admired Christine for her courage and 'great gallantry', but he did not always admire her judgement. 'She was very Polish', he

than to the Polish authorities. See Anna Potocka, *Through Hills and Valleys . . .* (2011), p. 140.

* Despite constant caution and occasionally hostility towards Christine from the Polish VI Bureau (Polish military intelligence), Christine was listed as a VI Bureau courier under the 'pseudonym' of Gizycka, in 1941, receiving a small amount of 'danger pay'. Ledóchowski was listed in the same report. See TNA, HS7/183, 'Polish VI Bureau', Captain Venner to Colonel Perkins (21.2.1946).

later commented, 'in the sense that she was very romantic.'[19] Christine's fierce, almost blind, pride reminded Davidson of the courage demonstrated by the Polish cavalry that rode against the German Panzers in the full knowledge of their fate. Davidson resisted the temptation to tell her about his own clandestine work. Instead he let Christine upbraid him, as a young man of military age, 'for sitting in Budapest apparently doing nothing except drinking in bars and dancing in night clubs where I had no right to be, instead of fighting for my country'.[20]

Soon the exiled former editor of the *Polish News* group commissioned Christine to take some funds into Warsaw, along with a quantity of propaganda material assembled for the underground press.[21] Then, despite the official intelligence attitude towards Christine, an attaché at the Polish consulate gave her a large envelope of glossy photographs showing General Sikorski decorating Polish officers in Paris, and even meeting Winston Churchill, all to be republished in the Polish underground press as evidence of continued Allied support. It was all the encouragement she needed.

Given that his artificial leg prevented him from making the crossing himself, Andrzej agreed that Wladimir would make the best escort for Christine. Wladimir was also keen to get back to Warsaw, but when the expected commission from the Budapest ZWZ was slow to materialize, Christine decided to wait no longer. In the first week of June, she set off alone.* Just before she left, while Andrzej was out buying cigarettes, Wladimir gave her a parting gift, 'a necklace of flint glass which cast tiny coloured flecks of light', that he had bought having pawned his watch that morning.[22] 'Are you mad?' Christine had exclaimed, with a furtive glance in the mirror. 'You would have done better to buy yourself a pair

* Christine's SOE personal files state that 'in the course of her duties Mme Gizycka, operating from Hungary, undertook four journeys to Poland on foot via Slovakia in circumstances of great danger and hardship'. However, the reports contain inaccuracies, and conflicting dates are given for these journeys. On 31 May 1940 the British reported she had made two successful trips into Poland, but elsewhere only one is recorded. The most likely sequence is a first journey in February/March, two attempts in June, and a successful journey in November 1940. She made additional trips across Hungarian borders as part of her and Andrzej's evacuation work.

of decent shoes.'[23] Both her lovers then saw her to the station. Afterwards Andrzej and Wladimir went to Budapest's Palais de Danse to get drunk together on slivovitz, the local plum brandy. It was a rare emotional truce, and by the end of the evening they had agreed that if the situation in Hungary continued to deteriorate they would help each other to get out.

Two days later Christine was back. The border guards had been increased, the fields were flooded and the rivers bursting their banks with spring rain. She had not been able to get across. 'Not a mouse could have made it', she told the men, and Wladimir thought she looked defeated, her self-assurance gone.[24] Full of pent-up frustration, she was outraged when she heard about the pact that he and Andrzej had made in her absence, shouting 'To hell with you both', and bursting into tears like an angry child.[25] It was not her finest moment. Although she loved risk on her own terms, for someone who could be remarkably cold-blooded when occasion demanded, she was also incredibly thin-skinned; any knock to her pride revealed a surprising insecurity. But perhaps this time something deeper had been triggered: the realization that Andrzej and Wladimir had both entertained the possibility that she might not return. She steeled herself to try to cross again, as soon as possible. 'The news I have from my wife is not encouraging', Jerzy Gizycki wrote to Section D. 'It does not look as if my desire to be with . . . or at least nearer to her, should be fulfilled soon.'[26]

Just after Christine's return, Wladimir's orders at last came through. He had been commissioned to smuggle in microfilm of papers, signed by Sikorski, that confirmed the promotion of commander Tadeusz Bór-Komorowski to the rank of general.* After a furious morning studying maps and collecting materials, Christine, Wladimir and Andrzej headed out of Budapest to the honey-scented acacia woods beyond for a last carefree afternoon. Leaving Andrzej on the lower slopes, Christine tugged Wladimir into the flowery

* Bór-Komorowski would later give the orders for the Warsaw Rising, become Commander-in-chief of the Polish Armed Forces, and for a few years serve as prime minister of the post-war Polish government-in-exile.

trees, where he kissed her passionately. They were both intensely happy at the thought of returning to Poland and of resuming their romance. That evening the three of them packed two rucksacks with maps, compass and peppermints, the microfilm hidden inside a torch, clandestine mail, propaganda material, false identity papers and passes with Gestapo stamps, American dollars, Polish zlotys, Czech koruna and Hungarian pengos, 'any of which' (apart from the mints), as Section D noted, 'in the event of her arrest, might have seriously compromised her'.[27] For Andrzej, however, the Sikorski photographs were too blatantly incriminating. The risk of what might happen to Christine if she was found carrying them was more than he could bear, and he quietly removed them from her rucksack. Then he drove them to the station.

Christine spent a long time saying her goodbyes to Andrzej, and when the train finally started moving she and Wladimir sat opposite each other 'like enemies'.[28] Before nightfall they had completely fallen out. Wladimir bitterly told her how much pain she had caused him, but added that at least now he finally felt free of her. It was an inauspicious start. Meanwhile, when Andrzej got back to Budapest he found that, despite his best efforts, Christine had repacked the glossy propaganda photographs.

At dawn the next day, Christine and Wladimir took a taxi towards the mountains. In the foothills they started hiking up the most sheltered tracks, walking between fields of green wheat and budding blackthorn hedges until they entered the forests that lay across the border. It was midnight before they stopped to sleep, Wladimir lying restlessly in Christine's arms. Starting off again at dawn they found that they had travelled in a circle the day before and were back near the Hungarian border, close to a Slovak checkpoint.

By now the Hungarian police were more or less completely controlled by the Gestapo, and were especially vigilant in the frontier areas. Czechoslovakia, like Poland, was occupied by the Germans. Unwilling to lose another day, however, Christine and Wladimir decided to bolt across the road where a dip in the terrain was just enough to keep them below the seated border guards' line

of vision. Wladimir went first, 'sprinting the one hundred metres in a stylish way, except for my half-bent posture'. Looking back he saw Christine, leaning against a tree, silently applauding. A while later, tired of waiting for the signal to follow, Christine started crawling after him. Wladimir's fingertips were starting to sweat when he saw the border guard stand up, screen his eyes against the slanting rays of the sun, and with his other hand clutch the leather strap of his rifle. 'Run', Wladimir shouted, as 'there was a loud report of a shot, then another one, the next ones fired blindly, showering us with clipped off twigs and leaves.' 'Bloody bastards', Christine commented, when they finally stopped to catch their breath.[29] She was living up to her Musketeer code-name, Fly: irritating, but fast, and hard to catch.

On the Slovak side of the border the climb quickly grew steeper, and as the day heated up they started to peel off coats and jumpers, stuffing them into their bags. Seeing that Christine was tiring, Wladimir discreetly shifted the heavier stuff into his own rucksack. By midday they were above the lower forests and momentarily out in the hot June sunshine, but they were moving too slowly. Dizzy and sunburnt, Christine suggested they take a train, but Wladimir's ZWZ training made him reject the idea. Stopping at a house for milk, they learned that Paris had been taken by the Germans. Wladimir was deeply shaken. If France had fallen then England would be next, he predicted, and there would be no safe place in the world for the Poles.[30]

After two more hours' hiking, they were exhausted as well as demoralized. When Wladimir took Christine's bag and water bottle against her will, she sat under a tree in protest, tears streaming down her face at both her own situation and the whole course of the war. Coerced and cajoled, she pulled herself together, and Wladimir agreed to head for the nearest railway station for the final stage of their journey, the crossing into Poland.[31]

It was dusk when they hid behind the station's goods sheds, but the stationmaster's dog barked at them, so they pressed on down the line and finally crossed an iron railway bridge spanning a deep river, towards the next station. As it was now pitch-black, and about

to rain, they risked sheltering on the platform. Perhaps they dozed off. Either way they were quickly held at gunpoint, and told, in Slovakian, to put their hands up. Wladimir explained that he and his sister had escaped from an internment camp outside Budapest and were heading home to Poland. Then, as Christine painted a sorry story of their life in Hungary and begged the guard to let them go, Wladimir discreetly clicked the torch in his pocket to expose the microfilm and dropped some of his forged travel papers on the fire. The guard seemed to soften as Christine spoke, but he still called the police, telling them that if their story was true they had nothing to fear. Soon an armed patrol arrived to escort them to the local police station, and then on to the nearest Gestapo headquarters the following day.

As they approached the iron bridge, Christine began to limp and, stopping for a moment, she bent down to rub her blistered feet. Wladimir quickly leant forward and offered to get a bandage from her rucksack while he slipped the bulky envelope of propaganda material and Sikorski photographs from her bag into his coat. Once on the bridge he threw the package into the river below. Chaos erupted. One guard ran to retrieve the envelope. Another hauled Wladimir to the other end of the bridge, demanding he tell them what was in the package if he did not want to be shot 'like a dog'.[32] Christine threw herself between them, screaming that it was some money and magazines; stuff of hers that Wladimir knew nothing about. For a moment the envelope hovered on the water, just out of reach of the shore, then it disappeared. The guards were furious, shouting that it would be better if Christine and Wladimir confessed to being spies now, before the Gestapo arrived and forced the truth out of them. Either way they would be shot. 'Your story stinks', Wladimir recorded one officer screaming. 'It's shit!'[33] 'They cross-questioned us, keeping me up against a wall for several hours, covered with revolvers,' Christine later reported, in an account clearly tailored for her British handlers, 'but I swore I did not know the English.'[34]

Soon all of Christine and Wladimir's possessions were laid out on the grass: peppermints, tea, torch, the different packages of zloty

and other currencies, Wladimir's wallet, Christine's forged travel
documents, lipstick and even, Wladimir noticed with astonishment,
a bottle of perfume. Dollars and Czech korunas quickly disappeared,
but it was Wladimir's Madonna that caused the most excitement –
too many people had been caught crossing the mountains with the
same pendant round their necks for it to be coincidence. The medal
was indeed a ZWZ tag, and with growing horror Wladimir realized
he was now a liability. 'Feeling he was ready to die', he started to
consider how, should it become necessary, he could share with
Christine the cyanide powder hidden deep in his pocket.[35]

By 2 a.m. there was still no sign of the Gestapo and the first
shock of their arrest had begun to pass. The forest was fifty metres
behind them, and in between was a guard on the tracks. Wladimir
measured the distance with his eyes and decided that, given enough
of a distraction, they could make it. Christine, her hair 'falling
charmingly' around her face, was talking softly with the guards who
were counting out the money. Two minutes later Wladimir noticed
one of the men holding up her glass necklace to examine it in the
beam of his torch. A small fight ensued as Christine snatched for
it, breaking the string of what she loudly called her 'diamonds',
and scratching the officer's face. The sergeant slapped her, but
also tried to grab at the falling stones. In the confusion Wladimir
knocked the torch from his hand and grabbed Christine, dragging
her up the embankment. They heard the wind in their ears as they
ran, jumped over the track and threw themselves down the other
side. There was shouting and gunshots behind them as the cold
wet branches of the first trees hit their faces, and then they were
climbing and crawling, holding on to branches and tree trunks as
their feet slid across the damp needles, until Christine crashed down
a slope and straight into a tree. She did not get up. 'So that's it',
Wladimir thought.[36]

Christine had not killed herself, but she had injured her leg.
Nonetheless, with Wladimir's help she managed to keep going.
Amazingly he still had his compass, and Christine had some loose
tea-leaves and sugar in her rucksack, which somehow sustained
them. After another close encounter with a mountain patrol who

fired a few shots at them the following day, they reached a rocky
outcrop near the top of the mountains where they could rest a
while. Here they sat, watching the mist clear. 'Do you know',
Christine said, getting to her feet, 'that I've only just this moment
understood what Saint-Exupéry meant when he told me that on
his solitary flights, high above the clouds, he felt like opening the
canopy of his plane to lean out and shake hands with God.'*[37]

Two days later Christine limped over the Hungarian border,
and the next evening they were back in Budapest with Andrzej.
Wladimir would always maintain that Christine had saved both
their lives when she brought out her 'diamonds', but Christine was,
as usual, more circumspect in her own report. 'Having found
145,000 zloty on me, and 75 dollars and 15,000 kronen on a boy
accompanying me', she wrote rather modestly, 'they apparently
preferred that to the 10,000 marks reward' they would have received
for two agents, 'and we were able to escape'.[38]

Despite having narrowly avoided being shot as spies, Wladimir
and Christine felt they had failed. The only valuable intelligence
they brought back was that the route they had taken should
temporarily be closed, and that the medal of Our Lady was no
longer a safe identity tag for the ZWZ. They had lost the money
they had been entrusted with, along with Christine's travel docu-
ments bearing her photograph. It was later reported that her image
was posted in every railway station in Poland, with £1,000 reward
on her head – 'dead or alive'.[39] Nevertheless, Christine announced
that she was determined to return to Poland permanently, and
support the underground resistance *in situ*. It seemed like a death-
wish. On average, the women engaged in liaison and courier work
inside Poland could expect to survive, at most, a few months, and
most of them were anonymous, at least at the beginning.[40] Know-
ing, however, that danger was not likely to put her off, Andrzej and

* The French aviator and writer Antoine de Saint-Exupéry was best known for his
book *The Little Prince*. He was famous in pre-war Poland, and Christine probably met
him during her French travels with Jerzy Gizycki. They might have crossed paths
again in Algiers in 1943 before Saint-Exupéry disappeared on a flying mission in 1944,
never to be found.

Wladimir discouraged Christine by arguing that her languages, and her good relations with the British, gave her greater potential to work with Polish intelligence elsewhere in Europe. But the prospect of languishing in Budapest held no appeal for Wladimir either, and a few days later he moved to Belgrade. Once there he accepted a posting with the Polish army to Latrun, in Palestine. He would go on to fight with exceptional courage in North Africa.

By the time Wladimir left Hungary, France was being evacuated. Jerzy Gizycki had already arrived in London, from where he hoped to move to Canada 'to prepare there some sort of a home to which Christine could come when she gets out of her . . . predicament'.[41] His appeals for information about his wife now went unanswered, partly because Hubert Harrison had failed to return to Budapest after his most recent trip to London, preferring instead to resume his old job at the *Daily Express*.* Jerzy's last letter in Christine's British file states with moving brevity, 'Am going away on official mission. Do not know when shall be back. If should not be back – kindly take care of my wife.'[42] He had abandoned his Canadian plans and departed instead for West Africa, where he had taken a posting with Polish intelligence.[43]

Eastern Europe, like the rest of the world, was badly shaken by the fall of France that June. The Polish community in Budapest might no longer feel as humiliated by their country's earlier defeat, but they also saw that the whole tide of the war had shifted in Germany's favour. And Hungary's puppet government, which had recently introduced its own version of Germany's Nuremberg laws, preventing Jews from working in the civil service or marrying outside their own communities, now knew that sooner or later they would have to give way to German pressure to abandon their neutral status altogether. Recognizing this, the Polish intelligence team left Budapest for Belgrade. As a result the British now needed their agents in Hungary more than ever, both to provide a link to

* Harrison arrived back in Britain on 3 June 1940, and never returned to Budapest. In October SOE decided his services were no longer required and he left the firm the following January. See TNA, HS9/668, SOE personal files, Hubert Harrison.

Poland, but also to help evacuate British and Polish POWs, particularly pilots, who were now desperately needed to fight in the Battle of Britain. That summer two fighter squadrons of 145 Polish pilots, escapees from Poland, France, or Hungarian internment, shot down 201 enemy aircraft. This was the highest number of kills by any Allied squadrons in the battle, and a decisive contribution to the victory. Thirty Polish pilots lost their lives, but the Battle of Britain marked Hitler's first major defeat and a strategic turning point in the war.

Christine and Andrzej were ordered to Belgrade on 30 June, but their work in Budapest had entered a key phase.[44] They had developed their courier networks to smuggle money, arms and explosives into Poland, and intelligence out, using well-connected contacts including a Jesuit priest, 'a little, worn man' with broken boots, called Father Laski, and Prince Marcin Lubomirski.[45] Andrzej, his assistant, Antoni Filipkiewicz, and others, were also driving vast numbers of Czechoslovakian and Polish officers, many of them pilots, across the 'green frontier' from Hungary to Yugoslavia, often in groups of twenty or thirty men, barely hidden in Andrzej's enormous Chevrolet, as well as the lorries and farm trucks that had previously brought in supplies of vegetables, flour and explosives.

By now Andrzej had unrivalled knowledge of the frontier, and had organized a number of courier posts on the borders. That summer he and Christine extended the routes that would later become famous as part of the secret 'underground railroad' that took escapees out through the Balkans and Turkey, and so to Greece or on to Palestine and Egypt to join the Allied war effort. Christine would make the clandestine arrangements on the Polish and Slovakian side, and Andrzej and his team would drive the men out of Hungary to the south.[46] Andrzej was too security-conscious to keep a record of his movements, but his passport contains over twenty visas, mainly between Hungary and Serbia, and many for multiple entry. The British later estimated that he was responsible for the transfer of 5,000 internees over the course of 1940, with Christine crossing the Polish border six times and the Slovakian

border eight times in support of this work.[47] Clearly they worked extremely effectively together, making a huge contribution to the war effort both in terms of providing men to fight the Nazi advance and by undermining the Germans' sense of security in the territories they occupied.

Andrzej's summer journeys along the dusty roads lined with budding mulberry bushes and the poppies whose black seeds would later flavour the country bread were in many ways idyllic, but he was under increasing surveillance. On one occasion he was captured by a border patrol on the Slovak frontier while awaiting the arrival of some British escapees from Poland. Although 'severely handled' by the police, he managed to get away, and immediately returned to the frontier to finish the job.[48] Not long afterwards he was sent to collect men from the Polish–Russian border. Ever resourceful, he obtained a Hungarian Ministry pass and official car to drive into the frontier zone, in exchange for smuggling out the young relatives of a Hungarian colonel.* With this permit, and Christine's press pass, the pair of them could now also carry the microfilm received from her Polish contacts further across Hungary, usually hidden, with cartoonish audacity, either inside her gloves or behind a secret panel in his wooden leg.

Their adventures were soon the stuff of legend. Alone, on the run from a border patrol, Christine met a sympathetic forester who, with great presence of mind, took her in and hid her, pretending she was his daughter, sick in bed.[49] Weeks later, as she hiked to the crest of the mountain range serving as the border between Poland and Czechoslovakia, a Luftwaffe pilot reportedly spotted her dark figure beneath him, 'trapped like an ant on a tablecloth'.[50] For hours she was forced to play hide and seek, shielding herself behind a large rock to escape the stream of machine-gun fire that streaked towards her.[51] Once she talked her way out of arrest by telling some suspicious frontier guards she was on a picnic, even getting them to help push-start her stalled car.[52] In another story she and Andrzej were driving three Czech pilots across the border when some police

* Masson *Christine, SOE Agent*, names the colonel as Zoltan Schell, p. 81.

opened fire. Although they sped away, two of the Czechs were killed, one shot in the head, the other in the spine, leaving 'the interior of the car ... spattered with blood, its back riddled with bullets'.[53]

Sometimes their activities seemed to take on a darkly comic dimension. During another dramatic car chase Christine is said to have optimistically tried to shield Andrzej's head from a volley of bullets with her bag. Later he joked that her knickers would have served as a better talisman.[54] And in Budapest they once had to shelter the well-known socialite turned secret agent, Prince Eddie Lobkowitz, then working for the French underground. Bored at their safe house, the prince simply pulled down his hat and went off to drink coffee in the best cafés, where he watched the waitresses through a hole in his newspaper, burnt for the purpose with his cigarette. They laughed afterwards, but were glad to pass him on swiftly.[55] As the German position strengthened, Budapest grew ever more dangerous, and neither Christine nor Andrzej had diplomatic immunity. She was 'a person of quite remarkable courage and intelligence', the British reported that August.[56]

Christine was also busy enlisting the help of the British Minister in Hungary, Sir Owen O'Malley. Sir Owen had arrived in Budapest from London less than a year earlier, his imagination fired even on the drive over as he watched 'the brave way the silver snipe on the bonnet of my Humber car flashed on the great plain of Central Europe'.[57] Patriotic, romantic but essentially conventional, at Harrow O'Malley had played Antonio, the merchant of Venice, opposite Rupert Brooke's Portia, and he would later live in a house rented from the Byron family. But Sir Owen was also an opportunist. When war broke out he had sent as many British subjects home as possible, and then launched a daily information service, using trusted staff and his attractive eighteen-year-old daughter Kate to take shifts sitting on a cork-topped stool in the Legation bathroom to monitor the powerful radio receiver.[58] He also encouraged members of his staff to rent flats overlooking the West-Bahnhof rail tracks so they could report on the long munition trains full of tanks, tracked vehicles and guns passing through the city, the shapes

clearly recognizable under their waterproof covers. Despite this, he was punctilious in keeping to the Foreign Office line of maintaining cordial relations with so-called neutral countries. He was, therefore, initially reluctant to support the work of Section D in Hungary.

Christine's friend the British journalist and intelligence officer Basil Davidson described Sir Owen as 'an Anglo-Irish gentleman of impeccable diplomacy whose views . . . were that the war was probably lost and that, this being so, nothing should be done to make bad into worse, above all nothing irregular, and in his own Legation'.[59] When Sir Owen discovered that Section D had been secretly using the Legation's cellars to store sacks full of high explosives until they could be used to blow up enemy shipping on the Danube, he sent for Davidson. He had 'pale blue eyes, and pale spectacles rimmed in gold', Davidson remembered. 'All these he turned away from me.'[60] Sir Owen was livid, and had ditched the explosives in the Danube lest the Legation's diplomatic neutrality be compromised. Davidson was *persona non grata*, and lucky not to be in the Danube himself. 'We were totally amateurish', he admitted later, 'very amateurish and very ignorant.'[61]

But Sir Owen did not avert his eyes from the 'young, beautiful and gifted' woman, as he described Christine, who cornered him at one of the Legation's regular Monday evening cocktail parties; his daughter Kate was just as taken with Andrzej.*[62] Sir Owen's news bulletin was his pride and joy, and it did not take Christine long to smooth over the strained relationship between the Minister and Basil Davidson, giving both men the chance to share 'watered-down news of a pro-Allied colour' to the Hungarian press and radio.[63] Christine was of 'considerable assistance to the British Minister', Section D reported, although it might be argued that the boot was on the other foot.[64] Sir Owen was not entirely uncritical of Christine, describing her as 'extremely obstinate, individualistic, attractive

* There are various stories as to where Christine and Sir Owen first met. In her novel *The Tightening String* (1962), Ann Bridge, Sir Owen's wife, described these Monday events as being attended by 'a few Poles who had managed to escape to Hungary', some British, Hungarians and a few Allied diplomats. They may have been introduced here by a mutual friend, the Polish consul in Budapest.

and moody', but he was completely won over by her 'unexampled courage', reporting that 'she was ready to risk her life at any moment for what she believed in'.[65]

As a result, both Sir Owen and Kate O'Malley were soon helping, 'as unobtrusively as possible', with the 'exfiltration' of Polish soldiers and pilots, and British POWs interned in Hungary and Poland.[66] Sir Owen applied to the British Foreign Office in London for funding, and was 'staggered' when he was told that he had an unlimited budget.[67] His daughter Kate, meanwhile, was able to meet Christine and Andrzej in the Budapest bars, cafés and cheap boarding-houses to which her high-society parents could never go, slipping in and out of buildings in her fashionable little Budapest shoes 'with the familiarity and ease of a little mouse', her mother later wrote, before confessing she had been 'rather aghast' when she learned how closely her daughter had been involved in the underground.[68]

Like her increasingly besotted father, Kate worshipped Christine, even noting the 'grace and ease' with which she moved. 'There was something almost animal in it,' Kate commented. 'Something antelope-ish.'[69] Sharing great risks almost daily, but also gossip and light-hearted intimacy, she and Christine were soon as close as sisters. However, Christine was not entirely happy about Kate's equally fervent admiration for Andrzej. That summer Christine and Andrzej had finally moved into a flat together, but now it was Kate and Andrzej who wandered round the flower market, Andrzej teaching Kate songs about the frontier, along which 'the corn is so green, oh so green, that a man may pass through it unseen, all unseen'.[70] Meanwhile Christine was left lecturing one of her few other female friends in the city on how 'you have to love a man so much you don't mind ... helping with his gammy leg, or giving him an enema'.[71] (Andrzej was still driving huge numbers of men out of the country, and as security tightened he was often forced to walk long distances to make contact with his smugglers, causing terrible problems with his leg, which had received no medical attention since the start of the war.) But if some of the romantic spark had gone, Christine's relationship with Andrzej was still

deeper and more intimate than any she would enjoy with any other man.

At the end of September 1940, as the situation in Hungary worsened and Wehrmacht officers started lingering ever more territorially over their coffee in Budapest's railway stations, Christine and Andrzej began to amass information on troop and freight movements through the country. At the request of the British they organized surveillance of all the main rail, road and river traffic, particularly noting the build-up of the frontier guards on the borders with Romania and Germany. Christine was later credited with sabotaging communications on the main Danube river route, as well as providing vital information on oil transports to Germany from Romania's Ploieşti oilfields.[72] Both she and Andrzej also distributed British arms and explosives to exiled Poles in Hungary and in Poland itself, and on at least one occasion that autumn made good use of the weapons themselves.*

Incensed at seeing Romanian petrol being shipped via Hungary into Austria, Andrzej and a friend limpet-mined some of the barges on the Danube one night, swimming out into the icy river with the heavy magnetized mines while Christine, who could not swim, waited impatiently, with Andrzej's leg, in their fastest available car. The barges later blew up spectacularly too far from port to be salvaged.† By now even Sir Owen had overcome his dislike for SOE sabotage work. Deeply impressed, he would later claim that Christine 'had a positive nostalgie [sic] for danger . . . [and] could do anything with dynamite, except eat it'.‡[73]

* The Romanian Ploieşti oilfields were eventually bombed by the RAF and US Air Force, with considerable loss of life.

† The limpet mines used time-delay detonators that were originally concealed inside Woolworths aniseed balls whose dissolving rate had been vigorously tested in Bedford Modern School swimming pool the year before, before the sweets were replaced with corrosive acid. See BBC WW2 People's War, 'Aniseed Balls and the Limpet Mine', article A4376153 (6.7.2005). Later the British used 'sticky bombs' to sabotage many more German oil barges on the Danube: see Jozef Garlinski, Poland, SOE and the Allies (1969), pp. 25–6.

‡ Plastic explosive developed at the Royal Arsenal at Woolwich just before the war could be safely eaten, 'though it can hardly have been either tasty or nutritious'.

But such proceedings could not go unnoticed. Polish intelligence were filing reports on their activities, but Andrzej was also under more hostile and almost constant German surveillance. Soon the Nazis began to pressure the Hungarians to arrest him. Fortunately Andrzej had developed excellent relations with some influential Hungarian officials, and when he was arrested for a third time the police released him with the strong advice that he leave the country. Not long afterwards several other members of his network were arrested and interrogated. Realizing that they had been infiltrated, Andrzej discovered that one of his newer recruits had been seen talking with a member of the German Embassy. He started to feed the man false information and, when he was sure, felt no compunction about calling on a group of Hungarian thieves sympathetic to the Poles to look after his 'inquisitive friend'.[74] Having got the informant paralytically drunk on slivovitz while they knocked back water, the thieves left him on the nearest public bench. He was found stiff and dead the next morning after a night when temperatures reached minus 20, his body giving off the distinct smell of bitter almonds from the plum kernels in the slivovitz.

At the start of October 1940 a Musketeer courier arrived from Poland with news that sixteen British pilots and airmen were hiding, as they spoke no Polish, in a Warsaw 'asylum for the deaf and dumb'.[75] Christine at once asked the British for the money and backing she would need to go to Poland and lead the men out. Fears for the men's safety grew as rumours circulated that Hitler was planning to implement 'mercy killings' of the disabled, but Christine was urged to wait until the November snows, which would reduce the effectiveness of the frontier patrols and enable her to ski across more easily. 'I waited for five weeks', Christine later reported, before deciding that if the British would not help, 'I would do it myself.'[76]

Christine finally left on 13 November, accompanied by Father

M. R. D. Foot, *SOE: An Outline History of the Special Operations Executive 1940–1946* (1999), p. 107.

Laski.[77] They chose a more easterly route than the one she had taken with Wladimir, over the high Czarnahova, now in the Ukraine, and she carried Ukrainian identity papers made out in a false name, along with $500. By the time she reached the Warsaw asylum, five days later, she found that, amid growing fears that Hungary was about to join the Axis, the Polish underground had decided not to risk the old escape route. As a result the airmen had been taken into the Russian-occupied zone of Poland, and through Kiev into Russia itself. Soon after two of them reappeared in Warsaw, with the news that the Russians had handed the others over to the Germans. Christine was now asked to bring these last two pilots out, but they were too exhausted to travel. Instead she handed them over to the Musketeers with $200 to pay for a doctor and sanctuary for three weeks, before they could be taken over the border. It was Father Laski who finally got them to Budapest, where he made contact with Kate O'Malley. Sir Owen was having an after-lunch nap when his daughter told him she had two RAF pilots who needed to be taken south over the border. 'Body-smuggling was generally taken to be below the dignity of a British diplomat, and contrary to HMG's regulations to boot', Wladimir noted when he heard of the incident, but Sir Owen nevertheless agreed to help them.[78] Having hastily provided the pilots with passports and visas under the rather conspicuous names of Hardy and Willis, Sir Owen took them to Belgrade listed as members of his staff.[79]

Christine had not been able to wait for them because she had been asked to take a large consignment of urgent information to Budapest. The bulkiest item was an Anglo-Russian dictionary with a special code, call signs and wavelengths hidden inside its pages. Going against the usual security precautions, she was also given a detailed description of the number and locations of radio stations in Poland, and instructions for how to establish regular direct radio communications between Warsaw and London at specified times, using the information in the dictionary. Witkowski must have been short of couriers to entrust both of these documents to the same person, but that was not all Christine was carrying. She had the formulae for two new gases being produced by the Germans, and a

second report which, in her own words, provided 'further up to date information on ammunition factories in Germany and Poland, detailed plans of aerodromes, aircraft factories, the number of planes which existed in Poland, details of torpedoes, U-boats and a new torpedo invention'.[80] The extraordinary detail of the intelligence had been provided by sixteen engineers placed among the Polish workers forcibly sent to Germany to work in munitions factories and at railway stations. Like almost all the information Christine brought out, these reports had been photographed onto 35mm film, the rolls of which she carried inside her gloves.

Christine had also made the time to undertake some personal missions while she was in Poland. Andrzej had written a letter for his mother, Maria, which Christine delivered to her at Zamosc, in the south-east of the country. And having learned that her Skarbek cousins from Lwów had escaped to Hungary, she now wrote to them, giving them the first definite, if circumspect, information they had had about their father since the fall of France.[81] Despite the risks, Christine also visited her own mother again, who told her that her brother had been arrested by the Gestapo. Once again, she tried, vainly, to persuade Stefania to leave Poland, or at least Warsaw and her work as a teacher in a clandestine school. Strive as she might, she could not persuade her mother of the very real danger she faced. Stefania was convinced that her social status as a Skarbek would protect her – in a society that had never really accepted her, and which was now disintegrating. The ghetto, bordered on one side by the empty building of the former Goldfeder bank, now enclosed in less than one and a half square miles over 400,000 people, nearly a third of Warsaw's population, mainly Jews. Were Stefania to be discovered living outside the ghetto she could be shot instantly. She could also be shot just for giving classes. When the Gestapo discovered that secret lessons were taking place in another Warsaw flat, 'they seized all of them', an underground officer wrote, 'and hanged them straight away from a balcony in Leszno Street'.[82]

Determined to protect her mother, Christine spoke to Witkowski about her, and also sought out her father's old friend

Stanisław Rudziejewski, the young war hero whose odorous feet had so offended the fine ladies at the Warsaw opera twenty years before. Stanisław had been sent to a camp in Latvia in 1939, from which he had been rescued by his wife Irena, just before his unit was transferred to the Russian forests near Katyn. A forester by trade, both he and Irena had now joined the Polish resistance, and Christine asked them if they would hide Stefania in their isolated forest house until she could get her out.[83] After some discussion they agreed, but Stefania was obdurate. Still blindly clinging to the belief that as an aristocrat she would be safe, she refused to abandon Warsaw, her Goldfeder relatives locked inside the ghetto, and her pupils. Christine could win the confidence and financial support of the British, she could secure the devotion of Polish officers working both in and outside the official resistance, she could even talk a Gestapo officer into carrying a 'black-market package' for her, but she could not persuade her Jewish mother to leave Nazi-occupied Poland. To Christine's profound distress, Stefania disappeared a year later, having been arrested by the Gestapo and confined in Warsaw's infamous Pawiak prison.

It was a bitter irony that Pawiak had been built in the 1830s to the design of Fryderyck Skarbek, prison reformer, godfather of Chopin – and Christine's ancestor. Following the Nazi invasion of Poland, Pawiak was turned into a Gestapo jail, its name becoming 'a spectre' throughout Warsaw, according to one Polish underground army officer.[84] Roughly 100,000 men and 200,000 women passed through the prison during the course of the war, mostly members of the resistance, political prisoners and civilians taken as hostages in street round-ups. Of these, 37,000 would die there.

The prison's records provide a stark picture of what Pawiak was like when Stefania arrived there on 31 January 1942: the last known trace of her. Fifty-six people, including five family groups, had arrived at the prison the day before, and only ten left, including a child 'transported to the city morgue'.[85] Stefania was one of four new arrivals, and as a Jew she would have received harsher treatment than the resistance suspects, hostages, POW fugitives and smugglers

that comprised most of the rest of the inmates, but conditions were very poor for all of them. Pawiak's cells were dirty, cold, dark, crammed with people and riddled with vermin. Windows – where the cells had any at all – were generally covered, further limiting access to light and air. Prisoners slept on planks or straw mattresses, and buckets served as the only toilets. There was no soap or water. Meals supplied only a few hundred calories a day, so most prisoners were starving. Routine maltreatment ranged from beatings to forced walks across glowing cinders. Disobedience led to solitary confinement, or immediate execution.[86] For most inmates, Pawiak was a stop preceding deportation to the concentration camps at Auschwitz, Ravensbrück, Stutthof, Majdanek, Sachsenhausen, Buchenwald or Gross-Rosen, but there is no evidence that Stefania was sent to a camp. Thousands of Pawiak prisoners, mainly members of the Polish intelligentsia, were executed by the Nazis, and it is likely that Stefania was among these, possibly killed by machine gun in the Palmiry forests just outside the city, or otherwise dying of disease or starvation in the prison itself. She was in her mid-sixties.

Christine had left Budapest by the time her mother was arrested at the start of 1942, but at least two independent accounts, both seemingly informed by Christine herself, tell a different story.[87] According to Wladimir, just after Christine arrived in Warsaw, in November 1940, a cousin told her that Stefania had been arrested either because she had failed to register as a Jew and move into the ghetto, or because she refused to identify Christine in the false papers taken from her daughter in Slovakia earlier in the year. Burning with guilt, Christine evolved a plan to buy her mother's freedom, provide her with Aryan papers, and smuggle her out of Warsaw to somewhere she could be hidden until the end of the war. A Goldfeder cousin, a pianist at a café in the ghetto patronized by crooked Wehrmacht officers, put her in touch with a Gestapo officer called Grüber, who was known as 'the uncrowned king of the black market', and 'a mighty skirt-chaser'.[88] The next evening Christine danced with Grüber in the café, and later, over drinks, he agreed to look through her mother's files. The next day he left

Christine a note saying that he regretted he could not help, as her mother had already been transferred to Auschwitz.* In another account, the Gestapo officer demanded $300 and a night with Christine for her mother's life, and only told her she was too late after both payments had been taken.[89]

By late 1940 Christine was used to telling stories to cover her tracks. She changed the route of her first train journey into occupied Poland, and Wladimir's ability to work out her identity from her regularly repeated tale of the bodies in the snow had shown her how important it was to vary any story, however painful or seemingly innocuous. Later Christine's war stories would grow more and more contradictory. From time to time she indulged 'in the most outrageous fantasies when talking to people whom she was not disposed to take seriously', one of her close British friends and colleagues later admitted, thinking of her tales presenting herself 'as a gun-toting female who would happily toss hand-grenades whenever the occasion demanded'.[90] But people's stories usually have some vestige of truth, and it is possible that Christine did try to rescue someone from Pawiak or the Warsaw ghetto. Women *were* using sex for this purpose in Warsaw in 1940. Or perhaps the story stemmed from Christine's eternal regret that although she would have done even this to save her mother, she never had the chance.

Christine arrived back in Budapest on 25 November 1940, physically and emotionally exhausted. She spent Christmas with Andrzej, working on plans to return to Warsaw but too ill to do much more. She had flu, and a hacking cough, and Andrzej was concerned about her. He was also increasingly worried about the situation in Hungary, whose military police, press and policies were all now dominated by the Nazis. By the end of November the Gestapo had even established an independent presence in Budapest.

* Stefania Skarbek (Goldfeder) is not listed in the surviving Auschwitz records. According to Pawiak Museum archives, Edmund and Józef Skarbek were sent from Pawiak to Auschwitz in 1940, and Tadeusz, Menaszel and Zofia Goldfeder were interned in Pawiak between 1940 and 1942, before being sent to Auschwitz and Sachsenhausen, but their relationship to Christine, if any, is not known.

Andrzej wanted to leave the city, but Christine was waiting for a final delivery from a Polish courier. Towards the end of January 1941 Andrzej realized they were under almost constant surveillance. Above all he was concerned that they should not be arrested together, as this would leave no one to warn other members of the network, and because if their cover stories were not entirely watertight they might be made to contradict one another. At 3 a.m. on 23 January, knowing that the military police typically called in the early hours, Andrzej left Christine in the flat on a practice escape run. It was cold and miserable but the streets were deserted. The next night they went out for dinner with Kate O'Malley and some other friends. They were woken by banging on their door at four o'clock in the morning. They looked at each other. Christine grabbed a dressing gown. Andrzej put on his leg. Neither of them had any illusions, but to Andrzej's amazement he noticed that Christine seemed almost cheered by their impending arrest. After weeks of illness and nervous anticipation 'she was smiling to me . . .' he reported, 'as merry as if she was going to a cocktail party!'[91]

6: TRAVELS IN AN OPEL

'Christine suddenly stood up on the bed, holding the edge of the sheet with her teeth', runs one account of the arrival of the Hungarian police. '"I'll make you some tea," she told them, "but turn round first, all of you . . . "'[1] Whether or not the bed-linen was raised, Christine certainly managed to put the police off their guard. A moment later the whistling of the kettle could not entirely disguise the sound of the toilet flushing away incriminating pages of her diary. 'Why did you pull the chain?' one of the policemen demanded furiously in Andrzej's version of the story, provoking Christine to smile, and reply 'in her normal voice, "Isn't it usual to flush the loo after use?"'[2] When Andrzej tried the same trick he was given an unblinking escort, and was reduced to using some smart sleight of hand to stow his coded notebook in the pocket of his jacket. The police searched the flat for an hour but found nothing incriminating. Even so, Christine and Andrzej were driven to a fortified house in Horthy Miklos Street to be interrogated.

Andrzej was ushered into a large upstairs room, where a Gestapo officer ordered him to remove his clothes. His overcoat was immediately searched down to the inside of its seams and left on a peg. Having stripped to his underpants, he managed to slip his notebook from under his folded jacket into a pocket of the coat, where it hung, untouched, throughout the questioning. His leg and his person having been thoroughly checked for microfilm, he was 'brutally interrogated' for nineteen hours without break but stuck doggedly to his usual cover story.[3]

At midday on the second day the interrogators finished their shift and were replaced. Andrzej was exhausted and losing his grip. Hoping to break him, the Gestapo showed him the bloodied mess

of a man they were working on in the next room. Then the interrogation began again. The Gestapo officers wanted to know why he and Christine had spent so much time at the British Legation, to which Andrzej replied that he did not think that the German Minister would have welcomed them. His sarcastic response only provoked them into beating him. However, he clung to the growing conviction that the Gestapo needed to prove that he and Christine had been working directly against the Reich, for the British or for someone else, before they could be extradited to Germany. That evening Andrzej was confined in Budapest's notorious Hadik prison. The situation seemed hopeless. The next day, back in the interrogation suite, he was amazed to see Christine ushered in, looking 'as pale as paper'. 'The doctor says I am not well', she told him pointedly.[4]

Christine had faced a similar ordeal to Andrzej and, like him, she stuck to their story. At times it was almost too well rehearsed: she even made the same joke about the German Ambassador not being likely to welcome them, although, she added drily, Andrzej's frequent presence at the British Legation might have something to do with the Minister's attractive daughter. Most importantly though, she later reported to Section D, 'I again denied having any dealings with the British', adding with typical aplomb, 'other than a flirtation', possibly referring to Sir Owen.[5] Christine's interrogators wanted to know how, and how often, she had managed to visit Poland, and showed her a copy of her 'Zofia Andrzejewska' identity papers with her photograph attached. 'One can't deny that the likeness is striking', one admirer later pictured Christine responding after a steady inspection of the papers. 'However, it seems to me that the girl on that picture is much prettier.'[6]

Christine had been ill before she was arrested, and despite her courage Andrzej could not imagine how she would hold up under twenty-four hours' interrogation. But, not for the first time, Christine made a virtue of her apparent weakness, hamming up her hacking cough until her eyes were streaming. With what the British later called 'great presence of mind', she then bit her tongue so hard, and so repeatedly, that it soon appeared as though she was

coughing up blood.*[7] It was a searingly painful but brilliant tactic that brought immediate results. The Germans were, rightly, terrified of tuberculosis, which spreads rapidly through the airborne droplets expelled by coughing, sneezing or even speaking. A prison doctor was quickly called in to diagnose Christine's condition. As casually as possible in the circumstances, Christine mentioned that she had been enlisting the help of her aunt, who was related to Admiral Horthy, Hungary's regent, to find a lung specialist when she had been arrested. Christine did indeed have a tenuous connection to the Horthy family through a distant aunt, and while it is doubtful that by 1941 the Gestapo had any concerns about this, it might have given the Hungarian doctor another incentive to help her. Although it is unlikely that he was taken in by her coughing, the doctor arranged for Christine to have a chest X-ray. She could not have hoped for a better result. Dark shadows were clearly visible across her lungs: the impact of the garage fumes from her job at Fiat fifteen years earlier. The doctor conspiratorially 'confirmed' tuberculosis and urged her immediate release on humanitarian grounds.[†]

Christine's sangfroid paid off. After a brief consultation she and Andrzej, who was considered likely to be contagious, were released – under certain conditions. Followed by two plain-clothes policemen, they were told to go to their regular rendezvous, the Café Hangli, before returning to their flat, which they were then not to leave without permission. They were not to take any form of transport except a tram, and were to report to the police every three hours by phone. Fortunately word of their arrest had got round, and in any case one look at Christine and Andrzej's swollen faces would have served as a clear signal. No one greeted them at the café. After coffee, and their first meal in two days, they walked

* Christine may have got this idea from a British leaflet entitled *How To Fake An Illness*, which recommended simulating internal bleeding by biting lips or gums – although how to bite your own gums is not fully detailed.

† It has been speculated, but never confirmed, that a bribe may have been paid for Christine and Andrzej's release, or that Sir Owen O'Malley pulled a few strings with Admiral Miklos Horthy, Hungary's regent.

slowly back through the icy streets to their flat. It was only when they realized they were still being followed and their phone had been tapped that they finally started packing.

Andrzej's pride and joy was his sandy-brown, two-door Opel Olympia, nicknamed 'Paul Opiel', which he had kept topped up with petrol but hidden in a dirty greenhouse in the gated courtyard behind his and Christine's flat. This was the same car that he had driven out of Poland the year before, and in which he had escaped the Hungarian internment camp. The SS had raced Opels in 1938, and the following year the convertible became a favourite of high-ranking SS officers.[8] It is entirely possible that Andrzej's beloved car had once belonged to a discerning Wehrmacht officer, as his sister later proudly referred to it as his 'spoils of the war with Germany'.[9] But because Andrzej had never used the Opel on his border excursions, or driven it much round Budapest, it was not known to the Hungarian police. When, blithely ignoring the team watching the flat, a friend arrived with a bottle of slivovitz to welcome them home, the three of them came up with a plan. That evening, as the police followed Andrzej's Chevrolet out of the city, Andrzej revved up 'Paul Opiel', filling the cold greenhouse with clouds of fumes, and drove off in the opposite direction. The Opel had a four-cylinder engine capable of at least 60 miles an hour and made short work of the roads around their flat. Soon they were parked outside the old, yellow-plastered houses round the corner from the British Legation. A quick call to Kate O'Malley and they were through the snow covered porte-cochère, which led from the street to the Legation's large inner courtyard.

During the seventeenth-century Turkish occupation, the British Legation at Buda had been a palace complete with harem, and its gardens ran right up to the medieval bastion that surrounded the Old City. At the top of the stone steps from the porte-cochère was a long passageway leading directly to Sir Owen's study. Here Christine and Andrzej sank wordlessly into armchairs. Sir Owen took one look at their bruised and swollen faces and helped them to a drink from the tray that stood permanently on his desk between red diplomatic boxes, a few old copies of the *New Statesman*, and

his telephone, which he kept in a baize-lined wooden box in case it had been bugged to enable his private conversations in the room to be overheard.[10]

Sir Owen had suspected for some time that the Gestapo, working through the Hungarian police, were closing in on Christine. 'I begged her and implored her to leave the country while there was still time', he later claimed, 'but she was obdurate.'[11] Now he was determined to get her safely out, and if Andrzej, of whom Sir Owen vaguely disapproved for eliciting his daughter's affections, could be evacuated too, then all the better. Sir Owen's plan was to hide Christine in the boot of a Legation car the following day, and get a junior member of his staff to drive her across the border into Yugoslavia, and on to Belgrade. Andrzej was to follow in the Opel, which they would need to take them on through Europe.

'On Sunday, after breakfast,' Sir Owen later wrote with remarkable lack of drama, 'I noticed signs of perturbation in the courtyard.'[12] None of the available Legation cars had a boot large enough to hold Christine. Fortunately Sir Owen's car was a generously proportioned Chrysler. The boot was hastily cleared and its diplomatic pennants attached as the tank and some spare jerrycans were filled from the huge petrol storage tank that Sir Owen had thoughtfully had sunk in the Legation courtyard.[13] Sir Owen now pressed his guests, with growing urgency, for the new names and other personal details that his clerk required to complete the false passports and visas needed to take them across the border and on through Europe.

Andrzej as yet spoke only two words of English, and they were 'double whisky', but he opted for the name 'Andrew Kennedy', in honour of both Sir Owen's Irish roots and a relative of his own who had married an Irish Catholic émigré whose story he could appropriate. Christine, hastily advised by Kate, picked the more ambiguously European, almost aristocratic-sounding, 'Christine Granville'. Her cover story, that she was born of French parents in the Channel Islands, was designed to supply a reason for her perfect French but shaky and heavily accented English. In return for her new name, Christine gave Kate her talisman of the Madonna of

Częstochowa that she had carried with her since childhood, saying, 'Keep this for me, I shall probably never need it again.'[14]

The farewells were taking too long and even Sir Owen began to get agitated, but Christine was unfazed. When the clerk pressed her for her date of birth she smiled, looked up at him, and coolly took the opportunity to knock seven years off her age. From then on Christine would always give 1915 as her birth year. Perhaps she was simply completing her disguise, but it is equally likely that vanity played a part. Seven minutes later the ink was drying on her new passport, and an apparently twenty-six-year-old Christine Granville was ready to be delivered to the free world.*

They had to move fast. While the police at the Legation's wrought-iron gates, who were used to getting hot cocoa in the porter's lodge on snowy nights, looked the other way, Christine practised folding herself up 'like a penknife' in the boot.[15] There was no time for any further attempt at concealment. Stifling her cough, she was driven out of the Legation, out of Budapest, and swiftly down the nearly deserted roads through southern Hungary. As agreed, Andrzej, in the Opel, arrived at Lenti, his chosen frontier checkpoint, just ahead of the Chrysler. Seeing it drive up, flags flying, he waited respectfully for the Legation car to cross the border first. With his heart in his mouth he watched as the Hungarian customs official leant his palm on the Chrysler's boot, and ordered it to be opened. Then, noticing the British pennants, the official touched the visor of his cap with one hand and waved them through with the other.[16] In high spirits, Andrzej, who had no exit visa in his Polish passport, then cheekily asked the border guards to help push his little Opel across the frontier, ostensibly to be collected for hard currency by a buyer on the other side. Once

* Christine was not the only one to exploit the minor advantages of living under a false identity in this way. In his unpublished memoirs, her husband, Jerzy Gizycki, states he was born in 1889, but in his 1941 application to serve with the British he gave his date of birth as 1895. But if Jerzy thought he could reduce the considerable age gap between himself and his wife, at least on paper, he was wrong. Christine had beaten him to the same trick, even as the Gestapo were combing the streets of Budapest for her.

over the border he jumped in and drove off at top speed, waving his new British passport out of the window.

When Andrzej and Sir Owen's driver released Christine from the Chrysler's boot, some distance inside Yugoslavia, she simply stretched, laughed, kissed them both, and suggested a small celebration. Andrzej produced a flat bottle from his hip pocket and they toasted Yugoslav freedom with Hungarian brandy. To Christine it was as if the whole escapade were just a big adventure, Andrzej later proudly recalled, 'like it was a picnic'.[17] Arming themselves against the freezing January air with further nips of brandy, Andrzej then drove the much-loved but unheated Opel non-stop to Belgrade. They arrived in the city, cold and stiff, late that evening.

An atmosphere of menace hung over Belgrade in early 1941. Hitler was rapidly extending his grip on the Balkans and threatening Yugoslavia more openly, but the Yugoslav population was still resolutely defiant. While hoping to avoid direct provocation, small military units marched through the capital most days, often followed by groups of well-wrapped schoolchildren singing martial songs, as residents watched from behind the closed windows of the classical apartment blocks that typified the city.

On arrival Christine and Andrzej presented themselves to the British Legation, briefed by Sir Owen to expect them, and then headed for the bar of the Hotel Majestic, which famously stayed open until five in the morning. Here they blended in with the expats, among them a number of Poles sitting around reading *Time* magazine, smoking endless cigarettes, discussing the increasingly bleak future of the Balkans and drowning their anxieties in glasses of slivovitz.[18] One of these turned out to be an old friend, Andrzej Tarnowski, who had once helped to save Kowerski from an avalanche. Despite Christine's nagging cough, they felt safe and welcome. 'Here I sit in a little café with a cup of Turkish coffee', Christine began her first letter to Kate the next morning, but as their visas were good for only seven days, she added, 'all is uncertain, come quick'.[19] 'Finally . . . we can sleep and sleep without fear of the sirens', Andrzej continued the letter. 'Christine is busy

reading guidebooks to the city, finding the best places to eat oysters, but we miss you and our beautiful days in Budapest.'[20]

Sir Owen arrived a few days later.* Together they spent a celebratory evening drinking champagne in Belgrade's nightclubs and belly-dancing bars: 'low haunts' as Sir Owen described them. Coincidentally they met the two RAF pilots that Christine and Sir Owen had helped to evacuate from Poland some weeks earlier. Christine's delight that they remembered her added to the festive spirit of the occasion. 'I did not embarrass the Foreign Office by reporting to them Christina's escape', Sir Owen later recorded drily in his memoirs; it 'was not part of a Minister's duties', any more, presumably, than entertaining escaping airmen in Serbian belly-dancing clubs.[21]

Sir Owen did, however, continue to champion Christine with the British. Having helped to save her life he felt responsible for her, he told Harold Perkins. But he also had a great respect for Christine's abilities, and was more than a little in love with her, 'devoted to her' as Andrzej put it.[22] 'She is a rare and peculiar character and for all her attractiveness not everybody's cup of tea', Sir Owen wrote, perhaps thinking of Peter Wilkinson's reaction to Christine, or possibly the feelings of his wife and other women in the Legation who found Christine intimidating or simply infuriating. He then went on to characterize Christine as a true patriot, ready to give her life for the causes she believed in. She had 'an almost pathological tendency to take risks', he continued, saying that one of his difficulties now was to find her work that was 'sufficiently risky and bloodthirsty to appeal to her'.[23] In fact this was not Sir Owen's responsibility, and the British were in any case only too happy to keep Christine, and now Andrzej, on their growing books.

In 1940 Section D had been closed down. Its best people were integrated into the new Special Operations Executive, or SOE, a politically led sabotage organization modelled in part on the IRA,

* Kate's daughter Jane later wrote that this was the weekend of 10–12 February 1941, and that 'doubtless' Kate would have gone too. See O'Malley papers, Jane O'Malley, 'Christina' (nd).

and which was famously launched by Winston Churchill in July 1940 with the rousing injunction to 'set Europe ablaze'. This was 'easier to command than achieve', Wilkinson later commented drily. Indeed SOE 'sometimes came nearer to setting Whitehall ablaze'.[24] The problem was double-edged. In operational terms, with the exception of Poland, most of occupied Europe in 1940 was not 'smouldering with unchannelled resistance', but rather stunned by defeat.[25] Meanwhile SOE faced huge internal resistance from the other service chiefs and the Foreign Office, and only survived through Churchill's personal support.

Churchill had become Britain's prime minister only two months previously, 'at a time', noted Gubbins, later head of SOE, 'when British fortunes and hopes were at their lowest'.[26] As minister of defence, as well as PM, Churchill was directly responsible for the conduct of the war in all its military aspects and he gave 'special consideration' to the possibilities of irregular types of warfare, which had held an almost romantic appeal for him since he had himself witnessed guerrilla action as a young soldier and war correspondent. The secretive new organization, known publicly only as the 'Joint Technical Board' or the 'Inter-Service Research Bureau', and simply as 'the firm' to insiders, was charged with conducting guerrilla warfare against the Axis powers. This was to be achieved through instructing and aiding local resistance groups to facilitate espionage, sabotage and reconnaissance behind enemy lines. After a first successful drop of agents into Poland, SOE slowly began to grow. Operations were controlled by sections dedicated to specific countries, sometimes with more than one section per country, depending how unified or disparate the various national resistance movements were. Most were run from London, but SOE's operations in the Middle East and the Balkans were controlled from Cairo, and further stations were later set up in Algiers to support southern France, and in Italy for the Balkans. Christine would get to know them all, but it was her old contact George Taylor, the man who had first approved her for Section D work in December 1939, who now met her in Belgrade, as head of SOE's Balkan Section.

Christine was keen to re-establish contact with the Musketeers, the independent Warsaw-based resistance organization. But before she could do so, Taylor wanted to reactivate the links with Andrzej's courier and 'exfiltration' organization in Hungary. Someone had to be found to replace her as the Budapest contact. To Andrzej's dismay, Christine suggested her husband. Jerzy was indeed the perfect candidate. He spoke fluent Polish, Russian, Ukrainian, French, German, Italian and English; he was a good organizer, a great skier, intelligent and charming; and he had been angling for a posting in the Balkans since November 1940. To date the British had been cautious. 'I think you will find that 4826 [Jerzy Gizycki's] anxiety to return to the Balkans is to find his wife, who is one of our agents and a very charming woman', Taylor had advised in December 1940. 'My impression is that if we pushed 4826 out to the Balkans, and his wife, as is quite possible, has gone into Poland, we should not see 4826 for smoke.'[27] As a result the British stalled Jerzy, but in January 1941 he had taken it upon himself to terminate his Polish mission in West Africa and head for the Balkans – and Christine – via the British base at Cairo. With Taylor's blessing, Christine now wrote to her husband, arranging to meet him in Istanbul, where she hoped to persuade him to take over her Budapest role.

In late February, Christine and Andrzej set off again in the valiant Opel, still with its Polish number plates but its nose now pointing south-east and ultimately, they hoped, for Egypt, via Bulgaria, Turkey, Syria and Palestine. The car was crammed with luggage and cans of petrol, and Christine had a wad of official letters in her bag, providing introductions to various British contacts on the way. Just before leaving she also collected another parcel of microfilm from a Musketeer courier who had reached Belgrade. She shoved it unceremoniously into her gloves – the car was not warm enough to travel in without being well wrapped up – and off they went on the Belgrade–Sofia Rally route, and, as it turned out, not far ahead of the Nazi advance.

Sofia, the capital of Bulgaria, is 250 miles south-east of Belgrade. In 1941 the roads were winding and often unsurfaced, and in

February that year the weather was miserable, with incessant rain turning much of the route into a river. Christine found the radio grating – she did not care much for music except for occasional bursts of Chopin – and preferred to talk or be left to her own thoughts, so most of the drive was punctuated only by increasingly gloomy news reports. At some point the Opel lost its exhaust-pipe, among several other underpinnings, but as dawn broke, the rain eased and they could see the outlines of the trees and houses on the outskirts of Sofia. As they drove into the city, its beautiful tree-lined avenues, flanked by pink and white stucco buildings, seemed to reflect the first promise of spring but, as throughout Eastern Europe, life in Sofia was becoming unseasonably tense. The city was crawling with journalists, intelligence operatives, and agents from all sides. The British Ministry of Foreign Affairs alone had doubled its presence over the past month, and the city's main hotel, the Bulgaria, was so full of Nazis that it had become unofficially known as the 'Brown House'.

Christine and Andrzej reported at the British Legation on the last Sunday of February 1941. Aidan Crawley, the young air attaché, was more than a little surprised to have his quiet weekend disrupted by 'a beautiful young Polish woman' and a 'round-faced, jolly ex-Polish officer', who claimed they had just driven from Budapest, but his 'two unusual visitors' wasted no time in handing over their letters of introduction from Sir Owen, and several rolls of micro-film.[28] Christine was as impressed with Crawley as he was with them. 'Blonde, big, blue eyes . . .' she wrote to Kate mischievously. '. . . If I wasn't so old and hadn't sworn to shun affairs of the heart until the end of the war . . . I'm not making any rash promises, though. If the war doesn't end soon, I'll run the risk of remaining a virgin until I'm middle-aged – and after that it will be too late.'[29] It is a comment that reveals both her easy intimacy with Kate and, at the very least, a slight frustration with Andrzej.

The microfilm Christine had given to Aidan Crawley had the potential to change the entire direction of the war. It was footage of hundreds of tanks, Wehrmacht regiments, Panzer divisions and stores of ammunition, being amassed along Russia's eastern borders.

There was also an impressive list of petrol depots, apparently organized to support a mechanized invasion.* In Crawley's opinion there could be no doubt that Hitler was making large-scale preparations for an aggressive campaign against his Soviet ally. He was aware that Christine was 'officially working for the other organisation' – the Musketeers, who were subject to growing suspicion from Polish, and correspondingly British, intelligence. As a result any information she delivered had to be treated with caution. However, he also recognized the significance of a possible Nazi invasion of Russia.[30] Since the fall of France, Britain's primary allies had been two exiled leaders reliant on the remnants of their armies also in exile – hence the investment in resistance and sabotage within occupied territories. Should Hitler now alienate Stalin there was the potential for an alliance with a world power whose military and economic resources might well prove decisive for the outcome of the war.

Hitler's rationale for invading Russia was not only to defeat the 'Jewish–Bolshevik conspiracy' and protect Nazi oil interests in Romania, which the Soviets appeared to be threatening; he also hoped that his ambitious plan to defeat Russia in six weeks would 'clarify to the British the hopelessness of their situation'.[31] Instead, the prospect of a conflict between Germany and Russia gave new hope to the Allies; hope that at first they hardly dared credit. 'This was the first positive evidence of its kind', Crawley later wrote, and once Christine had entrusted him with the films he sent them to the British Air Ministry, who passed them straight to Churchill. 'That Germany should at this stage, before clearing the Balkan scene, open another major war with Russia seemed too good to be true', Churchill recorded.[32] Despite further reports on extensive troop movements towards Russia from 'Ultra' – the German intelligence signals decoded at Bletchley Park – and other sources, it was not until the end of March that Churchill became convinced that Hitler was resolved on what he called 'mortal war' with the Soviets.

* The Polish resistance officer Kazimierz Leski later claimed that the Musketeers stole these microfilms from the ZWZ. See Larecki, p. 137.

Once she had been thoroughly debriefed by the British in Sofia, Christine's report was filed, and Andrzej was officially recruited to SOE.[33] Crawley had already sent urgent reports to both Cairo and London, and he now warned his Polish colleagues to press on towards Turkey before Britain severed diplomatic relations with Bulgaria in the wake of the Nazi advance. Early the next morning, Christine and Andrzej folded themselves stiffly back into the Opel, to which Andrzej had made some rapid repairs, and headed optimistically towards Istanbul.*

After a long day trailing behind ox carts, and pushing the Opel out of swathes of mud, it was nearly dusk when they reached the last village before the Bulgarian–Turkish border. The Ottoman Empire had supported Germany in 1914 and, as a result, lost all its European territories. Now a republic, Turkey would remain neutral throughout the Second World War. Within sight of relative safety, Andrzej was determined to get Christine, who had still not shaken off the flu, across the border that evening. Polish number plates, white with dark lettering, were very similar to their German equivalents, and in the half-light the Bulgarian frontier guards mistook the Opel for a German car. Andrzej took care not to disillusion them, asking in German what time the border closed. To his relief he was told it would be open all night. Once he had handed over their British passports, however, the story quickly changed: the border had just closed, he was told; they could not go on. Andrzej started to bristle. 'Keep calm', Christine whispered in French, squeezing his hand. It was, she said, just 'a ruse to annoy subjects of His Majesty King George VI', but they had a long night ahead of them.[34]

The guards insisted that they unpack every piece of their luggage, including the petrol cans, and that it was all taken to a shed at the customs post. There they went through everything, even the powder in Christine's compact. They found nothing, but

* In his book *Leap Before You Look: A Memoir* (1988), p. 162, Crawley says that he arranged for Christine and Andrzej to take their films to Egypt via Istanbul. Other sources say that Crawley relieved them of the films in Sofia.

were still not satisfied and told Andrzej to bring the tyres from the car. It was now raining hard, but despite the severe pain in his leg, Andrej had no option but to fetch and then refit each of the tyres. Christine was incensed, but refused to give the guards the pleasure of showing it. Then she found a subtle revenge. One of the guard dogs, a fierce Alsatian, snarled and lunged at Andrzej whenever he came back into the hut, making the guards roar with laughter. Christine went up to the dog, soothed it with a few quiet words, put her hand on its head and waited for it to look up at her. Then she sat down, cross-legged, beside the animal, and started scratching its ears while it contentedly pawed her – to the guards' undisguised dismay. The following day, after endless phone calls to the Bulgarian police headquarters in Sofia, the border guards finally agreed to raise the barrier and let them through. Halfway across no-man's-land, Christine asked Andrzej to stop the car. To his astonishment she got out, and stood there, in the rain, whistling. Suddenly the Alsatian bolted from his handler and bounded up to Christine, nuzzling her face when she knelt down to him. It was a small triumph, but satisfying. Friends later said that she flirted with animals as she flirted with men, exercising an uncanny power over both.[35] After enjoying the moment she sent the dog back, but it would not be the only trained patrol dog she would subvert in her wartime career.

On the Turkish side of the border it was the Opel that stole all the attention. One of the customs officials, complete with rifle and bayonet, climbed in to escort them through before confiscating the car. Andrzej was loath to part with his car but he and Christine were both exhausted, and eventually he agreed to swap it for a receipt and a taxi to take them to the Park Hotel in Pera, the historic heart of Istanbul, recommended by Aidan Crawley. Here they washed, ate and slept, 'diving', Andrzej later wrote, 'into the blessings of idleness'.[36]

Some time later Christine looked out of her hotel window to see old Istanbul rising steeply from the crowded waters of the Golden Horn. Another agent who stayed at the Park described the view of 'the great mosques of Bayazid and Suleiman surrounded by

a maze of houses . . . straight in front rose the six minarets of the mosque of Sultan Ahmet and beside it the vast dome of Santa Sofia. From there the ground ran down to the exquisite Seraglio Palace jutting out into the sea . . . Then . . . across the gleaming blue of the Marmara, lay the coast of Asia with Scutari guarding the entrance to the Bosphorus and the mountain of Chamblidja above it'.[37] Not everyone was struck by Istanbul's beauty, however. Crawley thought that, apart from some picturesque old wooden houses along the Bosphorus, the city's architecture was 'ugly and without character'.[38] But, for once, Christine found it hard to drag herself away.

While Western Europe was being torn apart, in Istanbul things seemed strangely calm. The great domes and minarets piercing the mist on the Sea of Marmara, the regular refrain of the calls to prayer echoing and anchoring the streets sellers' cries, combined with Turkey's refusal to be directly drawn into the war, lent the city an air of immutability. At the same time, Istanbul was living up to its historic reputation as a centre of international intrigue. Hardly a nation involved in the war went unrepresented in the cafés along the Bosphorus or in the hotel registers of Pera. Germans and Italians, British, French and Russians passed in the same narrow streets, avoided the same stray dogs, bought books and ordered drinks, olives and Marmara mackerel in the same shops and restaurants.

Christine's SOE records state only that 'in Istanbul she assisted our Polish Section in their courier and contact work'.[39] 'We are waiting for all sorts of answers', she wrote to Kate, but in general things were going well.[40] Her first priority was to ensure that the courier routes to Poland were maintained, and that up-to-date information and funds were sent back to the Musketeers. Polish refugees often came through Istanbul on their way to join the Polish army in the Middle East, or to offer their services to Britain, and she soon received a further consignment of microfilm. She and Andrzej set about meeting as many Polish and British contacts as they could. Among them was a young oil engineer, Alfred Gardyne de Chastelain, or 'Chas' as Christine soon knew him. As SOE's man

in Bucharest, de Chastelain had been responsible for trying to sabotage Romanian oil supplies to the Third Reich. He was now running the Istanbul office, and was still engaged in sabotage. This time his targets were the warehouses full of Axis equipment, and Italian tankers docked on the Bosphorus, which were taking Romanian oil to the German armies in Greece. Crawley soon joined his team, having fled Bulgaria the day the Germans arrived in Sofia, but not before he had secretly photographed the most high-ranking Nazi arrivals at the airport. The other British Embassy staff from Sofia followed.

Although Christine and Andrzej's work was still risky, being in Istanbul had removed them from the front line of the war. Christine's biggest headache was where to hold meetings in the city without attracting the attention of the Turkish police, or of the German and Italian secret services. Most of the hotels were under surveillance, along with the SOE base housed in the former servants' quarters of what once had been the British Embassy to the Ottoman Empire. She and Andrzej were also still being watched by Polish intelligence in Istanbul. Accordingly Christine would meet her contacts among the groups of European sightseers that still resolutely gathered in the courtyards of the mosques, on pleasure boats, or over little dishes of meze in the many cafés along the banks of the Bosphorus. This gave her plenty of time to regain her strength, soaking up the sun while wandering the streets of the old city, watching the wild birds flying in the great dome of Santa Sofia, or exploring the city's huge covered bazaar. In March she sent Kate O'Malley a bracelet to protect her from the evil eye, along with a rosary that, she wrote, 'smells like an old cathedral' for her father.[41] In the evenings she and Andrzej would go to diplomatic or journalists' parties, or dancing in the city's nightclubs, happily checking the seals on the bottles they ordered in case of German skulduggery.

Although Christine was having a wonderful time, Andrzej was feeling rather less comfortable. It was not the Nazis in Istanbul that bothered him, as much as the thought that Christine's husband, the redoubtable Jerzy Gizycki, was on his way. Even the most hardened SOE officers found Jerzy intimidating: de Chastelain later described

him as both the most difficult and the most capable man he had ever met, undoubtedly charming but 'with chilly grey eyes in which a smile never appeared'.[42]

On arrival in Istanbul on 17 March 1941, Jerzy was given Christine's address by his new SOE bosses. 'She was glad to see me, she responded to my kisses, yet something was wrong', he wrote.[43] A very nervous Andrzej now met Jerzy for the first time since he had bought a pair of his old skis in pre-war Zakopane. Jerzy later claimed to have immediately understood the dynamics of the situation. 'They were lovers and we had to part', he wrote, before adding cryptically that 'knowing my wife, I was sure that sex played a very small part in her decision or, even, no part at all'. While it is possible that he was simply protecting his own vanity, his last comment on the whole affair was certainly extremely generous. Andrzej was 'an upright, fine man', Jerzy wrote, adding that he obviously felt rotten about the whole mess. 'I told him not to take it hard, that it was not his fault but the war's, and that I understood how it had all happened.'[44] In fact it seems likely that, at this point at least, Christine coolly kept Jerzy in the dark about the true nature of her relationship with Andrzej. There were certainly fireworks later. For now, however, Jerzy agreed to take over Christine's former role as the British contact in Budapest for the Polish underground, and she and Andrzej spent some days briefing him.

Jerzy was given a British passport in the name of Gordon Norton, Norton being the name of a cowboy he had particularly admired in the American West twenty years earlier, and a diplomatic pouch with secret documents to be delivered to the British Legation in Belgrade at his first stop. Having enjoyed the charms of Belgrade, although the girls were 'a little on the hefty side' for his full approval (Christine's slender figure still setting the standard), he caught the train to Budapest, arriving on 1 April.[45] Here he spent a week posing as a cipher clerk in Sir Owen O'Malley's Legation, while being further briefed by Sir Owen's daughter Kate. With an open-ended budget from the War Office, and the help of Helena Marusarz, the sister of the Olympic skier who had previously worked with Christine, and herself 'a very pretty girl with

lots of spunk', Jerzy then helped to smuggle people and information out of Poland, and British money, a wireless set, codes, propaganda and explosives back in.[46] Recognizing the 'extremely hazardous' nature of this work, the British put him forward for the King's Medal for Service.*[47] The situation was indeed getting more dangerous by the day. Helena Marusarz was caught on a return trip to Poland, and shot on the spot. Not long afterwards Jerzy learned that, for reasons he never discovered, one of his three sisters, and her children, had all been murdered by the Nazis in what is now the Ukraine. From that moment, the war became at once both deeply personal and almost unbearable. 'His rage against the Germans has now reached a pitch where he would do almost anything to deal them a blow', his SOE handler reported.[48]

The war was escalating fast across the Balkans. Having watched Hungary, Romania and Bulgaria slide towards alliance with Hitler, Yugoslavia's regent, Prince Paul, succumbed to pressure to join the Axis on 25 March. Two days later a popular military coup, encouraged and supported by SOE agents in Belgrade, replaced him with the anti-Axis king Peter II. 'Hitler was stung to the quick', Winston Churchill later recorded rather proudly in his history of the war.[49] At 7 a.m. on 6 April, hundreds of turtle doves suddenly started 'circling in agitated manoeuvres' above Belgrade: the Luftwaffe had begun saturation-bombing the city.[50] Hitler had been so enraged by the Yugoslav coup that he launched the campaign, code-named 'Operation Punishment', without a declaration of war, or even waiting for talks with the new government.[51] Caught by surprise, Belgrade's residents huddled in cellars, school basements and the bars of hotels. The British Minister reportedly took shelter under the grand piano in his drawing room. Some 4,000 civilians were killed, many buried in the rubble, and the country's key communications were destroyed. Despite a courageous defence, Yugoslavia could not stop Hitler's Panzer divisions streaming in through Hungary. Eleven days later, the country surrendered and

* The British were careful not to let the Polish administration know about the award, in case complications arose from their employment of a Pole.

was immediately divided between its German, Hungarian and Italian invaders.

Britain formally broke off relations with Hungary the day after the invasion of Yugoslavia, and Jerzy was evacuated with the rest of the British Legation staff on 11 April 1941. While travelling through Soviet-occupied Polish territory he telegraphed Istanbul, asking Christine to wait for him there.[52] But when he returned to Istanbul in late May, Christine – and Andrzej – had gone. His earlier telegram had been received as, 'Please notify Granvil [sic] not to wait'.[53] Jerzy was furious, convinced that the text had been changed deliberately. Nevertheless, he kept working, contacting the Budapest network through the Polish radio he had supplied. He also volunteered to be sent into Poland or Russia, but the British declined to use him in either country. Finally, believing that he was being poisoned by pro-German White Russian waiters in his favourite Turkish restaurant, Jerzy agreed to move on to Cairo.

The Budapest network continued to operate effectively for some time, working directly with the official Polish Intelligence Service.[54] Father Laski kept the courier routes open under the cover of getting information on the persecution of the Church in Poland, with the unwitting help of an ecclesiastical office providing religious and social support to Polish refugees. He was arrested in October 1941 and died in a Nazi concentration camp in Poland. Michal 'Lis' Gradowski, 'the Fox', was caught trying to cross into Yugoslavia but escaped by jumping from a moving train. Managing to pass himself off as a Baltic German baron of Estonian nationality, he found himself entertained in a German airfield mess in Belgrade, where he was able to observe all the aircraft. He then accepted a lift to Istanbul from the German consul. In the early morning of the day he arrived Christine introduced Gradowski to de Chastelain, who enlisted him formally into SOE while still in his pyjamas.[55] Marcin Lubomirski and Andrzej's personal assistant, Antoni Filipkiewicz, continued to support the 'exfiltration' of British POWs from Poland, sometimes temporarily hiding the men in their homes. It was only in 1944 that the Gestapo broke the organization, with tragic results.[56] The eight key remaining circuit members were all

arrested. Only Lubomirski and Filipkiewicz would survive their incarceration in Mauthausen concentration camp, being released in 1945. The other six met their deaths in the gas chambers. 'They were the best of the bunch,' a report in the SOE files notes, but 'as none of them has . . . any surviving relatives, posthumous awards in this case would seem to have no point.'[57]

Not long after Jerzy left for Budapest, Christine and Andrzej moved on to Cairo, where the British had a regional command base. They had somehow secured visas to travel through pro-Vichy Syria and Lebanon, then part of the French Mandate. According to SOE files, it was at the time possible to buy Hungarian, Bulgarian and German passports and visas 'in blanco' in Istanbul.[58] On the other hand SOE specified that 'only travel with a genuine passport is recommended. Other methods are still in the experimental stage, or are so hazardous as to be impractical'.[59] In Andrzej's account it was Christine who secured the visas, fluttering her eyelashes at the Vichy officials in the French consulate. The apparent ease with which she did so later caused a great deal of speculation about her contacts, but at the time Andrzej was more worried about retrieving his Opel from the Turkish authorities. A hefty bribe finally reunited them, and Christine and Andrzej were able to set off. When they stopped briefly at the British Embassy in Ankara they met Julian Amery. A British agent, who like Aidan Crawley later became an MP, Amery described Christine as 'one of the gentlest looking girls I have ever met', and found it hard to credit her with some of the exploits that had already earned her a fine reputation in intelligence circles.[60] In mid-May, Christine and Andrzej quietly crossed into Syria.

Having wrapped up in coats and gloves as they drove through the wintry Balkans, Christine and Andrzej now wound down the Opel's windows to try to catch the sea breeze as they drove through Syria on the narrow coastal road towards Beirut. Andrzej cursed the oppressive heat but Christine turned her face to the sun. Stopping in villages, or beside golden fields darkened by purple thistles and deadly nightshade, they lingered over figs, goats' cheese, baklava, and local wine, soaking up the views of the Mediterranean and the

crusader castles that dominate the Lebanese coast. At one point they stopped in silent admiration to watch thousands of storks gathering to migrate north, before pressing on in the opposite direction, the Opel sparkling in the heat, its chrome fittings too hot to touch. As they drew closer to Beirut, the monotony was broken by Christine's shrieks whenever she saw a dog or cat dart across the road, until she became 'almost hysterical' if she thought one had strayed too close to their wheels, though Andrzej swore he always swerved in time.[61] Once they reached the city, they headed for the St George's Hotel, only to find it full of smartly dressed German officers. Seeing their British passports, the receptionist loudly offered them the best rooms at the standard rate, and Andrzej spent the whole night expecting to be murdered.

Next day they started early for Palestine. Unable to face the long hot queue at the border controls, Andrzej revved the Opel and made a final break for freedom. They were stopped by the police, of course, but when they handed over their passports the officers saluted them. The British authorities in Turkey had sent word that they were to be expected and they were quickly furnished with ration books, petrol coupons, and a room in a hotel in Haifa, on the northern slope of the great plateau of Mount Carmel. In the morning Christine insisted on taking some time to walk barefoot on the beach, curling her toes and smiling for Andrzej's camera, and, with her tanned skin and dark sunglasses, looking as carefree as any tourist anywhere. Eventually Andrzej dragged her back to the car, and they followed the rising tide of military traffic moving towards Jerusalem. Now it was Andrzej's turn to be the tourist, marvelling at 'the weight of history which seemed to seep from the very stones' of the ancient city.[62]

Having checked in with the British authorities, headed here by the sociable Peter Porter, Christine and Andrzej felt they could finally relax for a while. Christine arranged to meet Zofia Raczkowska, the sister of her journalist friend, Florian Sokolow. Like Florian, and their father Nahoum Sokolow, Zofia was a great advocate for an independent Israel, and she had toured Palestine for several years, promoting the Zionist cause. Andrzej and Christine

also met Zofia's twenty-year-old son, who was active in the Jewish underground, and many of their local comrades, as well as British military personnel and civilians working for the British civil service in Palestine. Even as the war against the Nazis continued, tensions were growing between the Jewish underground, fighting for a future state of Israel, and the British authorities, who had still not endorsed the idea. The British were well aware that Zionists were successfully smuggling arms into Palestine, but as Gladwyn Jebb told the head of SOE, 'we simply cannot afford to alienate the Jews at this particular moment'.[63] Despite, or perhaps partly because of, Poland's own historic anti-Semitism, the Poles were more supportive of the idea of a Jewish state and had provided finance and training for Jewish insurgents since the 1930s. Half-Jewish, Polish, but working for the British, Christine must have had some interesting evenings at Zofia's house in the hills overlooking Jerusalem. All Andrzej recorded of this time, however, was that she 'fell in love with the family dogs, two fine boxers, which we used to take for drives'.[64]

Less than two weeks later Christine and Andrzej were summoned to Cairo. After another long, hot drive, the Opel was again waved through the border, this time into Egypt, and they were directed to the rambling Continental Hotel, whose bars and shady verandas had been all but taken over by the services. Here they were met by Peter Porter, who told them, rather stiffly now, to rest and relax while their future was being decided. It was not the welcome they had anticipated, but they knew the Cairo office had other priorities: the Germans had reached North Africa, the siege of Tobruk was in full force, and Vichy France was in the process of giving Germany access to its military facilities in Syria. Christine and Andrzej were soon surrounded by old friends including Andrzej Tarnowski and Kowerski's cousin, Ludwig Popiel, recently returned from service in the desert with the Carpathian Lancers. The Lancers were commanded by Colonel Władysław Bobinski, whose horses Christine had ridden when she was just fourteen, and who was also stationed at the Continental along with many of his officers. And yet, given the number of people they knew at the hotel, the atmosphere surrounding Christine and Andrzej was surprisingly tense.

Stranger still, apart from Ludwig, Tarnowski and Bobinski, none of the Polish or British officers at the Continental, or even the Polish Ambassador, whom Christine knew well, were talking to them.

Having driven fairly blithely across hundreds of miles of Nazi-sympathizing territory, often carrying incriminating letters and sometimes microfilm, and just weeks or at times days ahead of the Nazi advance, they were finally safely in British controlled territory. But two days later they were interrogated, separately, and at length, at SOE's Cairo office, then a small villa on the banks of the Nile. Something was terribly wrong.

7: COLD IN CAIRO

'X & Y are now in Cairo', the Middle East branch of SOE informed London at the end of May 1941, glad to have an unassailable fact to report concerning the pair. X and Y were, of course, Christine and Andrzej, currently sheltering in the bars of the Continental Hotel both from the city's increasingly oppressive heat at the start of the long summer and from the unexpected chill of their welcome. It was obvious that they were being cold-shouldered by both the Poles and the British in the city, but far from clear why. Although complicit in this treatment, the British in Cairo were little better informed than Christine and Andrzej. A few weeks earlier they had been keen to embrace their returning agents, Peter Wilkinson telling Colin Gubbins, now head of SOE Military Operations, that they were 'under a very considerable obligation to these people'.[1] But by late May, Wilkinson's tone had changed and he was referring to Christine and Andrzej as 'rather a problem'.[2] The problem stemmed from a top-secret Polish intelligence report claiming that at least one Polish agent had been killed as a result of what were described as Christine's 'indiscretions'.* Although the Poles refused to elaborate, and this accusation was never either effectively substantiated or disproved, they demanded that Christine and Andrzej should not be employed again until there had been a full investigation. Both of them were 'very well thought of' by Colonel George Taylor, the SOE office in Cairo informed London, but 'viewed with grave suspicions' by Polish intelligence. 'Please

* This allegation was made by the Second Bureau officer Lt Col Jozef Matecki, under his operational pseudonym of Jakob Alec. See TNA, HS4/198, MX to M (28.5.1941).

discuss fully', they begged, and telegraph by return, 'what to do with X, Y'.[3]

'Nobody who did not experience it can possibly imagine the atmosphere of jealousy, suspicion and intrigue which embittered the relations between the various secret and semi-secret departments in Cairo during that summer of 1941', the SOE officer Bickham Sweet-Escott wrote.[4] Internal relations between the various British services were strained enough, but tensions between the Poles and the British were in another league. Christine had a foot in each camp, which left her open to suspicion and politicking from both sides. From the British perspective, she had proved herself a valuable and trustworthy agent; ironically it was her Polish nationality – her greatest asset to them – that was now causing difficulties. The Poles had fought hard for independence from their rather overbearing British allies from the start of the war, securing the right to run their own operations, and to send their own signals using their own codes. In 1940 British secret services had agreed that all their clandestine communications with Poland would go through official channels. Arguably, in directly employing first Christine and then Andrzej the British had failed to honour this arrangement. With Christine now being monitored by the Poles themselves, her presence in the British offices in Cairo was a decided embarrassment.

The official Polish intelligence and counter-espionage unit, known as the 'Second Bureau', had far greater concerns, however. They had been keeping Christine under surveillance ever since she had appeared in Budapest. It was no surprise to them that she was reporting to the British, but they had recently begun to suspect that she was hiding something more sinister: that she might be a double agent working for the Nazis. These suspicions were seemingly supported by the apparent ease with which, in Istanbul, Christine had secured visas for Andrzej and herself to travel through pro-Vichy Syria and Lebanon, both then in the French Mandate. The British knew that visas could be obtained at a price, but it seemed impossible to the Poles that anyone other than a German spy could have achieved such a thing. This was just seen as corroborating

evidence, however; the Second Bureau's concerns about Christine had much deeper roots.

The fundamental issue was her close working relationship with Stefan Witkowski and his clandestine Polish intelligence group, 'the Musketeers'. Ironically it was precisely because the Poles had considered Christine a liability, and had refused to use her as a courier between Hungary and Poland with the mainstream ZWZ, that she had first started working with the determinedly independent Musketeers. In 1940 the British had been desperate for intelligence on the German position inside Poland, and were delighted to employ Christine to bring out information that had not been sourced by official Polish intelligence and filtered through the Polish government-in-exile. Christine meanwhile, pleased to have found a job valued as much by her compatriot Witkowski as by the British, if anything became over-enthusiastic about her role. In early May 1941, Peter Wilkinson, who was censoring her letters, described the information they contained as 'rather good stuff', but was shocked to find one enclosing photographs of documents committing the British government to unreserved support for the Musketeers. 'These latter rather alarming', he reported. 'We mustn't make this sort of mistake again!'[5] Christine was perhaps naive about the sensitivities of her position, but to the British her commitment to the Allied cause and to Poland seemed beyond doubt. However, by early 1941 the ZWZ and the Second Bureau were beginning to have serious doubts about Witkowski's activities – and his loyalties.

At their height, the Musketeers had around 800 members, with agents operating inside the Russian-occupied area of Poland and across Europe, including over 200 actually inside Germany. Witkowski himself had travelled around the Reich purporting to be senior SS officer 'Artur August von Tierbach', while gathering high-quality intelligence for both the Poles and the British. His ambition and effectiveness reportedly enraged his official Polish intelligence rivals, who were determined to discredit him unless he agreed to pass all intelligence exclusively to the Second Bureau in return for a monthly budget and continued operational independence. Nonetheless, tensions continued to mount. Witkowski complained that

the Second Bureau was not giving the Musketeers due credit for their intelligence reports. The Second Bureau in turn became furious when Witkowski bypassed them and gave intelligence directly to General Sikorski, now head of the Polish government-in-exile and commander-in-chief of the Polish forces, and indirectly to the British. A significant part of this intelligence went through Christine.

In an attempt to stem such intelligence rivalries, in early 1941 the Musketeers were officially merged with the ZWZ. But although Witkowski had been sworn into the fold he remained impossible to control, continuing to develop independent contacts with White Russian organizations, and becoming involved in secret talks with unnamed German commanders. Like Christine, and indeed many Poles, Witkowski saw Soviet Russia as just as great a threat to Poland as Nazi Germany. With contacts in both camps, he was unable to resist exploring ways to play the two aggressors off against each other, or to cut deals to try to ameliorate the harsh terms of the Nazi occupation. Not only did this undermine the authority of the Polish government-in-exile, inevitably it also left the Musketeers open to enemy infiltration, and certainly to claims of this. Several Musketeer agents were later reported to 'gradually change their stories until finally they would admit to working for the Germans' in the hope of cooperating with White Russians against the Soviets.[6] In May 1941 Sikorski decided to withdraw all support from the 'unsatisfactory and harmful' Musketeers, and, for the sake of continued good relations with their Polish allies, Britain officially supported this decision.[7] Christine, well known to be Witkowski's little 'Fly', had arrived safely in Cairo, against all the odds, right in the middle of the crisis surrounding the Musketeers. It was no wonder that she was subject to suspicion, and soon fell foul of the bitter jealousies and personal rivalries that followed. As her close companion, although never a Musketeer agent himself, Andrzej was tarred with the same brush.

A series of signals and telegrams now crossed and recrossed between Cairo, London and Istanbul, and between Polish and British intelligence, until at least one British message complained

of 'getting fed up with the bloody chaos'.[8] According to Julian Amery, 'there was a good deal of spy mania at the time and the authorities were taking no chances'.[9] For a while the idea was mooted of sending Christine and Andrzej to London and offloading them onto the Polish administration there, but it seemed a waste of valuable assets. On the other hand, although SOE might have little doubt about Christine's loyalty, the British were anxious to preserve good relations with the Poles. With the Baltic states steadily falling to the Axis, France already lost, Russia still treaty-bound to Germany, and the USA studiously avoiding being drawn into the conflict, Britain could not afford to alienate its ally. For Wilkinson this was the critical point. 'The disadvantages of giving support to an organisation which is not collaborating with the Polish Government are obvious,' he wrote with regard to Christine and the Musketeers, 'and, in my opinion, outweigh all possible advantages.'[10] It was decided that Christine and Andrzej should remain in Egypt, at least temporarily, but were not to be used in any connection with Poland, and were not to renew contact with the Musketeers. This last proved more tricky than it seemed, as a series of reports and microfilm still filtered through to Christine, carried by escaping Polish servicemen hoping to rejoin their army in the Middle East, and which she passed on regardless of her official position.

It was June 1941 before Colonel Guy Tamplin, the British liaison officer with the Polish authorities in Cairo, finally explained the situation to Christine and Andrzej. 'Christine and I were appalled', Andrzej remembered.[11] Since the start of the war the two of them had risked their lives for Poland, only to be denounced and blacklisted as suspected double agents by their fellow countrymen. Christine felt thoroughly let down. 'I am so fed up with everything and everyone that I am becoming a desert island', she wrote to Kate O'Malley.* In Belgrade, George Taylor had promised to look after

* She also half told Kate a story that Andrzej had 'saved my life by taking me out of the sea, and at the risk of his own life. It's quite a funny story although it nearly ended tragically.' Sadly she provides no more information. See O'Malley papers, Granville to Kate O'Malley (30.1.1942).

them, she continued, but 'now he says he can do nothing, and has left us on ice'.[12] And yet the situation continued to be so confused that at times it seemed farcical. Christine had to fend off constant insinuations, but no direct accusation, that she was a Nazi agent, while at the same time contending with the low-key anti-Semitism that was prevalent in Cairo. Andrzej learnt that he had been awarded the Virtuti Militari, Poland's highest military honour, on the same day that he was officially denounced as a spy by the Second Bureau. Both of them were hugely relieved when they learnt that Peter Wilkinson was arriving from London later that month to resolve their seemingly impossible situation.

It was only when Christine and Andrzej were sitting opposite Wilkinson that it became apparent the news was not going to be good. According to Andrzej, Wilkinson dispensed with their services without a word of explanation, suggesting only that Christine hasten to join the Red Cross and Andrzej to sign up with the Polish armed forces. Both of them were stunned, Andrzej in 'a furious rage', Christine 'pale and silent'.[13] When Andrzej dutifully started to hand over their last rolls of microfilm, Wilkinson abruptly rose to see them out, announcing sharply that 'Your microfilms are of no interest to us. Good-day.'[14] In Wilkinson's account of the meeting, however, he made clear that there were serious concerns that the Musketeers' 'amateur operations' might compromise the 'infinitely more clandestine activities' of the official Polish resistance; an explanation which he believed Christine and Andrzej accepted 'philosophically'.[15] Perhaps Wilkinson was simply more optimistic about Christine's shocked silence than the occasion warranted; later he admitted that it had 'proved a painful interview', and one that he had 'handled badly'.[16] In the space of just five minutes he had made lifelong enemies of both Christine and Andrzej, something he would later sincerely regret. Christine did not apply for a job with the Red Cross, and she swore that she would never again be dictated to by a man behind a desk. Wilkinson did, however, give them both a lifeline by neglecting to have them struck off the SOE payroll. A shrewd judge of both character and situation, he had taken apparently decisive action, while ensuring

that ultimately the British retained control of their impressive and still potentially useful Polish agents.*

It was now mid-June, well into the long Cairo summer that would stretch through until October. Rising early, before the stifling heat of the day started to hang in the air, Christine and Andrzej would head to 'Grey Pillars', the massive building also known as 'Hush Hush House', to petition the SOE office for an update on their status. As the days ran into weeks they also fired off letters to every senior British and Polish officer they knew. Top of Christine's list was Sir Owen O'Malley, whose response to her pleas only had Wilkinson commenting drily that Sir Owen 'seems to have fallen a victim to Mme's well-known persuasiveness'.[17] The Poles showed no sign of changing their position, and without their support, her case looked hopeless.

Andrzej was less directly linked to the Musketeers than Christine, and, as a decorated officer, was also more generally employable. Gubbins, based in London, approached General Sikorski on his behalf, writing tactfully that 'I am anxious that this man should not suffer through any fault of ours', and suggesting that Andrzej should be allowed join the Polish armed forces in Egypt.[18] Andrzej meanwhile wrote to his former commanding officer, General Stanisław Kopanski. When Kopanski was appointed to the Carpathian Brigade, Andrzej cornered him at the Continental and, using an old Polish expression, asked if they could speak privately, 'between four eyes'. 'That is impossible', Kopanski told him, to the obvious delight of a contingent from the Second Bureau who were watching from across the lobby, only to add that with his war wounds they had only three good eyes, and three legs, between them.[19] After their talk Kopanski also fought Andrzej's corner, but there were still no job offers. 'He is a very decent officer,' one Polish report conceded, but he 'finds himself under the negative influence of Mrs G'.[20]

Christine and Andrzej both loathed taking a salary, however basic, without contributing anything to justify it, and they were frustrated and soon rather disturbed by their seemingly idle and

* Peter Wilkinson's decision was supported by George Taylor.

purposeless lives while they were surrounded by action. They spent
the long summer afternoons lying under the slow ceiling fan in
their dark room, shuttered against light and heat and insinuation.
When they could they listened to Polish radio, broadcast from the
Embassy in Cairo, or dozed on the verandas that ran the length of
the hotel. Most Cairo establishments closed from midday until five,
when the whole city lay in a motionless stupor of heat. These were
the lost hours of the day when, according to the author Lawrence
Durrell, who was also caught in Cairo, 'one feels walked upon by
the feet of dead elephants'.[21] Even the covered souks and the Muski,
the warren of lanes lined with open-fronted shops jammed between
massive gateways and ancient latticed windows, were quiet in the
afternoons; the shopkeepers sleeping in the shade until evening
brought some relief and some custom. Then Christine would join
the crowds of men in long white djellabas and women swathed in
black, small boys carrying trays of tea, and donkey-carts piled high
with goods, all pressed into the maze of narrow streets in Cairo's
Old City. She had little money to fritter in the fashionable palm-
shaded bar at Shepheard's Hotel, which occupied a villa where
Napoleon had once stayed, or in cafés like Groppi's that sold fresh
cream cakes, and few invitations to officers' parties. Instead she
would while away the early evenings petting the long-limbed Egyp-
tian street cats, pitying the city's exhausted and overworked horses,
and sipping tea with the Muski shopkeepers who could tell she had
no interest in buying. Andrzej meanwhile greedily eyed the silks,
bottles full of perfume, and above all the jewellery, wishing he were
in a better position and could buy a gift for Christine.

The rest of their evenings were mostly whiled away over a drink
in the Hotel Continental's roof garden, occasionally entertained
by belly-dancers but more often with repeated choruses of Lili
Marlene, and the loose security talk of the officers around them.
Sometimes they joined the civilian expats on the well-watered lawns
of the Anglo-Egyptian club on Gezira Island, but often they would
just stroll out to the pyramids together, watch the feluccas dipping
in the wind on the Nile, and listen to the long, wailing notes of the

muezzins calling the faithful to prayer as the kites rose to wheel above the city's mosques.

Cairo was a deeply cosmopolitan city. Here Muslims, Jews, Copts, Syro-Lebanese Christians and a mixture of European expatriates did business together 'over endless little cups of sugary coffee and glasses of syrupy tea'.[22] 'After the provincial quiet of Istanbul,' Christine's old SOE friend Basil Davidson wrote, between ferrying explosives around the region in diplomatic bags, 'Cairo had all the bustle of a strange and various metropolis.'[23] For their colleague Julian Amery, too, the city was 'astonishingly vital', and among the varied population the military were 'everywhere, dressed in the simple, tropical uniform of the desert, with every now and then the red tabs of a brass hat or the distinctive cap of a French or Polish officer. All was noise, bustle and hurry.'[24] The city's souks, cafés, hawkers, beggars, dogs and donkeys created a vibrant, and pungent, picture of Arab street life, but the Egyptian middle classes had long adopted a policy of British administration with a veneer of French polish. Most fellahin wore turbans and djellabas, but the well-to-do effendi landowners wore smart suits with their tarbooshes and drove limousines between the caravans of camels on the streets.

In 1875 Britain had become the largest shareholder in the strategically vital Suez Canal when it acquired the interest of Egypt's Ottoman ruler, the khedive. In the early 1880s Her Majesty's forces had intervened to help crush a nationalist revolt against European and Ottoman domination. Although Egypt officially gained independence in 1922, the troops had stayed, and Britain continued to dominate the country's political life. By the start of the war, however, as Cairo again filled up with British uniforms, Egyptians were divided in their sympathies towards their former colonizers. As Poles, Christine and Andrzej were viewed similarly – with polite suspicion. It was something they both hated but were fast getting used to. The main redeeming feature of these idle early weeks in Cairo was that they were together. 'We are in a perfect friendship', Christine wrote, and 'without him I think I would have already

gone into a lunatic asylum'.[25] It was then that Christine's husband, Jerzy Gizycki, arrived.

Jerzy had been in Istanbul when the British learnt that all links with the Musketeers were to be broken off. Impressed by his work in Hungary, Russia and Turkey, 'the firm', as SOE was known to insiders, was keen to keep him on its books. 'He speaks a number of languages fluently, is very debrouillard, and seems to hate the Germans as much as is humanly possible', one report extolled.[26] But the British also knew that Jerzy had a temper. Considering it unwise to inform a volatile man about their sudden change of loyalties while he was in neutral territory, de Chastelain quickly dispatched Jerzy to Cairo. However, nothing could have prepared the British for the extent of his fury when, en route in Jerusalem, he heard the rumours and accusations surrounding Christine, Andrzej, and – by extension – himself.

'I have been informed by my wife that Maj. Wilkinson has notified her that she, [Andrzej] Kennedy and I are as suspect as the organisation in Poland we were in touch with,' Jerzy stormed, 'and which counts between its members well known Polish patriots and friends of Gen. Sikorski!' Hardly lifting his pen from the paper he continued, 'This is the reward from the British government for all our efforts, our sincere desire to do some useful work, and the grave risks my wife and Kennedy were running!'[27] Jerzy was livid and, not satisfied with submitting this tirade in his official report, he soon began talking to all his contacts. For the British this was not good news; Jerzy knew senior diplomats in several countries, including the USA, and was a personal friend of Sikorski. Some of the wind was taken out of his sails by a hasty message from London confirming that it was well known that all three of them, now referred to as X, Y and Z, 'acted out of patriotic motives and are free from suspicion'.[28] Jerzy continued to protest 'most emphatically against this unfair, ungentlemanly attitude towards us' over seven closely typed pages, but he knew it was pointless.[29] Any future collaboration with the Poles now seemed impossible. 'As a former cell of the Witkowski organisation,' Wilkinson reported, 'they are barred, for good, from having anything to do with Poland or Polish affairs.'

Jerzy hung around Cairo for nearly five miserable months, but there was nothing there for him. As soon as they met, Christine finally told him that she no longer loved him, and intended to leave him. After an explosion of grief and rage, he never spoke to her again. 'His reaction was not what I expected', Christine wrote to Kate O'Malley, and was 'almost impossible to put into writing'.[30] She had forborne to tell him any sooner not because she doubted her feelings, but because she knew that Jerzy was unlikely to take over her Budapest network unless he believed that their relationship had a future. She might not love him, but she greatly respected her husband's energy and abilities, and must have felt sincere pity for the distress that she now evidently caused him. Christine was not intentionally cruel, but while excellent at bluffing she found sincerity more difficult and usually dealt with emotional conversations bluntly. Whatever she had anticipated, it was not surprising that her last meeting with Jerzy ended acrimoniously. It was a bitter double blow for a man who had stayed at least emotionally loyal to his wife, and absolutely loyal to his country, only to find himself betrayed by both in the same few weeks. In a series of written accusations, Jerzy now blamed the British for everything from his situation in Cairo to failing to pass on his earlier letters to his wife. 'He is terribly sore about the treatment he says he has received,' Guy Tamplin warned Gubbins, 'also I gather his personal life has gone wrong as XY is now own firm, and for this we are to blame!!'[31] Wilkinson also put in his own tuppence worth, writing: 'I gather that their marriage had never looked very permanent.'[32] It is fortunate, perhaps, that Jerzy was not party to British cipher telegrams. As it was, citing his impossible position, he turned down all British offers of work, including a role in Iran, then under British jurisdiction, and demanded repatriation to Britain, before, as a colleague noted, he told Tamplin to 'fuck himself' and left.[33] He finally returned to London in October 1941 and refused to have anything further to do with the SOE. The following spring he moved to Canada. His marriage, and his war, were both over.

On 22 June 1941, a week after Wilkinson dismissed Christine and Andrzej, Hitler had launched Operation Barbarossa, the German

invasion of Russia. Although the Musketeers' microfilm carried by Christine, and a range of corroborating evidence, had long since reached Churchill and the commanders-in-chief, the massive build-up of German forces from the Black Sea to the Baltic had generally been interpreted as a mere show of force, designed to push through a more favourable German–Soviet agreement. It was not until June 1941 that Churchill sent a personal message to Stalin, warning of the imminent invasion. Stalin dismissed the letter as a crude attempt to cause dissent between Russia and Germany. Ten days later the greatest invasion force in history tore though Stalin's ill-prepared border defences and ploughed relentlessly on towards Leningrad, Moscow and Stalingrad. Christine and Andrzej knew that they were to some degree vindicated – no Nazi agent would have provided warning of the invasion – but the rise of their personal stock was in direct correlation to the waning of Poland's status in the war. Until Hitler invaded Russia, Poland had been Britain's only effective ally. On 22 June 1941 Russia officially came to the Allied table, relegating Poland to a rather problematic acolyte.

Twelve hours after hearing the news of the invasion, Churchill broadcast his aim to help Russia in whatever way he could. Asked by his private secretary, as they strolled in the gardens at Chequers, whether this alliance presented difficulties for such an arch anti-Communist, Churchill replied, 'Not at all. I have only one purpose, the destruction of Hitler, and my life is much simplified thereby. If Hitler invaded Hell I would make at least favourable reference to the Devil in the House of Commons.'[34] General Sikorski must have envied Churchill his clear-cut position. On 30 July, strongly encouraged by the British Foreign Office, Sikorski signed an agreement to re-establish diplomatic relations between Poland and Russia, but for many Poles accepting an alliance with the Soviets would prove impossible. Poland had been carved up by Russia and Germany less than two years previously, and Russia still had clear territorial ambitions in Poland. Under pressure, in August the Soviets granted an amnesty to the surviving Poles they had interned since 1940, including 40,000 prisoners-of-war. Although notably few officers were among them, these 40,000, along with around 75,000 Polish

civilians, mainly their families, now left Russia for Iran, under the leadership of General Władysław Anders, a former cavalry officer and an old friend of Andrzej's. The whereabouts of the many thousand missing Polish officers would weigh heavily on Polish–Soviet relations.

With the launch of Operation Barbarossa the British felt both more certain of Christine and Andrzej's loyalties and less obliged to keep them on ice for the sake of good relations with the Poles. Aware of their obligation to Christine, they offered her passage to Britain, but she decided to stay in Cairo, where she felt she had a greater chance of an operational posting. She 'lacks nothing except employment', the SOE Cairo office reported. 'We are trying to remedy this.'[35]

In August, Christine and Andrzej escaped Cairo's claustrophobic heat for Jerusalem under arrangements made by SOE, but 'on their own private business', Tamplin informed Gubbins.[36] Their stated plan was to get medical attention for Andrzej's leg, which, Christine wrote to Kate O'Malley, was 'in a bad way'.[37] Christine took the opportunity to meet both with friends at the British Legation, and with Zofia Rączkowska. As a result she would have been perfectly placed to provide the British with an off-the-record dialogue with the Jewish–Israeli independence movement. In June and July this organization had played a significant role in the successful Allied campaign to prevent the Germans from using Vichy French Syria as an air-refuelling base and a springboard from which to attack Allied-held Egypt, and five years later SOE would credit Christine with having 'proved particularly useful during the Syrian campaign against the Vichy French'.[38] However, there is nothing further on this in the files.* Whatever the reason for this Jerusalem visit, it was short and seemingly not newsworthy and, perhaps partly because of this lack of fanfare, there was good news waiting for Christine and Andrzej on their return to Cairo.

* In his 2008 biography of Christine, Poland's Colonel Jan Larecki speculates that Christine might have been sent to Palestine as an agitator, to help form Jewish units to fight with the Allies, or for counterintelligence purposes to encourage cooperation with the British: pp. 165–80.

The British had agreed with the Polish Second Bureau that they would not employ Christine and Andrzej in any position that would bring them into direct contact with Poles or Polish affairs, but there was nothing to stop them being used elsewhere. Now that the Allies had secured Syria and Lebanon they also had strategic control over the main routes to the oilfields of Iraq, which had been held by pro-German rebels since April. As the summer progressed, and the Panzers pushed across Russia, it looked as though Germany might again burst into the Middle East, giving the oil routes renewed strategic importance.

At the end of August, Tamplin proposed that Christine and Andrzej should be sent into northern Syria. From there they were to monitor political developments in the region, in particular the volatile situation in neutral Turkey, and the security of the bridges over the Euphrates, with an eye to their suitability for sabotage should the Germans break through. Before instructing Christine, however, Tamplin cleared the mission with the Poles. As Polish investigations had unearthed nothing to further incriminate Christine on the basis of the allegations made in May, references to her earlier 'indiscretions' had now been dropped, and the green light came through in September. The rest of the month was spent in preparation. Christine was briefed on the political and military intelligence required, information which, Tamplin commented drily, 'I would imagine she would find it quite easy to get'. Andrzej was sent on a course in explosives, 'so that he could be in a position to deal with railways if and when necessary'.[39] Both of them were reminded in no uncertain terms that they were on unofficial probation.

In late October, Tamplin reported, 'X and Y have at last gone off – very pleased to have an occupation again', adding that 'they swore that they would not let their enthusiasm run away with them and lead them into indiscretion'.[40] They drove the Opel to Aleppo, the largest Syrian city near the Turkish border, well placed to monitor the likelihood of Turkey joining the Axis. Ultimately, as Turkey remained neutral and the Russian front held, Christine did not have much to report, but despite the lack of drama these were,

for her, some of the happiest months of the war. She was back in the field, however modest the role, and living and working with Andrzej. She was also winning admirers among the more distinguished residents of Aleppo, among them the son of the Emperor of Afghanistan, with whom Andrzej went fishing (with dynamite), and whom Christine teased about his solid gold signet ring being inferior to her Skarbek ring with its slice of iron.

Liberated from the disapproval and constant surveillance they had endured in Cairo, and back on an active-service wage, Christine made the most of her freedom, exploring the city's ancient souks, riding out into the dry and stony Syrian steppe, being guest of honour at a Bedouin feast and attending the birth of a camel. Andrzej was also enormously cheered by the apparent change in their fortunes. As soon as he had the opportunity he bought Christine a beautiful bracelet whose heavy gold links, inset with ivory, folded back on themselves to form a neat cube when not being worn. He also proposed to her. He knew she was not free, being still technically married to Jerzy, and perhaps this is what emboldened him. Christine did not accept Andrzej's proposal, although she did not reject him out of hand. But she kept the bracelet for the rest of her life – much as she did Andrzej.

At the end of 1941, the course of the war changed again as the attack on the US naval base in Pearl Harbour drew America into the conflict. 'The Japanese declaration of war on America eclipses all other news this week', Wilkinson filed in December, adding, in perhaps the greatest understatement of the war, 'it seems that Pearl Harbour was not a very pleasant surprise for them'.[41] The Allied position had never been stronger, but Poland's once strategic significance to the course of the war was over, and once again Christine's fortunes were to change in inverse correlation to those of her country.

8: THE BEAUTIFUL SPY

The scene is a military ballroom.
The gallant and fair are the dancers;
But who's the brunette,
Who with eyes black as jet,
Fascinates all the guards and the lancers?
Shame on you, shame on you!
Oh, fie, fie!
Olga Pulloffski, you beautiful spy![1]

In June 1942 Guy Tamplin prudently informed Peter Wilkinson that Christine 'seems to be regarded as our tame Olga Polofsky [*sic*] who spies on the Poles and reports all the things she learns'.[2] Olga Pulloffski, 'the beautiful spy', was the anti-heroine of a 1930s popular song which was once again enjoying considerable Allied air time, and whose name had just been appropriated for the glamorous honeytraps surrounded by fawning officers in the British government's 'Keep Mum' poster campaign. But behaviour that seemed rather romantically daring to the British was viewed as treasonous by the Poles.

Britain had officially entered the Second World War to defend Poland's borders, but during the course of the conflict the two allies' interests had diverged. Unlike Britain, Poland faced twin threats, from Nazi Germany and Soviet Russia. The British had now embraced Russia as an ally, but within the Polish camp there was huge discord about whether their aggressive neighbour should be resisted or appeased. Christine was deeply patriotic but she was not overtly political. She had no doubts about Soviet intentions, but she had lost her country, and many of her family, under the Nazis. She had also seen how divided the Polish authorities, home army

and exiled forces had become. Convinced that Britain offered the greatest hope for the deliverance of her country, Christine had repeatedly risked her life to bring intelligence out for the British secret services from the independent Polish 'Musketeers'.

Now, back in Cairo, she was playing a dangerous game, using her charm, social contacts and skill at securing and assessing information to report select bits of Polish political and military news and gossip to the British. SOE did their best to protect their source, giving both Andrzej and Christine new code-names. In all British ciphers and telegrams they now appeared as 'Forcible' and 'Willing', 'the latter name, by the way, an obvious libel', Wilkinson's team admitted.[3] In fact 'Willing' seems rather too passive for Christine, who had, throughout the war, sought out the most dashing lovers and dangerous missions. If she was frustrated at being reduced to the role of 'beautiful spy' in Cairo while waiting for another posting to the field, then she at least saw that pleasure and duty could to some extent go hand in hand, and as always she threw herself into the job.

Christine and Andrzej had returned to Cairo from Syria in early 1942. They moved into a boarding house in Zamalek, the leafy, residential part of Gezira Island in the Nile, run by a Jewish couple and 'infested by WAAFs' (members of the Women's Auxiliary Air Force).[4] Being largely undomesticated, Christine preferred living in a boarding house or hotel to having a flat, and she loved the café life that allowed her to come and go as she pleased. Most mornings she would stroll down Zamalek's wide shady avenues, lined by flame trees, nineteenth-century villas, restaurants, bars and cafés, on her way to the renowned Gezira Sporting Club, a well-maintained complex of parks, lawns, café, swimming pool and tennis courts leased to the British military command. Officially re-employed by SOE, she could now enjoy the benefits of club membership. If she arrived early enough she could watch the polo ponies being ridden on the lawns before the working day began. She had never learned to swim, but would settle down beside the pool to sunbathe, read, drink tea and enjoy being entertained by a wide range of admirers drawn from the city's large officer corps.

Most officers were 'buccaneering, swashbuckling types', remembered Laura Foskett, an SOE secretary who shared Christine's Zamalek pension for a while.[5] Some had come in straight from the desert, still in tattered battledress; others were freshly posted and eager to see action. They came to Cairo for briefings, training, weapons, pay, rest – and sex. The city was virtually a garrison town. Most wives had been sent to South Africa for their own safety in 1940, and attractive female company was in huge demand. Invitations might begin with tea in Groppi's large garden, or afternoon drinks on the shaded raised terrace at Shepheard's Hotel. In the evenings there were romantic dinners at Mena House in the lee of the pyramids, and dancing late into the night at the Continental, the Turf Club, Mohammed Ali Club or the Kit-Kat on a boat moored on the Nile. 'Your line of retreat to the powder room has been cut. Reinforcements sent to your aid have been intercepted at Groppi's, where after a futile struggle they unconditionally put down their arms . . .' read one flirty leaflet produced by the men of the 'King's Own 1st Pencil Pushers' for their colleagues in the First Aid Nursing Yeomanry, the women's voluntary corps better known as the 'FANYs'. 'There is no escape from this dilemma. You can't go on talking forever, and sooner of later the whisky will give out. Mother is far, far away . . . Think it over . . . follow your worst instincts . . . SURRENDER CAN BE FUN'.[6]

Young, single and pretty, Laura Foskett surrendered happily, making love by moonlight at the foot of the pyramids – although, she admitted, 'the sand could get in the way'.[7] She was not the only woman in the city having fun. According to the novelist Olivia Manning, 'Cairo . . . was like a bureau of sexual exchange', and Christine's husband, Jerzy Gizycki, reported that while he was in Cairo around twenty nurses had to be evacuated to England because they were pregnant.[8] 'There is nothing wrong with young couples sharing beds – especially in war time', Jerzy wrote. 'But one would think that nurses would be able to get some contraceptives and use them.'[9] But although a 'French letter' and a tin of ointment was given to every soldier entering the inappropriately named 'Berka',

Cairo's notorious red-light district, young women like Laura Foskett had no independent access to such luxuries.

Christine became the focus of attention as soon as she walked around the pool at the Gezira Club in her peep-toe platform espadrilles and well-cut shirt and skirt. Guy Tamplin's wife, Nina, described her as 'unusual-looking perhaps, but certainly not beautiful', though she had to admit that Christine 'had a wide choice of admirers'. Even her own husband was 'devoted' to Christine, Nina admitted, although, she stressed, his feeling was 'an emotion which transcended sex, and had its roots in admiration of her heroic qualities'.[10] However, Douglas Dodds-Parker, an army captain who had been posted to the city to coordinate SOE activities in the Balkans, believed Christine 'had some kind of magic in her that men could not resist'.[11] 'She wasn't really beautiful, but she was very attractive', Margaret Pawley, another of the Cairo-based FANYs, agreed. 'Men found her terribly attractive . . . but women would be rather fed up about the fact that she had such an effect on the men.'[12] One young British officer, Michael Ward, used to watch her at the Club in the afternoons. She already had a reputation as a courageous agent, 'so there was a certain atmosphere of glamour attached to her' and, as she was 'an attractive woman at that', he introduced himself. After two or three dates, however, Ward realized that Christine 'was hoping for something a little bit stronger' than their innocent chats, and nervously made his excuses.[13] Other officers were less circumspect.

She 'had many lovers' according to Laura Foskett. One evening, Foskett later recalled, Christine was in bed with company when there was an angry banging on her door. Watching her partner produce a gun and aim it at the unwelcome intruder, an affronted Christine exclaimed, 'You never told me you kept a loaded revolver under your pillow!'[14] Nina Tamplin meanwhile remembered Christine turning up to meet her on the arm of 'a splendid-looking Afghan major', and afterwards boasting that 'he would die for me'.*[15] Whatever the truth behind such stories, Christine did

* This was the son of the deposed emperor of Afghanistan, whom she and Andrzej had met in Aleppo the previous year.

nothing to curb them. 'She was an embroiderer', Nina Tamplin felt, 'not a liar ever, but she just had to cover her tracks.'[16] 'She was certainly mysterious', Margaret Pawley agreed.[17] Whatever the truth, Andrzej still worshipped Christine, but he was beginning to accept that their relationship would never be exclusive. To the FANYs and SOE 'cipherines' at the Club it was clear that Andrzej was off-limits, but British officers like Ward were 'rather surprised' when they found out that Christine and the handsome but heavily built and moustached Andrzej were in any way an item.[18]

Christine and Andrzej also had a social life outside of the British enclaves. Although still regarded with suspicion by the Second Bureau, Christine now treated the allegations against her with contempt. She and Andrzej both had influential connections in the Polish military including Bobinski and Kopanski, and Andrzej had many Polish friends and 'cousins' serving as cavalry officers in the Middle East. There were surprising reunions too. One day the former Musketeer agent Michal Gradowski, 'the Fox', turned up in Cairo, bursting with stories to be shared over a drink, and even Prince Eddie Lobkowitz, whom they had once sheltered in Budapest, arrived for some rest and recuperation having received a bullet in his backside. Cairo had become, in Olivia Manning's words, 'the clearing house of Eastern Europe'.[19] Exiled royals and their hangers-on, elected heads of state with their diplomats, officers, journalists and spies, all had arrived in Cairo to wait for the end of the war. Christine was soon moving in the most select circles, invited to drinks with Egyptian Jews connected to King Farouk's household, and Muslim dignitaries including Prince Ali Khan, the socialite son of Aga Khan III, as well as to dinners with British, Greek, Yugoslav, and even Polish officers and agents.*

That spring a childhood friend of Andrzej's, Zofia Tarnowska, arrived in Cairo. She was lent a luxurious villa by King Farouk's uncle, who had often hunted on her family estates. Zofia was

* Aly, as Prince Ali Khan was popularly known, was then married to Joan Guinness, but would later have an affair with Winston Churchill's daughter-in-law, before marrying Rita Hayworth, the favourite pin-up of the Middle East.

strikingly beautiful and had enjoyed a privileged and rather wild childhood in the Polish countryside, at Rudnik. 'Rud' means iron and, like Christine, Zofia proudly wore a family signet ring with a slice of iron embedded in its face. Like Christine, she too had a deep love of animals, had been expelled from her posh Polish boarding school for having too much spirit and had married young to escape the nest, although Zofia's nest was rather better feathered than Christine's had been. Zofia had married her cousin, Andrzej Tarnowski, who was now serving in the Carpathian Brigade and was also a close friend of Andrzej's. But their marriage, always tempestuous, had been shipwrecked by the war and the deaths in infancy of their two sons.* Arriving in Cairo to some degree liberated her from her traumatic past, and she seized the second chance. Perhaps she and Christine saw too much of themselves when they looked at one another, or perhaps Christine was jealous of Zofia's pre-war friendship with Andrzej and suspicious that he might be secretly in love with her. Whatever the reason, it took the two women a while before they embraced as friends. Once they had done so, however, they became as close as either of their fiercely independent natures would allow.

Zofia was a society beauty who loved huge house parties and fashionable nightclubs. Christine preferred smaller occasions, where she could turn all the heads if she chose, but still have intimate conversations in a quiet corner. Zofia was intrigued by Christine, and full of admiration for her. She felt Poland's loss just as keenly as her friend, and had even burned her passport in 1939 as a protest against being forced to flee. But she had never had any desire to serve in the front line. Instead she was happy to volunteer for the Red Cross, helping to trace missing Allied soldiers and serving at the military canteen outside Shepheard's Hotel. Christine, for her part, admired Zofia's strength and determination, and the natural aversion to discipline that chimed with her own. They would be friends for the rest of their lives.

* Both children died of natural causes, the eldest aged two, on the birthday of his younger brother.

Although she enjoyed soaking up both the sun and the admiration on offer in Cairo, Christine was intensely frustrated at her lack of active deployment. She had seen the impact of Nazi occupation, understood the terror and risks her countrymen faced, and knew that she flourished in providing support to the resistance. The atmosphere in Cairo was 'unbearable', she now wrote to Kate O'Malley. 'There are about 90,000 officers trying to have fun. You cannot imagine the way in which nobody here realizes the atrocities going on in the occupied countries, and the battles in the desert here are treated like a game. I am in despair. The offices are full of young, cheerful, unworried youngsters that see people like me as defeatists or spoilsports.'[20] She also wrote repeatedly about her regret at not returning to Poland. Over there her work had reaped clear results, but in Cairo it seemed to be all talk. SOE wanted to move her – and Andrzej – on as well. 'I can see no point whatever in leaving them in Cairo where they cannot be employed,' Wilkinson wrote, 'and where they are a potential source of disgruntlement.'[21] In private conversations 'disgruntlement' was rephrased as 'potential source of danger', and it was clear that in London at least Christine and Andrzej were again being seen more as a liability than an asset.[22] 'The perplexed question of X and Y' continued to 'cause embarrassment' over the next few months.[23] Yet at the same time Christine was bringing in some very useful local intelligence.

In April 1942 she warned Guy Tamplin of a rumoured assassination plot – 'a rather violent accusation' – indirectly linked to Józef Retinger, one of General Sikorski's more controversial personal advisers.*[24] By May she was regularly being asked to report on Polish officers and Second Bureau personnel. Libel not being a key concern in espionage, her comments were often refreshingly frank. Damning one Polish officer who had been described by SOE as 'tall, athletic and good-looking, with charming manners', Christine reported that 'his brother has for many years adorned a lunatic

* Retinger would be linked to the discovery of an unprimed explosive device in the plane carrying Sikorski to Washington in December 1942, and was later removed from Poland on a special British flight in fear for his life.

asylum', and implied that 'he might do worse than join him'.[25] Her
wry style was not unwelcome. 'Source venomous but probably good,
ie Willing', reads the comment at the bottom of a report on the
bruised pride of a Polish general in Tel Aviv.[26] However gossipy
her reports might seem, it was clear that the British valued them,
and they now tried to keep her in Cairo. SOE headquarters had
moved to Rustum Buildings, a block of flats on the edge of the Nile
so covert that every taxi-driver knew it as 'Secret House', and
shoeshine boys and other street vendors would stand outside shout-
ing 'Chocolates! Cigarettes! OBEs!'[27] At first Christine was offered
secretarial jobs; unsurprisingly, she refused them. Aidan Crawley,
who was also now in Cairo, lobbied on her behalf, saying that she
was not 'the type that can abide office work' and wanted 'work with
risk'.[28]

Andrzej also wanted work with risk, but he too had been out of
action since their return from Syria. His leg had still not received
medical attention and was now badly swollen and irritated by the
sand that infiltrated between his stump and his prosthesis, causing
considerable pain. In March he underwent an operation to remove
another three centimetres from his stump. It took him a further
month to be able to move about again on crutches, after which
Christine and Kate O'Malley connived to get replacement parts for
his artificial leg sent from London.

While visiting Andrzej in hospital, Christine met an old friend.
In September 1941, when she and Andrzej had been posted to
Syria, Wladimir Ledóchowski had been dispatched further west,
with the Polish Carpathian Brigade, to help relieve the Allied forces
defending Tobruk in Libya. The end of Wladimir's left elbow had
been blown away and he was lucky not to have had his arm
amputated. As it was, surgery left one arm shorter than the other,
and locked as straight as a stick. Although he loathed the sympathy
he detected among many of his visitors, imagining them gossiping
about him at the hospital gates, he was touched by Christine's visit.
'She looked at me with tears in her eyes', he wrote in his journal.[29]

A few weeks later Christine sat around a table at the Mena
House restaurant with her two crippled lovers, all of them staring

resolutely through the windows at the pyramids. Wladimir raised a glass of wine to their reunion, but it was a miserable occasion. 'Stiff?' Christine asked him, looking at his sling. He nodded. 'So the war is finished for you?' 'Just about', Wladimir answered.[30] And that was the end of the conversation. Although Wladimir would always cherish the memory of his months with Christine in Poland and Hungary, it was obvious to him that there was no longer anything between them. For Christine, however, the self-knowledge that came from this meeting was even clearer. She became absolutely determined that the war should not be over for her.*

Britain was now in the awkward position of having both guaranteed Poland's pre-war borders and committed to support Russian interests. Gubbins had a long-standing distrust of Soviet intentions, but with typical frankness Wilkinson summed up the thoughts of many when he told Tamplin, 'my own feeling is that it is high time we stopped molly-coddling the Poles'.[31] With British encouragement, General Sikorski was pursuing a pragmatic policy of rapprochement with Russia. Many senior Polish officers were critical of this position, and Sikorski now had to contend not only with occupation at home and war abroad, but with growing dissent among his own forces. Opposition was particularly strong among those who had experienced Soviet hospitality first hand, or who knew some of the nearly 20,000 Polish officers and intelligentsia who had been interned by Stalin and were still unaccounted for. 'The situation of the Poles in Russia is really very horrifying . . .' even Wilkinson admitted, and 'clearly not a very good argument in favour of Sikorski's policy of rapprochement'.[32]

It seems strange then that in April 1942, SOE sent a cipher telegram to Moscow, arranging for Christine and Andrzej's names to be passed to the NKVD, the Soviet secret police.[33] It was envisaged that Britain could help Russia through intelligence-sharing and a coordinated campaign of subversive activities. Having

* Wladimir in fact rejoined the Polish secret service, and was sent to Istanbul under the guise of being a diplomat. He was then posted to Ankara, where he lost his diary journal, which was only published posthumously. From Ankara he was sent to Paris. After the war he married the daughter of the Polish ambassador to France.

signed an agreement with Britain, in January 1942 NKVD representatives started arriving in various Allied-held territories in the Middle East to facilitate joint working. The Poles were rightly concerned that the Soviets were trying to penetrate their organizations, and it is possible that the NKVD were given Christine and Andrzej's names to distinguish them from other Poles they might be watching. Or Christine and Andrzej may simply have been convenient small fry, worth passing on to establish good relations.

Unaware of these arrangements, Christine now had her work cut out for her trying to keep the British in Cairo even partially up to speed with Polish intrigues. It did not help that she was politically naive. Christine was not working to any grand scheme. She was an opportunist, keen on action, who fell in with whichever personal contact would give her an assignment to work for the freedom of her country. She was loyal only to Poland. The Musketeers, and the British, were means to an end.

In January 1942, SOE reported that Sikorski was growing increasingly concerned about the Musketeers' political influence.[34] Their leader, Stefan Witkowski, taking an independent line on what constituted Poland's greatest threat, had become involved in highly secretive, possibly collaborationist, discussions with the Nazis. When it seemed likely that Germany would win the war, a clandestine mission was dispatched, with German knowledge and support, to the Polish general Władysław Anders, who was raising an army from Polish internees recently released in Russia. Microfilm hidden in a bar of shaving soap revealed a letter from Witkowski and other senior but independent Polish figures, ordering Anders to attack the Red Army from behind their own lines. Unwilling to act against his Russian 'allies', at least without direct orders from Sikorski, Anders ordered the arrest of the men he had welcomed just hours before.

Denials swiftly followed. The official Polish resistance confirmed they knew of the mission, but not of the military order. The couriers were tried before a military court and condemned to death for cooperating with the enemy. A spirited defence by the Musketeer agent Klementyna Mańkowska, from whom the British

were still secretly accepting intelligence, led to their sentences being commuted. Christine officially denied knowing Mańkowska.[35] In June, Witkowski sent Christine a warning that their reports were being intercepted, and told her he had been informed that she was in a concentration camp. Not long afterwards the Musketeers were disbanded, with most of their personnel joining the Home Army. Others, including Christine's friend Teresa Łubienska, were arrested by the Gestapo.

Witkowski was accused of insubordination, profiteering, conducting assassinations without investigations or trials, and collaboration with the Gestapo and the Abwehr. In August 1942 a Home Army Special Court passed a sentence of death on him and on 18 September Witkowski was assassinated by a Polish execution squad dressed in German police uniforms. Only a year earlier he had been recommended for the highest Polish military honour, the Virtuti Militari.* How independent Witkowski's actions were is not known, but less than a week before his death at least one British SOE intelligence officer, a friend of Christine's, had also been in conference with senior Polish officials and the Gestapo in Istanbul.[36]

General Anders and his troops and their families had now arrived in Palestine, where the men were drilled daily in the hot desert sun, while waiting to head to Italy. Visiting Palestine, Harold Macmillan was impressed by the Polish troops' spirit, describing them as having 'an extraordinary sense of romance – not gaiety exactly, but chivalry, poetry, adventure'.[37] Andrzej was an old friend of Anders, and when the general visited Cairo in May 1942 he agreed to arrange work for both Andrzej and Christine in Tehran. Christine was at first delighted, but as the possibility of working directly for the Poles edged closer she had to face some awkward truths. Despite her friends in high places, Christine was neither liked nor trusted by the majority of the Second Bureau. Her reputation, already tainted by association with the Musketeers, was now further jeopardized by her intelligence work for the British,

* There is no record of Christine's reaction to Witkowski's death, or even that she knew of it, although she must have suspected.

informing on her fellow Poles. 'The English have managed to position us on very bad terms with the Poles', Christine raged in a letter to Kate. 'I think I will never be able to return to Poland as they will treat me as a traitor and a British spy. And here I am, risking my life and those of others.'[38]

When the Poles specified that if Christine were to work for them she would first have to give up her British passport, she became intensely suspicious. In July she told Tamplin she feared that the Second Bureau would lose no time in having her interned 'on any convenient pretext', or that she would otherwise be 'deliberately compromised' or 'put in the cooler', should she give up the protection of her passport.[39] Later a friend, possibly Colonel Bobinski, who was deeply involved in Polish intrigues, wrote to Christine 'begging her for her own sake' not to accept any Polish assignment.[40] She now understood that she would never be able to work directly in the service of her own country. Despite his excellent military record Andrzej shared Christine's dim view of their situation, telling SOE that, if he worked for the Poles now, he too 'would probably be shot down at the first ... opportunity'.[41] When he was finally offered employment under his former commander, General Kopanski, he turned it down.

Christine now petitioned to join the ATS, the women's branch of the British army, offering to 'do any kind of duty, except office work, preferably near the front'.[42] Inactivity was driving her crazy, and she even applied for a job with the new American mission in Cairo. In mid-July she sent an SOS to a friend in Hungary saying she was reduced to working as a waitress in Cairo, and 'on the rocks'.[43] Hearing of this, Gubbins quickly telegraphed Cairo demanding to know what had happened to her and Andrzej. Within a few weeks Andrzej was employed as a transport officer with the SOE Middle East motor fleet, a job that could hardly have been more perfect for him. He was working 'in cars', Christine noted drily, while 'I am still waiting'.[44] Suggestions that she might serve as Andrzej's secretary left her 'very browned off' indeed.[45]

But there were distractions, at least. In June, Richard Truszkowski arrived in Cairo to temporarily take over from Guy Tamplin,

who had been promoted.* Truszkowski was a senior British SOE intelligence officer of Polish extraction, usually based in London, who had accompanied Gubbins on his first military mission to Warsaw. Hungry for Polish conversation, he now moved into the same Zamalek boarding house as Christine and Andrzej. In the evenings, while the resident WAAFs and FANYs were out dancing at the Continental or the Turf Club, Christine, Andrzej and Truszkowski would eat at Shepheard's or at the Gezira Club where there was dancing on an outdoor terrace, under lights among the trees. Back at the pension they would stay up talking in French and Polish late into the night over whisky that Truszkowski described as 'almost pure fusel oil, with a headache in every drop', and gin that was 'faintly corrosive'.[46] Sometimes they wrapped up against the sand-flies and slept under the brilliant night sky on the building's flat roof, counting the stars and discussing the kind of Europe that might emerge from the war.

Christine was soon providing Truszkowski with full organizational overviews of both the Musketeers and the ZWZ, as well as specific nuggets of local information. Once she informed on the mistress of a Polish officer whom she suspected of being a German double agent. SOE investigations revealed that the woman was 'definitely suspect', using the diplomatic post to send uncensored letters to Hungary referencing particular pages from a specific edition of Goethe.[47] When the officer involved was reprimanded for 'mixing business with love', he angrily telegrammed Sikorski, demanding that those who accused him of 'working for the Gestapo' should be disciplined.[48] Instead, he was removed to 'an insignificant post in East Africa', clearly showing the importance attributed to Christine's intelligence.[49] The incident also reveals that Christine was not the only beautiful spy in Cairo. Soon the British had a nickname for the German equivalent of Olga Pulloffski: 'Venal Vera . . . from Gezira'.[†50]

* Guy Tamplin died of a heart attack at his desk in November 1943. 'His funeral in the desert was a sad affair.' See Annette Street, *Long Ago and Far Away*.

† There was so much intrigue that in 1942 MGM released a spy spoof, called *Cairo*,

In July 1942 Tamplin's permanent replacement arrived. Gubbins had appointed Captain Patrick Howarth, a comparatively junior officer in the Intelligence Corps who spoke fluent Polish. As Howarth arrived at Shepheard's Hotel he overheard some Sudanese waiters teaching each other German. It was not an encouraging start. There was now heavy fighting in the Egyptian desert as Rommel's advance halted just sixty miles from Alexandria. Recognizing that many Egyptians were not unhappy at the prospect of a change of European guest, Rommel's Afrika Corps Radio broadcast to the capital: 'Get your party frocks out, we're on our way.'[51] Allied Egypt suddenly seemed at risk, and the whole of Cairo was soon in a flap. On the day that would become known as 'Ash Wednesday', Christine walked to Rustum Buildings through a swirl of charred papers as the British and other embassies burnt their most sensitive files. Story has it that Andrzej was among those selected to stay behind enemy lines in Cairo should the Germans take the city. Certainly, although the huge crowds heading for Jerusalem filled the stations and jammed the streets with traffic, neither he nor Christine packed their bags. Nor did their headstrong friend Zofia Tarnowska, who, refusing to be displaced again, took a train to Alexandria, where she went to the best restaurant and ordered a bottle of their finest wine. Before the end of the month, however, the Axis advance was halted at the first battle of El Alamein. Patrick Howarth, who had a weak stomach, found it all 'a bit of a strain'.[52] From then on he survived in Cairo on a diet of weak tea, boiled rice, Stella beer and whisky, which in no way prevented him from socializing with his Polish agents.

During his London briefing, Howarth had been shown files leading him to believe that Christine and Andrzej were people best avoided, but in Cairo Richard Truszkowski firmly told him to look after them. 'Christine was a very remarkable woman,' Howarth soon decided, 'we became very close friends.'[53] He would never forget the first time he saw her, 'stretching in cat-like delight with

in which a warbling Jeanette MacDonald is mistaken for a Nazi agent by an American hack who follows her between the souks and the pyramids.

the Gezira sun' in her 'dull dark-brown jacket, dull light-brown skirt, [and] brilliant brown mobile arresting eyes'.[54] She had just flatly turned down another offer of office work from Tamplin. When Howarth asked her reasons she replied that while she had plenty of physical endurance, she had no intellectual stamina. Howarth believed her real reason was her determination never to accept anything second-rate. 'In issues that were important to her,' he wrote, 'she wanted the best or nothing.'[55] Later he would describe her aversion to office work as 'almost pathological'.[56] Truszkowski, however, believed that Christine's fear of being desk-bound came from a deep-seated 'inferiority complex'.[57] She was proud and, being surprisingly thin-skinned, likely to 'burst into tears' at the slightest criticism, giving 'the worst possible impression of herself', he wrote.[58] 'I am incapable of working in an office', she admitted.[59] In the field, Christine's self-belief and determination were steely enough to overcome the most extraordinary challenges; but she had little interest in, or aptitude for, paperwork and, unsuited to the faintest shadow of constraint, the etiquette of an office left her cold. She was, however, quite prepared to guide Howarth on the intricacies of Polish politics, provide background on particular officers, or discuss the possibilities for getting Polish workers to defect across the Balkans. She even proposed Michal Gradowski for an SOE mission in Albania, but Christine was also still holding out for a mission of her own, and 'the more difficult and dangerous', Howarth recognized, the better.[60]

It did not take Howarth long to see that Christine's considerable talents were being wasted with her 'salamander existence' at the Gezira Club, and he made up his mind to rehabilitate her.[61] Later he would claim, only half-joking, that 'the most useful thing I did in World War Two was to reinstate Christine Granville'.[62] It was also perhaps one of the more difficult. A man of his time, Howarth was not a natural advocate of treating his female colleagues on the same terms as their male counterparts. When his secretary undertook to darn his socks he praised her initiative alongside her complexion and 'tinkling voice'.[63] But although

'thoroughly feminine', Christine was clearly exceptional: she had worked for British secret services in the field for two years before SOE was officially given the green light to recruit women for operational duties.[64] She herself, Howarth noted, had no time for any kind of discrimination. 'She set her own standards, which were high ... [and] would treat a General or a Sergeant with exactly the same courtesy and, if she thought their human qualities merited it, the same degree of attention', and she had an 'aristocratic disdain' for differences of creed or colour. She was never intolerant of failure or inadequacy, but she was tersely dismissive of people she found pretentious, sending them away with such comments as 'bloody fool' or 'quel poltron'.[65] Howarth judged Christine to be at once attractive, intelligent, passionate about her country and her people, experienced, able and under-utilized. With support from Churchill, the first female SOE agents had been dropped into France the previous autumn. It was time to get Christine ready to return to the field.

As a first step, Howarth arranged for Christine to be recruited into the FANYs. In 1943 women in the British military were not allowed to carry guns or explosives. To get around this Gubbins enrolled female SOE agents into the FANYs, which officially operated outside the Armed Forces but still offered some protection under the Geneva Convention in case of capture, and provided pensions should the women become casualties. For a couple of weeks Christine was placed in the care of Gwendolin Lees, who was soon captivated by this 'most remarkable' woman.[66] Christine practised her cover story on Lees, presenting herself as a penniless patriot, married at the age of just seventeen, and so now unable to marry the love of her life, 'Andy Kennedy'. But her passion and patriotism were undisguised. She was completely dedicated to helping SOE to liberate Poland, Lees reported, hugely impressed.[67] Although the two women spent only a short time together, years later Lees would name her eldest daughter after Christine.

Apart from this Christine had little to do with the FANYs, either operationally or socially. The only time she wore the uniform

was for the photograph for her papers, and then she had to cadge the correct buttons from a friend's summer drill set. Christine carried any uniform well, but the resulting photo was a far cry from the naked-beneath-a-fur-coat shot that had once graced her Polish identity papers; there would be little chance of even the most efficient card-index putting the two together. Her once deliberately provocative beauty was now hidden behind a clean face, beret, khaki uniform with shirt, tie, and borrowed brass buttons. Only her signature, squashed up against the document's spine as it overran the allotted space, hinted that there was more to this woman than could be contained on paper.

By September 1942 Howarth was working to find Christine a job as a wireless operator in the field, sending information, and messages for drops of men and supplies to aid national resistance, back to base in London or Algiers. The idea appealed to her, but Howarth was concerned that training would be difficult to arrange, as she would be 'the only woman housed with some 300 thugs' in Rustum Buildings.[68] Nonetheless Christine started a course in October and was soon reportedly 'very happy with her Morse alphabet'.[69] She had much to smile about. Her teacher was a handsome young half-British, half-Italian sergeant-instructor called Dick Mallaby, known at least as much for his 'gentle, almost dreamy manner', as for his fine record of service.[70] Her greatest source of pleasure, however, was an offer of employment in Turkey on completing her training. But despite many weeks spent on the roofs of various Cairo buildings with her SOE suitcase transmitter bleeping and whispering on its dials as she sent practice transmissions to Baghdad, Christine could not get the hang of her wireless.[71] After early sessions she would throw her hands in the air, her skin flushing, and exclaim loudly to all around that she could not do it; it was impossible.[72] It was not an office job, but it was the kind of repetitive work she abhorred, and when, in August, her proposed mission was cancelled because it was decided that she was too well-known in Turkey, her patience with the authorities who were still forcing her to remain away from active service began to wear perilously thin. But 'slowly and with some difficulty', she at last

began to master her wireless set, and was able to send a decent
fifteen words a minute by the end of the year.*[73]

She now needed to work on her coding, 'the deadliest of parlour
games', as SOE's Head of Coding, Leo Marks, put it.[74] The best
signallers and coders were 'girls straight from higher education
schools . . .', Gubbins wrote, who 'had not lost the classroom'.[75]
Once again Christine was not a natural, and once again her
famously courageous, and now infamously temperamental, figure
became a familiar sight in Rustum Buildings, where, to the irritation
of the other FANYs, even the most taciturn officers would fall over
themselves to be introduced. She 'had the most extraordinary grace
and a casual sort of chic', Margaret Pawley remembered, along with
'qualities of fascination which men found irresistible'.[76] 'As soon
as she came in all the men stopped to look at her, even the very
austere Colonel, who usually had his nose in his books, would leap
up to offer her a seat.'[77]

In the autumn of 1942 relations between Poland and the Soviet
Union were rapidly deteriorating. General Anders's army was now
more than 75,000 strong, including plenty of Soviet spies and
agitators. Soon rumours began to circulate suggesting that the tide
of support was shifting to Anders from Sikorski. By mid-September
Sikorski felt compelled to denounce plotters in a speech to the
National Council. If anything, however, the intrigues became more
complex. Anders was a brilliant professional soldier, not a natural
conspirator. According to Richard Truszkowski, now in London,
when told by the Polish authorities that 'if he stuck to straight
soldiering he would be a howling success, but that he was a mere
child where politics was concerned', Anders reportedly 'took it all
like a lamb and promised to be more circumspect in the future'.[78]
Christine, however, reported that 'cavalry officers of her acquain-
tance' all believed that the established Polish authority's days were
numbered.[79]

In December, Truszkowski outlined the 'numerous' difficulties

* Twenty words a minute was considered good, but some operators could send up to
thirty. See Patrick Howarth, *Undercover: The Women and Men of the SOE* (1990), p. 79.

still surrounding the operational deployment of both Christine and Andrzej. The main problem was 'the violent opposition to them by practically all Polish organisations', a position exacerbated by what he called 'their somewhat complex personalities'.[80] But there were also other concerns. The two of them had stated that they were little known to the Gestapo and would be able to move around occupied territory without risk, but Truszkowski had his doubts. 'Their somewhat striking personal appearance', combined with Andrzej's wooden leg, made them 'the sort of people who once seen are never forgotten', he wrote very reasonably, and to make matters worse they had 'literally hundreds if not thousands of friends [and] enemies, all over Europe, Africa and Asia Minor', increasing the risk of recognition.[81] 'They would shine under conditions in which personal courage and determination are essential', Truszkowski noted, but he continued, rather unfairly given the amount of information Christine had been passing to the British in Cairo, neither of them 'have any special talents for conspiratorial work'.[82]

As a result of Truszkowski's report it was suggested that Christine should be kept in the Middle East and found work as a nurse, preferably within a danger zone, as a wireless operator, or with prisoners-of-war. Christine was happy with all of this, asserting only that she could not countenance the humiliation of receiving any further pay for no active service. Then a radical new idea was floated. George Taylor reported that Christine was 'convinced she could live in France as a Frenchwoman', and that Andrzej might pass as a French Pole.[83] The Poles could have no objection to them being dropped into France or French North Africa. With the prospect of a new mission, Christine, Andrzej and Patrick Howarth celebrated Christmas at a flurry of charity balls and military dances. The future suddenly seemed worth looking forward to.

1943 started optimistically. Christine was still waiting for orders, but while she did so she took classes in English and Italian. When Howarth had first arrived in Cairo he noticed that she always spoke French as, 'her English was not very good'.[84] In fact she spoke English charmingly, if not very accurately, with a lilting accent and similarly seductive turn of phrase, often translating idioms literally

if she felt it added impact. But then even her French was 'fluent but rather breathy', a friend noted, and her natural manner was to speak in what Wladimir Ledóchowski had once described as a 'halting . . . panting fashion'.[85] Always conscious of the power of language, when she felt charm would not help her Christine would simply petition friends to write 'in your King's English' on her behalf.[86] While preparing for an unknown future, she also now took the opportunity to re-establish contact with old friends, exchanging letters through the diplomatic post with, among others, Kate and Sir Owen O'Malley. The next month Sir Owen was appointed as the British Ambassador to the Polish Republic, represented by the Polish government-in-exile in London under Sikorski, a position he retained until the end of the war. 'Do you think he loves me still', Christine asked Kate, 'for months I have tried to write, but the problem of how to begin defeats me'.[87] She need not have worried. Christine could 'still rely absolutely on his undying friendship', SOE reported, having read their exchanges.[88]

Andrzej's prospects were also improving. In March he was sent on a paramilitary course in Haifa in Palestine. Despite his false leg, he did well. Happy and popular, he was soon being considered as a potential instructor. While Andrzej was away Christine shared a small flat with Livia 'Pussi' Nasta, the daughter of a well-known Romanian journalist, and who worked for the British, broadcasting news back to her country despite being terrified that her voice would be recognized and harm would come to her family. She would later marry Bill Deakin, who ran SOE's Yugoslav section.* Christine still moved in an international crowd, although more and more of her British officer friends had arrived in Cairo, among them Aidan Crawley, Alfred Gardyne de Chastelaine, Ivor Porter and Ted Howe.

One new face was Colonel Cookham, a British officer who had rented a fine villa near to Christine, with a garden overgrown with bougainvillea and poinsettia, and lawns sloping gently down to the

* See William Deakin, *The Embattled Mountain* (1971) for an account of his work in Yugoslavia.

Nile. By day Christine joined Cookham on tours of Cairo's mosques and historic sites and, story has it, by night on 'excursions by felucca' to watch the flamingos and ibis in their evening flight upriver, eat kebabs, and drink red wine beside the water.[89] Cookham was, Truszkowski reported, 'a very decent sort', but he was not a permanent fixture.[90] Having tried unsuccessfully to persuade Christine to marry him, he was parachuted into Yugoslavia on a mission to Marshal Tito. There he was killed in action. After news of his death reached Cairo, Christine never mentioned his name again.

Throughout everything, Christine kept up her private information service for the British SOE, providing 'a good deal of valuable information' despite being under surveillance herself by the Polish Second Bureau, who were keeping 'a long account' of her activities.[91] The Russian victory against the Nazis at Stalingrad in February 1943 – 'surely', in the words of SOE's chief coder, 'the most effective eviction notice ever served on an invader' – turned the tide of the war.[92] Terrified that Stalin and Hitler might negotiate an independent peace treaty, Churchill and Roosevelt put increasing pressure on the Poles to accept the Soviet–Polish frontier changes. Dissent within the Polish forces increased correspondingly.

Christine was now approached by General Anders's aide-de-camp, Captain Klimkowski, whom SOE, with their usual dry humour, had code-named 'Plague'. Christine agreed to meet Klimkowski at the Continental Hotel. She was followed, she reported, by a fat Second Bureau agent with a limp, who managed to sit at the next table despite her frequent moves. Sadly there is no record of their conversation, but SOE understood that Klimkowski's star was in the ascendant. 'Nobody . . .', they wrote, 'dares to oppose Plague openly for fear he may be the coming man'.[93] Two weeks later there was an abortive coup, aiming to replace Sikorski with General Kazimierz Sosnkowski. Klimkowski, who belonged to a different faction of conspirators, warned Anders about the intended action, and Anders remained loyal to Sikorski. However, SOE now reported that rumours had begun circulating 'to the effect that if Gen Sikorski pays a visit to the Middle East he will be assassinated'

by a group of extremists led by Klimkowski.[94] Patrick Howarth called for urgent action, and British concern that 'an "attempt" is contemplated' by a secret military clique 'on the life of General Sikorski' led to a significant increase in security around the general in London.[95]

By April 1943, Cairo was again humming with stories of 'impending crises' and 'tales of calamity'.[96] April was the month when the hot desert wind, the khamsin, blew through Cairo's streets, choking the city with sand and dust, which camouflaged the buildings and trees in the municipal parks. This year a khamsin of rumours whirled through Cairo at the same time, obscuring the intelligence picture just as effectively. Truszkowski urged London to treat Christine's reports with caution. 'Willing is certainly a most delightful person', he wrote, 'and I have no doubt that she believes very much of what she says', but she is 'very highly strung', and her information 'coloured by its emotional context and by feelings of friendship'.[97]

No doubt this was true, but something was going on and Christine was caught up in it. The Poles suddenly wanted rid of her, and offered her unconditional work in Romania. Christine was 'distinctly suspicious', and Truszkowski conceded that he saw why the Poles 'would be very glad to have her out of the way at this particular moment in view of the extent to which [Anders, Klimkowski] and the rest of them talk to her'.[98] Klimkowski's conversations with Christine had by now confirmed British opinion that he was 'fanatically' anti-Sikorski.[99] Despite her doubts, Christine offered to take the Polish job and then report directly to the British from Romania, although her real aim was to get back to Poland and file reports from there. Truszkowski argued against such a move. Double-crossing was a 'dangerous game', he wrote. 'Willing would be very foolish if she started any such game.'[100] So she stayed in Cairo, where the Polish political intrigues were becoming ever more involved.

On 13 April, Berlin radio broadcast the discovery of 'a ditch . . . 28 metres long and 16 metres wide, in which the bodies of 3,000 Polish officers were piled up in 12 layers'.[101] German military forces

advancing into Russia through the Katyn Forest, near Smolensk, had uncovered the first mass grave of the nearly 20,000 officers and representatives of the Polish intelligentsia who had been missing since their internment by the Soviets in 1939. They had been taken from their prison camps into the forest in groups of around 200, restrained, and shot in the back of the head. Some still carried diaries and letters home. It was a war crime of appalling magnitude. The Germans accused the Soviets of having carried out the massacre in the spring of 1940. After initially suggesting that the find was an ancient burial site, the Soviets claimed the Nazis were responsible. Sikorski demanded an independent investigation by the International Red Cross. In response, Stalin cynically accused the Poles of bad faith and collaboration with the Germans, and used this as an excuse to break off diplomatic relations.

As British Ambassador to the Polish government-in-exile, Sir Owen O'Malley wrote two reports on the 'Katyn massacre', the first in May 1943, detailing the horrific last moments of the murdered men, and passionately presenting the evidence that this was indeed a Soviet act of genocide. These documents caused consternation in the British Foreign Office, but Churchill was unwilling to risk alienating Stalin, and instructed that 'the issue was to be avoided'.[102] After a limited circulation, Sir Owen's reports were buried in the archives. 'In handling the publicity side of the Katyn affair we have been constrained by the urgent need for cordial relations with the Soviet Government . . .', Sir Owen wrote; 'we have in fact perforce used the good name of England like the murderers used the little conifers to cover up a massacre'.*[103]

One week after news of the massacre broke, the Nazis launched their operation to clear the Warsaw ghetto. A year earlier it had been the largest Jewish ghetto in occupied Europe, but over 250,000 residents had already been sent to the extermination camp at Treblinka and a further 100,000 had died from disease, starvation or random shootings. Although there had been some coverage

* In November 2011 the Russian parliament declared that the Soviet dictator Stalin had personally ordered the Katyn massacre.

of the deportation and subsequent disappearance of hundreds of thousands of European Jews in the British and Palestinian press, Christine must have held on to the possibility that Stefania and some of her Goldfeder cousins might still be living in the ghetto. On 19 April 1943, the eve of Passover, 2,000 Nazi troops entered the ghetto, systematically destroying buildings block by block despite being fought all the way by a courageous, organized and armed resistance. The battle lasted twenty-eight days during which over 50,000 people were murdered or sent to Nazi concentration or death camps. 'By the rubbish bins, lay women, girls and children in a sea of blood', one survivor later testified. 'An abandoned heap, like old and useless rags, a pile of old clothes.'[104] Patrick Howarth, so close to Christine, later called the destruction of virtually the entire population of the ghetto 'the greatest single act of genocide in the war'.[105] Whatever faint hope Christine might have held out for her mother now died. From this moment onwards she rarely spoke of Stefania, even to her closest friends, and always completed any personnel forms by clearly listing both her parents as dead.

In late May, Sikorski embarked on a month-long military tour of inspection, visiting Polish units in the Middle East, most of whose men had come from prison camps in Russia. His intention was to make his government's policy on the Soviet Union clear, and to calm the tensions that had been growing in the ranks since the discoveries at Katyn, fuelling rumours of a coup. Howarth would later testify that the British uncovered a Russian plot, linked to the NKVD, to assassinate Sikorski in the Middle East: 'to kill him then'.[106] However, after visiting the troops, and holding lengthy discussions with Anders and other Polish military leaders, Sikorski returned safely to Cairo.

Christine had planned to introduce Andrzej to Sikorski, to promote his chances of deployment, but the general was preoccupied. On 2 July, Howarth reported that Sikorski seemed to have 'gained a palpable victory, but more by purges and a show of force than by wooing or the redress of grievances'. Anders had demanded military control, but the wind was taken out of his sails when

Klimkowski, his main backer, was posted to the USA.* Christine's old friend Colonel Bobinski now bore 'along with other conspirators a slightly sheepish air', Howarth noted.[107] 'General Sikorski left today direct for England', the British Foreign Office filed on 3 July. 'Although at one time there were indications of dangerous disagreement between Sikorski and Anders . . . these difficulties have now been surmounted' and Sikorski felt 'thoroughly satisfied'.[108]

On 4 July 1943 the converted Liberator bomber flying Sikorski back to Britain crashed into the sea within minutes of take-off from its stopover in Gibraltar. The general, his daughter in her sealskin coat, the British MP Victor Cazalet, and all those on board except the Czech pilot, were killed instantly.[†] Evidence considered by an RAF inquiry, attended by a Polish Air Force officer, pointed to an accident as a result of a technical fault and ruled out sabotage, although the full details could not be determined. Inevitably conspiracy theories quickly circulated, including suggestions, fuelled by Axis propaganda, that Allied secret services were behind the accident. Other theories blamed the Soviets, or the various Polish factions.[109] Gubbins was deeply affected by the death of his friend and ally, and rebutted any suggestions of British involvement in the most 'forcible language'.[110] Howarth was also keen to debunk any theory that the British were behind the crash, reportedly once writing to *The Times*: 'Sir, if General Sikorski had been murdered, I would have had to do it. I didn't. Yours etc, Patrick Howarth'.[111] But Howarth remained unconvinced that there was no connection between the Polish–Soviet assassination plans in the Middle East and the Gibraltar air-crash. As Howarth's confidant, Christine no doubt had her own suspicions, but if so she wisely did not broadcast them.[‡]

* In September 1943 Klimkowski was arrested on charges of embezzlement. He was later prosecuted as a Soviet spy and removed from the Polish army.

† Major Victor Cazalet replaced Peter Wilkinson on the flight.

‡ Although no evidence of foul play has been found, conspiracy theories still surround General Sikorski's death. After the war Captain Klimecki, one of Anders's adjutants, returned to Poland and accused Anders of Sikorski's assassination, only to later face accusations of being a Communist agitator himself. In 1947 the military governor of

Sir Owen O'Malley was among the first to express his condolences to Madame Sikorska on both a personal and a diplomatic level. Winston Churchill heartened the rest of the Poles with a powerful BBC broadcast. 'I shall not forget you', Churchill told the Polish people. 'My own thoughts are with you and will always be with you.'[112] But the death of Sikorski, arguably the only Polish leader that the Allies respected, was a huge blow to Poland's hopes.

This latest tragedy, at the end of months of trauma, left Christine 'periodically depressed'.[113] She had been at the heart of the Polish political intrigue, talking to, and reporting on, the key conspirators in a series of plots against Sikorski, almost until the moment of his death. Yet how much she knew, suspected, missed or was deceived, and how much she reported to her British bosses, will never be fully known. Ultimately her reports had achieved little of definite value: the removal of a probable German double agent and exposure of some other dubious contacts and conspiracies, the placement of Michal Gradowski in Albania where his work earned him a Military Cross, and better-informed British decision-making in general. She had certainly proved a great asset to Patrick Howarth, and her determination always to maintain an independent assessment of any situation had – when she turned down the offer of the Polish mission to Romania – probably also saved her life.

But Christine placed no great value on her life if it were not to be used for the good of her country. Over the past year Witkowski had been assassinated, the atrocity at Katyn had been discovered but effectively ignored, the Warsaw ghetto had been razed to the ground, General Sikorski had died, and Poland was still occupied. Christine could no longer justify remaining in Egypt. The war in Europe was coming to a head and the pain of the last two years could only be anaesthetized by an injection of adrenalin. Christine was no longer 'Willing'; her role as a 'beautiful spy' was over.

Warsaw made the same accusations against Anders in the Polish parliament. Some years later Moses Szapiro, an intelligence officer also known as Edward Szarkiewicz, confessed to planning the assassination attempt in Cairo, although his testimony is also open to question. It is quite possible that Christine met all these men in Cairo, but there is no record that she knew of any assassination plans.

9: OUR WOMAN IN ALGIERS

Colin Gubbins was not a man to sugar-coat his opinions. 'Cairo was a sink of iniquity', he wrote, 'with an evil atmosphere which permeated every service'.[1] The autumn of 1943 was exceptionally hot and sticky in Egypt, but plenty of fresh air was blasted into SOE when Gubbins was given the code-name 'M' and promoted to head 'the firm'.* According to the SOE codebreaker Leo Marks, Gubbins's eyes 'didn't mirror his soul or any other such trivia. The general's eyes reflected the crossed swords on his shoulders, warning all comers not to cross them with him'.[2] From the moment he received news of his promotion, Gubbins knew that his 'first priority was to sort out Cairo'.[3]

Gubbins arrived in Egypt in October 1943. He immediately announced that most of the staff were to be transferred to Italy. Cairo SOE was not being completely closed down, but it had lost its regional significance. 'Operation Torch' in North Africa had secured Algeria for the Allies, and soon Vichy Morocco was forced to abandon its position of neutrality, paving the way for the Allied invasion of Italy. Mussolini had been deposed in July 1943. The surrender terms were finalized in Algiers by Douglas Dodds-Parker, who had kindly lent his bedroom to the Italian delegates for their private talks, his foresight in bugging it taking 'much of the surprise out of the subsequent discussions'.[4] The required radio link to Italy was provided by Christine's former wireless instructor, the 'dreamily'

* The 'M' came from Gubbins's middle name, McVean, as the initial 'C' was already taken. Ben Macintyre suggests that Gubbins was one of the inspirations for Ian Fleming's 'M' in the Bond series, as was Fleming's mother, who also signed her letters to her son 'M'. See Macintyre, *For Your Eyes Only: Ian Fleming and James Bond* (2008), p. 63.

handsome Dick Mallaby, who was, conveniently, in prison in Verona having been captured after parachuting into Lake Como. 'We rolled up the Italian Empire in a year', Dodds-Parker later commented with satisfaction.[5] Algeria and Italy were better placed than Egypt or Britain for managing operations into southern and central Europe, and Christine was determined to be part of one of these ops.

Having helped create SOE in the face of considerable opposition, and now come blazing in to sort out the Middle East office, Gubbins was, in Lord Selbourne's words, 'not universally popular'.[6] However, he had the gift of inspiring confidence, and spent as much time as he could with the younger agents in Cairo, by whom he was accepted not only as their commanding officer but 'as a battle-scarred member of their own tribe'.[7] He, Christine and Andrzej got on like a house on fire, sharing not only their love of Poland, but a great belief in honour through action. In a rare bit of long-term planning, Gubbins and Christine even pledged to go skiing together on Poland's free slopes once the war was over. Before he left, Gubbins threw an all-ranks party to which he invited the FANYs as well as agents and officers. Having knocked back a few whiskies he led the dancing in his kilt, keeping going into the small hours. The more robust even witnessed his party trick. Taking off his jacket, Gubbins stood on his hands with a pint of beer on the floor in front of him. He then slowly let himself down until he could get the glass in his teeth and drain it while still standing on his head . . . all while dressed in his kilt. How he managed this, and how he discovered his remarkable ability, remain among SOE's deeper secrets. Having reorganized the regional structure, and inspired the agents, Gubbins returned to London. 'Please give my love to Forcible and Willing,' one of his messages ran, 'and tell them how much I miss them.'[8]

A few weeks later Andrzej put in an official request for a transfer. The reason cited was that sand kept working into his artificial leg, damaging both the stump, which had ulcerated again and needed re-dressing several times a day, and the prosthesis, which had to be regularly removed for cleaning. The pain and discomfort were considerable but there were other, supporting, reasons that made Andrzej apply for a transfer. His relationship

with Christine, although close, had never regained its old intimacy after his trip to Haifa in February 1943. After his paramilitary training he had stayed on as a parachute packer and assistant instructor while she found other admirers in Cairo. When he returned in the late spring they digested the terrible news of Katyn, the destruction of the Warsaw ghetto and General Sikorski's death together, cementing their deep bonds of friendship and mutual support. But they could never resolve the fundamental imbalance between Andrzej's adoration of Christine and her need for freedom. Then, that summer, Andrzej received more news from Poland.

In July the London *Gazeta Polska* published a story about a massacre in Zbydniów, in Galicia, then south-eastern Poland, where Andrzej's uncle lived. 'Can you discover the truth of a report...', Howarth telegraphed Perks in London, 'that all Forcible's family were killed by Gestapo?'[9] Andrzej 'with his usual lightness ... doesn't believe it', Christine wrote, but she was not so confident herself.[10] The truth was almost unbearable. The previous month, friends and relations had gathered at the Kowerskis' country house for a wedding. Late that evening, when only the most tenacious guests were still up playing bridge, the SS arrived. Andrzej's mother, Maria, opened the door, and was immediately shot dead. Of the twenty-one people in the wedding photographs, including the seventeen-year-old bride, only two would survive the evening – brothers who had been quickly hidden in the attic by their mother, from where they heard their thirteen-year-old sister shot dead as she knelt by her bed, praying. The massacre had been arranged by a Nazi official who coveted the estate. The Polish Underground Army issued a death sentence, and the two surviving boys were part of the execution squad that shot the official and his family. In retribution, ten Poles from Kraków jail were shot by the Germans. Both the young brothers were later killed in action. The only members of Andrzej's family to survive the war were his sister Barbara, who had not been at the wedding, and an older cousin who was already in the Underground Army.*

* The surviving cousin, Dominik Horodyński, later married Wladimir Ledóchowski's

Grief-stricken, Andrzej could no longer bear to tread water in Cairo. In November, the moment his transfer was approved, he went to Ramat David, just outside Haifa, to undertake SOE parachute training. At first there was some resistance to his joining the course, in case his artificial leg broke on landing. Undeterred, he offered to pay for any damage and secured the permission of his doctors. First they practised rolling off the back of a truck moving at 40 mph. Then they were taught to jump harnessed from a tower, and after that through the floor of an old Wellington bomber. Two Red Cross lorries were put on standby when Andrzej did his first real jump. He landed perfectly, but a colleague broke a collarbone. After five jumps from a Hudson, the lowest from 500 feet, Andrzej earned his wings. There were 'some very colourful people' on that course, one of the other trainees later remembered. Andrzej was the most colourful of all, 'a splendid person' and, the instructors noticed, a hugely comforting presence, jumping out of the Hudsons with his wooden leg 'just as merrily as the rest of us'.[11] 'He is as happy as a King', Christine now wrote to Kate O'Malley, 'and I am as light to him as a butterfly because he has been given some purpose again.[12] Andrzej was the first one-legged parachutist in SOE, but he was barred from dropping in the field because of his disability, which enraged him.[13] Instead he was posted to Italy as a parachute liaison officer, but only after a trip to London to get his artificial leg adjusted.

It was December by the time Andrzej arrived in London from the Middle East. Although not a sun-worshipper like Christine, over the last two years he had gained a deep tan which emphasized what a friend once described as his 'hot blue eyes', so he made a striking figure in London's wintry streets.[14] But he didn't stay there long. He had kept in touch with Kate O'Malley, who was now in her early twenties and living between London and Surrey. Kate had been deeply impressed by both Christine and Andrzej in Budapest, feeling that they embodied the romantic and courageous spirit of

niece, and became a well-known journalist. After the fall of Communism in Poland he was allowed to build a memorial to his family at their estate.

resistance, and she had even written a novel based on their exploits.*
However, while Christine described Kate as 'my best and only
friend', Kate's most especial esteem was reserved for Andrzej, and
by the time he returned to London he had persuaded himself that
he was more than a little in love with her too.[15]

The last time that Kate had seen Andrzej they had just helped
Christine fold herself into the boot of Sir Owen's car, to be
smuggled across the Hungarian border to safety in Yugoslavia.
Andrzej had then driven off in his fabulous Opel, with a gun and a
bottle of Hungarian brandy in his pockets, to take his chances alone.
Kate had left Budapest not long afterwards, travelling with her
father, the other Legation staff and Christine's husband, Jerzy
Gizycki, through Russia to England ahead of the Nazi advance.
Now Andrzej turned up on her doorstep in the Surrey village of
Ockham. Andrzej's English was much improved, but his voice had
not lost its strong Polish accent, and when he talked passionately
on any subject its deep timbre 'made his utterances seem to emerge
with compressed force'.[16] Indeed everything about him seemed
forceful: his pride in his country, his determination to serve, and
particularly his zest for life, his humour, and his gift for catching
laughter despite bearing the deepest tragedy. Kate was swept off
her feet, while Andrzej in turn found her freshness and doting
admiration 'adorable'.[17]

They only had a few weeks together. At the end of January,
Andrzej was sent to Italy to take up his post at the Polish parachute
school in Bari, before being moved on to Ostuni. Although he sent
Kate silk stockings and love letters, written with the aid of an
English dictionary, in which he professed to be 'missing you
terrible', it was clear that his commitment to her was already
wavering. 'Write to me as much as you can without waiting for my
elaborate replies', he told her, adding that should Christine be sent
to London, 'you must not tell to her about us in any circum-

* Kate O'Malley burnt the manuscript of her novel, but ten years later helped her
mother, the author Ann Bridge, to rewrite the story. It was published as *A Place to
Stand* in the 1950s. See Ann Bridge, *Facts and Fictions* (1968), p. 83.

stances'.[18] The end of the affair left Kate pining, Sir Owen furious, and Christine unjustly hurt and angry at what she saw as Andrzej's 'betrayal'.

Christine had no excuses for resenting Andrzej's fling: she was up to her neck in new romances of her own in Cairo, and ironically Kate's brother, Patrick O'Malley, was one of her distractions. It was fortunate, Christine told Kate, in a letter carried by a friend and so free from being 'deciphered by thirty-six people', that she had met Patrick on the eve of his wedding, as 'otherwise I would have fallen madly in love with him . . . and as here young blondes are difficult to find . . . I assure you that I am not joking, in fact you know a bit about my tastes and you know he is my type'.[19] As it was, although Christine clearly liked and admired Patrick, 'so spontaneous and kind . . . a very handsome boy', she was unusually intimidated by his fiancée. Their first meeting was 'unfortunate', she reported. It was at Shepheard's, 'the most snobby place in town', and Christine was in 'a dirty ugly dress' while Patrick's fiancée was 'very elegant and wore make-up . . . a woman of the world and a Londoner'.[20] After five minutes Christine made her excuses and left. Two days later she bumped into the happy couple again, and having fought back her initial impulse to flee, she suffered a 'crisis of shyness', finding herself suddenly unable to pronounce a word in English to them. 'All the fragile scaffolding of our friendship . . . has collapsed', she told Kate, 'Voilà!'[21] But, as ever, Christine had other admirers waiting in the wings.

Michael Dunford was a tall, blonde British officer, who had been seeing Christine's former flatmate, Laura Foskett. But once he met Christine he was smitten. Dunford was a radar specialist and expert in communications who had travelled widely in the Middle East working in diplomacy, and he implicitly understood the need for tact and patience in negotiations. Recognizing that he could not pin Christine down, he decided he was prepared to wait for her.

Christine's friend Zofia Tarnowska had meanwhile fallen for Bill Stanley Moss, a former captain in the Coldstream Guards who had joined SOE after returning from the final defeat of the Afrika Corps in Tunisia. Tall, good-looking and 'devilishly languid', Moss

fought bravely, danced beautifully and drank enthusiastically.[22] Back from the front, treated like heroes, and with a fortune in back-pay, he and his friend Paddy Leigh Fermor wasted no time in moving out of their barrack-like Cairo digs, popularly known as 'Hangover Hall', to rent a Zamalek villa. Soon there were six young SOE officers living in the house between missions, and 'all pretty pleased with ourselves', Moss admitted.[23] Zofia joined them that autumn, moving in with a fictitious chaperone, a swimming costume, evening dress and her two pet mongooses. They called the villa 'Tara' and, for a few months in late 1943 and early 1944, their wild parties made it the most exciting venue in Cairo. Glasses were smashed and chairs broken. When the sofa caught fire it was thrown from a window, and Zofia's prune vodka, infused in the bath with alcohol bought in gallon containers from a local garage, once rendered her friends blind for several days. Guests included King Farouk, who arrived with a crate of champagne, Egyptian princes, Allied generals, diplomats, journalists, writers and actors. 'The Poles, of course, were the worst', one Tara inmate, David Smiley, remembered. 'They used to come and let their pistols off and shoot bottles . . . they were a bit wild.'[24] It was here too that Moss and Leigh Fermor dreamt up their plan to kidnap the German commander of Crete, mapping out their moves on Tara's steamy bathroom tiles for the operation that would later be made famous by Moss's book *Ill Met By Moonlight* and the film based upon it, starring Dirk Bogarde.

Paddy Leigh Fermor remembered Christine slowly 'dawning' on him at Rustum Buildings, where he once pushed through a crowd to see her and Andrzej being refused entry by the security guards in 1941. Later he noticed her at the Gezira Club and then at Tara. 'Her beautiful looks . . .', he wrote, 'were gentle and unobvious; the charm lay in the quietness'.[25] In late 1943 Christine was still reeling from the horrific reports from Poland, and Sikorski's death. While the high-spirited Zofia distracted herself from her own grief by living life to the full, Christine hovered somewhat uneasily in the social margins. 'Christine was solitary, she hated parties and rarely accepted an invitation', Laura Foskett wrote, and although always very conscious of her appearance, Patrick Howarth

noted that while Zofia was turning up at parties dressed as Scarlett O'Hara, Christine 'frequently dressed in a manner that attracted little or no attention'.[26]

Christine had always had what Howarth called a 'chameleon quality', which had helped her to be so supremely successful as an agent in Hungary and Poland.[27] Now she picked her moments to shine socially. Moss remembered her once entering a room 'hunched like a drowned rat', and only standing up straight when he pinched her behind.[28] That evening she made her excuses for not dancing by telling her would-be partner that a man she had been madly in love with had once died in her arms on the dance floor, and she had sworn thereafter never to dance again. The real reason, Moss believed, was that she was tone-deaf and could not dance at all. 'She only knew one song', he wrote mischievously, 'and would whistle it out of tune.'[29]

But if the mood took her, Christine had what Moss called a 'mesmeric power of "switching on" her personality'.[30] Paddy Leigh Fermor was drawn to her by her courage and flair, rooted, as he saw it, in 'patriotism and a sense of pity, backed by a love of adventure'.[31] For others the appeal lay in her dark good looks, once described as 'la Beauté du Diable', the Devil's Beauty.[32] For Moss though, her attractiveness lay in 'a blend of vivacity, flirtatiousness, charm and sheer personality . . . like a searchlight' which when she chose 'could blind anyone in its beam'.[33] Nevertheless, he declared, 'I would never become involved with Christine. It would be like buying a Hispano-Suiza.'[34] The Hispano-Suiza company was famous for producing luxury cars crafted in rosewood, but during the war focused entirely on aircraft engines and high-performance automatic weapons. Moss tried to objectify Christine, but what came to mind conveyed not just class and quality but power and danger. He knew that Christine was no longer simply whiling away her days round the Gezira Club pool. She was, like the other agents, being trained in preparation for a return to the field.

SOE was launched, one agent later wrote, in the face of 'bitter political opposition to using women in a combat situations'.[35] Women were still restricted to non-combatant roles but Gubbins

had successfully argued the case for using women as armed couriers in occupied countries, securing Churchill's backing in April 1942. Gubbins was considered 'a lech' by some of the female staff, and admired for his way with women by several of the men, including the young Kim Philby.[36] But he also recognized the potential contribution of able and determined women, like Christine, who had shown that they could move more freely around enemy-occupied territories than any able-bodied man, and could bring valuable results. By 1943 women had proved so successful as couriers that, unknown to the public, the decision was taken to use them in other capacities, such as wireless operators, one of the most dangerous roles of all.

SOE's basic training programme owed much to Gubbins's 1939 manual *The Art of Guerrilla Warfare* and its companion text, *The Partisan Leader's Handbook*, which were full of concise and practical advice on how to organize an ambush, sabotage telegraph lines, contaminate water supplies, set fire to cinemas, and stop enemy informers – 'they must be killed'.[37] In Britain, training took between six to nine months as students progressed through a four-stage series of 'schools'. The process started with an assessment, which was followed by weeks of paramilitary training in the Scottish Highlands where trainees built up endurance, learnt to live off the land, were taught fieldcraft and received commando-style training in weapons and explosives, silent killing, raid tactics, demolition and signals. Those who stayed the course went on to parachute training, and finally to what Christine's Cairo friend Ivor Porter called the 'ancient and modern tricks of subversion', which were taught at Beaulieu Abbey, popularly known as the SOE 'finishing school'.[38] In North Africa, however, Howarth believed that training 'could transform the enthusiastic volunteer into an effective agent within two to three months', which was fortunate – that was all the time that Christine now had.[39]

Christine, typically, seemed to be doing the right things in the wrong order. She had already started her training in Morse codes and wireless signalling when she was sent on a parachute course, probably at Ramat David near Haifa. Like Andrzej before her, she

slowly progressed from throwing herself from moving trucks until she was deemed ready to undertake three practice drops from an aircraft. Each time she dropped perfectly, her parachute billowing into a silken cloud above her until she braced to land, rolled, and gathered it up. But, as a woman, she was not expected to take the final practice drop that would enable her to earn her coveted paratrooper's 'wings' after her fifth 'op' jump. This was a constant irritation to female SOE agents, giving the lie to claims made by Maurice Buckmaster, Head of SOE's F (French) Section, that 'we didn't make any differentiation' between the genders.[40] But the training was still both rigorous and exhausting.

By the end of March 1944 she had also received training in elementary explosives, and had undertaken an SIS (Secret Intelligence Service) course in firearms, in particular pistol handling and use of the SOE weapon of choice, the Sten gun. Although Christine had grown up with guns at her family estate, she had preferred racing to hunting and had little shooting experience. Now she was taught to shoot from the hip, aiming intuitively at a target and firing two shots, in the style taught by Major Bill Fairburn and Captain Eric Sykes, SOE's two combat experts, previously employed by the Shanghai police force. Although a brilliant technique, what Christine mainly learnt was that she hated firing guns, finding them too loud and too shocking. Fortunately Fairburn and Sykes had also developed the 'ideal' fighting knife, with a seven-inch, double-edged, steel blade that could easily penetrate a ribcage, and which was issued as standard. Christine's fitted neatly into a leather sheath designed to be strapped to her thigh.

The SIS course also covered personal security and silent killing, the extreme version of unarmed combat using only a knife, a noose or bare hands. The methods were a mixture of karate, ju-jitsu and what Fairburn had learnt 'from hard practice on the Shanghai waterfront'.[41] Such training not only gave the slender Christine more physical confidence, it was designed to drill into her that her task might, at times, have to be aggressive. 'This is *war*, not sport', the SOE training manual instructed. 'Your aim is to kill your opponent as soon as possible.'[42]

She was also taught 'tradecraft', ranging from simple personal disguises such as changing her hair or putting bungs in her mouth or nose to alter the shape of her face, to the art of covert surveillance. Finally she was trained to organize dropping grounds for arms and explosives, and prepare reception committees for Allied agents being sent in to support specific actions. For this she needed to know how to identify suitable fields, organize a landing committee, arrange communications with London or Algiers and, if necessary, control an aircraft landing with the use of pocket torches. It was work she loved and in which she excelled.

Officially 'the Liberation of the Continent' had started on a small scale with the landings at Anzio in Italy. In February 1944 Gubbins found a telegram in his in-tray, informing him 'with regrets' that his eldest son, Michael, had been killed by a shell at Anzio while moving into no-man's-land in advance of the Allied landings. 'A totally useless death', he told Wilkinson.[43] Yet his professional focus did not falter. By the spring preparations were well under way for the Allied invasion of Europe, and numerous SOE missions were taking place in Yugoslavia, Romania, Albania, Italy, Greece and France.

Throughout the early months of 1944 Zofia threw a series of parties at Tara, and other suitably flamboyant venues such as the Cairo racetrack, whenever one of their group was sent on a mission. At some point in the evening a car would come and quietly collect whoever was due to be dropped into enemy territory. The unspoken rule was that no one was to feel anxious, as that would have been 'to accept the possibility of something dreadful happening to them'.[44] Even the SOE secretaries put a brave face on the farewells, writing poems like 'Darling Joe, Please Go' – Joe being the secure code-name given to all agents in transit – which begged them to stop 'hanging around the office, waiting for the planes, slowing the arrangements, of our fertile brains'.[45] For Christine, however, each departure raised a different anxiety; that her turn to be dropped would never arrive and she would be left hanging around the office for months to come. But in March 1944 'Operation Kris' was tailor-made for her.

SOE's plan was to drop Christine back into Hungary, without the knowledge of the Poles, to reactivate the networks that had lost contact with London and the British base in Istanbul earlier that year. The aim was to encourage national resistance, and specifically the sabotage of vital communications, transport lines, industry and oil installations. To achieve this they needed to re-establish wireless communications and make reception arrangements for SOE agents and supplies to be dropped into the country. It was, Howarth wrote, 'an operation involving the greatest risks and only a slight chance of success', and yet the strategic importance given to Hungary was deemed great enough to warrant the attempt.[46] Christine was SOE's only trained wireless operator with knowledge of Hungary, and 'the requisite personal qualities' to 'stand at least a chance of survival'.[47] She was delighted. Building her case, she told SOE she had a number of close personal friends in Hungary, mostly among the landed gentry although also some of a 'more left-wing nature'. The drawback was that she could only speak a few words of Magyar but, Howarth concluded blithely, this was compensated for by the fact that 'she is a person of quite outstanding courage with exceptional charm'.[48] Christine, someone scribbled at the bottom of the page, had 'obviously worked overtime' on Howarth.[49]

The first hurdle was getting her into Hungary. She could be parachuted into Slovakia, either to a reception team or 'blind' (without any support), and then cross the border on foot. But, given the mixed loyalties of the Slovakian population, the risks involved were deemed too great. Sending her into Poland, however, undercover as a refugee escaping the Russian advance, meant involving the Poles, and so inevitably 'creating too many unnecessary difficulties for ourselves'.[50] In any case, SOE admitted, as *persona non grata* with the Polish community in Hungary, Christine was 'likely to be betrayed'.[51] The only option was a blind drop. This, Howarth now argued, 'would probably amount to little short of homicide, and while this would not deter the operator [Christine], the advantages likely to be derived are so slight that this course cannot be conscientiously recommended'.[52] Nonetheless, 'as it has been agreed that Hungary must be penetrated, and as Christine is

willing to take the risks involved', it was decided, 'we must adopt the courses which would offer the greatest chances of survival'.[53] Christine was immediately put forward for a further 'SIS and short sabotage' course.[54]

At the start of April 'Operation Kris' was designated 'most urgent', and Christine had been given a new name and cover story. In her papers she was to be 'Marja Kaminski', from 'Lwowun', born in 1914 – a year older than Christine was believed to be by the British, but still six years shy of the truth.[55] One week later, to Christine's intense frustration, the operation was cancelled. 'In view of the fact that she is well known to Hungarian police and speaks little Magyar [I] do not feel justified in taking large risk involved', the new head of the SOE Balkans section in Cairo, Bickham Sweet-Escott, reported to London. 'If therefore you have some other project in mind for her, for example FRANCE please let us know soonest.'[56]

Sweet-Escott was another of Christine's many Cairo fans. 'She is a Polish lady of considerable beauty and great courage . . .', he wrote, 'as brave as a lion', and he refused to sacrifice her on what he considered an ill-thought-out mission.[57] Instead he repeatedly suggested she should be dropped into France, a country she knew well from before the war, and whose language she spoke fluently. Sweet-Escott knew that Christine's morale had taken a serious blow with the cancellation of Operation Kris, and yet at the end of April, as D-Day loomed ever closer, her future was still undecided.

It was only in May 1944 that the decision was finally taken to send Christine to the SOE base in Algeria, code-named 'Massingham', in preparation to be dropped into occupied southern France. Before she left she was given a temporary commission in the RAF, in the hope that if captured in the field she would be treated as a prisoner-of-war, rather than shot as a spy. Her one concession to the danger of her new mission was to send a message to Andrzej in Italy, letting him know her movements. Then, impatient to be off, she wore her steel-blue RAF uniform to her Cairo farewell party, a 'merry affair' at which 'vodka flowed and cucumber sandwiches were munched', and laughter quickly drowned

out the familiar din of the city that could be heard through the open windows.[58] 'I do not think I ever saw her look happier', Bill Stanley Moss later remembered.[59] She left at midnight.

Massingham, the British base at Guyotville, just west of Algiers, had been established a year earlier at the once luxurious 'Club des Pins' among the sandy dunes of the Mediterranean coast, on the beach over which the main assault had come a year earlier, and behind hundreds of miles of barbed wire. Originally a resort for rich Algerians and French families escaping the heat of the capital, Massingham's offices and messes were set up in a series of marble villas, whose grounds ran from wooded inland hills right down to a sheltered bay. A bar was built on piles above the water. A couple of hundred men and about thirty FANYs were already billeted there. The women worked as wireless operators, coders and teleprinters, and at night, when not on duty, they had parties on the beach and swam naked in the warm sea.

Beach aside, conditions were tough. There was no hot water, except that scrounged from the cooks, and Christine was lucky to arrive in the summer, as there was no heating in winter. But the army rations of spam, corned beef and peanut butter were cheered up by dates and other local fruit, and the villas were covered in the beautiful bougainvillea that grew like a weed all over the camp. Under the exceptionally well-connected Douglas Dodds-Parker, 'an antelope of a Colonel', Massingham was a highly efficient HQ.[60] The working day began with a compulsory run before breakfast, and with all the sea-bathing, bare knees and general enforced enthusiasm, the atmosphere was 'somewhat reminiscent of a racing north Oxford preparatory school'.[61] Having helped to coordinate the Italian surrender, Dodds-Parker was well respected, and he was now preparing for 'Operation Dragoon', the Allied invasion of France. Christine would become his only active female agent.

But Dodds-Parker had no immediate plans to drop Christine. 'It was decided', he wrote diplomatically, 'that her courage was best restrained until nearer the time of liberation.'[62] Later he admitted that she was held back because she was still considered 'too flamboyant' to work undercover effectively.[63] In the meantime Christine

underwent more training alongside other agents being prepared to drop into France. Among these were the ever-kilted Havard Gunn, tall, thin, quiet but charming, and just back from Yugoslavia; Leonard Hamilton, who had escaped from a POW camp in northern Italy; the chipper Paddy O'Regan, just back from ops in Greece; and John Roper, on his first mission, whose 'pudding face' was constantly animated by the effort of delivering stories from 'a mixture of the Tatler and Scots Guard magazine'.[64] Roper was soon under Christine's spell, and took to carrying a clean handkerchief for her and, if possible, 'a twist of tea', whenever he thought he might meet her.[65] All of them would become lifelong friends.

Christine was taught her personal cipher code, and true and bluff passwords, by Paddy Sproule, the senior FANY coder at Massingham, who was more used to working with American officers who brought treats of butter, bacon, eggs and waffles, than penniless Polish aristocrats. To help Christine remember the three unpublished poems she would need for coding messages, they were written for her personally. One was a nostalgic tribute to the lost happiness of her pre-war life, the others more optimistic in tone, celebrating the 'bliss of a gentle existence' and the 'luminous hearth of a woman adored'.[66] Considered 'very bright' by Paddy, Christine learnt her poems and complex personal code in less than half a day, building on the long hours of training she had undertaken in Cairo.[67] Her wireless skills, however, although satisfactory, were not up to the twenty words per minute that FANYs were expected to achieve. Now the process of numbly translating and signalling Morse was drilled into her until she could hardly hear a bird sing without trying to catch its meaning, but the high speeds needed for time-effective signalling remained beyond her. Dorothy Wakely, the Signals Planning Officer, astutely surmised that Christine was simply too old to be trained as a good Morse operator. Nevertheless Christine learnt to repair wireless sets, and was taught security measures such as hooking her radio to car batteries rather than town power supplies so that her location could not be isolated by systematically turning off power zones. Her parachuting skills were also reinforced with test jumps from a fragment of fuselage rigged

up in the hills, and at the RAF facilities established at Blida, sur-
rounded by vineyards a few miles to the south. As a result, unlike
so many female SOE agents, Christine did earn her prized para-
trooper's 'wings'.

She also worked on her small-arms and explosives skills. Hours
were spent on target practice with a revolver, pistol or German
machine gun, and at certain times at night the whole beach was out
of bounds for target practice with whatever firearms the agents
were carrying. Louder explosions were caused during demolitions
practice, when Christine and the men learnt to mould plastic
charges, add primers and tie them in bundles using sticky paste
before the fuses were lit and the group ran to hide behind the
dunes. Paddy O'Regan found 'the bang and the result very satisfy-
ing', but Christine still hated the noise.[68]

She was better at picking up courier skills, learning how to
arrange appropriate rendezvous for meeting different types of
people, how to find sites where a radio might be safely operated,
drop prearranged passwords into conversation, and set up live letter
drops (where someone would receive her post without asking
questions), and dead letter boxes (where messages could be passed
on without any personal contact). In Algiers she learnt to find and
follow a contact or, conversely, shake off a tail. Finally she was
taught how to survive exhausting interrogations by the police, or
the Gestapo, designed to break her morale and resistance, and how
important it was to hold out for at least the first forty-eight hours
to give any colleagues a chance to escape. This 'boys'-own' stuff,
demanding intuition, courage and determination, came as second
nature to her, and she thrived in the competitive, and very male,
atmosphere at the camp.

Most SOE agents, regardless of working towards the same end,
were independent creatures, and often rather solitary. But being
able to work in a team was crucial and Christine completed her
training with a three-day hike around Blida, at the base of the Tell
Atlas mountains, as part of a team-building exercise. Carrying heavy
rucksacks, she and her partners had to slide down scree hills in the
hot sun, before walking in the shade of the pines that covered the

deep valleys cut by zigzagging streams, and scrambling under wild rhododendrons, their branches heavy with flowers, whenever they heard a noise.

After their shifts the FANYs would go to parties in the Officers' Clubs but, for security, the agents led more secluded lives. The enforced distance suited Christine. She had no interest in FANY parties and was pleased to disappear from observation for a while, spending more time with her fellow agents while trying to cultivate the anonymity required for her undercover work. As the only female agent, however, she inevitably stood out. Dorothy Wakely, the Signals Planning Officer, remembered meeting her occasionally around the camp. Although she thought Christine's looks were unremarkable, her 'hair, face and skin colour generally the same uniform brown', she was still struck by her 'remarkable grace of movement and charm, and something about her which made one look longer'.[69] Christine would have been disappointed.

Christine spent most of her free time with Gunn, O'Regan and Roper. Although its climate was as hot as Cairo, Guyotville had the benefit of the coastal breeze. In fact, that spring the weather was 'unbelievably bad' in North Africa, taking some of the pleasure out of Christine's habitual sunbathing.[70] Instead she and some of the men drank coffee in the quieter Officers' Club, went for picnics along the coast at Tipaza among the ruins of a Roman city, or walked the mile to the Massingham gates and hiked up into the hills. Determined not to be the weakest link, Christine would often leave her companions behind. Gunn strode along more casually, taking off his shirt to soak up the sun, and, O'Regan remembered, 'occasionally talked mysteriously of our crusade'.[71] O'Regan suspected, too, that Gunn was 'falling in love with Christine'. He certainly called her 'a wonderful, wonderful person', chose his codename, 'Bambus', in memory of a clump of bamboo that he and she had once encountered during training, and accepted her dare to drop into France with a teddy-bear she bought him as a passenger.[72] But when Gunn asked Christine about her post-war plans she refused to be drawn.[73] She could not envisage what her life would be like in peacetime and in any case, she told him with a laugh

before striding off, she preferred to concentrate on the here and now, and on getting as fit as possible. 'She was vital and full of fun ... [with] a marvellous sense of humour', Gunn later commented, but 'strangely, she did not appear to have any sense of roots. She lived entirely for the moment, and appeared to look upon the future with some trepidation'.[74] Gunn's impression of Christine speaks volumes. To the men she was different for being female, but she had otherwise proved herself to be one of the lads. The implications of her being Polish, the pain of her past and her unimaginable future, had not registered. Christine was keeping herself very private.

Sometimes, if she could get a lift along the coast in a jeep or on a motorbike, she would go alone to visit the old pirate port of Algiers. The FANYs were advised not to go to the Kasbah, the Arab quarter, but most ventured into the fringes. For some the market was disappointing, 'totally bereft of any buyable thing', but Christine had little interest in material possessions.[75] After the souks of Cairo she was completely at home, chatting away in French over sticky dates and glasses of tea with the shopkeepers and stallholders. Eventually she bought three leather wallets, one for Andrzej, one for Patrick Howarth, and one for herself, all for a few small and colourful Algerian notes.

As soon as he was able, Andrzej secured two weeks' leave and flew to Algiers to join her. While he could not help noticing that in her RAF uniform Christine 'looked even more attractive than usual', he tried to focus on redeploying some of her time from hiking, picnicking, sunbathing and sightseeing towards learning to swim, cycle and shoot accurately – all, astonishingly, talents she still lacked.[76] In these endeavours he was helped most of all by the unseasonable weather, which curbed some of her enthusiasm to lounge about in the sun, her 'inherent laziness' she called it.[77] But despite Andrzej's best efforts Christine never would learn to swim, or master many of her other weaknesses.

Christine took a deep dislike to bicycles, which, after a while, she refused to ride at all. It was not that she found them unladylike, or worried that cycling might lead to excessively bulging thighs and muscular calves. On the contrary, she was very conscious of the

importance of keeping fit, and often cursed how thin she was, fearing it might undermine her physical endurance. But she had ridden astride horses from her earliest childhood, and simply found them stronger and better at jumping fences and testing unsteady ground. Bicycles might be faster than walking, and able to make even the strangest-looking packages seem quite innocuous in a basket or pannier, but for Christine they were flimsy, unreliable and apparently hostile.

Her dislike of guns was similarly tenacious. After weeks of training she still closed her eyes whenever she fired, claiming to hate the noise. 'Anyway, I could never bring myself to shoot anyone!' she told Andrzej.[78] Howarth later swore that she never did, preferring to employ other weapons in emergencies, above all what he called 'her formidable powers of persuasion'.[79] These, he believed, derived from a combination of her 'feminine charm', her 'controlled indignation which, it was easy to believe, might suddenly erupt into fury' and 'her ability to persuade any man on whom she was working that he was unusual in being perceptive enough, not only to understand the arguments she was advancing, but to agree with them'.[80] Christine was certainly possessed of an almost reckless self-confidence in most respects. She knew she had a number of basic gaps in her repertoire of espionage skills but, typically, she refused to spend time mastering anything that did not either interest or come naturally to her. To make matters worse, she had been allocated a briefing officer who, according to Andrzej, 'rubbed her up the wrong way'. This was putting it mildly.[81]

Francis Brooks Richards, head of Massingham's French section, had arranged for Christine to be briefed by Major Benjamin Cowburn, code-name 'Tinker', and 'one of the most gallant and courageous SOE agents', who was temporarily in between missions in France.[82] Sparks flew immediately. Cowburn was a short and stockily built, taciturn Lancashire oil technician, altogether the very picture of 'a dour north-countryman'.[83] Furthermore he liked to answer back. Maurice Buckmaster, SOE's London head of F (French) Section, found Cowburn's 'directness of manner as stimulating as it was disconcerting'.[84] Although Cowburn had proved he

had all the personal resources and determination needed to provide Britain with the first direct intelligence from occupied France, he could not make a connection with Christine. Whether this was because he was a fan of what he called 'blue stories', or an even greater fan of bicycles, is not known.[85] 'I think, in retrospect, that there were displays of temperament that were to be expected of a "diva", even when attending master-classes by another great performer', Brooks Richards later wrote.[86]

In fact, whoever had to sit Christine down to learn about life in occupied France, from political nuances to police uniforms and cultural details such as never to ask for a café-au-lait in case she should be betrayed by not knowing there was no milk, was going to have a hard task. Agents in Britain were sometimes given seven weeks of this kind of 'head cramming'; Christine could hardly sit still for a couple of days.[87] The course was full of exactly the sort of life-saving minutiae that drove her mad, and it took not only Andrzej, but a flying visit from Howarth, to calm her down and get her to pay the lectures, and her own detailed cover story as the fictional 'Jacqueline Armand', the level of attention they required.

One evening, a month after arriving at Massingham, Christine pinned down Dodds-Parker, demanding to know when, exactly, she was to be dropped into the field. 'I want to go to France, I am going to France', she told him, and when he protested that she was too flamboyant, too brave, and that she would get caught, she told him, her voice heavy with emotion, 'I'll keeeel you.' 'Kill me?' Dodds-Parker echoed, and quickly sent her over to see General Stawell, the new regional head of SOE, who was on a visit. After dinner, Christine and the general disappeared behind the sand dunes, and when he came back Dodds-Parker noticed that Stawell was 'knocking at the knees, and said she had better go to France'.[88] At last, and not without some personal intervention, Christine had full clearance.

Francis Brooks Richards was given complete discretion as to where to send Christine. Like so many men before him, he was not impervious to her charms. 'She was a very handsome woman,' he said, 'a woman of great presence', and he accepted unquestioningly

her personal 'cover' story that she had been Miss Poland in 1937, as well as a skiing champion, and the wife of 'the Polish Consul General for the whole of Africa'.[89] During his assessment of her, he reported, Christine made it 'quite clear she was perfectly prepared for cover purposes to become fictively married to somebody'.[90] Immediately he thought of Francis Cammaerts, one of F Section's best agents, running a highly effective resistance network in south-eastern France. Cammaerts had put in a request for a new courier to replace the female agent caught by the Gestapo a few weeks earlier. Danger, drama, a fictional romance: it could hardly have been more perfect.

Christine was now one of SOE's most highly trained, experienced and motivated agents, but she still faced an agonizing wait while on standby to depart. Parachute drops could only take place during a fourteen-day moon-period. Even when the moon was bright, flights might be held up by 'a thousand accidents of politics, weather or war'.[91] In Christine's case something more personal delayed her at the eleventh hour. 'She was pretty impatient and we had an awful dilemma,' the officer in charge of her departure tactfully reported, 'when at a certain time of the month, her physical condition and the moon coincided.' When her drop was delayed on this pretext, 'it took the whole of the unit to keep her pacified and occupied' until the next flight opportunity arrived.[92]

Finally, on 7 July 1944, Christine was driven to the airfield half an hour before take-off. She was dressed in a shirt, skirt and jacket cut to a French pattern by a tailor in London's Margaret Street. Her hair was set in the latest French style, and even her teeth had been checked to ensure they complied with French dental practice. Now she had her clothing searched for old bus tickets, small change or any other tell-tale evidence that might give her away, and was fitted with her parachute suit. A FANY gave her some sandwiches and a flask of tea for the journey. She was also given Benzedrine, to keep her awake for a few extra hours should she feel exhausted at the wrong moment, and her 'L' tablet: a little cyanide pill coated in rubber so that it would not melt in the mouth unless bitten.

In October 1942 Hitler had ordered: 'all opponents engaged in

so-called commando operations . . . are to be exterminated . . . all quarter is to be denied on principle'. To ensure there was no misunderstanding, a supplementary directive added that 'all sabotage troops will be exterminated, without exception . . . the chance of their escaping with their lives is nil'.[93] Christine was about to be dropped into France, one of the most dangerous theatres of the war, where few SOE agents were expected to last more than three months before being brought back to England if they had not already been caught, and where wireless operators had an average life-expectancy of only six weeks.[94] She felt alive again at last.

10: A FRENCH OCCUPATION

In 1944 Francis Cammaerts was twenty-eight. Tall, lithe, with serious dark eyes and a serious attempt at a moustache, when he relaxed with a cigarette he was distinctly handsome. The youngest child of a Belgian poet and his English actress wife, famed for her 'voice like figured satin', he was born in Kensington during the First World War and his earliest memories were of being brought up 'under the shadow of poison gas, absent fathers and one-legged lovers in the park'.*[1] Thoughtful and confident, at sixteen he became a socialist and a pacifist, even renouncing his Belgian citizenship to avoid national service. Later, he would personally execute one man and plan the deaths of many others, but he would never entirely relinquish his belief in the value of either democracy or the pacifist cause.

When war was declared Francis was a history teacher. His brother Pieter enlisted immediately, but Francis registered as a conchie. Convincing the Conscientious Objection Tribunals of the sincerity of his views, he avoided both active service and jail, and spent the next two years working on the land in Lincolnshire. Over Christmas 1940, Nancy Finlay, the sister of a friend, visited. Nan, as she was only ever known, casually walked in on Francis in the bath as he was washing off the blood of a goose he had just slaughtered. That evening they made love in his car and they were married three months later. Nan's friend, the journalist Katharine Whitehorn, claimed she valued Nan above all for her human wisdom and emotional strength. They were qualities that would be sorely tested over the coming years.

* Francis Cammaerts's parents were Émile Cammaerts and Helen Braun.

Three weeks after Francis's wedding, his brother was killed in action. In his grief, Francis began to question his absolute position. Nan was already pregnant and their first child was born in January 1942. When Francis held his daughter in his arms he knew he could no longer stand aside. That spring he decided to take an active part in the war, but he was not prepared to give up his freedom of conscience to do so. 'I might be ordered to kill people in a way that was entirely wrong', he argued. 'Once you'd accepted the notion of the discipline of an armed force you were bound to accept the probability of stupid and ridiculous orders which you'd have to obey.'[2] Passionate, moral, abundantly qualified but fiercely independent, Francis, like Christine, was tailor-made for SOE.

Francis was interviewed in a War Office annex by Selwyn Jepson, author of popular detective stories and SOE's F (French) section recruiting officer, who characterized him as 'a man of the highest principle'.[3] Bilingual, highly intelligent and fit after his work on the land, he was an ideal candidate. MI5 signed him off with their standard 'nothing known to his personal detriment', and months of intensive training followed.[4] Curiously for a man who was to prove so successful in the field, he was assessed at first as 'rather lacking in dash', 'a plodder', and 'not suitable as a leader', perhaps because he seemed so 'very quiet and unimposing'.[5] But Francis was also a good shot, strong at close combat and 'highly intelligent, very keen and completely reliable'. For Leo Marks, SOE's head of coding, there was 'nothing plodding' about him, and whether it was 'the quality of that smile, or the penetration of that look', Marks found himself 'feeling very sorry for anyone who made the mistake of writing this man off. Unless he happened to be a German.'[6] Like a headmaster signing off a school report, Gubbins then upgraded Francis, concluding he was 'an excellent man . . . one of the best types we have had', and arranging for his immediate transfer to the field.[7]

Christine was still kicking her heels in Cairo when, one moonlit night in March 1943, Francis, now code-named 'Roger', was slipped into France in a single-engined Lysander monoplane. He had been tasked with the challenging mission of preparing for the Allied

invasions by building a cohesive resistance movement in the south-east. He was sent first to André Marsac, second-in-command of the 'Spindle' circuit run by Peter Churchill and Odette Sansom. The same Lysander that delivered Francis to a hop farm in Compiègne also collected Churchill, who managed to convey one warning during their exchange: always carry a newspaper as France was light on lavatory paper. Then Churchill was up the aircraft's fuselage, into Francis's still warm seat and away to breakfast in London. The operation had been perfect. The Lysander stopped just twenty yards from the reception committee on the ground and was airborne again within 150 yards and three minutes. But once Francis was on occupied soil, with no possible means of return, everything quickly spiralled towards disaster.

Despite the night-time curfew, the French reception team drove to Paris. As a 'security measure' they threw Francis's revolver and papers out of the car window into a river. Francis could not help feeling that this was all 'slightly risky', but his concerns were soon allayed over a flask of rum with Marsac.[8] He spent the next day browsing Paris bookshops and acclimatizing himself to the sight of German officers strolling along the pavements. 'Paris is grey and gloomy,' he reported, 'total black and white photography.'[9] After an unsettling random body search outside a Métro station, he returned to the flat to wait for Marsac. But Marsac did not return. Nor did he make their rendezvous in a café the following day. After forcing down a lonely meal and a few cups of acorn coffee, Francis picked up his suitcase and headed, at rather a brisk casual walk, for the Gare de Lyon. Marsac had been arrested that morning and, just one day in, Francis was already a wanted man.

Things did not improve when he arrived at the beautiful lakeside village of Saint-Jorioz in rural south-west France where Peter Churchill had his HQ. Here Francis was met by 'a lot of very nice, very brave young men ... dressed like young résistance people', who took him to a building that, he felt, might as well have been signposted 'Résistance Clubhouse'.[10] Hearing that a new British agent was criticizing the security of the circuit, one of the young French leaders arrived, 'breathing fire, and threatening to shoot

everyone'.[11] In the midst of the ensuing scene a letter arrived from Marsac, written from his Paris prison cell, to introduce a disillusioned German 'Colonel Henri' who wished to be flown to London for talks. To Francis this was clearly madness: one of the first principles of SOE training was that, should enemy agents or informers present themselves to try to win your confidence, they must be killed.[12] Unable to dissuade Odette Sansom from exploring what he called this 'impossible fantasy', Francis left that evening to start a fresh circuit further south.[13]

Francis's instincts were right. The mysterious 'Colonel Henri' was really Sergeant Hugo Bleicher of the Paris Abwehr, German armed forces intelligence. The day that Peter Churchill returned to Saint-Jorioz, Bleicher arrested both him and Sansom. Churchill's pocketbook, containing several contact details, was also taken, and the circuit was effectively destroyed. Although both agents survived the war, Sansom refusing to talk even in the face of horrific torture, several others lost their lives as a result of the operation, the second successful sting of its kind by Bleicher. Only Christine's detested Ben Cowburn had evaded Bleicher before, later claiming he knew he could not be a colonel as 'he wore such cheap shoes'.[14]

More than a dozen SOE circuits were active in France at this point, each organized around three key roles – leader, wireless operator and courier, all of whom were usually trained in Britain. Francis had been assigned to lead the 'Donkeyman' circuit in the upper Rhône valley but, unwilling to trust anyone linked to the Spindle network, he elected to establish a new group of his own. Hoping that it would have more success than 'Donkeyman', the new circuit was code-named 'Jockey'.

The only Donkeyman contact Francis used was Auguste Deschamps, better known by his code-name, 'Albert'. Albert was a principled man who, along with his family, had been a resister from the start. A brilliant wireless operator, he had been trained in London but was accepted as a French peasant wherever he went. His wireless set, eight inches wide by three deep, fitted, with headphones and aerial, into an artificially aged attaché case, with the dials and plugs all fixed into the upper lid. When his

prearranged transmission time approached, Albert would open it up and fix the aerial across the ceiling with the earth connection perhaps attached to a water pipe and the power lead plugged into a light socket if he did not have a battery. Then, with paper and pencils at the ready, he would tap out his message, and twiddle the dials until he picked up the incoming signal from London or Algiers. Having captured several radio sets, along with their operators, the Germans knew exactly how the system worked. Once they had picked up a signal they would listen in, sending out cars fitted with direction-finding equipment to find the source. Whenever he was transmitting Albert knew that the Germans were 'after him like sniffer dogs'.[15] This meant he was constantly on the move, and more than once Francis would drive up to find no trace of his friend who, not waiting for a car he recognized, had already made himself scarce. Over fifteen months Albert would send over 400 messages to London – an SOE F Section record. He was never caught.*

Together Francis and Albert started recruiting potential saboteurs through the freemasons, whose secretive practices came into their own during the occupation, and other groups more recently forced underground like the Communist party and the trade unions. For a while all the Jockey members seemed to be working in the local industry – manufacturing rabbit-fur hats – which had limited strategic value. Francis then recruited Pierre Agapov, a young French radio engineer who became his second-in-command, along with the leader of the local resistance, a corn merchant called Raymond Daujat. Soon he had several hundred men and was responsible for an area larger than Wales, which stretched from

* Francis called Auguste 'the best man and most reliable friend I had', and regularly pressed for him to be decorated for his 'heroic work'. Despite having the longest record of unbroken wireless service in France, Auguste did not receive British decorations. In his February 1945 SOE debrief, the interviewer concluded: 'Informant gave the impression that he had been over cautious during his clandestine activities . . . did not give the impression that he ever took those risks which have to be taken if positive results are to be obtained.' All of Auguste's family had been arrested by the Nazis and his wife and teenage daughter were sent to Ravensbrück. See HS6/570, Deschamps, interrogations (27.2.1945).

Lyon to the Swiss border, down to the Mediterranean and along to Marseille.

Knowing the fate of the Spindle circuit, Francis was obsessed with security. He kept his true identity a secret from everyone. He never slept in the same place for more than three nights in a row. His organization was cellular, with each group operating independently, and while he knew how to reach all the local leaders, no one knew how to reach him. The telephone was forbidden. Writing information down was forbidden. And, once recruited, no one could resign or be sacked from the organization; if there was any of what Francis vaguely called 'bad discipline', the person in question would be shot.[16]

By the end of May 1943 Francis had prepared the first of his drop zones, and began receiving arms and equipment. Training began in the men's own homes but later moved to the hills where they could use explosives, anti-tank PIATs, and bazookas without attracting unwelcome attention. Francis had courage and determination, men and munitions, a clear mission and growing experience. He even had a price on his head and, after the arrest of Agapov, his photo in the Gestapo files. The one thing he did not have, and needed desperately, was a trained female courier to take messages and supplies between his different teams, and to keep in contact with the 'Maquis', the resistance fighters who had left their homes to form a permanent base in the hills, after whose scrublands they took their name.

It was June before Francis's courier arrived. Cecily Lefort was an Englishwoman who had married a wealthy French doctor and divided her time between Paris and a fishing village in Brittany. When France was invaded, Cecily went to London, joined the WAAF, and gave the use of her Breton villa with its secluded private beach to SOE.* She then volunteered to return to France for special operations. She was brought in by Lysander, the pilot commenting,

* The officers evacuating compromised agents and resisters from this sheltered bay to Falmouth were using the same route as the real-life Scarlet Pimpernels of the French Revolution.

rather unhelpfully at this juncture, that her accent was poor and she looked flustered, like a 'vicar's wife'.[17] Keeping cool under pressure was not something that came naturally to Cecily. Francis respected her, and she was useful, but it was clear to him that she 'looked forward with terror to the next day', and every day 'anticipated failure'.[18]

Cecily's arrival coincided with a sabotage push by the Jockey network, which drew German attention to the area. One team successfully took out the hydroelectric station in Durance, interrupting power supplies and the plants producing aluminium for the Luftwaffe. A series of operations followed, putting railway turntables, locomotives and communications pylons out of action. The plan was to cut off local Abwehr forces from their HQ in advance of the Allied invasions, but progress was not achieved without the loss of several men and the arrest of Albert's wife and daughter. Then, just three months after she arrived, Cecily broke security protocol when, stuck late at night, she called at a safe house despite warnings that the address was compromised. The Gestapo arrived immediately. Alone inside, she panicked and hid in the coal cellar. It was too obvious, and by the time Francis arrived it was too late to help her. 'If she sticks to her story,' he reported as positively as possible to London, 'I feel sure she has a chance of being released.'[19]

Cecily was carrying nothing incriminating and refused to name names either at Lyon prison, or under further interrogation by Bleicher at the Gestapo headquarters in Paris, the infamous 84 Avenue Foch. Apparently ignorant, she began the long journey to Ravensbrück, the concentration camp built by Himmler exclusively for women and known by the French as 'L'Enfer des Femmes' – Women's Hell. Its function was to work the women to death, while extracting maximum profit from their labour. Over 130,000 women and children would be incarcerated there, including Odette Sansom, who was being held in isolation when Cecily arrived, and Paulette Deschamps, Albert's teenage daughter. Over 90,000 of the inmates would die from starvation, beating, execution by hanging, gas or firing squad, or from medical experimentation. Soon after her arrival, Cecily was diagnosed with cancer of the stomach and

ironically underwent a successful operation before being given the pink card that designated her as 'sick', and of no further labour value. She missed an opportunity to escape, trying to persuade a friend to join her, and was gassed in February 1945.[20]

Cecily had lasted almost twice as long as the average female courier in France and her arrest spooked London, prompting Buckmaster to recall Francis. During debriefing he gave a critical report of Cecily, claiming she had shown 'little initiative' and concluding bitterly that 'it is quite useless to send into the field a man who cannot be relied upon to keep calm or at least preserve an appearance of calmness in an emergency'.[21]

While in London, Francis lobbied for more air deliveries and a new female courier. He had seventy-five cells waiting for supplies. Despite Gubbins's commitment to air support for France, which he rated as 'strategically by far the most important country in the Western Theatre of War', he had not been able to divert aircraft from Bomber Command. Without arms and explosives it was impossible for the units on the ground to get results. It was also difficult to keep the teams motivated – and pointless trying to recruit more.

Francis spent a difficult Christmas with Nan in Harrow. He enjoyed his first cuddles with his new baby daughter, the only person outside 'the firm' to whom he could talk about his work, but managed to give Nan trench mouth, which cost her several teeth. In January 1944 Hitler used his New Year Proclamation to declare that 'the present struggle overrides all the inhibitions which purely humanitarian considerations imposed in the past, because at the end of it there will in any case be no victors and vanquished, but only survivors and annihilated'.[22] It was a chilling reminder of the danger faced by SOE agents throughout Occupied Europe. And a few days later Albert contacted Francis with bad news – one of his cell leaders had been killed during an attack on a train.

In February, Francis's return flight was forced to turn back because of snow. On the way back he thought he could hear 'hard things' hitting the outside of the plane.[23] A moment later one of the engines was on fire. It is possible that ice was the cause, but a solitary British plane flying over occupied France would have

been a mouth-watering sight for any alert German gunner. When a second engine caught fire the crew dropped their containers, and soon they and Francis were forced to jump from the burning plane at 10,000 feet, 100 miles from their intended destination. Minutes after he landed in a snow-covered potato field, he heard the plane crash into the hills close behind him.

By now Francis had three million francs on his head, a sufficiently flattering sum for him to joke that the Germans apparently 'attached greater value to him than the War Office', so he was taking a calculated risk when he walked up to a farmhouse and knocked on the door.[24] Fortunately, seeing a British airman on their step, the farmer shouted to his wife to 'get the wine out'.[25] Over the next few months the farm would become one of Francis's most reliable safe houses. In another stroke of luck, the canisters bailed from the burning plane were picked up by a small resistance group who had been waiting sixteen months for supplies. It was all put to good use. Francis's first thoughts, however, were for the five aircrew, uniformed officers, who had been forced to bail out with him. It took him four days to find them and several weeks before he could put them on the escape route through Spain. Meanwhile, despite speaking no French, the twenty-one-year-old flight engineer, Sergeant Len Gormal, disregarded his squadron leader's specific instructions to lie low, and insisted on supporting Francis's operations, at one point helping to save the lives of four French resistants.*

By March 1944 Francis was up to his neck in preparations for the planned Allied invasion. The Wehrmacht were moving reinforcements into his area, supported by both the Gestapo and the crack troops of the Waffen SS, and as measures against the resistance intensified several of his local leaders were arrested. 'Passing very difficult days', Francis filed. 'Germans are attacking all . . . reign of terror, farms burnt, shootings and hangings . . . picture is black.'[26] Hitler's proclamation was already being translated into action, but things were about to get infinitely worse.

* Francis lobbied for Gormal to be decorated, but having returned to Britain with rest of the crew he was shot down and killed twenty-four hours before VE day.

At dawn on 6 June 1944 the Allies invaded northern France. Bombing raids and local resistance circuits had already damaged much of the German coastal defences and radar installations. More than 100,000 troops arrived by air and sea, while further south, Jockey rail-cutting teams immediately went into action. Every train with German troops or supplies leaving Marseille for Lyon after D-Day was derailed at least once by Francis's resistance groups, and over 800 lines were cut during June alone. The same pattern was followed across the country as SOE circuits attacked enemy troops moving towards the Normandy beachhead. The Nazi reprisals were swift and brutal. On 10 June the SS entered the village of Oradour-sur-Glane and murdered 642 people, including 190 schoolchildren. If the aim was to inhibit further resistance, the result was inevitably to instil an even greater determination. Francis knew that if the Jockey circuit were to maintain its level of attack against Nazi production, troops and communications, and the respect and loyalty of the 10,000-plus local resistants, mainly the Maquis in the mountains, he needed more arms, more equipment, and many more officers – and in particular a new female courier. His requests to London became ever more urgent and eventually he got what he wanted.

As 'Jacqueline Armand', code-name 'Pauline', Christine had been issued a rubber-lined crash helmet, loaded revolver, razor-edged commando knife, torch, and round, brown, rubber-coated cyanide tablet sewn into the hem of her skirt. She had French papers forged near Harlow by the cream of British and Polish professionals, who happened to be out of prison when recruited, and a money belt stuffed with gold sovereigns. In some accounts she was given a square of silk printed with a local map, a compass hidden behind her hairclip, and a magnifying glass placed in the end of a cigarette.

As a 'Joe', her flying suit, pack and harness reduced her mobility but helped to keep her warm and cushioned her bumps as the plane lurched through both turbulence and enemy flak. Occasionally she and her fellow Joes were knocked sideways and down between the packages that were carefully wedged along the floor. The larger

metal containers were carried in the modified bomb bays. Christine was travelling with three officers of the 'Paquebot mission', led by Captain Jean Tournissa, an engineer who had been detailed to supervise the construction of a new airstrip in the Vercors region, south-west of Grenoble. Soon they were playing sardines, squashed together in the metal belly of the plane, the noise of the engines drowning out any attempt at conversation. As the hours in transit wore on, the light oily, tinny, smell that is peculiar to military aircraft was soon competing with the more pungent odours of fear, brandy and thermos tea. It was 7 July 1944, a windy, moonlit night. Christine was thirty-five years old, although her passport said twenty-nine, the same age as Francis Cammaerts.

As the plane approached the reception field, the RAF dispatchers attached Christine's static line to her parachute. For stealth and accuracy, she and her fellow officers were to be dropped too low for their canopies to open unaided, so the bags in which they were stowed were tied to the aircraft fuselage. When Christine dropped, her line would be pulled taut, holding back the bag and freeing the canopy just below the plane. Now they learnt they were facing near gale-force winds. As the dispatcher opened the exit hatch, blasting the passengers with a rush of cold air and the deafening roar of the engines, Christine could see the moonlit ground below. There were few lights to confuse with the landing torches. Christine was not worried about finding her reception committee or starting work in Nazi-occupied France; she was not even anxious about whether she might smash her face on the circular exit hole as she jumped, or break her legs on landing. She was, quite simply, exhilarated. Anything less dramatic than this stormy flight would have seemed inappropriate after all the build-up and delays in Algiers. Laughing, she tapped out 'an excessively rude' Morse code message on an old Aldis lamp in the plane, before swinging her feet into the hole, watching for the red signal light to change to green, and plunging into the air, like a hangman's victim, just 150–200 metres above the arranged drop zone.

Christine was immediately blasted sideways on a torrent of wind. Swept four miles off course, she finally hit the ground with

such force that her revolver was smashed and her coccyx and one ankle fared only slightly better. While other agents talked of the beauty of their chutes opening like flowers above them, of swinging in ever-decreasing arcs like a pendulum through the sky, and of the silence and the bright moonlight, Christine simply said she dropped 'like a wet dish-cloth'.[27] Later she embellished the story of her landing, saying that she fell straight towards a church spire, which she only avoided with 'supreme effort', and that her head was still 'battered' by the gravestones in the churchyard.[28] But if the truth was less dramatic, it was also more impressive. The gale had completely separated Christine from her fellow officers, one of whom, it later turned out, had broken an arm and fractured his skull on impact. Landing alone in a wheat field, she immediately buried her parachute and broken revolver in the hard summer earth and was met the next day looking as though she was on a regular morning stroll through the nearby forest. Her plain clothes looked perfectly French, and her manner seemed perfectly easy despite the searing pain of her twisted ankle. Once she had verified that her new companions were indeed her reception committee, however, 'her language shocked several of its more conventional members'.[29]

That afternoon Christine was reunited with Jean Tournissa. Together they caused quite a stir as they sat beneath the apple tree shading the entrance to the town hall at Vassieux-en-Vercors, the largest town on the imposing Vercors plateau. Here they were given their local French forces permit cards, a telling indication of how strong the resistance was in the area.[30] Although their French was fluent, their accents were obviously not local and the villagers were intrigued as to where the 'commandos' came from. Tournissa was thought to be Canadian, and a rumour quickly spread that the pretty 'Pauline' was Irish. Everyone knew better than to ask un-necessary questions, but the town's schoolteacher, Jeanne Barbier, who had been baking a 'victory cake' with her friend Suzy Blanc, could not resist making a note in her diary wondering about the sole young woman among the men who had just dropped in.[31] Christine was already causing a stir.

She met Francis, now Major 'Roger', a few days later when they

were collecting canisters of explosives and equipment that had been dropped the night before. 'I saw a beautiful, slender, dark-haired young woman', Francis remembered. 'Even in those rough conditions I was impressed by her features and bearing. Her face was sensitive and alert . . .'[32] Later he refined this impression to describe her as 'structurally very beautiful', but at the same time 'an actress' who could 'pass completely unnoticed' at will, or draw people's eyes 'with a tremendous magnetism'.[33] Slim, fresh-faced and suntanned from her months in Egypt and Algiers, she was fit and attractive, and despite her sore ankle she moved with the fluid grace that was one of the legacies of her convent schooling.

Christine, meanwhile, saw a young, handsome man, whose trim military moustache was surprisingly similar to Andrzej's, but whose height – and enormous feet – were in a league of their own. Indeed, Francis's field names included 'le Diable Anglais', but he was best and most affectionately known as 'Grands Pieds'.[34] His feet had even defied the infinite care that went into ensuring that all agents' clothes were either originally, or apparently, French. Suits and underwear were always of French cut, French haberdashers' labels were carefully added, telling hat-bands removed, and even buttons were sewn on 'in the French style'. But Francis could not find French shoes in his size, and he was always concerned that his brogues, of a style and colour rarely seen in France, might give him away.

Francis, like Christine, was neither vain nor showy, but he was charismatic, and good to look at in his faded blue shirt, especially after months of walking in the mountains of the Vercors. He was also reassuringly meticulous given the situation, and he had great determination and a clear sense of right and wrong. Christine took a shine to him immediately. Soon they were laughing together as they searched for packages in the fields. Eventually they made their way down the stony hillsides, occasionally missing their footing as they struggled with the heavy metal containers, while the wind whipped Christine's hair across her face.

Francis found his new courier a cottage at Saint-Julien-en-Vercors, a small village where he had a command post, just beyond

the town of Saint-Martin where the local Maquis had its head-quarters. Although she and Francis grandly christened it 'la maison de Miss Pauline', the single-storey building was little more than walls and a roof, but Christine liked it all the better for that. Never a home-maker, she preferred to keep her possessions stowed away in a knapsack and a large canvas bag, and 'yet', Francis said, 'she always managed to look immaculate'.[35] Christine did little more than sleep at her 'maison', hang up her few clothes, and very occasionally drink weak tea there with a pretty, russet-haired nurse called Sylviane Rey, who had been brought up in Algeria, and whose husband Jean was with the Maquis. Sitting on Christine's step, Sylviane thought her friend's almond-shaped eyes gave her 'the look of a Siamese kitten'.[36] Here the two women would steal a few moments to listen to the sounds of bees and cicadas, and watch the peacock and painted lady butterflies visiting the wild flowers in Christine's untended garden. There was no time for any greater commitment to the place; Christine was working flat out from her first day.

She had been sent to France with two operational objectives. She was primarily a courier for Francis, the local resistance leaders and the Maquis. But she had also been tasked with helping to subvert any Polish or other foreign units fighting for the Germans. It was now just over a month since the Allied invasions in Normandy, and the Wehrmacht officers and troops in the south were getting increasingly nervous. Francis believed that his chief aim should be 'to persuade everybody who was willing to help our cause, to join us', and Christine did a fair bit of that, too. 'She created a climate of warm friendship so rapidly that one felt one had known her forever', Sylviane Rey remembered of their first meeting. 'She was always calm, smiling and happy, and she was full of fun . . . modest about her own achievements, and generous in her praise of others.'[37] Christine's vitality, and her contagious ability to relax, were huge assets. Whether she needed to discuss the storage of guns or could just chat away about the pleasure of sunbathing, there was something at once open and conspiratorial about her, and she quickly won the confidence and devotion of her audience.

One of her earliest tasks was to support the drops of arms, explosives and detonators, both for Francis's network and for the increasingly active Maquis groups in the hills. Liaising with Francis and Albert, she helped organize local reception committees of six to eight men to be on standby with bikes, mules or, if possible, a truck, and torches. Then she would sometimes join the designated reception leader and his family for an evening meal while they listened for the BBC radio message to confirm that night's drop. Most agents agreed that sharing such moments was a privilege. New recruits were often thrilled by the idea of the mighty BBC broadcasting their message to all who chose to listen, a message that made sense to no one but them. But it was also the moment when the adventure became real, and dangerous, no longer owned by the team alone but also involving RAF pilots risking their lives to deliver supplies, and Bomber Command who were supporting the diversion of aircraft to the field. Christine would intuitively tune in to the mood in the room, reading how deeply the men drew on their precious cigarettes and how quick the women were to smile, and her natural self-assurance helped to calm their nerves. For this reason as much as any other she would sometimes join the reception teams, occasionally climbing high into the hills for hours, to help to count the parachutes bursting like spores from the back of the plane, and collect the packages and containers that landed with tinny clunks and rolled down the hillsides, sometimes over a radius of several miles.

As these night-time deliveries were dependent on 'Charlotte', the rather romantic code-name for the full moon, and the moon-period that lasted a few days either side, Christine enjoyed some surprisingly busy nights in the remote fields and grazing pastures of rural south-west France. Occasionally the team might find themselves surrounded by cows as the curious animals came to get a closer look. Once while waiting for a drop, Francis saw other figures wandering around a building in the middle of 'their' field. Creeping up behind them he found himself facing a man with a Sten sub-machine gun just like his own. 'We looked at our Stens and we said, I think we must be on the same side', he told Christine, laughing.[38]

But usually it was quiet work, with just the sounds of insects and low calls between the team as they prepared to light the torches, bicycle lamps or the small creosote and oil fires made in biscuit tins that guided the supply planes to the drop site. Sometimes the moonlight was so bright that the men joked they should have brought newspapers to help pass the time before the sound of an engine – memorably described by Ben Cowburn as 'a 5000 hp roar of defiance' – finally heralded the arrival of a small dark shadow in the sky.[39]

It was not unusual for at least one of the parachutes to fail on these sorties, especially if the flight came from Algiers, where a shortage of silk meant that parachutes were sewn from heavier Egyptian cotton. If a chute failed completely, its metal container hit the earth with such force that it would be practically unrecognizable. Even when no one was killed or injured as a result, excavating these flattened containers was demoralizing work, as once prised open they usually only offered up rifles with their butts broken, or the barrels bent. Cardboard packaging, also used by the teams in Algiers, would often break up in mid-air, sometimes showering Christine and the team with explosives and detonators and leaving much of the munitions unusable. But on good evenings they might find eight or nine undamaged containers, and many more of the lighter packages, which had treats shoved among the supplies: cigarettes, tobacco, slabs of chocolate, jars of butter, tins of food, warm clothes, and even notes of encouragement.

Once collected, the containers and packages were stowed in old houses or under fodder in barns, in caves or in wells. A few nights later the team would be back, unclipping the containers lengthways like ripe pea-pods, and checking their haul. Christine then arranged the deliveries: guns, ammunition, explosives, detonators and chocolate for small bribes to the sabotage teams; silencers to those men 'who could not be trusted to use a knife successfully'; extra Stens, heavier arms, clothes and any parachute silk that could be made into clothes or tents to the Maquis; radio batteries to Albert, whom she daily blessed for saving her from the necessity of putting her own wireless training to the test; bicycle tyres, ration cards and cash

to Francis.[40] There was never enough of anything, but the only items missing from the shopping lists sent to London were extra lethal tablets. A contact in the hotel where the Luftwaffe local HQ was stationed had floated the idea of lacing the soup. 'No', London pencilled against the suggestion; that level of indiscriminate killing was taking things too far, even for the makers of exploding bicycle pumps and detonating horse manure.[41]

As a courier, Christine was also responsible for conveying messages between the well-dispersed members of Francis's network, and between them and the Maquis. Travelling almost constantly through enemy-held territory, within a few weeks she had made contact with the more than fifty cells of the Jockey circuit, making her the only person besides Francis who knew all the key personnel. She 'worked hard', Francis noted, and had quickly become invaluable.[42] For security, all messages were delivered in person and usually from memory, although Christine would sometimes carry an annotated cigarette paper that, if need be, she could easily lose, or even swallow. As a woman she avoided the suspicion that any able-bodied man moving around France by train now generated, but the constant travelling was suspicious in itself and with her dark eyes and hair she was still an obvious target for Nazi guards on train or road controls. Francis suggested she cycle but she absolutely refused, telling him that bikes made her 'shudder' and she would 'rather make twenty parachute drops than accompany him twenty yards on a bike'.[43] Staying in cheap lodging houses, and always dressed in a modest but immaculate blouse and skirt, Christine spent the whole time trying to play down the glamour attached to being a British agent in France, the very glamour that Francis admitted he found 'a tremendous advantage' in the field.[44]

Good communications were vital, not only to coordinate operations, but because resistance circuits were networks 'irrigated by personal trust'.[45] It was not just about personal security; it was about staying sensitive to the various political allegiances of the different groups: Communists; Socialists; Gaullists who like their general felt that nobody should operate in France without their knowledge and consent; regular soldiers 'who were the best of them'; those Francis

called the 'Dynamic Active' who were attracted by pure patriotism and the need for action; and the natural outlaw element whom he described as 'Marseilles gangsters in port-loafers with a taste for adventure'.[46] The Communists were criticized for taking overt actions that might lead to civilian reprisals, but when it came to getting things done they were generally considered the most effective, and not above hijacking an operation, stealing the explosives and equipment for the job, and doing it first.

Above all, Christine had to keep the men motivated while continually reinforcing Francis's policy of sticking to targeted hit-and-run operations and deferring any overt uprising until the Allies had landed in the south, when their combined work would have maximum impact. It helped that she made friends everywhere, partly because she was brave and reliable, and always willing to stop and listen, but also because she was an outsider. Christine's motives were clear: she was, like the French, working with the English voluntarily to defeat a common enemy, but she remained, to Francis's deep admiration, 'a completely independent human being, answerable to nobody'.[47] In addition, she was more experienced than just about anyone there, a professional among amateurs. Francis soon noticed that 'any society Christine moved in, a group of formidable orthodox French officers, or a group of extremely simple peasants working under Communist leadership, the same reaction would be felt: here is someone we can rely on without asking a single question, with no hesitation . . . she was admired by people who'd only met her for two or three minutes, as being someone quite out of the ordinary'.[48] Christine was able to talk to anyone, from any walk of life, with neither false humility nor haughty self-satisfaction. In fact she seemed to disregard herself entirely, always giving her full, flattering, attention to those she was with, and fixing them with her 'searchlight' gaze as effectively as she had the officers in Cairo.

As well as the active groups, Francis believed that the great majority of the French population were passive resisters. SNCF railway staff provided overalls, spanners and travel passes, actively sabotaged tracks and locomotives, drained engine oil, and misrouted

German troops and supplies. Large numbers of the Gendarmerie supported the resistance, too, and would occasionally arrest members of the Jockey circuit on one side of Nazi checkpoints only to release them safely unsearched on the other. Only a tiny proportion of the population, 'a very bad type indeed', Francis wrote bitterly, actively collaborated.[49] These ranged from barbers, barmen or brothel-keepers paid to inform on their clients, to the Milice, the uniformed paramilitary police force created by the Vichy government – possibly the most loathed of all Free France's enemies.

On a hillside overlooking Guillestre, a few days after de Gaulle had issued instructions to the resistance to execute every member of the Milice, a Jockey team brought a *milicien* to Francis. The man's hands were tied at the wrists. A few questions elicited his name, that he was just twenty years old, had joined the Milice of his own accord, and did not know what this meant for him now. Francis told him it meant execution. Then he shot him in the back of the head. The young collaborator was buried on the spot. 'I had to do that because I couldn't ask someone else to do it', Francis later said with obvious difficulty about the execution.[50] With no facility to keep the man a prisoner, and the names and addresses of the circuit compromised, the principled pacifist had had no other option.

Over time, the Jockey cells had become cleverer and more daring in their operations. It was far more effective to put a train out of action inside a tunnel, requiring the engine to be pulled out before repairs could be made, and if the crane coming to the scene could be hit too, so much the better. Christine supported certain sabotage attacks, helping to disrupt most of the roads and the main railway lines along which the Germans were sending reinforcements north, including the Route Hannibal and the Route Napoléon. As well as trains, the circuit was now attacking aircraft, bridges and oil and petrol depots, and increasing their ambushes on Wehrmacht troops. Smaller 'mosquito bite' operations, involving ripping down phone lines, pouring sand into oil containers, and changing the destination labels on German supply trains, kept up the groups' spirits while they waited for the delivery of munitions. By midsum-

mer even a tree across a road could cause the enemy hours of delay
as they searched the surrounding woods, firing into the under-
growth. An excellent shot, Francis always carried a Mauser. He had
been issued with a Colt .45 both times he left for the field, only to
watch one thrown into a river the night he arrived, and report the
second as 'lost'. Christine, whose revolver had smashed on arrival,
preferred not to carry a gun.*

All in all, the Jockey circuit was proving a 'serious menace to
the enemy', and Francis's personal leadership in both organizing
and carrying out the actions was endearing him greatly to his men,
and to Christine.[51] Delighted to be in the field again, with a renewed
sense of purpose and a regular rush of adrenalin, Christine was
thoroughly enjoying herself and, Francis noticed with a hint of
pride, even 'in the most difficult situations, she would sometimes be
shaking with laughter'.[52]

Christine and Francis were the perfect partners in crime. Need-
ing next to no direction, she was soon in effect acting as his second-
in-command, usually on her own initiative, and becoming notably
cooler the tighter the situation. 'Christine is magnificent', Francis
signalled Brooks Richards in Algiers a few weeks after her arrival.
'What couldn't I have done if she had been here three months
ago!'[53] His wire almost crossed with one from Christine filing her
own, similar report. 'Dear Brooks, "Roger" is a magnificent person.
The unity of the whole of the south of France depends upon him',
she enthused before demanding, 'you must support him and back
up his prestige'.[54] Brooks Richards didn't mind the lecture; he
trusted Christine's judgement, and was delighted that this difficult
but brilliant agent was so effectively employed.

Magnificent, magnificent. There was a strange symmetry to
the partnership between Christine and Francis. Both were highly
trained but essentially self-motivated, guided above all by a deeply
held moral code. Both were superb at self-preservation, positive,

* The Imperial War Museum has a Polish Vis Radom gun, displayed as having
belonged to Christine Granville, but without any provenance. There are no references
to this gun in her files, but she may have acquired it in Warsaw, Budapest, Cairo or
Algiers.

popular, cool-headed in a crisis, but at the same time hugely vulnerable, being hunted by a Gestapo who not only had both of their photographs but were offering large sums for their arrest. And both were absolutely dedicated to their countries' shared cause: the defeat of Nazi Germany. The British would later maintain that Francis was 'one of the most successful agents we ever sent into France', and his partnership with Christine would make SOE history.

11: THE BATTLE OF VERCORS

On the beautifully clear morning of 14 July 1944, less than a week after arriving in France, Christine and her new friend Sylviane Rey took part in a defiantly patriotic Bastille Day parade in medieval Die, in the Drôme valley. Although it was not yet half past nine, the air in the little mountain town was already warm and the tables outside the café-bar were busy, when the now familiar drone of engines made Christine glance up. Soon everyone was watching in awe. Seventy-two silver American 'Flying Fortresses', with a fighter escort circling round the heavier four-engine bombers, were coming in, very low, twelve in a line, bringing supplies to the Maquis camps up on the wooded plateau of the Vercors. The planes ejected their containers which separated, caught on their parachutes and drifted momentarily in the haze. The local curate estimated there were over a thousand red, white and blue chutes, the different colours indicating their contents but also making a powerful statement on the first Bastille Day since the Allied invasion of France. It was a historic moment. In June, thirty-six British-based American Air Force Liberators had brought a few hundred containers, but this was the largest daylight sortie of the war, and the Allies' greatest effort to help the French Maquis. The seventy-two planes at Vercors were part of a force of 400 Flying Fortresses organized by Gubbins with authority from General Eisenhower. 'The effect of these great planes flying in swarms low over the centre and south of France, dropping their loads to selected areas', Gubbins wrote proudly, 'was like an electric shock of stimulation.'[1] Certainly Christine, Sylviane and half the village were galvanized to set off at once and help collect the supplies.

Up in the Vercors hills the maquisards were elated, literally

shouting in joy. 'The sky was filled with a hundred Allied planes glittering in the sunlight', one recorded. The planes flew over the landing strip while fixing their positions, and then circled round again, flying low this time, and 'sowing hundreds of parachutes which burst open in the blue sky like the corolla of white flowers, descending joyously ... it was a magnificent fête!' 'A splendid spectacle!' another wrote in his diary, 'the noise filled the whole plateau and must have been heard in the plain of Valence.'[2] Then the planes dipped their wings in salute, catching the sun one last time, and 'vanished into the clouds'. More containers were dropped in this sortie than in all the preceding months, over a thousand altogether, and among the Sten guns, ammunition and clothes were boxes of cornflakes and packets of American cigarettes tied with tricolore bands and handwritten messages: 'Bravo lads. Vive la France!'[3]

But the drop had taken place in daylight, the 'parachutes clear as hell against the sky', Francis commented bitterly.[4] Within half an hour a German reconnaissance plane flew over and strafed the drop zone. Everyone ran for cover except Christine who, looking up at them with her hand shielding her eyes from the sun, 'seemed so serene and unconcerned', according to Sylviane, that those around her almost questioned their own reactions.[5] Half an hour later two more fighters appeared, this time heading for the hills. 'Les Amerlots!' the cry went up.[6] It was only when the planes' swastikas were clearly visible that the maquisards realized these were not more Allies. The planes flew low, skimming the roofs of the Vercors towns to empty their machine guns. Seven hours of bombing followed. In Vassieux-en-Vercors the town's schoolchildren were caught among incendiary bombs that sent flames thirty metres into the air, but most managed to hide in cellars and the local caves. When they dared to come out again, at eleven that night, 'the town had been destroyed', rubble and bodies lying in piles where houses, church and boulangerie had stood that morning, and the Vercors plateau was surrounded by Wehrmacht troops.[7]

The Vercors is an immense, blue-grey limestone plateau in the shape of an arrowhead, about forty miles long, eighteen wide, and

in places reaching heights of 1,000 metres. Sitting between the departments of the Drôme and the Isère, this high plain marks the connection of four major communication routes from Grenoble to Aix, Marseille and Nice. Breathtakingly beautiful, on most sides the plateau is bounded by sheer chalk cliffs; elsewhere the landscape is almost Alpine. Its huge river gorges and dense beech and pine forests, full of wild chamois, protect several small villages with rich orchards and farmlands, and its many rocky outcrops hide extensive caves below. It is hard to imagine better territory in which to shelter a growing clandestine army.

By early 1943 Germany's diminished labour force was straining to meet its production requirements. The Nazis had already brought over Polish workers, who were doing a good job of limiting their useful output while, wherever possible, sending supplies back to the Polish underground. On 15 February 1943 Germany put into action the Service du Travail Obligatoire, or STO, in France, to tap into French labour resources. The Vercors, which had already been used as a training base for local resistance groups, now became a magnet for thousands of young Frenchmen avoiding conscription for forced labour in Germany or even dispatch to the Russian front. Many set up camps among the dense forests on the Vercors plateau. They were not paid and had no false papers or ration cards, so they, and the families they had left behind, somehow had to be supported. Most were dressed in civilian clothes, with heavy-duty boots, baggy trousers and jumpers over open-necked shirts, and blue berets or flat caps on their heads. Others wore faded pinstripe suits, or a few bits of uniform kept from the last war. Some had no shoes and had to make moccasins out of tough parachute silk. At first they also had very few arms. Nevertheless they formed into units with strong chains of command and communications, arranged supplies of food, clothes and equipment through local farmers and existing resistance networks, and trained their dogs to bark at strangers from further down the slopes. The French Maquis had been born.

By May 1943 there were several hundred Maquis in the hills. 'Vercors has a finely organised army,' Francis reported to London,

'but they need long-distance and anti-tank weapons.'[8] The response was ambiguous. Experience in Yugoslavia had already demonstrated the Wehrmacht's ability to deal effectively with guerrilla forces, and yet there were clearly the makings of a significant resistance army in the Vercors, one that could be hugely valuable in hampering Nazi communications and troop movement in the run-up to the Allied invasion. As a result, light arms were dropped, and carried into the camps by foot or in farm carts but, to intense French frustration, no heavy weapons followed.

Francis too had mixed feelings about the Maquis. On the one hand he recognized their potential as a guerrilla army which, if organized into small groups, armed and trained, could mount effective sabotage and ambush attacks. To this end he joined local leaders from the Forces Françaises de l'Intérieur, or FFI, the well-organized French resistance loyal to de Gaulle, to give advice, and instruction in the use of Sten sub-machine guns and revolvers. He even loaned them Albert and his radio. But Francis was also critical of this army-in-waiting, believing it was more useful, if more dangerous, to stay at home, derailing trains by night and returning to work as usual the next day, 'than to sit in the woods and behave like a boy scout'.[9] Nonetheless, by the end of 1943 there were eight large camps, each with eighty to a hundred men, sleeping in hastily constructed huts, lean-tos or tents made from parachute silk, and hundreds more living in shepherds' huts, in the villages, or on local farms across the Vercors.

As far as possible Francis was determined to keep his Jockey sabotage network separate, while encouraging the Maquis to develop along similar lines. He felt that the value of the Vercors plateau lay mainly in its potential as an Allied landing site, and as a shelter for a shadow army able to attack German forces repeatedly in small ways, in a hundred different places, without ever showing where they could be attacked in turn. The basic tenet of guerrilla warfare was, after all, never to try to hold a position, but to do as much damage as possible and disappear. Furthermore, SOE agents had been directed to take 'particular care . . . to avoid premature large-scale risings of patriots'.[10] However, by the autumn of 1943

the French had started working on a grander plan. The Vercors plateau was now being referred to as 'an impregnable citadel', to be championed as free territory before Allied reinforcements arrived.[11] In the spring of 1944 news came, via a BBC radio 'personal message', that General de Gaulle had personally approved the idea, and that up to 4,000 paratroops would be dropped into the Vercors.

Over a few optimistic weeks, dropping zones were prepared on the plateau, code-named, strangely, after articles of stationery. 'Pencil sharpener' was to serve parachute deliveries from Algiers, 'dividers' was to receive those from Britain, and 'paper-weight', 'gummed paper' and 'paper-knife' were all made generally available. At the same time, emboldened by the sanction of de Gaulle as much as by the sheer cliffs that formed a natural protective barrier between the Vercors interior and the surrounding countryside, the Maquis's sabotage operations were becoming increasingly daring. Not only were consignments of food and fuel being captured, train tracks, bridges, telephone and telegraph cables were sabotaged, power pylons brought tumbling to their knees, and key roads blocked by felling the most strategic of the thousands of trees planted by Napoleon to provide shade for his marching soldiers over a hundred years before.

Horrendous reprisals then began. After one attack on a convoy on the Route Nationale that left nearly sixty Wehrmacht soldiers dead, a captured maquisard was tied to a village post to be made an example of. He insisted that he was a regular soldier with an American unit, which saved the village, but then his eyes and tongue were torn out before he was bayoneted in front of the villagers. Despite such atrocities, by the early summer of 1944 the plateau was home to an irregular army of over 3,000 men, with more streaming in from across the region and some from as far as Paris.

FFI leaders, and Francis and his Jockey circuit, were now stockpiling supplies in preparation for the major push to support the Allied invasion, but there was still great confusion around the timing of that invasion. At the start of June, Colin Gubbins, his American counterpart Colonel David Bruce, and the French hero General Pierre Koenig, the newly appointed commander-in-chief

of the FFI, were still in London discussing the plans. The original intention was to mount two concurrent assaults: a major invasion on the north-west coast and a secondary operation in the south. When the southern invasion was delayed Koenig assumed that the resistance rising in the south would be put back correspondingly. Now he reluctantly agreed that, to prevent warning the enemy where they should concentrate their battalions, the resistance should be called into action simultaneously across the country, at least for a few vital days.

On 5 June, as the 'Overlord' armada neared the Normandy beaches, the BBC broadcast seventy coded messages mainly for the circuits operating in the north of France, such as 'Giraffe, why do you have so long a neck' and 'The cats mate in the front garden'.[12] The next day the resistance swept into action with nearly a thousand acts of sabotage undertaken in twenty-four hours. The precise date for 'Dragoon', the Allied invasion of the south, was still under wraps, and further south there was some dispute as to whether the specific call to the Vercors, 'The Alpine chamois leaps', had been included.* But there was no doubt that a nationwide rising had been signalled and Francis had received the call to action for the Jockey network.

After years of bearing the humiliation of defeat and occupation, and witnessing the arrest and execution of friends, the desire to make a stand proved irresistible for men impatient for action across France. Among them were the leaders of the Vercors Maquis. 'The supreme battle is being fought . . .', De Gaulle broadcast to the French nation the following night, laying their fears to rest. 'For the sons of France, wherever they are, whoever they are, the simple and sacred duty is to fight the enemy by every means at their disposal.'[13] In a bold statement of intent, a tricolore flag bearing the Cross of Lorraine, the symbol of the resistance, was raised over the Vercors plateau on 7 June.

* It has been claimed both that de Gaulle used the phrase in his broadcast of 5 June 1944, but that it was not included in the list of transmitted messages in the BBC archives. See Michael Pearson, *Tears of Glory: The Betrayal of Vercors 1944* (1978), p. 42.

On hearing of the Allied landings in Normandy, Francis and his friend Gilbert Galletti, a resistance leader in the Hautes-Alpes, had trekked into the hills to recover hidden munitions and prepare for action. A few days later Francis was informed that his circuit was now officially part of the French Forces, and he was in effect deputy to Colonel Henri Zeller, the FFI regional commander for the south-east and one of the 'moving spirits' of the French resistance.

A series of what Brooks Richards called 'increasingly pathetic and desperate calls' to Algiers for heavy artillery, anti-aircraft guns and anti-tank weapons followed.[14] None were available, and in any case it would have been impossible to supply sufficient ammunition for a sustained battle for anything heavier than a bazooka. 'They had got the impression that paratroop reinforcement might be expected within a very short time', Brooks Richards said later, avoiding any notion of conceding Allied responsibility. 'Well, of course it was quite irresponsible . . . No one had consulted the US or Great Britain as to whether they could supply the Vercors.'[15] The extent of the breakdown in communications between field and HQ became apparent not when Brooks Richards replied to Francis, blaming atmospheric conditions for preventing sorties, but when Koenig in London defied all expectations with the order, 'Send the men home because mobilised prematurely'.[16] The thousands of Maquis would be arrested immediately if they went back home, and in any case they were already far too committed to stand down. London clearly had little understanding of the situation on the ground, while the expectations of the Maquis were hopelessly unrealistic.

That same week a group of men working with Francis received an order to hand over all their recruits, arms and explosives for the defence of Barcelonnette, a medieval town in the Basses-Alpes that was strategically placed on the principal route in and out of Italy. As the note was not signed by anyone they knew, Francis told his men not to comply. He received an immediate response informing him that if he did not obey orders he would be 'court-martialled and shot'.[17] Nerves were fraying, but an apology soon followed, with a request that Francis himself come to Barcelonnette.

Francis was amazed to find the tricolore decorating Barcelonnette's faded stone town hall. The local German garrison had been temporarily overcome and the town was now being defended by the FFI. Colonel Zeller, just arrived from Lyon, met Francis on the town hall steps, along with local resistance leaders and Captain Hay, a British officer recently dropped from Algiers. Hay believed the Allied landings in the south were due within a week, and liberating columns could be expected in less than ten days. The town was being held by 600 men, all in high spirits and some in uniform, with 600 tricolore armbands, but arms and equipment for only 250, some of which were the men's own hunting rifles or relics from the Great War. They had just twenty rounds of ammunition each. It was a pitifully small force with which to face Nazi tanks, regardless of anticipated reinforcements. To make matters worse, neither Francis nor Zeller was expecting the southern invasion imminently.

Francis was astonished when Zeller demanded that he hand over his stock of arms and explosives. It was, he said, impossible. The arms had been distributed, some to people who had been waiting years for them. 'If you have a nice but fierce dog and you give him a bone,' Francis argued, 'you don't put your hand out and take it away again.'[18] In any case he felt that they would have been giving up all their equipment, simply 'for the Germans to capture'.[19] Seeing that the situation was critical he did, however, agree to send a small force across the mountains to attack from the rear. He also sent urgent signals to Algiers resulting in the drop of over a hundred containers of anti-tank arms on 11 June. Unfortunately many of these supplies were collected by enemy troops. Four days later the Germans moved in – too fast for Francis to bring his reserves to bear. 150 men were killed defending Barcelonnette, including Captain Hay, who was mown down by machine-gun fire during a heroic bid to take out a third German tank with the only PIAT anti-tank weapon that Francis had been able to provide.

Undeterred by the tragedy unfolding at Barcelonnette, the Vercors Maquis managed to repel several attacks, during each of which the Wehrmacht suffered disproportionately high losses.

Then, in a ceremony on 3 July, the civilian leader of the Vercors resistance, Eugène Chavant, proclaimed the plateau 'the free Republic of Vercors'. All Vichy laws were immediately rescinded. It was the first democratic administration in France since the start of the German occupation in 1940. It was also a courageous act of outright defiance, and one the Nazis could not ignore. Francis, who had not been consulted, was furious. He was now left with the difficult task of transporting arms across country to a known resistance stronghold.

On 7 July, the night that Christine crashed into France, Francis sent his first report to London since the Allied landings and the tragedy at Barcelonnette. 'There has been a complete lack of understanding . . .', he raged, 'which amounts to criminal negligence against which shot hostages, raped women and burnt villages can bear witness.' 'You must treat us as a serious military force . . .', he concluded. 'Don't let the French down again.'[20] It was a voice that would only become more familiar to SOE HQ over the next few weeks.

For the Maquis, the arrival of Christine's travelling companion, Jean Tournissa, and orders to build an airstrip, seemed to indicate that the heavy armaments that could only be delivered by plane, and possibly paratroop reinforcements, must surely follow. Francis and Christine spent the next few days crossing the plateau with whatever supplies they could coordinate, while sending increasingly desperate signals to Algiers and London for the artillery, anti-aircraft guns and anti-tank weapons that the Maquis so urgently needed. Daniel Huillier, the sixteen-year-old son of one of the original Vercors Maquis, remembered having an aperitif with Christine in a café at Saint-Martin. Daniel was struck by how at ease she seemed, the only woman among all the men, and wondered what on earth she could be doing there. 'She was truly beautiful', he sighed, 'a fine person, a great woman . . . magnificent.'[21] Christine knocked back her drink while Francis started the engine on his motorbike, then, grabbing her rucksack, she swung one leg over the back and they were off to the next unit without a backwards glance.

A week later Christine found herself in the middle of the crisis that followed the Bastille Day sortie at Die. By ten o'clock the Germans were carpet-bombing the plateau in a concerted attempt to stop the Maquis from collecting the light arms and supplies dropped by the planes. 'By eleven our communications were cut', one of the maquisards noted. 'Having sprayed us lavishly with bombs, the enemy planes then inundated the plateau with dozens of grenades . . . Vassieux was on fire.'[22]

Christine, true to form, stood her ground calmly in the face of the Luftwaffe fire and set to work, cutting away the fallen parachutes that gave such clear targets to the Nazi bombers, collecting those canisters that could be gathered in daylight and unloading supplies, stripping the weapons of the grease in which they were packed and preparing them for use. Soon there were stacks of cartridge boxes, round cases of explosive, and piles of grenades shored up against the empty containers, waiting to be distributed. She then helped to deliver arms, and Francis's advice, to the quickly assembling units of Maquis, and worked to keep a secure line of communication between Francis, Zeller and Albert.

Christine's friend Sylviane Rey was also hard at work. With a starched pinafore tied over her grey skirt, she was busy moving among the many casualties, administering first aid. The church at Vassieux, with its massive wooden doors, was already in ruins, one of the bombers' first targets, and all the towns of the Vercors were soon under fire. Makeshift hospitals were quickly set up in schools, and buses and lorries converted for use as ambulances. The air attacks continued all day.

In between directing the response, the Vercors military commander, Major François Huet, hosted a surreal lunch, discussing strategy in the face of the assault, and proposing a series of patriotic toasts as bombs exploded around his HQ in Saint-Martin. At midnight Francis and other senior officers attended a crisis meeting at Huet's villa, in a room thick with cigarette smoke. In the early hours he retreated to Saint-Agnan, the next village south, where Christine joined him in what Francis described as 'a burning hotel'.[23] It was here that they spent their first passionate night

together. Bombs were still falling as they climbed the stairs, and just a few miles away enemy troops were massing for a final onslaught. They were physically and emotionally shattered but, as Francis put it, 'absolutely certain that we were going to die the next day; it was all over, this was the end', each considered the other's arms an excellent last sanctuary.*[24]

Standing by the window in the first light of dawn, they watched a Nazi bomber heading directly for them. When the plane was close enough to see the pilot's face Francis bent his head slightly and said quietly to Christine, 'If they release a bomb now it will come right in through the window next to us.'[25] As Francis said 'now' the pilot let a bomb fly. Francis was not often wrong, but he was about three feet out on this. The bomb skidded over the roof, so close they could feel it brushing the tiles, and buried itself in the dry earth bank beyond without exploding. Gripping his hand, Christine led Francis out of the room, down the stone stairs and round the back of the building to find it. Then, glancing up at the already busy morning sky, she laughed, exclaiming, 'They don't want us to die!'[26] It was typical Christine, no mention of God and no sign of fear, just defiant *joie de vivre*.

Over the next few days, constantly under fire, Francis and Christine continued their efforts to coordinate, collect and distribute supplies, support the preparation of Tournissa's landing strip, which was still being levelled with a steamroller, and generally maintain the Maquis's communications and morale. Many hours were spent at the command post at the top of the plateau, watching the troop formations through heavy binoculars. By counting the lines of soldiers neatly forming into reconnaissance patrols, Francis hoped to work out where they planned to break through the Maquis's lower defences and begin their push up into the interior of the Vercors both on foot and with tanks. Despite his continued and increasingly desperate requests to Algiers and London for

* Their affair was kept quiet. Maurice Buckmaster, SOE's Head of F Section, said agents were organized into groups 'that would get on well together, but not too well. I mean, in other words, that the organiser wouldn't want to go to bed with the courier all the time . . . we never had any problems of that kind'. IWM, Sound Archive, 8680.

anti-tank weapons, mortars and paramilitary reinforcements, there were no further deliveries.

Part of the problem was that the SOE had never won the respect or support of the RAF. The British Air Marshals believed that their limited resources should be at the full disposal of Bomber Command. 'The dropping of men in civilian clothes for the purpose of killing members of the opposing forces is not an operation with which the Royal Air Force should be associated', Sir Charles Portal, Chief of Air Staff, had written early in the war.[27] As the battle for air resources intensified the relative merits of acts of sabotage on the ground versus bombing from the air were considered, with Portal now claiming that 'my bombing offensive is not a gamble. Its dividend is certain; it is a gilt-edged investment.'[28] In retrospect sabotage was shown to have been more effective at targeted impact, but until the summer of 1944 Britain's only visible contribution to the war in Europe was through the bombing offensive, and it was therefore vital to maintain Allied credibility. Repeated lobbying by Francis and others had, however, resulted in an increase in the amount of air support for SOE agents. And in June 1944 Churchill announced that 'every effort must be made to supply the Maquis at once with rifles, Bren guns, Piat guns, mortars and bazookas with ammunition' – but there were never enough pilots or aircraft.[29] A month later, with the Allies advancing into Normandy, and the second invasion imminent, Britain was still not in a position to risk reducing air coverage of the invading army, even for the established French resistance. At the same time, Algiers was facing a barrage of demands for supplies, all of them urgent, from resistance groups across the country.

The lack of air support for the Vercors Maquis might have been strategically justifiable, but neither London nor Algiers seemed even to acknowledge the desperate situation on the ground or give serious consideration to the possibility of evacuating the plateau. As the Maquis fought off the first assaults from the local German garrisons, a series of weakly apologetic signals sent from Algiers ended 'love to P', short for Pauline, Christine's alias. Such flippant niceties incensed her. '*Psiakrew!*' (Dog's blood!) Christine cursed,

as a colleague beside her swore that he 'would gladly break their necks, we have no time for love here'.[30]

On 20 July, Francis and Christine sent a signal in the name of Colonel Zeller: 'Fierce battle for capture of Vercors imminent. Without your help result uncertain . . .'[31] As well as reinforcements in the form of a parachute battalion and mortars, they repeatedly requested the immediate bombing of the German airfield at nearby Chabeuil, where fifty to sixty Luftwaffe planes were assembled, before ending rather pathetically, 'Come to our aid by every means.'[32] But no attack came and the following morning the Nazis launched a full-scale assault on the Vercors Maquis. It would be the biggest operation undertaken by the army of occupation in France. A major air offensive was followed with strategic attacks by highly trained commando units against whom the lightly armed Maquis, so effective at ambush and sabotage, could offer little sustained resistance. 'Massive attacks by airborne troops . . .', Francis signalled Algiers. 'We hope to be able to maintain radio link . . .' But he signed off 'adieu', suggesting a more permanent farewell than his more usual 'au revoir'.[33]

That morning the defenders of the Vassieux airstrip would at first mistakenly welcome twenty enemy gliders containing at least 200 SS troops armed with flame-throwers, believing them to be Allied support. The landing strips had just been completed, but the British considered them too short to be used. The Germans did not. It was, in Brooks Richards's words, a total 'cock-up'.[34] The gliders descended steeply and very rapidly, the pilots maintaining a steady stream of machine-gun fire as parachutes slowed their approach for landing. Two were shot down and two more damaged. The rest discharged ten Waffen-SS soldiers each, who dispersed 'like flies', allowing the defenders little time to take cover.[35] Heavily wounded, Jean Tournissa, the airstrip engineer, crawled into a shallow trench. Within minutes a hundred people lay dead on his landing strip, slumped across the few machine guns and under wheelbarrows where they had run for shelter. Christine reported that she was in a barn at the far end of the airstrip, en route to deliver a message from Francis to Tournissa, when the gliders came

in. Shaking violently, she managed to retreat, taking news of the airborne invasion back down the hill.[36] Later accounts would have her using a machine gun and hand-grenades against the gliders.*[37]

The ensuing slaughter was not restricted to the Maquis. Despite attempts to keep the conflict zone away from the local population, many of whom had taken shelter in the Vercors caves, Wehrmacht troops and SS units progressed mercilessly up the roads and farm tracks cutting into the forests and mountains, and through all the villages, killing indiscriminately as they went. The intermittent sound of machine-gun fire echoed across the plateau, punctuated by the screaming of cows that had not been milked. Still no help came. Over the next few days the Nazi troops pressed into the Vercors interior, forcing local women and children to walk ahead of their columns as human shields. Hostages were shot, farms burnt down, and the Maquis were forced into isolated positions deep within the forests while enemy reinforcements arrived at Die.

Francis, Albert and Christine now put themselves entirely at Zeller's disposal. Albert almost slept with his headphones braced over his head and his aerial harnessed round his chest, and Christine spent hours coding and sending increasingly desperate signals to Algiers and London. There were occasional victories: the blocking of a strategic pass, the routing of the enemy in one sector by throwing hand-grenades from a beauty spot, and the capture of some heavy artillery with at least one big gun dragged higher up the plateau with a maquisard riding gleefully on its barrel. 'Morale of our people excellent', one message to Algiers began, 'but they will turn against you if you do not take immediate action. Those in London and Algiers understand nothing about the situation in which we find ourselves and are considered as criminals and cowards. Yes repeat, criminals and cowards.'[38]

By 21 July it had become clear that, unless the remaining maquisards either forced a passage through the enemy line, or rapidly dispersed in small groups through the forests, they would all be killed along with any civilians who were believed to have

* Captain Jean Tournissa, alias Paquebot, died a week later, on 18 August 1944.

sheltered them. A summer storm had blown in and the paths and
fields were slick with mud. The Maquis were still a few thousand
strong, but German reinforcements greatly outnumbered them, and
they had been massively under-armed from the start. On 23 July,
with defeat inevitable and driving rain making rivers of the moun-
tain paths and washing through the remaining camps, the order to
disperse was given, followed by the release of the Maquis's pris-
oners. Many in France would later regard the abandonment of the
Vercors as treason. It was certainly a disaster in terms of morale
and the loss of the region's most strategic base for guerrilla raids.
Nonetheless the Vercors Maquis had forced the Germans to deploy
11,000 men in the area for six weeks, at a time when they were
badly needed in Normandy. By the end of July there seemed to be
little honour in the prospect of certain martyrdom, rather than
regrouping to fight again elsewhere. As it was, most of the exits
from the plateau were already blocked and several hundred maquis-
ards were caught trying to fight their way out in small groups.
No prisoners were taken.

The Maquis lost over 600 men at Vercors. As their line retreated,
over 200 local villagers, young and old, men and women, were also
summarily murdered or raped in reprisals that compare with some
of the worst Nazi atrocities. The horror of the messages reaching
SOE HQ was so great that the young woman who decoded them,
in safe and leafy Grendon Underwood, in Buckinghamshire, had to
be transferred. Captured maquisards were burned alive in buildings
or left hanging by piano wire. 'The Germans would eat their lunch
in front of the struggling men', read one report.[39] Villagers were
tortured and shot. Corpses were mutilated and trampled on. In one
village on the plateau a nineteen-year-old secretary was disembow-
elled and left to die with her entrails round her neck.

On an isolated farm twelve-year-old Arlette Blanc was pulled
from the ruins of her home where she had been trapped between
the decomposing bodies of her family – including her aunt Suzy,
who had been baking victory cakes just a few weeks before. Also
dead were her grandmother and younger sisters Jacquie and Danie,

aged just seven and four, and her eighteen-month-old baby brother, Maurice. Her mother had taken several days to die, begging for water until the end. Wehrmacht troops had passed by, but, she said, 'gave me nothing, and left mocking me'.[40] Arlette was eventually freed and taken in a wheelbarrow to a neighbouring village, where she was washed and her wounds tended to. She ate, slept, asked to write to her father, and then died in great pain the following day, tormented that she had not seen her father and did not know where she would be buried. Ten members of Arlette's family had been killed in four days. Houses, livestock and harvests were systematically looted and destroyed. In Vassieux only ten properties were left out of the village of 150 houses, and even in tiny Saint-Julien, where Christine had made her home, thirteen buildings were razed to the ground. Putrefying corpses lay everywhere.

On 27 July, a Red Cross camp in the one of the larger Vercors limestone caves, the Grotte de la Luire or 'Gleaming Cave', was surrounded by the Wehrmacht. It had been set up by a doctor, priest and six uniformed nurses only a week before, and tended to both Allied and enemy injured, their stretchers lying between the boulders. Any of the wounded who could support themselves had already been taken further into the forest in small groups led by nurses including Christine's friend Sylviane. Some of the others had been driven to safety by Daniel Huillier's uncle, in a bus with its seats ripped out. When asked to help, Daniel, the sixteen-year-old boy who had been so struck with Christine drinking her aperitif in a café a few days before, now refused to drive to the cave, insisting that he did not want to 'die in that hole'.[41] That instinct may have saved his life.

The two Polish patients in the cave, who had been serving with the Wehrmacht forces, came out first, requesting mercy for the thirty casualties left inside. The French wounded, and one American officer, Francis Billon, who had parachuted into France from the same plane as Christine, and had broken his leg on landing, were then ordered out. Those who could not walk were dragged across the rocks by their hair and legs. Most were then shot. After interrogation the doctor and priest were also shot. One survivor

recorded that 'the bodies were driven away and thrown into ditches along the roads. A group of sixteen men who were gravely wounded, covered in blood and supporting themselves on improvised crutches were marched off to a wall and mown down by machine-gun fire ... [Later] some fifty men who managed to crawl into a thicket were found by a troop of SS men and beaten to death, one by one'.[42] The remaining nurses, still in their once starched caps and aprons, were interrogated and sent to Ravensbrück. 'How savagely these people were killed by us. We completely exterminated a hospital of partisans, with doctors and nurses ...', one German soldier wrote home, the letter later found on his own dead body, 'but those pigs deserved nothing more'.[43]

Over the next few weeks several desperate groups of maquisards who descended from the limestone peaks seeking water were also massacred by waiting Wehrmacht troops. But some, surviving on a diet of clover and the water sucked from moss, managed to break through the German lines, re-form and restart ambush and sabotage operations, and there were many small insurgencies. It was not until 18 August that the last German troops pulled out of the Vercors as the Allies landed in the south.

The tricolore flew over the plateau for six heady weeks, but the 'Battle of Vercors' lasted only four days. Francis, Albert and Christine did not see its conclusion. Once the order to disperse had been given they could serve little further purpose on the plateau, and their responsibilities with the Jockey circuit across the region were too great to risk capture or a purely heroic death. Before first light on 22 July, they, Zeller and a few key contacts escaped covertly, driving to one of the tunnels that gave a route out of the plateau, before abandoning their car to struggle down the steep surrounding hillsides. On the road from Die, they watched a Wehrmacht column headed by three tanks moving in, and above it a Luftwaffe plane. Halfway down the hillside they heard the tunnel they had come through being blown up, cutting off one of the few escape routes for the Maquis left behind. They still had to cross the main road, guarded by patrols, and wade across the Drôme river before they could consider themselves out of immediate danger. Eventually

they covered a distance of seventy miles, sixty on foot, in twenty-four hours. Christine and Francis headed for the small town of Seyne-les-Alpes. Albert carried his wireless set, still in its battered leather suitcase, to a house in a neighbouring village. Zeller went on to Algiers to demand a meeting with de Gaulle.

The following day SOE sent a short note to Nan Cammaerts: 'Francis is doing splendid work.'[44] In truth he and Christine were holed up together in a safe house, trying to recover their energies while absorbing the horrendous knowledge that they had just left over a hundred courageous young men to face their deaths, 'to be slaughtered like sheep', as Christine put it.[45] 'Many officers have disappeared, believed killed', ran Zeller's last transmission via Francis. 'Troops and commanders curse failure to provide air support. Hope for early landing in the south. Send me news.'[46] 'Fully understand your sadness and your feeling of isolation . . .', Algiers responded. 'Confident that Vercors troops despite dispersal will have success and revenge through action as guerrillas.'[47] It was bitter comfort. The Allies would not land in the south of France until the middle of August.

Today, the Battle of Vercors is held to be the most heroic resistance stand in occupied France, but for Francis and Christine it was simply their first, sickening, experience of total war.

12: SWITCHING ALLEGIANCES

For Christine, scrambling down the goat tracks that led away from the Vercors battleground towards the relative safety of Francis's temporary base at Seyne-les-Alpes felt like a shameful betrayal of the Maquis. Few words were exchanged as she and Francis pushed on, fear and determination holding their exhaustion at bay. When not completely focused on their own immediate safety, both absorbed themselves with how best to help prepare for the imminent Allied invasion in the south.

Francis believed that the main threat to the Allied advance was the unknown quantity of Wehrmacht troops, perhaps as many as seven divisions, stationed in northern Italy and ready to attack over the Alpine passes. Nevertheless his immediate priority was to coordinate the Jockey circuit's sabotage of key German communications and troop transport routes within south-eastern France. Part of Christine's mission, however, was to support the arrival of 'Operation Toplink', a joint British, French and American special force being prepared to coordinate the work of the partisans on both sides of the high Alps, in order to protect the Allied landings. Fifteen officers, including Christine's friends John Roper, Paddy O'Regan and Havard Gunn, were due to drop from Algiers in early August. Her focus therefore turned to making advance contact with the Italian partisans. While she was doing so, she thought it could do no harm to try to coordinate the concerted harassment of German garrisons in the Alps and attacks on any convoys that ventured on to the roads.

Christine also hoped to fulfil another part of her brief – to secure the defection of some of the thousands of her Polish compatriots who had been forcibly conscripted and deployed locally

by the enemy. In Cairo, SOE had learnt that there were consider-
able numbers of Poles among the German garrisons in France,
most of whom feared that desertion would lead to reprisals among
their families. 'They do, however, take every opportunity to become
prisoners-of-war', Harold Perkins had noted in 1943, before going
on to suggest that there might be an opportunity to organize
deserting soldiers and other such prisoners into units.[1] Christine
had first discussed the possibilities for effecting large-scale deser-
tions among the foreign troops in the Italian border areas with
Patrick Howarth in Cairo, and later with Brooks Richards in
Algiers. She had already made some inroads before the situation in
the Vercors deteriorated. Now arriving at Seyne-les-Alpes she ate,
slept, washed, changed clothes and ate some more. Then, impatient
to justify her retreat from Vercors, just twenty-four hours after
arriving, Christine left Francis and their Seyne safe house for the
north-western Italian frontier.

Until the end of July 1943 Italy had been a hostile power, and
Germany would remain in effective control of parts of the country
until the end of the war. After the Italian collapse Hitler had
ordered several Wehrmacht divisions into southern France and
north-western Italy to try to persuade the Italians to keep fighting.
They met with little success. The Italian 51st Alpini Division turned
against the Nazis, and eventually over 50,000 Italian troops were
disarmed and sent to the French interior as forced labour units.
Many deserted, especially those near the French border, most
joining the Italian Maquis or other resistance networks including
the Jockey circuit. Released or escaping prisoners-of-war added
to partisan numbers. Francis believed that much more could have
been done to encourage desertions, and was disappointed not to
have been able to collect more Italian arms and supplies. That
said, significant resistance did not begin to emerge until both the
British and US armies were established on the Italian mainland.

Christine set off on her journey into the Italian Alps dressed in
peasant-style sandals, a short-sleeved shirt, plain skirt, jersey tied
around her waist, and a headscarf to keep back her thick dark
hair. On her back was a haversack full of bread, cheese and hand

grenades. After some miles she caught a lift in a *gazogène* car, converted, like most French cars in wartime, to be powered by a coke-, wood- or coal-fed boiler rather than petrol. Her first stop was Gilbert Galletti's base in Bramousse, an obscure hamlet 10 kilometres north-east of Guillestre. Galletti, a former garage proprietor, was one of the key local resistance leaders on the French side of the border and was working closely with an inspirational young leader, Paul Hérault, to coordinate the defence of the Italian frontier in the Hautes-Alpes. Both were in close contact with Francis. Confident and cheerful, Galletti was a reassuring figure in his faded blue army shirt and shorts, every pocket of which was weighed down with supplies. His tanned face regularly lit up with a broad smile, and although he was deadly serious about his work he could rarely resist clowning around to raise a laugh. Francis, and soon Christine, too, doted on him.

Paul Hérault was different. A skilled cabinetmaker by trade, he was also a mountaineer who, before the war, had taught young people to appreciate their local landscape. Fit, handsome with a thin, wiry frame and long dark hair, Francis thought that he looked like a 'Red Indian'.[2] Thoughtful and softly spoken, Hérault had quickly won the trust and admiration of everyone he met, civilian or military, Communist, Gaullist or simply patriotic. By 1944 he was the departmental chief of the FFI and, according to Francis, not only 'the greatest resistance leader' but 'the greatest man' he had ever met.[3] Francis would often stay at Hérault's apartment, where they simply booby-trapped everything before going to sleep as 'it was well known that entry to his flat would blow him and everyone else up'.[4] Later Francis would name his only son Paul in his friend's honour, and he quickly guessed that he would become a 'very special friend' to Christine.[5] Both were essentially loners, with few strong emotional ties to the people around them, even those who adored them. Theirs was a rare meeting of minds. 'Christine recognized the purity and perfection of his personality', Francis wrote. 'She needed his level of grace.'[6]

Galletti's men knew several of the trails over the Alps, and were already in contact with some Italian partisans, although not with

the most important local leader, a hero known as Marcellini. Marcellini commanded over 2,000 men and held the heights between the two main roads leading into France at Briançon, making his, in Francis's opinion, 'the only partisan group in the Italian Alps capable of being useful'.[7] Clearly contact was essential. Hérault, meanwhile, was enthusiastic about the idea of persuading conscripted Polish and other foreign troops in the region to defect. Together they discussed Christine's best route through the mountains, the opportunities that might present themselves, the likely outcomes of her work and her strategy for retreat.

From Bramousse a local ski instructor, Gilbert Tavernier, drove Christine into the foothills of the Alps on the back of his motorbike. At one point they were stopped and ordered off the bike by a Wehrmacht detachment controlling the roads. Christine waited politely, the picture of ease, sitting in the sunshine twiddling a stick while Tavernier was searched; she knew he was not carrying anything incriminating. Only when invited did she pull herself up, smile, and climb back on the bike behind him, the hand-grenades in her rucksack softly clunking as she moved.[8] Simply being a woman – calm, charming and modestly dressed – was still excellent camouflage.

Once in the foothills Christine made her ascent alone, sticking mainly to the higher forest tracks above the roads. It was hot, and the climb hard going, but no more demanding than her hikes in the hills outside Algiers. The trees at first provided welcome shade, but as she climbed higher the snow-capped mountains shimmered in the heat and clouds of dust blew up along the paths. At one stage, Andrzej must have been intending to join her, because she sent a message to Brooks Richards saying that his leg would not be up to it. 'The conditions now on the . . . frontier are too difficult for him,' she signalled, 'there are no means of transport at all and everything has to be done on foot.'[9] Christine spent two weeks trekking back and forth across the mountains, which were rapidly becoming a battlefield, reporting back on enemy troop movements, resistance plans and general morale. Stopping at villages on both sides of the border she saw how unpopular the conflict had been locally.

Whether they were French or Italian, people in the Alps were shaped by the same cultures and traditions, and sometimes even shared the same family names. Crossing the German lines, she noticed that the guards looked increasingly nervous; everyone knew the tide of the war had turned and the Wehrmacht troops had lost their certain faith in victory. 'The morale in the German army is bad,' she reported, 'they know the war is lost. Propaganda is almost unnecessary.'[10]

Christine was always on the move, pushing herself to the limit, and glad to re-establish contact with her friends in France every few days, where she might stop for some ersatz coffee, made with ground acorns or grilled barley, or, better, some tea or a glass of local wine. It was in these kitchens and cafés that her stories began tumbling out. Once, she said, she had been stopped by a Nazi frontier patrol as she was openly carrying her SOE silk map of the area.* Unable to run, or to hide what was in her hands, she calmly shook the map out and used it to replace the scarf tying back her hair. Paying no more attention to it she then greeted the soldiers in fluent French, persuading them that she was just a local village woman running errands in her sandals.

Her sangfroid paid off again one evening in Piedmont, on the Italian side of the Alps, when a border patrol caught sight of her with some French partisans some way ahead. They flung themselves under some dense bushes in a wood near the road, but were quickly sniffed out by the patrol's vicious Alsatian dog, trained to bite and break necks. Christine quietly put her arm around the animal, and as she did so it lay down beside her, ignoring its handler's whistles. Christine's former lover, Wladimir Ledóchowski, later laughed at her pride in her ability to connect with animals, and the way that Christine would tell her dog-charming stories 'right and left, to whoever was willing to listen'.[11] Francis, however, was less cynical, believing 'she had a magic with dogs'.[12] 'A dog, like any human being, would simply be drawn to her like a magnet . . .', he mused.

* MI9's Christopher Hutton created silk maps so that they would not rustle inside clothes should an agent be searched.

'There are people like that who draw your eyes; she was an intensely compelling personality' and 'had a sort of electricity which was not only human but animal'.[13] Gilbert Tavernier, who had been with her, however, thought that in this instance Christine's compelling personality was supplemented by her quick thinking. She had been using chicken-fat to stop her heavy sandals from rubbing blisters on her heels, and had quickly smeared some on to her hands, giving the dog something good to lick while she whispered Polish endearments in its ears. Permanently switching allegiance, the dog remained with Gilbert Galletti for the rest of the war, only leaving his side to greet Christine by rolling at her feet whenever she appeared.

But perhaps the most repeated story is that Christine was once stopped by two Italian conscripts while she was guiding one of their partisan compatriots to the nearest Maquis group. Ordered to put her hands above her head, she slowly raised two live grenades, threatening to blow everyone up. Then she retreated into the trees, momentarily losing her partisan charge, who, fearing she had lost her nerve, was unsure whether to join her. Later Christine would cheerfully claim that she always preferred grenades to a gun. 'With a pistol you can defend yourself against at most one person, with a hand-grenade – against five, perhaps ten', she bragged when in the mood. 'I always had hand-grenades.'[14] Whether or not the story is true, and different versions have her giving her ultimatum in Italian or even German, neither of which she spoke with any fluency, it is clear that Christine had become an expert in the valuable art of bluff.

Throughout this period, Christine was sending back information on troop movements to Galletti and Francis, and identifying the partisan bases to receive arms drops and be linked up with the new 'Jedburgh teams': groups of specially trained British SOE, American OSS and French resistance leaders, being dropped in under Operation Toplink. She also arranged to provide what supplies she could by mule to local Maquis who were harassing those German convoys that ventured along the vulnerable mountain roads. She was in her element. 'We need as many Jedburghs and

Missions as possible, and for God's sake do not wait until the war is over', she signalled to Brooks Richards in late July, her familiar tone conveying both her natural inclination to command and her renewed belief in the importance of her role. 'Send at least one Jedburgh . . . to each department and instruct them all to listen to "Roger's" orders.'[15]

The Toplink Jedburgh teams started arriving over the next few days. The first, Leonard Hamilton and Paddy O'Regan, parachuted in on 1 August. The naturally good-humoured O'Regan had been given false papers identifying him as a pig dealer, and had deliberately frowned for his photograph, hoping that it would make him 'as fascist looking as possible'.[16] Hamilton, who looked twenty-five although he was in fact forty, towered over him, and as he tended to stand assertively, with his hands on his hips, O'Regan felt that he never seemed like anything other than a resistance fighter. With them came a French wireless operator, and two Italians, lieutenants Ruscelli and Renato. 'One a little Sicilian with the heart of a lion, the other a large Neapolitan Teddy Boy with the courage of a consumptive mouse', O'Regan commented after Renato had drawn his revolver on the Frenchman who ran to gather him in.[17]

As Christine was in the Alps, Francis, 'smiling, slim, competent, alert and energetic', came to welcome the men himself.[18] All of them were detailed to support Paul Hérault. Sitting together in a farmhouse kitchen that evening, with large cups of milky coffee that had been warmed over the fire, O'Regan thought how strange the moment was, 'a world within world'.[19] The next morning he, Hamilton and their team were woken early, piled into an old truck fuelled by a log-burning stove, covered with a tarpaulin, and driven to the Italian frontier with a gendarme ahead on a motorbike, and occasionally a couple of bicycles hitched behind. Eventually they arrived at Galletti's base. After a few hours of drinking they set off on what they thought would be half an hour of light climbing up to the Maquis camp. Four hours later O'Regan began to stumble, and Galletti had to carry his jacket, equipment, and eventually the humiliated new officer himself, into the camp.

O'Regan was not just tired; he had contracted dysentery. When

he woke he found that Hamilton and the Italian officers had gone ahead up the Col-de-la-Croix, a high Alpine pass, leaving him behind to recover. He borrowed a shaving kit, washed in a stream, and caught a lift down to Bramousse, where he was delighted to meet not only Francis, but Christine. 'I jumped off my motor cycle and we kissed enthusiastically', O'Regan remembered.[20] For him, Christine was 'the gayest and most alive person I have ever met'. She was also an inspiration. 'With women like that around,' he said with an inward sigh, 'there was nothing to do but bottle up one's incompetence and go through with it.'[21]

Christine was delighted to see O'Regan, but she was 'dead tired' herself. She had come straight from La Rosière, in the heart of the Alps, where she had been trying to track down the elusive Italian partisan leader, Marcellini, to arrange for him to coordinate plans with the Toplink teams. Walking over the Mont Genèvre pass, and through German lines, she had heard sustained gunfire. The Nazis had been forced north through Italy by the Allies pressing up past Rome, and they were now conducting an effective clean-up oper-ation in the Alpine area with the aim of securing the mountain passes. Realizing that Wehrmacht troops must be facing significant resistance close by, Christine followed the noise and quickly found herself in the middle of a major skirmish as a large Wehrmacht division laid siege to Marcellini's temporary base. This time the Italian partisans held their ground triumphantly. As the enemy retreated Christine clambered down from her vantage point. The partisans welcomed her by shooting into the air. She had succeeded in making the first Allied contact with Marcellini.

Francis wrote that Christine 'realized at once the possibilities of Marcellini as a leader, and did all she could to help him'.[22] He in turn informed her about German troop movements across the mountain passes, showed her his groups' positions and, as he prepared for a strategic retreat, implored her for help in the form of arms and reinforcements. Christine then hurried back to Gal-letti's base, having to pass German lines under fire, with several small bits of paper hidden around her person detailing Marcellini's

news, positions, and urgent need for ammunition, shoes, uniforms and 'packed meat'.[23]

Perhaps prompted by this last request, Francis insisted they eat steak for lunch before asking Christine to hike back through the pass with him and O'Regan, to pass her strategic information on to Hamilton and his team. A driving mist had by now blown in across the valley. Halfway down they met two Italians coming up who warned them that the Germans were not far behind. Francis didn't believe it, and they pressed on. When they were the best part up the other side they found Hamilton and his officers haring back down, having been forced to retreat by approaching Wehrmacht soldiers. Unlike Christine, Hamilton had not found Marcellini, only scattered pockets of Italian partisans in retreat. Together they now climbed wearily back, Christine and Francis 'almost passing out' according to O'Regan.[24] While they rested in a ruined ski hut, depressed and cold, the impressive Hamilton, who had escaped from a prisoner-of-war camp in northern Italy on a previous mission, before walking 600 miles to rejoin Allied lines, went off and returned with some meat and rice. Christine then briefed the whole team on the news from Marcellini. Eventually they made it to an Italian village at one o'clock in the morning.

By now Christine, who was still in skirt and sandals, was soaked and shaking. She changed into some dry trousers donated by a villager, and joined the others to eat potatoes and eggs in front of a blazing fire. O'Regan sat so close that he singed his beret. It was here that Christine learned that on the first of August, the same day that Hamilton and O'Regan had been dropped into France, the civilian population of Warsaw had risen up with the underground Polish Home Army in a courageous attempt to drive out their Nazi occupiers. Their aim was to free the city ahead of the advancing Russian troops, so as to be able to welcome them as Allies and equals rather than as liberators to whom they would be indebted. For a moment the courage of her countrymen, and the real possibility of Polish liberation, filled Christine with unspeakable hope. What little news she heard of the desperate turn of events in

her home country over the next few weeks only heightened her determination to share the fight and help rout the common enemy in France.

The next day they set off again, climbing up past the snowline to the deserted village, high in the Alps, that Galletti had recommended both for their HQ and as a possible site for arms drops. The calm and beauty of the ruins in the snow made a deep impression on Christine, who spent some time in the little chapel while the others set up camp. Seeing them together that evening, O'Regan decided that Christine was in love with Francis. They almost certainly shared a bed again that night, in one of the ruins. The following morning O'Regan set off with his wireless operator, and a note of introduction from Christine to Marcellini. 'Commander, I present to you the English Commander who works with me and is head of the British Mission', Christine scrawled in blunt pencil across a sheet of the squared notepaper they carried for coding. 'I regret I cannot keep working for you myself as my work calls me elsewhere. I hope you meet and get all the help . . . you desire. Goodbye and "in bocca al lupo", Pauline'; the last literally meaning 'in the mouth of the wolf', a pleasingly appropriate idiom for 'good luck', given their surroundings.[25]

Aware that more Jedburgh teams were due to be dropped into the fields below, Francis and Christine now returned to Galletti and his group at Bramousse. On 4 August, Havard Gunn, still proudly kilted beneath his flying suit, had been parachuted in with a French officer, Christian Sorensen, and the teddy-bear Christine had given him in Algiers. After a short reunion, during which he discreetly showed Christine the flattened remains of the bear that had taken the full impact of his landing, Gunn set off to work further south at Colmars. Sorensen, however, had injured his leg on landing, and was forced to stay in Seyne. Three days later John Roper arrived. Roper had fallen for Christine in Algiers and had last seen Francis as a schoolboy on the rugby pitch at Harrow, making him one of the few people in France who knew 'Roger's' real name. The two men now embraced each other in a mountain valley in occupied France, and Francis was delighted to see his old friend's 'engaging

smile' again.[26] With Roper came John Halsey and Robert Purvis. Christine 'was on top of the world', Purvis noted, thriving on her work and forming great friendships wherever she went.[27] 'The work done by all this personnel was invaluable,' Francis later added, 'but in most cases they only had a fortnight or so in which to do it.'[28] The Allied landings in the south of France were now scheduled for 15 August, so the pressure was on.

On the evening of 9 August, Francis and Christine arranged for the Jedburgh officers to meet the local FFI resistance leaders at a safe house in the forest near Gap. Here Paul Hérault outlined his detailed plans for the liberation of the region. These were approved unanimously. Francis then proposed a vote of confidence in Hérault's leadership, and everyone left, inspired, and clear about the role that each must play.

The next morning Hérault learnt that one of the local leaders who had been at the meeting had since been arrested. Leaving a message for Galletti, he left Gap at midday on the back of a local gendarme's motorbike to see if he could secure the man's release. Half an hour later they were stopped by a Wehrmacht convoy that was, unusually, travelling on a minor road. Hérault immediately sprinted into a wood near the road, making it to safety only because the troops were not expecting anyone to run. There he lay, face down, as bullets shredded the bushes around him, and one was fired at point-blank range into the skull of the gendarme he had left with the convoy on the road. Frantically, Hérault started tearing up all the incriminating papers still on him from the night before. Having pressed them into a tight ball, he lobbed them away among the trees. He then crawled to the edge of the wood, waited until some time after the firing had stopped, and made a second run for it. He was brought down in a hail of bullets. His ball of paper was later retrieved by the resistance.

Hérault's death threatened to rupture the precarious alliance between the various local resistance groups, but his legacy – the regional liberation strategy – proved strong enough to ensure effective action. Hamilton's team assisted in blowing up the strategic bridges between Briançon and Gap, and at Prelles. He then

moved on to fight at Briançon until he was forced out of action when his leg was broken in a car accident. O'Regan eventually met up with Marcellini and his men, whom he described as 'young, nervous, and bearded'.[29] But before support could be dropped the Italians were forced to temporarily disband after 'putting up determined resistance against several thousand German and Fascist troops for a fortnight'.[30] As so often, Allied offers of help seemed too little, too late. Undeterred, and supported by Hamilton in France, O'Regan used forty mules to ferry a huge amount of ammunition through the Col-de-la-Mayt pass to the Italian partisans. He also took part in several unsuccessful engagements, at one point leading a group of 150 men, only to have all but three desert into France overnight. Marcellini did regroup, however, for a while setting up his command post in the old barracks at the Col-de-la-Mayt. Francis later credited him as being 'the only leader capable of stopping the Italian partisans from running away immediately they are attacked'.[31] By then O'Regan had moved on into the area around Turin where his work in the last weeks of the war made him a local 'figure of legend'.[32]

Like Francis, and so many others, Christine was deeply affected by Hérault's death and, taking her last conversation with him as an unofficial order, she decided to now prioritize securing the defection of key foreign troops conscripted into the Wehrmacht locally. She had already sent a note to Brooks Richards in Algiers, brought out in person by Zeller, in which she told him that 'there are very few Serbians and Checks [sic], some Ukrainians, Russians and Armenians', but 'the only important groups are Poles'.[33] On several occasions she had even managed to contact these units of foreign conscripts. However, this work became increasingly difficult after the Wehrmacht was alerted to the strategy.

Nevertheless, in early August, Christine made contact with the Polish garrison at Briançon. Initial talks with the 400 conscripted troops convinced her that they would be willing to surrender to the Maquis if certain conditions were fulfilled. Unfortunately one of these conditions was the liberation of Poland. 'I cannot promise them a free Poland', she wrote sadly to Brooks Richards, before

asking for 'authoritative propaganda in Polish language', to help press her case.[34] Encouraged by the willingness of the Poles in Briançon to at least engage in talks, she now broached discussion with other Polish strongholds, both in France and further into northern Italy, to try to influence Poles and Russians serving in the Oriental Legion of General Friedrich Wiese's 19th Army. Again many of these troops had been forcibly conscripted to protect their wives and children, or as their only livelihood. Was she to 'demand' immediate action from them, she questioned Brooks Richards with typical aplomb, or just get information so a specialist could follow up? Already hundreds were beginning to desert, often joining local resistance units. But Christine was soon presented with an opportunity of particular strategic value.

One of the key German frontier garrisons was at Col-de-Larche, a 2,000-metre pass that dominated the surrounding terrain and effectively controlled the military route down to the large French garrison town of Digne. Marcellini had informed Christine that the fort was manned mainly by Poles, 'recruited' from forced labour camps or on the strength of threats to their families. Uncertain of the loyalty of these troops, particularly in the light of the growing number of piecemeal desertions, Wehrmacht officers had redeployed any French speakers, and moved the rest of the men around regularly to try to avoid their subversion. They had not reckoned on a Polish speaker in the mountains.

After Hérault's death, Christine had agreed with John Halsey, the senior Toplink officer at Barcelonnette, that she would make a preliminary approach to the Poles at Col-de-Larche on 11 August. Unfortunately the new local FFI commandant was unwilling to cooperate with the operation. Unsupported, it took her, and the local gendarme who offered to serve as her guide, the best part of two days to climb the steep goat tracks through the forests up to the Col-de-Larche garrison, often slipping back on the swathes of dry needles that covered outcrops of sharp rock. Because she was slight, Christine often surprised her friends with her physical fitness and what Gunn referred to as her 'reserves of strength'.[35] But despite the weeks she had recently spent trekking through the

mountains, her muscles were soon aching and her legs were swollen and covered in cuts.

Christine knew that the Germans were now extremely nervous and on the lookout for local partisans aiming to subvert their troops. Dressed in sturdy army boots and uniform trousers, albeit rolled up above her knees, and with a loudhailer slung over one shoulder, she was clearly no longer going to pass as a local peasant. But her experience in moving about in hostile country proved invaluable, and they reached the huge concrete, stone and strengthened steel garrison undetected, carried out a careful recce and made contact with one of the Polish guards. Having got the information she needed, most specifically the place and time of roll-call, their partial descent to a village further down the Col was much faster.

Two days later the order came through to block the passes on the Italian frontier, soon followed by a warning that Wehrmacht troops were approaching quickly from the south. Christine now climbed up to the garrison again, this time alone. 'Working entirely on her own . . .', Francis later reported, 'this was work of extreme danger'.[36] Once directly below the first fort platform she used the loudhailer to address the sixty-three Poles who were among the 150 officers at the garrison. To win their confidence Christine carried a red and white scarf, the colours of Poland, and even revealed her true identity, greatly adding to the likelihood of her being shot as a spy should she be caught. In the more colourful versions of the story she 'jumped over the iron fence' that surrounded the platform and was lifted shoulder-high by her compatriots, who 'knocked the revolver from the Major's hand as he aimed it at Christine'.[37] Whether or not a German revolver clattered on the concrete, in less than an hour Christine had persuaded the Poles that, when the time was right, they should sabotage the military installations, desert, and join the FFI. She then gave them a pre-typed A4 note with instructions to remain at their posts until they received the order to move, how to then descend in groups of ten behind white flags, what to do should their Nazi or fascist commanders order them to leave the zone before the order to desert came, and finally assuring them that if any were unwilling to join the resistance they

would be treated honourably as prisoners-of-war.[38] Then she
returned to report back to Halsey.

Halsey and Roper arrived at the garrison with around fifty
maquisards on 19 August, less than a week after Christine had done
the groundwork, and four days after the Allies landed in southern
France. There was a short exchange during which a German soldier
in charge of some Polish work crews trying to repair the pass road
was wounded. Halsey and Roper then informed the garrison com-
mander that his communications were cut off, he had no guarantee
of reinforcements from Italy, half of his men were mutinous, and
he needed a doctor for his wounded soldier. They then gave him
an ultimatum to the effect that 'to avoid useless bloodshed, we
advise you to give orders to your troops to surrender. Terms will
be conveyed to you.'[39]

At first the commander refused to countenance surrender but
instead, with surprising courtesy, he accepted Roper's suggestion of
inviting them for dinner. 'We went up by bike', Halsey later
reported and, after their unlikely meal, 'the commander assembled
practically the whole garrison . . . and we argued'.[40] As the evening
wore on the Polish troops deserted en masse, first rendering the
German heavy weapons useless by removing the breech-block firing
pins, as specified by Christine, and then abandoning the garrison,
bringing as many mortars and machine guns as they could carry
back down to the French and Italian partisans. Christine had already
'persuaded the Polish troops to steal all the arms of the garrison
and . . . hand them over to us', Francis wrote with obvious admir-
ation.[41] At half past two in the morning, with his men fast deserting,
the garrison commander finally accepted terms. 'It was a Hollywood
scene,' one of the men later remembered with evident delight,
'with general handshaking, flag-raising and conducted tours of the
spacious German quarters'.[42] The German officers were then
moved under guard to a local château, their commander and his
dog being led away personally by Halsey.

'Both Christine's personality and the enormously rapid series
of "happenings" in the area', Francis later recorded, made the
surrender of the Larche garrison 'the subject of divergent and even

contradictory reports'.[43] But whether or not Christine had stood beside the flagpole on the platform and, 'fingering the rope ... started to pull down, slowly at first, and then faster and faster, the black Swastika sprawled indignantly on its red background', as she did in one version of the story, she was certainly responsible for securing the garrison.[44] It was by Christine's 'own personal efforts' that she achieved 'the complete surrender of the LARCHE garrison', Francis reported to SOE.[45] Her work 'has not been short of remarkable', General Stawell added in his later citation for her, 'and of the greatest value to the Allied cause'.[46]

Christine's clever and courageous action at the garrison had not only cost no lives but had seriously impacted on German plans for an attack over the Alps. The sixty-three Polish officers were all brought into the FFI as a heavy machine-gun company, and later fought with the Maquis to prevent the Larche pass from being reoccupied. The Maquis were also left free to blow up the main road with the Germans' own explosives, so helping to prevent the possibility of motorized troops crossing over from Italy and down to Digne to attack the advancing American columns in the weeks that followed.

Francis had long recognized that Christine had extraordinary qualities. What struck him most now was what he called the 'inevitability' of the Poles deserting and changing allegiance once Christine had set her mind to it. It was not just that she spoke their language. She shared the motivations, fears and aspirations of her countrymen, forcibly 'recruited' to serve an enemy who was at that moment razing Warsaw to the ground. Like highly trained frontier dogs, indeed like most men, 'they were amenable to her charm', Francis commented, but, more importantly, when they deserted they did it with immense enthusiasm. For the Poles, Francis said, Christine 'was an avenging angel'.[47]

1. Trzepnica manor house, 2011: Christine's childhood home.

2. The Skarbek coat of arms on Jerzy Skarbek's tomb, Powazki cemetery, Warsaw.

3. The Skarbek legend, 'Let gold eat gold'.

Nr **9**
KRYSTYNA hr. SKARBEK
Warszawa

4. Christine, as a 'Star of Beauty'
in the Miss Poland national beauty
contest,
Warsaw, 1930.

5. Andrzej Kowerski,
aged about sixteen.

6. Christine's Polish identity card, issued in Warsaw, December 1928.

7. Jerzy Gizycki,
Christine's
second husband,
Washington,
1922.

8. Andrzej Kowerski.

9. Count Wladimir
Ledóchowski.

10. Andrzej Kowerski's
Polish passport, issued
September 1939.

11. Christine c.1940.

12. Sir Owen O'Malley, Head of the British Legation, Budapest, 1940, later British Ambassador to the Polish government-in-exile.

13. Christine and Andrzej in Syria, 1942.

14. Christine and Alfred Gardyne de Chastelain at the Gezira Club.

15. The pool at the Gezira Sporting Club, Cairo, *c*.1943.

16. Christine, Andrzej seated behind, and an unknown officer, Cairo 1942 .

17. Zofia Tarnowska Moss, Cairo, *c.*1943.

18. Bill Stanley Moss, Cairo, 1940s. 'She throve on danger', Moss said of Christine, 'it was a tonic for her'.

19. Christine in Palestine, 1942.

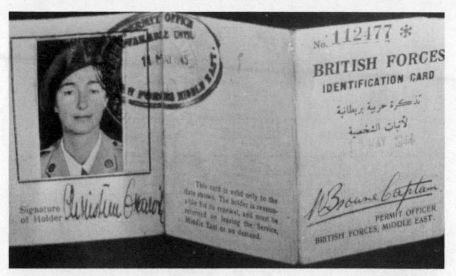

20. Christine's British Forces identity card, showing her in FANY uniform, Cairo *c*.1943.

21. Christine's code card. One of the three code-poems written for her roughly translates:
'Far behind me my southern French loves. My memories of happy years long gone. The weight and the hate, infernal desires, have destroyed my happiness and peace. I would like to forget.'

22. Christine's commando knife.

23. Major General Sir Colin McVean Gubbins KCMG, DSO, MC, Executive Head of SOE 1943–1946.

24. Lieutenant-Colonel Francis Cammaerts, DSO.

25. The Vercors Maquis, August 1944.

26. Christine sitting by a water duct near the blown up bridge at Embrun, Haute-Savoie, France, August 1944.

27. Gilbert Galletti, Paddy O'Regan, John Roper, Christine, Leonard Hamilton, Bramouse, France, August 1944.

— 1 — Cairo 25.III.45

Perks Kochany.

Thank you very much for your very nice letter. I was expecting something like that since our Polish scheme fell through - but you always put things in a kindest way. I am very grateful to you for the three month pay you are offering to me. I should like to stay here in Cairo for at least three three month and, in the meantime look around for another job. If I do not succeed - then I will again ask you for your help. I have already put in an application for a work with R.A.F. but I am afraid that it's too late. If I [get] it - will you write and tell them that I am honest and clean polish girl? I have got two other things in mind

and maybe one will come off. Anyway I should like to keep in touch with you and for God's sake do not strike my name from the firm till it exist - remember that I am always too pleased to go and do anything for it. Maybe you find out that I could be useful getting people from camps and prisons in Germany - just before they get shot. I should love to do it and I like to jump out of a plane even every day. Phone Perks if it's not for your section - maybe somebody's else.
I - thank you for the news about my brother. I have sent a parcel to him. Did you ever heard something about my husband? Please do look after Andrew and don't

32. Letter from Christine to 'Perks', Cairo, 25 March 1945, 'May be you find out that I could be useful getting people out from camps and prisons in Germany – just before they get shot. I should love to do it and I like to jump out of a plane even every day'.

33. Christine at a Vercors memorial event, July 1946.

34. Christine, Andrzej (*right*), Ludwig Popiel (*far right*), and possibly Dennis Muldowney (*left*), in front of the Shelbourne hotel, 1952.

35. Dennis George Muldowney (*below left*), photograph from his seaman records.

36. Christine's decorations: Musketeers' commemorative gorget in the shape of a shield; George Medal; OBE on civil ribbon; Croix de Guerre with one bronze star; 1939–1945 Star; Africa Star; Italy Star; France and Germany Star; War Medal 1939–1945.

PICTURE POST

Christine the Brave
by Stanley Moss

In 1940 a young Polish girl came to London to offer her services in the fight against the common enemy. Her qualifications were patriotic zeal and a readiness to run any risk—anywhere.

For the next six years, as a British secret agent, Christine Granville (one of many aliases concealing the true identity of Countess Krystyna Skarbek) undertook missions in enemy-occupied countries which won her, young other decorations, the George Cross, the O.B.E., and the Croix de Guerre.

The story of those breathless years and the reputation for daring and almost incredible bravery which she

earned among her colleagues is now told to PICTURE POST by one of them who knew her well.

Stanley Moss, author of ILL MET BY MOONLIGHT, operated from the same quarters as Christine for three years. From his own knowledge and from material collected from her closest associates, he has pieced together a record of heroism which might have remained untold—so little did the heroine herself trade on her achievements—but for the tragedy of her recent death in London. This tragedy brought her name and achievements for the first time to the attention of the British public who indirectly owed her so much.

37. Bill Stanley Moss, 'Christine the Brave', *Picture Post*, 13 September 1952.

38. Andrzej rushes to right the cross at Christine's grave, Kensal Green Roman Catholic cemetery, London, June 1952.

39. Oil portrait of Christine by Agniela Pawlikowska, c.1952.

13: OPERATION LIBERTÉ

On the day of the Larche garrison surrender, Sunday 13 August 1944, Christine heard that Francis had been arrested by the Gestapo. She set off at once to see how she could best attempt to secure his release.

Two days earlier, and just three days before the long-awaited Allied landings on the south coast, Francis had organized a reception committee at the small village of Seyne-les-Alpes, to meet new two agents being parachuted in. Xan Fielding, code-named 'Cathédral', short, dark and athletic, was an experienced British officer recently returned from helping to organize the resistance in Crete. His second-in-command, a 'suave, silent man with greying hair, neat dark features and a tired, urbane manner', was a South African gambler called Julian Lezzard. Xan had first met him across a baccarat table in Alexandria, and Christine had briefly coincided with him in Cairo. Lezzard was to operate under the code-name 'Eglise' ('Church') – though given that he was partly Jewish he joked that he should perhaps have been called 'Synagogue'.[1]

'Lizzie', as Lezzard was popularly known, cracked two vertebrae on landing. Fielding, who had braced his legs to receive the first shock, was lucky to avoid a fracture. Both of them had been dropped too high, got caught in the wind and were blown two kilometres off course onto a rocky outcrop. During his descent Fielding had kept his eyes firmly on the reception committee's landing lights, weak beams from four-volt torches with fading batteries, but even so, 'the only landmarks visible in any direction or dimension'.[2] As he was blown off course he watched these lights retreating diagonally across his field of vision, until they finally and abruptly vanished, leaving him alone 'in the dark unchartered sky' [sic].[3] The reception

committee was just delighted to watch them fall at all, having spent
the previous two nights waiting in the cold as the Lysander pilot,
unable to pick out their faint lights, was forced to turn back with
his uneasy passengers trussed up in their harnesses throughout the
eight-hour round trip.

Once both men had been found, Lezzard was handed into the
care of a young medical officer. He would be out of action for
seven weeks. A congenial liability, he cursed his injury for keep-
ing him away from the gaming in Monte Carlo that would be
picking up, he said, once 'this invasion business' was over.[4] Field-
ing was brought to a safe house, the home of the local grocer,
Monsieur Turrel, who had placed his property at the disposal of the
resistance since the start of the war at huge risk to both himself and
his family: the penalty for harbouring a British agent was summary
execution. And yet, 'Monsieur Turrel, fat and jovial in a waistcoat
three sizes too small for him, looked as carefree and contented as
an actor in a documentary film', Fielding thought, as he gratefully
accepted a glass of wine while Turrel's wife went to wake Francis
and Christine.[5]

'She and "Roger" were an imposing pair', Fielding remem-
bered.[6] Knowing Francis's reputation as a heavyweight field agent,
Fielding was somewhat surprised to see him bound into the room
like 'a smiling young giant', with a 'coltish appearance'.[7] It was not
long, though, before he realized that Francis's affability masked
great determination, and that he was a natural leader for whom
'resistance was tantamount to a new religion'.[8] Fielding was more
immediately impressed with Christine, though, whose reputation
had also preceded her, and whose 'heroic attributes' he fancied he
divined at once beneath her 'nervous gestures and breathless man-
ner of speech'.[9] Despite Christine's usual modest camouflage of an
austere blouse and skirt, Fielding was also quick to divine her
'glamorous figure', and decided that her 'short, careless-combed
dark hair and the complete absence of make-up on her delicately
featured face, gave her the appearance of an athletic art-student'.[10]
Christine had learnt to dress so as not to attract attention. 'It's
enough to pin on a flower', she once told a friend, 'for someone to

be able to say: "The woman with the flower".' And yet Fielding, like so many, thought she 'was so pretty that she could attract attention just by dint of that'.[11]

After breakfast the three of them spent the day in the Alpine pastures collecting the heavy containers and packages of supplies that had been dropped with the men that morning. As Francis briefed Fielding about the development and present state of the resistance movement in the region, to Fielding's mounting embarrassment, and Christine's amusement, it soon became evident that there was no obvious task for him to undertake, and Francis could only politely suggest he join a tour of his circuit the next day.

That evening, Christine left for the Italian frontier to organize the defection of the Polish unit at the Larche garrison. Once Fielding and Lezzard's containers had been collected and distributed she saw no point in hanging around. The men also moved on, but only to enjoy an excellent dinner and a comfortable night with Albert, the Jockey circuit's wireless operator, stationed at a house a few kilometres from the village. The following morning they were collected by Claude Renoir, grandson of the Impressionist artist, in his specially licensed Red Cross car. After picking up the injured French commandant, Christian Sorensen, code-name 'Chasuble', who had also trained at Massingham, they set off to meet the local resistance leaders. All the officers had fake identities, ration cards and other false personal papers, and if stopped they were to say that they did not know one another and were simply hitching a lift in one of the few cars on the roads.

It was an idyllic journey and Fielding had to keep reminding himself that he was not on holiday as they toured the dusty villages. Escaping the July sun he sipped wine under plane trees outside cafés while Francis conferred with the local leaders and boasted about the imminent birth of his second child in England. Realizing that he was carrying a suspiciously large amount of money, Fielding doled some out to Francis and Sorensen. His sole concern now was his uncomfortable 'baggy Charlie Chaplin trousers', which he had had to borrow from Monsieur Turrel since they had been unable to find the container with his own clothes and personal equipment.[12]

At about noon the next day the four men heard an air-raid siren as they were approaching the large garrison town of Digne on the return leg of their tour. Knowing that the Wehrmacht tended to man additional roadblocks during a raid, they arranged to meet Renoir at the other side of the town before taking cover with the rest of the local population. With the all-clear they made their way along the busy streets, mingling with the crowds emerging from the shelters, until they met Renoir as agreed. But just a few hundred yards round the next corner they found the road barricaded by soldiers with a sub-machine gun trained on the bridge across the river that they were due to cross. Already sighted, they could not turn back.

Francis was not overly concerned. The soldiers were some of the more than one million 'non-Aryans' – Armenians, Georgians, Mongols, Bosnians, and other men from the Caucasus – that the Nazis had reluctantly enlisted after suffering huge losses on the Russian front in 1942, and who now formed the Oriental Legion Against Communism of the Wehrmacht. None of them seemed to speak either German or French. They ordered Francis and the others out of the car, but after a cursory glance at the proffered identity cards, labour permits and ration coupons, they waved them on.[13] Renoir was just letting go of the clutch when a second car arrived, and Francis breathed 'Gestapo'.

Francis had often dismissed the Wehrmacht rank and file in France as 'extremely incapable'.[14] Officers who could be spared to preserve order in the French countryside were never going to be among the most able of the German ranks, and he had noticed that many were chiefly out for their own financial gain – each arrest meriting 'prize money'.[15] Once, at Avignon station, when some officers were spending rather too long studying his papers, Francis had bitten his lip and spat out some blood on to the platform 'My papers were returned very quickly and I was sent on my way', he later laughed.[16] Indeed there were numerous stories of Nazi incompetence, some more reliable than others, but the occasion that really tickled Francis was when he and a circuit member were stopped for fifteen minutes by specially trained SS troops. An American bomber

had been shot down nearby, the soldiers told them, and they were on the lookout for the crew. Francis's car was comically overloaded, and one of the soldiers now leaned in to poke at the back seat with his bayonet. 'You don't think we've sewn the bomber crew into our seats do you?' Francis's friend had joked. Within minutes they were on their way, the soldiers having failed to notice that the boot was in fact 'so full of arms and explosives that it was weighing down the whole back of the vehicle'.[17] With this in mind, Francis now remained pretty cool. He later claimed that he had never been able to 'identify fear' within himself, and in any case took the hugely practical approach that 'usually it's an advantage not to be moved by anticipation, by something that *might* happen'.[18]

Fielding, however, had not spoken French for several years, even though it was his mother tongue, and was not confident of his ability to bluff the *milicien* collaborator and trained interrogator who now descended from the car. In fact the Gestapo man was not French, but Belgian, and very precise. Horribly aware of an uncontrollable tremor in his right leg, Fielding handed over his wallet again, but was unable to explain why his Algiers-forged work permit, as a clerk at the electricity works in Nîmes, had not been stamped for the current month. As he was escorted to the Gestapo car, the soldier next to the driver turned and covered him with his machine-pistol. Fielding now felt his fear 'take the form of abject loneliness', and he realized to his shame that he was almost consciously longing for his companions to be arrested with him so that he would not have to face whatever was to come entirely alone.[19]

Francis, Sorensen and Renoir appeared completely unconcerned as they showed their documents and emptied their pockets, Francis 'with an expression of surprised amusement on his face', Sorensen 'with a look of contempt'.[20] But the *milicien* was diligent, and noticed that, despite the three passengers' claim that they did not know one another, the banknotes in their wallets were all from the same series. Two minutes later Francis and Sorensen had joined Fielding, leaving Renoir, whose papers were in order and who had not taken a share of the money, to drive back alone and report their arrest.

The three men were taken to Digne prison, 'a dreary barracks of a place' according to Francis, who was finding plenty to fuel his contempt for the Nazis.[21] Having stood for some time facing the courtyard wall with their hands above their heads, they were pushed into a stinking basement cell with four dirty bunks, one already taken, and a small barred window high in the stone wall, with a bucket of excrement and stale urine beneath it. Their cellmate had a heavy German accent, and Francis, insulted by the clumsiness of this attempt to flush them out with a '*mouchard*', or stool pigeon, simply suggested that they try to sleep instead of discussing their situation. After twenty-four hours with no food or water, and – for Francis – as bad if not worse, no cigarettes, they were woken by the metal door scraping open and orders to move.

Their next stop was the elegant Villa Marie-Louise on the outskirts of Digne – Gestapo HQ, and notorious as the place where resistants were taken to be tortured. Here their photographs were taken before they were locked into a first-floor room with another 'inmate'. Some hours later the door was flung open with 'intentional violence' to reveal the man who had arrested them, 'Herr Max . . . standing on the threshold with a theatrically menacing attitude'. He was 'a perfect young Nazi', according to Fielding. 'Blue eyes, fair hair, fresh skin, breeches and jackboots: not a single essential feature was missing from this typical example of Stormtrooper.'[22] In contrast, their interrogator, 'with his grey hair, dark suit and almost benign expression . . . looked rather like a provincial bank-manager'.[23] Francis soon had him down as 'not a very bright chap . . . his questions were stupid, not sharp at all'.[24] First he, then Sorensen, and finally Fielding were interrogated by this violent but inept individual, who hoped to loosen their tongues by punching them in the face and kidneys.

When they found themselves finally alone in their cell, Fielding still shaking, they discovered that all three had 'confessed' to smuggling contraband, a story helped by Fielding's stash of hundreds of the cigarettes that had been dropped with him. The Gestapo had no idea that Francis was British, let alone the notorious 'Roger', the major resistance leader in the region, for whom a

generous reward was offered. 'They were badly informed, no doubt about that', he would later recall. However, he was also aware that they could still be caught out by a call to any of their non-existent employers, and they decided to attempt an escape that evening.[25] The plan was to throttle their room-mate if he returned, break open the shutters and jump from the window – hoping that at least one of them would evade the guard dogs and get away. But before they could act they were moved back to a large cell in the central prison and knew, without being told, that this was the death cell. 'They simply decided that . . . it was better to execute us, and get rid of us', Francis realized. Even though no definite evidence existed, 'we were to be shot as spies . . . That was determined.'[26]

'I kept thinking of the poison tablet sewn into the lapel of the suit I should have been wearing', Fielding later confessed, 'and wondering at what stage of the proceedings I would have nerved myself to swallow it.'[27] Francis did not carry a cyanide pill. He had somewhat recklessly lost the one he was issued with, and had never asked to replace it. As with capital punishment, he was opposed to suicide on principle.

All three men knew that the Allies should now have landed on the Riviera, and that Digne, so near the coast, might be liberated within days. They also appreciated that this meant they were more likely to be shot quickly, perhaps after being tortured to find out what they knew about the invasion plans. Fielding particularly resented the prospect of dying under a false identity, and began to envy the American prisoners in the cell opposite, with their ID tags round their necks. But Francis resolutely refused to think about such things. 'Hours away from execution,' he later recalled rather prosaically, 'all I felt was – what a pity.'[28]

By the time that Christine had arrived back at base, Francis, Fielding and Sorensen had all been condemned to death. She spent the next few days at Monsieur Turrel's house with John Roper, who had just arrived from Briançon, desperately trying to persuade members of the local resistance to form a small commando group and raid the garrison. Christine offered to lead them, and Roper

tried to round up what gold coins and other bribes he could find, but the French commandant reluctantly decided that the risk was too great. It would probably have meant the death of the prisoners anyway, there was neither time nor transport, and, besides, the network was fully focused on preparations for the landings.

Christine was distraught, but never so distracted that she forgot her *raison d'être* in France. As soon as she arrived back at Seyne she had sent messages to the ten new agents dropped during Francis's absence to help subvert the remaining foreign troops within the German army. At a remote chalet the next afternoon she announced that following Roger's arrest she had taken over his work, and had arranged for a lorry to take the latest Jedburgh team to Gilbert Galletti's base at Bramousse, with their heavy kit to follow the next day. She then waited while the equipment was loaded, briefed the guide and the driver and, in view of recent events, passed on details of her key contacts to the new mission's leader in case she herself should be arrested. Christine was a little curter than usual, the new agents reporting that she was clearly working under great difficulties and had had very little sleep and yet, they stressed, 'it is impossible to speak too highly of Pauline's conduct at this time'.[29]

Francis's wife, Nan, nursing their young children alone in Britain, was at least spared Christine's more informed anxiety. 'Very recent news of him is still good', the latest SOE note she had received told her – three days before he was due to be shot.[30]

It was then, learning that Francis and the others were due to be executed on the night of 17 August, that Christine had to decide not only whether to risk her own life, something she had never baulked at, but whether – as a key SOE agent – that risk was justified by the slim likelihood of her plan succeeding. The importance of Francis to the Jockey circuit tipped the balance. 'Roger had the whole organisation at his fingertips', O'Regan agreed. 'His presence was essential.'[31] Christine could rest assured she was acting out of duty, and not just on impulse. Mastering her fear of bicycles, she set off on the twenty-five miles to Digne to check exactly where the men were being held. At first she wobbled and rose heavily on the pedals to climb the hills, before flying down the other side

with the wind whistling past her ears. She would get to know the route, and her calf muscles, very well over the next few days.

Once at Digne, Christine slipped through the prison gates among the daily crowd seeking news of their relatives inside. Circling the inner walls she loudly, if somewhat unharmoniously, hummed the tune of 'Frankie and Johnny', the hit song that she and Francis had often sung together to keep their spirits up. Inspired by the real story of Frankie Baker, who shot her man dead for making love to another woman, Frankie is arrested in the song, and in some versions executed, an irony that is unlikely to have escaped Christine as she paced round Digne prison. She soon heard an echo from Francis inside. 'As far as I was concerned,' he wrote, 'Christine was simply saying "I love you".'[32] But Christine had bigger ambitions.

That afternoon she managed to secure an interview with an Alsatian gendarme called Albert Schenck, who flirted as a double agent while using his languages to act as a liaison officer for the Gestapo, and therefore knew nearly everyone. Christine was aware there was a price on her head, and yet she strode straight into the Gestapo offices at the prison to meet Schenck. It was the sort of encounter that would turn most mouths dry. But it was exactly the kind of situation in which Christine naturally flourished and, almost revelling in the moment, she nearly overdid it.

To justify her interest in Francis without revealing his strategic importance to the resistance, Christine pretended to be his wife. This had always been a possible cover story, and came naturally to her now. Moreover, remembering the impact that being able to reveal she was related to General Horthy had once had in Hungary, she now also claimed, entirely spuriously, to be the niece of Field Marshal Montgomery and, for good measure, a relation of Lord Vansittart as well, whom she had at least met once, in London, in 1939.* As such, she said, she could reliably inform

* Paddy O'Regan was not surprised that the Germans believed these rather wild claims. 'I would have believed anything that Christine told me and done anything she asked. So would and did anyone who knew her', he wrote. His wife, however, pointed out that they would only have had to start speaking in English to catch

Schenck that the Allied landing was imminent, and that he was
due to be 'handed over to the mob'.[33] It was, she later confessed,
'a shot in the dark', but it worked.[34] Schenck told her that the one
person who might be able to help was Max Waem, a Belgian who
acted as an interpreter for the Gestapo. Waem was the young
milicien, a Vichy-French paramilitary officer, who had first arrested
Francis, Sorensen and Fielding, so it did not look promising.
Schenck demanded a huge ransom of two million French francs,
more than he would have earned in twenty years of gendarmerie
service, ostensibly to bribe Waem. Christine agreed, coolly telling
him that if he reneged on the deal she would shoot him, per-
sonally. She then cycled back to Seyne. Radioed by Albert that
evening, Brooks Richards in Algiers arranged to deliver the money
within forty-eight hours; it would be 'the quickest response to a
request ever'.[35] Then he updated London. 'You could have heard
a pin drop' in the British SOE office the next morning, one of the
secretaries remembered.[36]

Two days later, and this time bringing some alcohol for the
guards, Christine again cycled to Digne to meet Schenck, who,
she recalled contemptuously, 'had done nothing'.[37] As the Allies
had finally landed she was able to enjoy terrifying him with exag-
gerated stories of their rapid advance up the Rhône valley, bluffing
about the proximity of American troops and the imminence of
heavy bombardments, and successfully playing on his fears about
retribution after German defeat. Only when she was confident of
his emotional commitment did she hand over the money, ten
bundles of rolled banknotes still in their rubber pouches from the
drop. Schenck then quickly arranged the meeting with Waem for
that afternoon.

As agreed, Christine arrived at Schenck's flat first, masking her
impatience with some difficulty until she heard a car roar up out-
side at about four o'clock. Hearing the men shouting in German,
she suddenly considered throwing her bag out of the window and

Christine out. See Liddell Hart archive, Paddy O'Regan papers; and Mieczysława
Wazacz (director), *No Ordinary Countess* (2010), Ann O'Regan interview.

making a run for it, but she kept her nerve. Waem then joined her, dressed in his Gestapo uniform.

'When he came he at first covered me with his revolver', Christine wrote in her official report, but it was not long before Waem put the gun down on the table between them.[38] As Schenck's wife brought coffee, real coffee, not even mixed with ground acorn, Christine openly told Waem that she was a British officer, parachuted in two years earlier. From her pocket she then produced some (broken) wireless crystals, the carefully calibrated pieces of quartz that make a radio resonate on a particular personal frequency, as evidence that she could make immediate contact with Supreme Allied Command. In sharp contrast to the Wehrmacht, which was increasingly isolated, she clearly had access to both money and communications. 'I began to work upon his fears by telling him of the extreme danger in which he and other collaborators were', Christine continued. Because every line of retreat was blocked by resistance forces, she argued that the garrison at Digne would have to surrender. Waem was well aware that no great number of German troops remained between Digne and the approaching Allied forces. He also knew that Wehrmacht soldiers would be sent to POW camps, to be freed once the war was over. Collaborators like Waem, however, Christine now made clear, would be handed over to the Maquis authorities, who knew that he was 'the chief of the Gestapo and one of the principal torturers', and who 'had a peculiar way of dealing with those found guilty of treachery'.[39]

By now Waem's hands were shaking so badly that he could not pour coffee without spilling it, and at one point he pathetically apologized, suggesting Christine tip the contents of her saucer back into her cup. Pressing home her advantage she quietly continued that Schenck and Waem could only enjoy enemy protection for a few more days at most, but that engineering the release of Francis and his fellow officers would guarantee them safe conduct to the nearest Allied base outside France. 'After three hours of that kind of talk,' she reported bluntly, 'he became obviously terrified.'[40] Finally Waem told her categorically that he would get all three men

released. It was seven in the evening. The execution was set for nine, just two hours away.

Three conditions were attached to Waem's compliance. He was to be saved from the vengeance of the French population; be treated as a free man and not put in a prison or camp; and would be actively rehabilitated by the British government informing the French or Belgian authorities that he had rendered the Allies an important service. He went on to claim that after the war he wished to return to France to convince people of his innocence, and even that he wanted to undertake some dangerous solo mission for the British that might take him into Germany or occupied Holland or Belgium. All of this, Christine could not resist suggesting, he might find difficult. The exact terms of the deal that was struck will never be known but, crucially, in the name of the British authorities, Christine gave her word that once the Allies arrived she would make sure he was protected. Waem nodded his agreement.

On the evening of 17 August, having had 'an ominously good meal' of vegetable soup and brown bread, Francis, Sorensen and Fielding were marched across the prison courtyard in a thin drizzle of rain by Waem, who again had his revolver at the ready.[41] Francis was the last in line and thought, 'this is it. It's something you've looked in the eye ever since you started on this lark. If it's going to be now, it's going to be now.'[42] Then, to his 'silent amazement', Waem complimented Francis on his wife, saying, 'what a wonderful woman you have'.[43] Nonetheless all three men were still sure that they were walking to their execution, especially as Waem now wore a Wehrmacht tunic over his civilian trousers, investing him with the same air of formality and ceremonial gravity, Fielding felt, 'as the black cap on the head of a judge delivering the death sentence'.[44]

Outside the prison gates, expecting to turn towards the football ground, the place used for executions by firing squad, they were surprised to be herded the other way. As the summer sky darkened with an evening storm, Francis realized that now, if ever, was their chance to escape, but after three days with little food or sleep and under the constant threat of death, they lacked the strength to make

a coordinated effort. Certainly for Fielding, events even seemed to be happening outside of himself, as though he were 'a disinterested spectator'.[45]

At last they reached a Citroën, and were sharply ordered to climb in. Slamming the door behind them, Waem got in beside the driver, and at once they were lurching round the nearest corner and heading straight for the roadblock on the edge of Digne. Seeing an official car approaching at high speed with Waem in his uniform leaning out of the front window, the sentries automatically drew back, and the car flashed past into the open countryside. Once round the first bend the Citroën stopped to collect a solitary figure standing silhouetted against the white wall of an isolated farm building. It was Christine. From her harassed expression as she squeezed into the front seat, combined with her lack of eye contact, Francis thought for a moment that she too had been caught and was trying not to betray knowledge of them by the slightest word or gesture. When the car next stopped it was at the edge of a muddy embankment, and here Waem got out and beckoned Fielding to follow him, slithering down to the riverbed. It was only after Fielding had helped to bury Waem's uniform jacket, and Christine turned to smile at him as they returned to the car, that it dawned on him too that this was a rescue.

'Did we say anything to each other?' Francis later looked back at that moment with Christine. 'I don't remember any conversations. Just holding her hand. It was part of the relationship . . . I think she was very much in love with me. And I felt as much for her.' But like Johnnie in the song, Francis had another woman – his wife in England had just given birth to their second daughter. As Christine already understood, and Francis now realized, 'it was, and is possible to be *totally* in love with two people at one and the same time'. Knowing this, talk was superfluous. They simply shared 'very strong feelings, deep emotions . . .'[46]

There were huge celebrations when Francis, Christine, Sorensen and Fielding arrived back at Seyne, with Waem and Schenck in tow. 'We all hugged her in turn', Fielding related proudly, while Francis praised her 'courage and wisdom'.[47] Not only were they

alive and free, but the Allied landings had taken place in the south of France, and American troops now controlled huge stretches of territory moving in from the coast. Francis was euphoric, and immediately threw himself back into finding the best use for the new teams of officers that had parachuted in during his absence. Even so, they all tuned into the stream of BBC personal messages that evening, which, among the many coded calls to action across the south of France – 'There's a rabbit in the garden', 'Jean loves Thérèse', 'My mother is not well' – still managed to fit in the wonderful words, 'Roger est libre; félicitations à Pauline' ('Roger is free, congratulations to Pauline').[48]

Christine concluded her official report with the earnest request 'that my promise to Waem is honoured', adding, 'I feel very strongly about this as Waem undoubtedly saved the lives of Roger, Chasuble and Cathédral'.[49] But her request for an amnesty caused difficulties. Waem 'was one of those most wanted by the Allies', Douglas Dodds-Parker tried to explain, at which point, he noted, 'Christine . . . understandably, blew up'.[50] Unable to meet the conditions she had agreed, Dodds-Parker told her the best he could do was put Waem as top priority for the daily shuttle to France and give him forty-eight hours, a decision for which Christine never forgave him. There are various stories as to what happened to Waem. One account had him 'probably executed by the French'. In another he was handed over to the British Parachute Brigade and sent to Bari in southern Italy, where he reportedly offered to take part in action in the Far East, before being repatriated to Belgium after the war. Other accounts had him 'taken over by the Americans', or being flown to Cairo for interrogation under secret orders from Major General Stawell, head of Special Operations Mediterranean.[51] The French Communists even accused Christine of having engineered Waem's escape, and though this goes too far she was certainly very bitter about his treatment. She had given him her word and it had been betrayed.

Schenck was found murdered shortly afterwards, it was widely presumed for the money, although Christine suspected it was really for his role in 'giving up' people to the Gestapo.[52] Interest-

ingly Christine made no reference to the two million francs in her official report, perhaps wishing to conceal the payment of the bribe, or the failure to later recover it. The following year however, Vera Atkins, Maurice Buckmaster's 'invaluable assistant', traced Mme Schenck, who apparently had no idea of her husband's many roles in the war, but was having difficulty cashing some large notes in post-war banks while being unable to explain how she came by the money. Francis had warned Schenck not to return to his home, advice which it turned out he had ignored, resulting in his prompt execution by members of the resistance. With typical honour, Francis and Christine helped Mme Schenck to return to Alsace with her family, and some money, so she would avoid 'persecution', as Christine put it, for her husband's work first with the Germans and then with the British.[53]

The story of Christine's courageous rescue operation rapidly became the stuff of SOE legend. 'Good reading', one SOE officer hand-wrote on the cover note of Francis's report. 'I am going to make sure that I keep on Christine's side in future.' 'So am I', another scribbled. 'She frightens me to death.'[54] Despite Christine's own quite modest official report, she did allow herself to dress the story up a little for her friends. At first Waem was 'outraged', she told Bill Stanley Moss, 'then threatening, then simply scared stiff'![55] Soon General Stawell was convinced that Christine had faced eight armed Gestapo officers, all 'fully intending to arrest her'.[56] Francis proudly had her telling the Germans that the Allies would be 'shortly shooting up the whole area, and that they and their families would be bombed to pieces'.[57] Douglas Dodds-Parker had her claiming to speak for the king, and as Brooks Richards told it, Christine had claimed that Francis was Winston Churchill's nephew.* Brooks Richards put the rescue down to a combination of the money and Christine's 'presence and her female charms'.[58] Maurice Buckmaster eulogized officially about both Francis's

* This ruse had already been played successfully, with more circumstantial evidence if no more truth, by Odette Sansom. After her arrest Sansom had claimed (falsely) to be fellow agent Peter Churchill's wife and (spuriously) therefore a relation of the British PM. It was a bluff that may have helped to save her life.

'sterling example of courage and reliability' and 'the daring ruse' of his 'lady courier', praising Christine's 'magnificent service' and 'brilliant performance' in securing Francis's release within a few hours through her 'initiative and dogged determination'.[59] He later included a romantic version of the events in one of his published SOE histories. In this telling Christine witnesses Francis's arrest as he leaves a café. Later the two are able to catch a glimpse of each other through an open door at Gestapo HQ. '"My dear Colonel", Christine said shyly,' in Buckmaster's account, '"Everyone knows. If you don't release your prisoner, it will be your funeral. And I mean exactly that . . ."'[60]

The truth was an even better story. Knowing the risk she ran as a British agent whose face and name were already in German files, the woman who had once been too shy to talk to her friend's handsome brother and his intimidating fiancée in British Cairo had walked straight into Gestapo headquarters in German-controlled France and demanded the release of three captured British and French officers with nothing but her own bravado and some broken radio crystals in her bag. On paper it looked suicidal. 'The way she handled these thugs, whom I had had occasion to meet myself, and who were entirely without normal human reactions, was unbelievably skilful', Francis testified two months later.[61] 'It was a tremendous bluff by a very, very courageous lady . . . she took voluntarily one chance in one hundred. Undoubtedly if it had not come off she would have been shot with us.'[62] To which Fielding, who would later dedicate his own war memoir to Christine, added, 'fortunately her courage was matched by her wits'.[63] In the words of General Stawell's citation for Christine's award for bravery, her 'nerve, coolness and devotion to duty and high courage . . . must certainly be regarded as one of the most remarkable personal exploits of the war'.[64]

Once the Allies had got through the southern coastal defences after the 15 August landings, they made their way quickly up the country. Some of the units followed Havard Gunn, either driving a little Fiat while dressed in full uniform with kilt, or sitting in a café with his feet on the table, waiting for the columns to catch him up. 'There

was no real resistance', Gunn reported. Progress was greatly supported by the work of the Maquis, both in uprooting the anti-glider stakes, known as 'Rommel's asparagus', designed to prevent the arrival of enemy air support, and in harassing the German retreat and even trapping some of the smaller garrisons that had been left isolated. Small groups of troops now began to surrender indiscriminately. Boys of fourteen and grandmothers in headscarves were seen with anything up to twenty German prisoners in tow. Francis's men covered the more dangerous right flank of the forces advancing towards the northern borders of Italy, and were soon in control of the hugely strategic Route Napoléon from Cannes to Grenoble. His organization was of 'inestimable value to the allied armies', SOE later recorded.[65] By 17 August the American general Patch had landed unopposed at Saint-Tropez with 100,000 men and 10,000 vehicles, and started driving north, quickly outflanking the residual German presence. 'Basically,' Gunn said, 'the Germans realized the war was over.'[66]

Digne was liberated two days after Christine's rescue operation, and she, Francis and Fielding joined the celebrations as the town applauded the Americans, some of whom drove by standing up in their cars, lapping up their warm reception. Lezzard, now officially a casualty of war, sat in a chair in the main street, where a queue of women lined up to kiss the injured hero. A few streets further up Fielding noticed a different procession had been organized, in which the main participants were being made to parade in front of a jeering crowd. At first, as their heads had been shaved, he could not tell if those being humiliated were men or women: 'sullen creatures ... they looked like frightened lunatics'.[67] But their half-dressed state soon revealed them to be women, each being punished for having spent some nights in the arms of a German soldier. It was a depressing scene soon being enacted across France, sometimes more horrifically with swastikas branded on the women's cheeks, as long-suppressed sorrows, political rivalries and petty score-settling surfaced in the first weeks of liberation.

On 20 August, Francis and Christine, driving a borrowed jeep and looking rather scruffy in makeshift uniforms 'with all kinds of

insignia, pips on one shoulder and none on the other', presented themselves to the American General Butler at Sisteron.[68] Their attire was far from unusual among their fellow British officers, who were standardly sent in with just a pair of boots, blue pants and vest, uniform, and an army groundsheet with a collar sewn on it so it could be worn as a mackintosh when required, and who had often lost much of that after a few weeks in the field. The Americans had arrived in 'gorgeous uniforms', complete with peaked caps, 'sun-tanned' shirts, rain-covers and macs.[69] To their eyes Francis and Christine did not look as if they represented much of a fighting force, and their offer of continued help met a curt response. 'He told me to bugger off, he didn't want anything to do with private armies [or] bandits, and turned back to his maps', Francis recorded furiously.[70] He and Christine, her quick temper ever sensitive to insult, had to be calmed down by one of the general's intelligence aides, who apologized, explaining that as there were still so few official reports of the role played by the resistance the general preferred to deal only with French military officers. As a result General Butler lost the support of the one Allied officer with years of experience in France and an unequalled knowledge of the area and its people.

Learning that the Americans' next move was to liberate Gap, Francis and Christine decided to get there first. They arrived ahead of the US forces only to discover that the Wehrmacht troops had already surrendered to a member of Francis's network, and had been herded into a cinema where they were being guarded by boy scouts while the resistance groups congregated to celebrate in the main square. Francis and Christine joined the party, and late that evening they stole back to their jeep, took off the handbrake, and rolled down the steep hillside, laughing all the way like a couple of kids. When American tanks arrived the next day there was nothing for them to do except to organize a parade.

A last German counter-attack the following morning lasted less than fifteen minutes. Three hundred men were captured, raising the local total to over a thousand – a logistical nightmare. Learning that several hundred of these were Poles, Christine was delighted to be

given a megaphone by a US captain and invited to address the men in their native language as they sat lined up on the bank of a river. 'She asked them if they were willing to fight with us', Francis recalled, and then told them that as, under the Geneva Convention, they could not fight in a foreign uniform, they would have go naked to the waist – at which hundreds of soldiers started to rip off their vests and shirts. 'They tore them off, exultant! Col de Larche all over again.'[71] But General Butler would not countenance this approach, and threatened to have Christine and Francis arrested and court-martialled if they did not leave immediately. 'Perhaps Butler simply didn't like our faces', Francis mused, but taking him at his word they moved on to report to General Patch at Draguignan.[72]

As the Allies continued their advance, liberating Avignon on 25 August, the German retreat was hugely hampered by the resistance. Francis's network now not only successfully held the entire Route Napoléon, but also closed off German access to the Alpine frontier passes. The Allies arrived at Grenoble within seven days, almost without any fighting. The local Wehrmacht surrender was accepted by the French commander Huet, the former military leader of the Vercors. Recognizing this extraordinary achievement, General Patch asked Francis and Christine to act as his liaison team with the resistance forces in the area.

The outcome of the invasion was no longer in doubt, least of all to the Nazis. Francis and Christine drove their open-topped jeep along roads bordered by piles of burnt and abandoned military equipment. None of the French guarding the columns of hundreds of prisoners that they passed had met any threats from enemy forces moving in the other direction, and there was no information on troop movements at any of the new town authorities on their route. Within two weeks French section FANYs from Massingham, who had sung the Marseillaise in Algiers as the first Allied troops landed in southern France, were heading towards the bomb-pockmarked runway at Aix-en-Provence. From here they drove to Avignon, the new international HQ. 'All along the route we were constantly stopped by excited groups of resistance workers, most of them armed with a motley selection of guns and all of them prepared to

fire if the answers were not in order', one FANY recorded. 'It was a hair-raising progress.'[73] But for Francis and Christine the immediate action in France was over, and they knew that their own intimate partnership would also soon be a thing of the past.

Arriving at a joyous, liberated Lyon, Christine was delighted to meet old friends including John Roper, who was clearly still deeply in love with her and very glad to find her in one piece, and Peter Storrs, who described her as looking 'very attractive, in a slim-greyhound sort of way'.[74] Even Sylviane Rey was there, having been liberated while still nursing wounded maquisards in the Vercors. Despite the long summer months working in the open, Sylviane's pale skin seemed untouched by the sun, but she had developed the 'sad amused smile' that was common to many veterans of the resistance.[75] Now she laughingly pointed out that Christine and Francis had arrived in a car with the number-plate 'MI5'. But the many friends who could not join them meant that celebrations were inevitably muted. Gubbins estimated that the resistance alone had lost 24,000 people, but, sitting in his Baker Street office, he neatly concluded that 'France had regained her soul.'[76]

'There were parties,' Francis remembered, 'but it wasn't feasting. The war was still going on.'[77] Above all, 'the tragedy of Poland', now suffering horrific losses as the citizens of Warsaw joined the underground Home Army in house-to-house fighting against the German occupiers, 'was driving Christine mad with impotence and impatience.'[78] Francis understood that Christine was 'passionately Polish', and felt her obligation to her country 'profoundly'.[79] As the people of Paris, Lyon, Avignon, and even tiny Saint-Julien-en-Vercors were toasting their liberators, in Warsaw thousands of Polish resistance fighters and civilians were still battling Wehrmacht troops. Being surrounded by cheering crowds, women throwing flowers and men handing out glasses of wine was a bittersweet experience for Christine. She was delighted to have helped defeat a common enemy and bring freedom to the French, but she could not help but be disappointed that she was not walking down a Polish street, wasn't bringing freedom to her people and her country, and that this was not the fulfilment of her dreams.

After forty-eight hours, Christine, Francis, Sorensen and Field-
ing reported to the Bristol Hotel in Paris for debriefing. Keen to
reclaim French national pride, de Gaulle had demanded the imme-
diate repatriation of British SOE officers, and brought FFI forces
under fresh army control. Roper had already driven north on his
motorbike. Fielding was posted back to Greece.* Sorensen took a
senior intelligence post in the city, and later became the mayor of
Algiers. Colonel Zeller, who had fought with Francis and Christine
in the Vercors, became the military governor of Paris. Christine
and Francis remained in the capital for a few days, meeting up with
friends and comrades. 'Paris was enjoying a brief revival of her old
self. There was . . . a sparkle and a gaiety that Parisians had not
known for a long time', wrote Laura Foskett, Christine's former
Cairo flatmate, who now also found herself in the capital.[80] But
although Paris 'seemed to be full of ex-spies', Foskett quickly saw
that Christine was finding it hard to adjust to the peace. 'She came
to Paris in search of new lovers and adventures', Foskett surmised,
perhaps unfairly, with a mixture of admiration and sympathy.[81]

Christine was not at a loose end, however. The immediate thrill
of clandestine resistance might be over, but she and Francis now
wanted to help set the record straight about the support that
members of the Jockey circuit had rendered to the resistance, which,
during the war, had had to be kept secret from their own com-
munities. They also started to distribute SOE funds to the families
and widows of those who had worked with SOE units and did not
initially qualify for French help. Later Francis would come back to
France on a 'Judex' mission to ensure that the families of those who
had helped the resistance were fully recognized and supported. He
also tried to help set the record straight for Pierre Agapov, his
former deputy who faced prosecution for informing under torture,

* Xan Fielding later returned to Digne as an adviser for the film of Bill Stanley
Moss's book, *Ill Met By Moonlight*. When the film team discovered that their hotel was
adjacent to the building where Fielding had been interrogated, they suggested moving
at once. Fielding laughed it off, saying he was glad to be back under such different
circumstances. 'This calls for a bottle of champagne', Dirk Bogarde responded. See
Daphne Fielding, *The Nearest Way Home* (1970).

and helped Albert, his radio operator, to trace his wife and daughter, both of whom had survived their incarceration in the camps.

With former resistants finally able to speak openly, Francis suddenly found himself heralded as a great man and Christine, his assistant, as a 'magnificent woman'.[82] Neither of them had sought or desired such praise, but for many Francis was as a brother or an uncle, and their doors would always be open to him. He was deeply moved, and maintained strong ties with the families he had once worked with, later making his home with them in the south of France.* Christine, however, shared none of Francis's feeling of belonging, or sense of closure. They had shared something fabulous in France, and his friendship was something she would always prize. But the liberation celebrations, and the many small dinners and tributes they received locally, brought home to her the great difference between them. To the people of France, and to some extent even to Francis himself, what mattered was that Christine was a woman of great determination and courage. Her endearing accent might have been Polish, or she might have been Irish, British or even French; her actions completely transcended the question of her nationality. But to Christine, she herself, her determination and her courage were all Polish. And, for her, the war was far from won.

In September, Christine finally hitched a lift on a small British plane flying to London. She was pleased to be wearing some new nylon stockings, then 'as rare as snowballs in summer', that had been given to her by Sylviane, and she was carrying the few British gold sovereigns she had not been able to put to good use.[83] To witness celebrations in Poland similar to those taking place across France was perhaps a wish too far, but Christine was determined to now at least play a useful role in the liberation of her own country.

* Francis stayed in touch with Vercors veteran Daniel Huillier, whose father had been 'like a brother' to him, sending a bottle of 'Don Chevalier Huillier' Bordeaux wine every year. Daniel remembered that in his last letter Francis 'considered himself French, he wasn't with you foreigners. He considered himself French'. M. R. D. Foot mentioned that at one point Claude Renoir gave Francis one of his grandfather's paintings, though Francis's daughter, Joanna, had not heard of this.

14: MISSION IMPOSSIBLE

'Please allot a code name urgently to Miss Christine Granville, who has been chosen to act as a courier in Poland', an SOE memo of 9 November 1944 requested.[1] 'Anxious for further work in the field', Christine had volunteered to join three mission teams of British officers who were to be dropped into Nazi-occupied Poland to observe political conditions and attempt the rescue of prisoners held in German camps.[2] Her proposal was gratefully accepted, and supported by both the British and the increasingly desperate Polish special services. She had been in Britain for less than a month.

Christine had spent a miserable first night in London, pacing the wet September pavements and sitting for a while on a doorstep in Regent's Street, as she refused to use the last of the SOE gold to pay for a room. She then moved into John Roper's flat, which she shared with his aunt and, more conveniently, his cook. When that felt too crowded she stayed with the O'Malleys at their London house in Cheyne Walk. Roper was also in London, and within a few days both they and Francis visited SOE HQ in Orchard Court, just off Baker Street, to file their reports and be debriefed. Punctual as she was, Christine's reputation preceded her. 'All the bigwigs wanted to question her', Noreen Riols, one of the SOE secretaries, remembered. 'She was known to be an incredible woman.'[3] Among those assessing Christine was Maurice Buckmaster, the Head of F (French) Section, who was particularly keen to hear the story of Francis's rescue, and to praise what he called Christine's 'wonderful record' of service.[4] Vera Atkins, Buckmaster's level-headed assistant, was more critical in her appraisal, finding Christine 'very brave, very attractive, but a loner

and a law unto herself'.*[5] Riols was more interested in what Christine wore: a well-cut tweed skirt, casually tailored open shirt and smart suede jacket. She looked 'rather sporty', with her hands in her pockets, but was distinguished, Riols decided, by her 'casual elegance'.[6] Christine was dressed like a typical well-to-do English-woman of the time, just up from the country, an image also cultivated by Atkins, who was usually found in 'a twin set or tweed'.[7] In fact both women came from part-Jewish families in Eastern Europe and, consciously or not, were repositioning themselves in wartime London. As Christine had arrived with no papers, she had to resubmit her personal details. With an eye to the uncertain future, she quietly listed her place of birth as 'London', appropri-ately entering it beside her equally fictitious date of birth.[8]

Christine did not feel much at home in London, however. Among her SOE friends there, Roper was still half in love with her, but had a local girlfriend and described his relationship with Christine as an exceptionally close 'straight friendship'. 'It would be absurd to say that her beauty added nothing', he qualified, but 'the fact of the matter was she was an exceptional person with an exceptional capacity for friendship'.[9] Francis, meanwhile, had quickly left London to be reunited with Nan and his two young daughters and, although he and Christine always met when he was in town, their relationship would never be the same. A greater advocate of full disclosure than Christine, Francis told Nan about their affair, and even asked if she would be happy for him to continue it. She told him that she would not. Francis had imagined Nan's war to have been 'utterly empty . . . except for the babies', while he felt that his own life had been expanded in every direc-tion.[10] Now he learned that she too had had an affair, with his own conducting officer, who would not return from active service. Somehow they had to find a way of rebuilding their marriage.

* Vera Atkins had a reputation for excellent judgement. Her eyebrows were 'as poised as a Georgian candelabra', one agent recalled, while Riols found her 'terrifying . . . very formidable' and only dared call her by her first name when they were both in their seventies, and then 'only at Vera's insistence'. George Millar, *Maquis* (1946), p. 19; Noreen Riols interview (October 2011).

Francis did, once, introduce Nan to Christine, contact that he felt to be 'necessary', but it was brief and never repeated.[11]

Christine's focus was now entirely on Poland. A national 'Rising', timed to coincide with a major landing of regular forces or Western air support for a final push to freedom, had always been on the Polish agenda. By July 1944 the Red Army, now officially Poland's ally, was marching from Russia to Berlin on its 'westward flood', as Gubbins ominously put it, and advancing rapidly towards Warsaw 'like a swift rising tide'.[12] The Polish Home Army aided their progress by attacking the German rear, and vital road and rail communications. At the end of the month Soviet troops had reached the River Vistula and the 'sound of Russian guns could be heard in Warsaw'.[13] The timing seemed compelling. Nazi Germany was still reeling from a bomb plot against Hitler; the Soviets had reversed the German advance; France was fighting towards liberation; and British SOE missions were increasing.* Britain had warned Poland that flight logistics prevented them from sending in the Polish Parachute Brigade or significant arms, or even from bombing German airfields. However, for some years, Wilkinson later confessed, SOE had been so deeply committed to the Polish cause that 'we funked facing them with the realities of their situation', making the limits of British support now hard to digest.[14] The citizens of Warsaw were impatient for action, hoping to welcome the Soviets into their capital as free citizens, and in late July the Polish government-in-exile authorized General Bór-Komorowski, commanding the Home Army, to announce a Warsaw Rising at his discretion. The Polish premier, Stanisław Mikołajczyk, then flew to Moscow to win Stalin's support for what they hoped would be a short and decisive action. On 29 July, Moscow Radio broadcast an appeal for the citizens of Warsaw to rise up against their German oppressors, urging that 'there is not a moment to lose'.[15]

On Tuesday 1 August, a light rain fell across Warsaw as women 'bustled along the pavements' carrying bundles of pistols and

* Colonel Claus von Stauffenberg attempted to assassinate Hitler on 20 July 1944. The plot failed and he was executed by firing squad shortly afterwards.

ammunition, while boys and girls 'shouldered rucksacks full of medical supplies and food' on their way to rallying points across the city.[16] At five in the afternoon the Home Army attacked, forcing the occupying Wehrmacht troops out of large sections of the capital. Their aim was to hold their ground for four or five days until Soviet reinforcements were negotiated. After nearly five years of occupation, much of Warsaw was suddenly a free city. The Polish flag was hung from buildings and the national anthem and other patriotic songs were broadcast through the streets. The sense of euphoria carried across Europe to Christine in France, who used the news to press home her arguments with the Polish troops forced into service with the Wehrmacht in the Alps, and later with the Polish prisoners-of-war held at Gap. Before she left France six weeks later, however, reports were coming in of huge Polish military and civilian losses.

The Polish Home Army had around 45,000 soldiers in the Warsaw district, mostly armed with pistols and grenades. But there were few heavy weapons. They faced a well-trained German formation of around 25,000 men, armed to the teeth and supported by artillery, Panzer divisions and the Luftwaffe. 'The action of the Poles is a blessing', Himmler reported to Hitler. 'We shall finish them off . . . Warsaw will be liquidated.'[17] Hitler responded by ordering 'every inhabitant to be killed . . . no prisoners to be taken . . . every single house to be blown up and burned'.[18] On 5 August, German troops attacked the city's western suburbs, sending units from house to house to shoot the inhabitants regardless of age or gender, in an attempt to crush the Poles' will to fight. Estimates of those killed within a few short days range from 20,000 to 60,000 people, among them shopkeepers, office workers, the elderly, and mothers with their children.

After a direct appeal to Churchill from the Polish president, on the night of 4/5 August fourteen RAF bombers flew from Italy to Warsaw. 'As the epic battle raged on, we did everything in our power to assist', Gubbins later wrote, but, although a limited amount of equipment and ammunition was dropped successfully to the insurgents, the high casualty rate forced the air commander-in-

chief, John Slessor, to cancel further flights.[19] His ban was rescinded after huge pressure from the Polish aircrews under his command. The pilots who had fought so bravely and effectively for the Allies in the Battle of Britain refused to be forbidden to fly to the aid of their own nation and people. 'Cannot accept RAF losses of 50% as being unacceptable, there are times when 100% is necessary', General Tatar, the Polish deputy commander for home affairs, based in London, supported his men. 'We do not ask for British crews, but Polish ones.'[20] Polish, British and South African aircrews went back into action, but losses mounted, and although the few successful drops brought hope to the insurgents they were far too few to affect the eventual outcome. Two weeks later any further flights were banned.

Churchill now appealed to Stalin for aid, or at least for the use of Soviet air space and airfields where RAF planes could land and refuel. Stalin refused, responding that 'the information given to you by the Poles is greatly exaggerated and unreliable . . .'[21] Having reached the banks of the River Vistula, only a few hundred yards from the action, the Red Army now abruptly came to a halt and stood idle for six weeks while Stalin denounced the revolt as the work of 'criminals' that was 'doomed to fail'.[22] The Soviets blamed military difficulties for their sudden lack of progress, but the real reasons behind what Gubbins called their 'callous and calculated refusal' to advance were political.[23] Stalin had no intention of relieving Warsaw while the Germans were doing such a good job of weakening Polish resistance. In late July he had appointed what the Soviets called the 'Lublin Polish Committee of National Liberation', as a rival authority to the Polish government-in-exile. This new Communist-backed 'government' took its seat in Soviet-liberated Lublin on the first day of the Warsaw Rising, leaving little doubt as to Stalin's intentions for post-war Poland.

Stalin, Roosevelt and Churchill had in fact already mapped out Poland's future at the Tehran conference of November 1943, at which Polish leaders were not present. Unknown to Christine in Algiers as she trained to drop into France, or to Poles fighting beside the British for what they believed to be a common cause,

the conference did not recognize Poland's territorial claims to its pre-war borders, and only Churchill committed himself to Polish independence. Roosevelt was angling for Soviet support in the Far East, and was almost literally already in bed with Stalin, having turned down an offer of hospitality at the British Legation in favour of an invitation from the Russians. At the end of the conference Stalin got out a map and the 'Big Three' carved up Poland along the 'Curzon' line, which was soon being described in *The Times* as 'the old Polish frontier'.[24] 'I have intense sympathy for the Poles . . .', Churchill told Parliament, 'but I also have sympathy with the Russian standpoint'.[25] A few idealists, such as Sir Owen O'Malley, who argued that the real choice was between 'selling the corpse of Poland to Russia' or 'putting the points of principle to Stalin in the clearest possible way and warning him that our position might have to be explained publicly with equal clearness', presented only the politest of threats.[26] Tehran had shown Stalin that he had nothing to fear from either Britain or the USA.

By the second week of August it was clear that, far from being a decisive action, the Warsaw Rising had descended into a relentless battle of attrition. Street barricades were built from rubble and broken furniture, pavements were torn up and trenches dug. Families of all social classes were caught in the fighting, lugging suitcases, blankets and food between the soldiers and the ruined buildings, and begging the fighters not to pull back. The resistance units were hugely resourceful, brilliantly improvising defences and weaponry, and supported by an efficient auxiliary service largely run by women and children. But medical supplies quickly ran out and dysentery was rife, food was scarce and horses, cats and dogs were soon being eaten. Day after day, despite their almost unbreakable spirit, Christine's compatriots were being slaughtered in scores on the hastily constructed barricades, and in the streets and ruins of their city. The Germans advanced steadily, demolishing buildings and mowing down the insurgents in the streets and courtyards by machine gun until there were tens of thousands of corpses across the city. The 'worst of all', wrote John Ward, the only British

officer on the ground in Warsaw, 'is the smell of rotting bodies, which pervades over the whole of the city centre'.[27]

Soon the insurgents took to navigating the city through its claustrophobic network of pitch-black sewers, the only safe route between the increasingly isolated pockets of Home Army personnel. At one point 1,500 fighting men, 2,000 walking wounded and 500 civilians including nurses and stretcher cases were navigating the filthy tunnels, slipping on the curved brick floors, wading through waste up to their shoulders – many drowning – while the enemy threw grenades down manholes and booby-trapped or blocked the exits. Sometimes the soldiers emerged from hours underground only to be rounded up at gunpoint as the German line advanced.

'We do not ask for equipment', the Home Army now desperately radioed London, keenly feeling the apparent injustice of failing to receive significant Allied support in their hour of need. 'We demand its immediate dispatch.'[28] Britain had warned the Poles that significant support could come only from the Soviets, and one Polish major now resigned in protest at the Polish administration in London continuing to give the Home Army too much reason to hope for material aid. His fears were borne out when Stalin's promised support arrived in mid-August, with the drop of hundreds of leaflets encouraging the population to cease resistance and describing the Rising as the work of an irresponsible clique who would be punished for provoking civilian deaths.

When the Russians continued to refuse the Allies air clearance, Polish aircrews insisted on resuming flights from Bari, in the heel of Italy, 960 miles as the crow flies and much of that directly over Germany. Fighter protection for the bombers was out of the question and, flying both to the limit of their planes' capacity and low over Warsaw's rooftops in the teeth of intense anti-aircraft fire, they sustained huge losses for minimal impact. 'You could see Warsaw from miles away, burning', one pilot recorded, while another remembered that those who returned arrived in planes 'holed like sieves' and branded the missions a 'suicidal waste of airmen'.[29] As their commander continued to demand 'the utmost

will-power and self-sacrifice', one Polish crew managed to make a further successful drop of supplies. The general rang to award the pilot the Virtuti Militari, but the whole crew had been burnt in the wreckage of their plane, which fell on roofs of Warsaw's Old Town.[30] 'The Poles just really committed suicide in an effort to . . . send supplies to Warsaw', one FANY wrote in distress.[31] Two squadrons of British Liberators followed, but when they arrived Warsaw was in flames. Only in mid-September did Stalin relent on air clearance and permit one group of American bombers to land. He even allowed Soviet supply drops, knowing it was too late. 'The relatively small amount of real help given is humiliating', Douglas Dodds-Parker wrote, voicing the thoughts of many in SOE.[32]

It was while 'Warsaw was', as Francis succinctly phrased it, 'blowing up', that Christine had arrived in London.[33] Her immediate instinct was literally to fly to the aid of her friends, family and country. Noreen Riols watched her storm into the SOE offices and demand to be parachuted back into Poland. 'She presented her request as a fait-accompli', Riols said, asking not whether but when it would happen.[34] The British hummed and hawed, not committing themselves either way. Riols assumed that they had no intention of sending Christine back, but in fact there was a possibility – not to drop her on to the burning roofs of Warsaw, but for her to join a long-anticipated uniformed military mission to Poland.

In February 1944 Stanisław Mikołajczyk, the Polish prime minister-in-exile, had written personally to Churchill, asking for a team of observers to be sent to the Home Army. This was not a new idea; Andrzej for one had discussed it with a key Polish courier when he had been in London at the end of 1943. The plan was to provide Britain and the USA with an independent source of intelligence on the situation inside Poland, while monitoring the shifting balance of power within the country and relations between the Home Army, the Wehrmacht and, later, the Red Army. As the months passed, the Polish émigré community in Britain maintained that the advancing Russians were arresting and liquidating Polish resistance soldiers as they came out to welcome them. Even John Ward, hiding in a safe house, described the first Russian forces as

'very drunk . . . they appeared to beat Polish men without provocation and some were shot'. Within a few days 'they had raped every female in the district over fourteen years of age'.[35] But the British foreign secretary, Anthony Eden, refused to consider any mission to observe 'political conditions' without Soviet approval, which was not forthcoming. Undeterred, Gubbins and SOE pursued the idea, getting ready for immediate action once clearance arrived. At the beginning of September, Churchill scribbled a note: 'This is a good idea, why not?'[36] A few weeks later Harold Perkins, Christine's old friend 'Perks', who was now the head of SOE's Central Europe section, received a pencil note saying simply, 'mission granted'.[37]

The plan was to drop three teams into Poland under the code-names Freston, Fernham and Flamstead. Freston was purely an observation mission, but the other teams were also briefed for the armed liberation of Polish prisoner-of-war and forced-labour camps. As Soviet troops advanced, huge numbers of prisoners were being marched west by the Germans, killed in reprisals or shot so that they could not testify. Christine was to serve as the courier liaison officer between the three missions, dropping with either the first or second team. Her role was to advise the officers on the political conditions and personalities in their areas, and to explain – 'without prejudice to her own position' – British policy regarding Poland. 'It is realized that this is a very difficult task', her briefing paper informed her. 'However, it is hoped that the Poles may be brought to an understanding of the expediency of the suggested solution.'[38] Christine was in effect being asked in part to serve as an apologist for the British policy of asking the Poles to welcome the Soviet advance. 'The Poles in Poland may be ill-informed . . .', an addendum struggled to qualify the position; the missions were to bring an understanding of 'the conditions ruling in world-wide politics today . . .'[39] As Christine was to report back by wireless, she was then given her own ciphers and, in keeping with the over-all theme of the operation, she was allotted the code-name 'Folkestone'.[40]

The Warsaw Rising ended only when all hope was lost, on

3 October 1944, after sixty-three days of intensive street fighting. As well as German losses, more than 18,000 resistants and 180,000 civilians had been killed.[41] In the last hours before capitulation tens of thousands of people fled into the countryside, many re-forming to fight on. Others were forced to surrender, held prisoner or dispatched to Germany as forced labour. General Bór-Komorowski was arrested and imprisoned in Colditz. Violating the terms of the surrender, German demolition squads then systematically dynamited those buildings still standing in the city. Over the course of the next four weeks they murdered another 33,000 Jews in camps across Poland.

The Rising had not been entirely without military impact, which almost added to the tragedy. Many much-needed divisions of the Wehrmacht had been tied to the city, sustaining heavy losses while unable to fight either on the Western Front against the Allies or in the East against the Red Army. 'What the Polish Home Army achieved with heroic bravery . . . represented an important contribution to the Allied victory,' Gubbins wrote, 'but especially to the Russian victory.'[42] Christine was determined that this should not be the final epitaph for Poland's war. There was still much to be fought for, and both the Poles and SOE were increasingly desperate to send in Freston and its sub-missions while there was still hope for an independent future for Poland.

Christine was confirmed for the operation, and after some lobbying she managed to get John Roper selected as a member of Fernham, the second mission team.[43] Her thoughts had also turned to Andrzej, now based in the Italian town of Bari, the centre of SOE activities directed towards Poland. On 19 October, Andrzej arrived in London and they had an emotional reunion. By the time he returned to Bari, two weeks later, he too was approved to drop with the Fernham team. Despite group briefings, his fellow team members never knew he had an artificial leg. The Freston team meanwhile, dressed in 'splendid fur-collared coats', was ready to drop, but it was repeatedly delayed by bad weather.[44]

At last allowing herself to believe, for the first time in months, that she was going home, Christine once again gave Poland as her

place of birth on the mission 'vetting forms'.[45] A week later Perkins sent a 'Top Secret' letter to General Tatar informing him of the mission and of Christine's 'special role'. 'I believe you are already conversant with her activities', Perkins wrote, knowing that Christine had long been *persona non grata* with the Poles. 'I would only state that she is one of the most intelligent and courageous operators with whom it has been my pleasure to work . . . and understands [the British] character and temperament as well as she understands that of her own people.'[46] Tatar ran the plan past the Polish administration and confirmed their support, hoping the missions would validate their demands for weapons, get the Home Army recognized as an official Allied Force, and provide independent witnesses to the atrocities taking place.

Although MI5 had already given Christine clearance in 1940, she was 'put through the cards' again, and on 21 November 1944 she was granted an honorary commission in the Women's Auxiliary Air Force and matching WAAF identity papers. SOE had described her as 'one of the most distinguished of our female agents' and 'a woman of very considerable influence . . . [who] should not be treated as a junior officer'.[47] As a result she was given the rank of Flight Officer, the equivalent of a Flight Lieutenant, although, irritatingly, no grant to pay for the uniform.

That same day Christine flew to Bari, buttoned up in her new uniform, and with John Roper at her side. She was delighted to see Andrzej's Opel at the airport. Although Andrzej thought Christine looked terribly thin, 'a bag of bones' as he called her, she was also 'glowing with success' at having engineered their return to Poland.[48] But Christine did not stay long. Her knowledge of her country and the Polish administration was needed back in London, and she returned a few days later leaving the men to check into the *trullo*, the conical stone house, traditional to Puglia, where they were to be lodged until the operation got final clearance. The worst winter in thirty years was just setting in.

The SOE base at the little fishing port of Monopoli, halfway between Bari and Brindisi, had been set up in late 1943, mainly by experienced hands from Algiers and Cairo. As soon as the Brindisi

airbase was secured, the 'handsome and dashing' colonel Henry Threlfall was sent out as commander, reporting to Perkins.[49] For a while Andrzej had served as Threlfall's liaison officer at a Polish training school, and the two men had formed a strong friendship. Throughout the Warsaw Rising, Threlfall had fought a desperate battle to get more support sent to the insurgents, constantly pressing the Polish point of view with the Air Force authorities. It was, he said, 'exhausting and heart-breaking' work that brought limited results.[50] Eventually he was reprimanded for submitting 'undesirable memoranda . . . which are essentially political in character'.[51] Undeterred, he now turned to supporting plans for Freston and its sub-missions.

The prospects for the operation improved in December, prompting Christine to make financial arrangements for an elderly Skarbek aunt living in France. Touchingly she also specified that 'if a sum of money is needed' it should be given to her husband Jerzy Gizycki, who, she was informed, had applied for aid to the Association of Polish War Refugees in Montreal, Canada.[52] Francis once said that Christine 'had no interest in money, for her it did not exist', but she also clearly had no illusions about the personal risks her mission involved, and wanted to settle her affairs as best she could.[53] She was now on a tax-free salary of £511.12.0 per annum, well above the national average and at the high end of the scale for a female agent. When she had been in France her expenses had been fully covered, so she had built up some savings. Now she would receive not only her salary but also danger and field pay. And yet she tried to secure even more. 'The claim for clothing lost by enemy action amounting to (gross) £240.7.0 is out of all proportion for such losses which can be allowed . . . The items included therein are on a luxury scale both as to quality and quantity', the finance department informed her curtly when she submitted a 'Misadventures of Jane' style claim for lost outfits.[54] Given Christine's penchant for a few plain skirts and well-cut shirts, she was definitely trying it on, but she received £155, to include her RAF outfit grant, while a junior officer reporting to Dodds-Parker was quizzed more thoroughly as to 'the circumstances leading to the loss of Miss

Granville's Operational clothes'.[55] Meanwhile, on 23 December, Christine signed out two white diamonds, $1,000 in gold, $500 in bills, and some thick Polish winter clothes for her 'Folkestone' mission.[56]

SOE knew, however, that Christine's worth was not all tied up in diamonds and lost dresses. Accordingly, they now attempted to extract what further value they could from their asset, inviting her input into a new 'Agent Training Manual', and arranging for her to liaise with the Polish Military at their London headquarters, where Christine was now received with the 'greatest respect' and the traditional kiss on the hand accorded by Polish gentlemen to ladies in lieu of a simple handshake.[57]

Finally, just after Christmas, the long-awaited signal that the missions could drop without Stalin's authority came through. The teams now hoped that their reports would show 'how the British government could best help the Poles in the face of increasing Russian pressure to abandon them'.[58] In the days before they left, the four officers of the Freston team, under the 'resourceful [and] highly experienced' Colonel D. T. Hudson, who had previously carried out a similar mission in Yugoslavia, learned new codes, drew their personal arms, and were issued with their cyanide tablets 'in an atmosphere of grim and silent sympathy'.[59] Moments later these lethal pills became muddled up with their aspirins and they were forced to destroy the lot.*

On the night of 26/27 December 1944, Hudson assembled his men for a cold but traditional Christmas dinner on the edge of the airfield before leaving, but atmospheric conditions again prohibited take-off. The SOE London office sent them consolatory Christmas cakes and a letter with Christine, who flew to Bari the next day, attaching her latest briefing papers so that Hudson could see her final instructions. These boiled down, SOE told him, to 'the duty of snooping on your behalf'. There was no need 'to eulogise

* This was not the only muddle that touched Hudson. Undercover in Yugoslavia in 1941, all his messages were indecipherable until the London team realized they were using a different edition of the *Reader's Digest* to code by. See Leo Marks, *Between Silk and Cyanide*, p. 85.

on her many various good qualities', the note continued; 'there is
no question about it whatever that she is better informed on Polish
political conditions . . . than almost any other single personality'.[60]
Freston finally got air clearance the following night, and their safe
arrival in south-west Poland was confirmed by the Home Army the
next day. The successful landing encouraged everyone, most of all
Threlfall, who now made feverish preparations for the dispatch of
the next mission, Fernham, comprising Christine, Andrzej, John
Roper and two other officers. 'Folkestone to proceed to the field as
quickly as possible', London ordered.[61]

Hudson and his Freston team had quickly run into difficulties,
however. Hudson had been knocked out on landing and was
concussed for some time afterwards, and another officer had been
injured and could not walk. After a warm and well-prepared recep-
tion from the Polish 27th Infantry Regiment, complete with farm
carts, clean sheets and cherry vodka, the team was on the road,
numb with cold and forced to bury their heavy kit, which they
never recovered. They saw the new year in at a party in a smoky
overcrowded room at a grand country house, getting drunk on
champagne that was not to be left for the Soviets, roaring through
the chorus of the Polish national anthem, and unwisely firing shots
into the air at midnight. Back in Italy, Christine and Andrzej could
only knock back glasses of cold Italian wine in Andrzej's quiet,
snow-clad *trullo*. The next morning Wehrmacht tanks, fighting a
bitter rearguard action, arrived at the Polish manor house. In their
hasty retreat the Freston team lost a wireless set and a courageous
member of their Polish reception committee, Janusz, who was killed
with his Sten gun in his hand in the ensuing battle. However, a few
days later they rendezvoused successfully with the 'clear-thinking
and confident' general Leopold Okulicki of the Home Army.[62] Over
tea and business, Okulicki suggested it might be wise to now send
in Andrzej and Christine who, as Polish nationals, could move
around more easily. Hudson radioed for them both to be dropped
in with extra kit but, before this could be acted on, in mid-January,
the Freston mission was overrun by a surprise Soviet offensive.
Hudson received radio instructions to report to the nearest Russian

formation, and there the team was promptly arrested. 'Too late to be of any public service', one of them admitted, they had managed only to witness Poland's 'death-throe'.[63]

The Soviet Army entered a devastated and deserted Warsaw on 17 January 1945. Having destroyed nearly every building, the Germans had retreated, carrying out horrendous atrocities against the remaining civilians as they went. With the capital reduced to vast mounds of rubble, the universities and museums bombed and looted, hundreds of thousands of books burned and the population decimated, the Communists easily seized control of Poland's future. In March, 'with a treachery rarely equaled in history', Gubbins later wrote, the Soviets arranged talks with the surviving Polish leaders at which they had them arrested and transported, or in some cases 'liquidated' on the spot.[64] When Okulicki ordered the dissolution of the Home Army, he implored his soldiers to keep the dream of freedom alive. Now thousands of Home Army soldiers were rounded up, interrogated, and required to join the Polish Red Army. Those who refused received death sentences as spies or collaborators. Okulicki himself would die in a Russian prison camp in 1946, and 'almost every day news was received in London of leading members of the Polish Resistance being arrested and summarily dealt with by the Soviet authorities', Peter Wilkinson recorded.[65] But the British Foreign Office was reluctant to intervene. Few leaders of the wartime underground, landowners, or members of the Polish intelligentsia still in the country would survive. 'In Lublin they were shooting them down in the cellar in the back of the head . . .', one officer reported.[66] Then the Moscow-backed Polish provisional government was moved from Lublin to Warsaw, and Soviet administration began.

Several of Christine's relatives had managed to get out of Poland. Her mother's brother, Józef Goldfeder, and his wife, had been killed during the German occupation, but their daughter had escaped to the USA. Another cousin, the son of her father's sister, had got to Britain, where he settled, and her more distant cousins from Lwów, Andrzej and Jan Skarbek, had been in Hungary with their immediate family from 1940 until they were old enough to

serve in Italy towards the end of the war. Christine's brother Andrzej had survived the war too. Having joined the Home Army in the early months of occupation, he had stayed in Warsaw, where he remarried in February 1942. He was later arrested, and spent the rest of the conflict in a German POW camp under false papers. His first wife, Irena, and their daughter Teresa Krystyna, named after the aunt she hardly knew, were also still alive and now faced a hazardous future.

The long winter weeks of early 1945 were the most traumatic of Christine's life. All autumn in London she had agonized over the unwillingness or inability of the Allies to assist in the Warsaw Rising as the BBC reported on the deteriorating situation and FANYs decoded 'heartrending messages' for help.[67] At the end of the year she had come so close to being sent out that Polish reports recorded her as number 317 on their 'parachute jumpers list', having 'dropped from Italy at the end of December'.[68] But in January 1945 she was still waiting in a Bari hotel for her mission to be given final clearance. The first few weeks after the departure of the Freston mission had been filled with drama. Christine was in frantic discussions with both Polish and British officers and, bluntly denouncing one proposed team member as 'useless', she supported some eleventh-hour changes to the Fernham and Flamstead personnel.[69] However, the strain of having to sit in idleness while keyed up for the operation eventually wore her down.

Every day Christine and the men would drive down the coast to the airbase at Brindisi or operational HQ at Monopoli to collect any messages. On 11 January she heard the first news of her brother Andrzej since she had last seen their mother, Stefania, in Warsaw in 1940. The unexpected possibility of seeing him again added to her frustration at the mission's delay. She started lobbying Perkins and Threlfall for action, but in return only received seemingly endless briefings and contradictory reports on the situation on the ground.

Her evenings were mainly spent with Andrzej, either glued to the radio for reports on the Russian advance or discussing the contribution that their mission might make, while huddled round

the stove in his *trullo* in the hills. Sometimes they played cards and, together with the Polish aircrews, cursed the infamy of the Soviets and their British and American allies, while avoiding the mess-hall full of empty chairs – of the thirteen Polish squadrons at the start of the Rising, there were now only two left. Occasionally they would take a jeep and explore Naples, or drive into the mountains to buy wine. Winter began to fade. Christine's original password to identify herself to her Polish reception committee, 'Have you got any plums for sale?', had clearly long passed its use-by date, and still the mission was not approved.[70]

It was no coincidence that the Soviets released Hudson and his Freston team on 12 February 1945, the day the Yalta conference ended. By then Churchill and Roosevelt had recognized the Communist provisional government of the Polish Republic, effectively ending the role of the Polish government-in-exile. Poland, it was agreed in absentia, should cede territories to Russia but be compensated with new land annexed from Germany. Churchill alone raised a voice for democratic elections, a request that was repeated at the Potsdam conference the following year, and with that, the Polish question was considered settled. Christine, and the 250,000 Polish servicemen still fighting with the Allies, saw Yalta as a betrayal. They now knew that they were no longer fighting for Poland's freedom, and there would be no free Poland for them to return to after the war. 'We were dumbfounded and bitterly resentful when news of the settlement reached us', one Polish officer wrote. 'Some just stared into empty space unable to speak, others wept openly, while others still raised their voices in anger and recrimination. How could our British allies and friends betray us so shamefully?'[71]

Christine's mission was finally cancelled in the early spring. 'The end of the war intervened', SOE brusquely noted in her file, and Christine was left devastated by her inability to help protect her country from either German or Russian aggression.[72] On finally hearing the mission was off, one account has her bundling up the heavy Polish clothes she had been issued with, and shoving them into an iron stove where she watched them burn for a while until she said to herself, 'That's the end.'[73]

Whether an SOE mission arriving six months earlier might have had any serious influence over events is debatable. Wilkinson, Gubbins's number two, felt not, but Threlfall, equally well placed to judge, believed that such an operation would have been of 'historical importance', as 'it is doubtful whether the Warsaw Rising would have broken out'.[74] At the very least, if successful, the mission might have provided some direct communication between the Home Army and the British, in the absence of which Bór-Komorowski's ability to judge the intentions and capacity of his Western Allies to support the Rising had been seriously impaired. Furthermore the mere presence of British observers might have limited the German reprisals when the Rising failed, and subsequently enabled them to act as human rights monitors with the Soviets. But perhaps the missions would simply have been arrested sooner and kept out of sight, as Freston was, until the intelligence they had gathered was out of date and could have no influence.

On a personal level, Christine would have felt greater solidarity with her compatriots had she been able to join them. As it was she was eaten up by feelings of impotence, anger and guilt. She could not stop thinking about the destruction of Warsaw – its opera house and department stores, the cafés and cinemas she had known so well, and the desperate last days of those who had lived in the city, her many friends among them. In the words of one Polish radio transmission, sent just after the fall of the city, 'absolutely everyone has lost absolutely everything'.[75]

Christine told Andrzej that she needed to rest, and he secretly booked a picturesque hotel on a nearby Greek island. He hoped that a change would distract her, restoring her energies and her old bold sense of self. Having shared such traumatic months, he also knew how deeply he loved her and how intimately they were tied to each other, as orphans and exiles together. Once again he planned to propose, hoping that they might face their uncertain future side by side. But Christine was still possessed of an 'almost violent independence', as Francis had once remarked, and she felt a desperate need to keep fighting on alone.[76] It was not that she did not love Andrzej: she did. But marriage had never been an answer

for her, and to marry him now would have felt like giving up. When Andrzej surprised her with his proposal and ill-timed plans for a romantic break, Christine shuddered and took to her heels. She had been offered work in the Movement Section of General Head-quarters Multilateral Force, dealing with displaced persons, and was flying via Naples to Cairo, where she still had many SOE friends, like Harold Perkins, who might yet be able to deploy her operation-ally. Andrzej waved her off, and seeing her leave him again he had the feeling that 'something had snapped between us – irrevocably'.[77] Two days later he returned to London alone.

Christine felt better just to be on the move. As she was stranded in Naples for a couple of days while waiting for her connection, SOE sent out an officer from Rome, Peter Lee, to keep her company at the villa in the hills, overlooking Vesuvius, where she was lodged. Far from meeting a desolate waif, Lee found a 'slim, oval-faced, rather olive-skinned, dark-haired girl with beautiful features' who kept him entertained over two successive dinner dates with her adventure stories from the field.[78] 'She was very free with her favours', Lee later commented on this 'amazing' and 'extraordi-nary' girl, not mentioning whether he spoke from personal experience.[79]

Christine found Cairo in a festive mood. Taking victory as being a mere formality away, there was a series of cocktail parties and receptions, and even formal balls. Her friends swarmed round her. Xan Fielding, who promptly lent her £150, a huge sum, and Zofia Tarnowska and Bill Stanley Moss, now a hero from his and Paddy Leigh Fermor's mission to Crete, headed the welcoming committee. Michael Dunford quietly slipped his arm back through hers, too, albeit slightly more shyly. The returning heroine was suddenly required to lend glamour and prestige to every event, a role for which she had little appetite but accepted to please her friends, ironing her best blouse, straightening the pleats of her Vercors skirt and pulling on a new pair of heels. It was Michael who now took on the role of observer, as Christine was swept away from him to recount her war stories to circles of admiring officers. Watching from across a room he felt that her conversation could

be transcribed as a series of Morse signals, intermittent flashes of brilliance, until the signal was abruptly halted as he lost sight of her. One night, having been deserted at an event, he drove angrily home through the Arab quarter only to catch sight of a new Morse code, 'flashed as she ran, by her bare heels'.[80] When he chastised her for her Cinderella-like behaviour Christine simply laughed at him and blamed the bores at the party and the pain of high heels. True to form, she refused to be disciplined, reprimanded or constrained in any way. Not long afterwards, when Michael introduced her to George Michailov, a Serbian pilot who was reputed to have stolen a German Messserschmitt in Zagreb, she disappeared with the hero, leaving Michael alone in the bar of Shepheard's Hotel, nursing 'murderous instincts' inside himself. 'I would have killed Michailov like a dog', he later admitted.[81]

But while Cairo society celebrated, for Christine the war was far from won. Although always happy to enjoy some romantic distraction, she had started manoeuvring for active service as soon as she arrived. She had already submitted an application to the RAF when in mid-March she petitioned 'Perks Kochany' (Dearest Perks) for work. 'I am afraid that the prospect of employing you in an operational capacity, either now or in the near future, have become exceedingly remote', Perkins told her. 'In view of the unhappy position of Poland there is obviously no possibility of an operational mission to that country.'[82] 'For God's sake, do not strike my name from the firm,' she replied earnestly, 'remember that I am always pleased to go and do anything for it.'[83] Her letter smacks of desperation, even including an uncharacteristically humble apology for her spelling. Dealing first with her RAF application she begs Perkins, in her imperfect English, to 'write and tell them that I am honest and clean Polish girl'. Should this prove unsuccessful her second plan was to parachute into Germany to 'get people out from camps and prisons . . . before they get shot'. 'I should love to do it,' she wrote, 'and I like to jump out of a plane even every day.'[84]

Christine was clearly thinking about the cancelled Fernham and Flamstead rescue missions to camps in Poland. She probably also knew that Andrzej was now standing by at Sunningdale golf course,

with Paddy Leigh Fermor, Havard Gunn and others, to be dropped in advance of Allied troops in Germany to prevent the many hurried executions that were taking place in the camps towards the end of the war.* 'Please do look after Andrew, and don't let him do anything too stupid', she told Perkins.[85] Francis Cammaerts had already been sent to Germany with SAARF, the 'Special Allied Airborne Reconnaissance Force' specifically created for this work. He would be present in April at the liberation of the Bergen-Belsen concentration camp, where 15,000 inmates died, mainly of starvation and typhoid, within days of their liberation.[†] It is doubtful whether Christine's offer to join these missions was given serious consideration, however, as SOE now ruled that no female personnel were to be sent into Germany 'under any circumstances'.[86] A few months later her former Cairo flatmate, Laura Foskett, witnessed 'the horror, the looks of incredulity on our faces, the numbed silence that fell over the office', when news of the concentration camps began to filter through from SOE's press section, followed by rolls of unexpurgated film.[87]

Christine's thoughts then turned to the people close to her. Perkins had managed to get an address for her brother in Poland and she sent him a parcel of food and clothing and, possibly, some of Xan Fielding's money. She asked for news of her husband, Jerzy Gizycki, and forwarded a letter for Alfred Gardyne de Chastelain, her friend and colleague from Istanbul and Cairo, who was starting to face questions about the political contacts he had made during SOE operations in Romania. 'If it is true that he is into troubles,' Christine wrote, 'there are people here who could give him some evidence which may be helpful to him.' With an eye to her future, she even sent her 'fondest love' to Gubbins.[88]

* Neither Andrzej nor Leigh Fermor were sent, and many prisoners were killed in early 1945, including the SOE female agents Violette Szabo, Denise Bloch and Lilian Rolfe. Andrzej ended the war with Leigh Fermor, 'swanning into Hamburg, Flensburg and Kiel and then, deliriously, into Liberated Denmark'. See the *Spectator*, Patrick Leigh Fermor, 'The One-Legged Parachutist', (1.1.1989).

† Cammaerts later also visited Ravensbrück, where he must have spent some time thinking about Christine's predecessor in France, Cecily Lefort.

The war, and life, went on. In April, Zofia Tarnowska married Bill Stanley Moss in a Greek Orthodox church in Cairo, having converted to secure her divorce from Andrzej Tarnowski. Their friends in the Egyptian royal family gave them a magnificent reception. The wedding was arranged partly because Moss was about to be dropped into Siam, and they knew he might not return. Inspired, Christine tried one last avenue to secure a mission herself. An SOE note from April records her report that she had been approached by the Poles to work for them. 'Christine is inclined to exaggerate at times,' the author wrote, 'but I feel that there is something in what she told me, very confidentially.'[89] But no Polish work followed, and if Christine had been trying a ruse to prompt SOE to employ her, it was a gamble that backfired. A month later a reply came back, saying that this 'would seem an admirable solution for her future'.[90] By then, though, Hitler had committed suicide as the Russians entered Berlin. The war in Europe was effectively over.

On 7 May 1945, when Germany signed the formal surrender, Christine was invited to a celebratory ball, but she was in no mood for rejoicing. Although the first of Britain's ultimately victorious Allies, Poland had suffered some of the greatest losses, including its independence, much of the territory in defence of which the war had been declared, and more than two thirds of the capital's buildings. Nearly six million Poles had died, the vast majority of whom, including a quarter of Warsaw's residents, were civilians. The country's total dead amounted to a fifth of the pre-war population. Another 500,000, mostly political and military leaders and members of the intelligentsia, were scattered around the world with no prospect of returning, Christine among them. VE Day, Victory in Europe, on 8 May, a day of triumph for the British, was one of the darkest of Christine's life.

After a week of celebrations came demobilization. British officers thought of home, their families waiting to welcome them, and interrupted careers that must now be resumed. As a member of the Polish landed gentry, who had fought with the Allies, and whose details had been given to the NKVD by the British, Christine had

absolutely no hope of returning to Soviet-administered Poland. Her British passport, issued to her in Budapest by Sir Owen O'Malley and twice renewed since, was her only identity document and was due to expire in July 1947. She was to all intents stateless, and almost immediately homeless. On 11 May, just three days after the Germans had ratified their surrender, Christine relinquished her commission in the WAAF. 'After the physical suffering and mental strain she had suffered for more than six years in our service . . .', wrote Xan Fielding, whose life Christine had saved in France, 'she needed, probably more than any other agent we employed, security for life. After her outstanding personal contribution to our victory, she deserved it. Yet a few months after the armistice she was dismissed with a month's salary and left in Cairo to fend for herself.'[91]

15: SECOND-CLASS CITIZEN

'Official intelligence in peace-time comes home to roost in White-hall, and is an office job . . .' one former SOE agent wrote scathingly after the war in Europe was officially concluded. 'Civilian clothes are no longer an intrepid disguise. The man who is caught is not shot at dawn. It is no longer a matter of life or death. It is, most of it, an exchange of files between the Foreign Office, the War Office and Scotland Yard.'[1] Basil Davidson, Christine's SOE friend from Budapest and Cairo, agreed, knowing from personal experience how difficult it was 'to get adjusted to the idea that you're not going to die . . .'[2] It was clear that Christine was not going to find the transition to peace easy.

Some of Christine's former colleagues fared better than others. June Darton, who had known her in Italy, was invited to stay in Sienna for a few weeks, before Henry Threlfall picked her up in his chauffeur-driven car and took her to the opera in Rome, 'a very thrilling thing to do'.[3] Other well-heeled FANYs from Cairo and Algiers 'had a wonderful time' on adjustment courses, with weekend lectures and trips to museums and galleries in Florence and Venice.[4] But for most servicemen with direct experience of war, demobil-ization brought little or no support, and often no work either. For Christine there was also no home to return to, no parents, no children, no career – no normal life at all. 'The cold winds of unemployment are beginning . . . to whistle rather drearily round the streets of London', one of her FANY friends wrote. 'Christine seems to have been one of the wisest as she's gone to ground in Cairo, saying she'd rather be poor there than anywhere else.'[5] But even in the sunshine, Christine needed an income to maintain her café lifestyle and, after living on a knife-edge for the last few years,

she also needed a new source of regular adrenalin. Like many who had fought with courage, belief and hope throughout the war, she became increasingly depressed by what she soon referred to as 'the horrors of peace', political betrayal, bureaucratic red tape and, perhaps most deadening of all, humdrum daily routine.[6] Denying defeat, Christine would not stand for any of it.

Barely a month after the Yalta conference in February 1945, Stalin made it clear that he had no intention of honouring his agreement to promote independent Polish democracy. International access to the country was restricted while mass arrests, deportations and executions effectively ended internal Polish resistance or organized opposition. In July, the same month that Britain enthusiastically elected a Labour government with whom to 'face the future', the Communist-installed Lublin administration was officially recognized in Poland. The following January, rigged elections sealed Poland's fate. The country would be a Communist state by 1949.

For the Poles who had ended the war overseas, these were agonizing times. Very few of the 30,000 servicemen and their families based in Britain risked returning home. After Yalta, Churchill had announced his support for Polish troops to be given citizenship and the 'freedom of the British Empire, if they so desire', declaring that 'His Majesty's Government will never forget the debt they owe to the Polish troops'.[7] The debt was indeed great: the Polish contribution to the war had been outstanding. Poland had produced the fourth-largest armed force in Europe, after the Soviet Union, the United States and the combined troops of the British Empire. Polish pilots had formed the largest group of non-British personnel in the Battle of Britain, and Polish troops had fought under British command in decisive battles in Italy, France, the Netherlands and Libya. In intelligence, the Poles had provided the Enigma machine to Britain's cryptographers and cracked the early version of the code; and they had supplied sample parts of Germany's V2 rocket. In recognition, in mid-1946 the new Labour government, under Clement Attlee, set up the Polish Resettlement Corps, offering Polish servicemen temporary jobs until they could find permanent work. But the popularity that the

Poles had enjoyed during the war quickly fell away when tens of thousands of Polish ex-servicemen contributed to flood the British job market, which was already struggling to cope with the five million Britons being demobilized.*

Insult followed when, in June 1946, only the Polish airmen who had taken part in the Battle of Britain were invited to join London's Victory Parade, while the Communist government in Warsaw sent official representatives. For Polish émigrés, having to live in a country where they felt so little welcome or respect was compounded by the trauma of not knowing what had happened to their loved ones left at home. Although sheltering in Cairo, Christine, like all her compatriots, faced a difficult and uncertain future, but she, at least, believed she could reasonably expect recognition for her service and some decent support in her transition to civilian life.

Christine's courage and achievements throughout her service were admired by everyone who knew her. In December 1944, General Stawell had recommended her for the George Cross, the civil equivalent to the Military Cross, for her 'nerve, coolness and devotion to duty, and high courage'.[8] But Christine was not impressed. The only medal that she would be proud to wear, she told Francis, would be a military medal. It was 'typical' of her, he said, that this was the one honour she could not hope to get.[9] Women were ineligible for British military honours, a situation that caused another female agent, Pearl Witherington, to protest that 'there was nothing remotely civil' about what they had done.[10] For reasons not recorded, General Alexander, the Supreme Allied Commander of the Mediterranean Theatre, then downgraded Stawell's recommendation for Christine to an OBE. This was subsequently raised to a George Medal by the War Office to 'make it obvious that she had been decorated for gallantry, as her courage was out-

* Although there were voices of support for the Poles, notably from the future Labour leader Michael Foot, in June 1946, 56 per cent of Britons polled were in favour of sending the émigrés back to Poland, while only 30 per cent felt they should be entitled to stay. See Lynn Olson and Stanley Cloud, *For Your Freedom and Ours: The Kościuszko Squadron – Forgotten Heroes of World War II* (2004), p. 401.

standing'.[11] At the beginning of June 1945, the recommendation was approved and the offer made.[12] Christine did not respond. Francis believed that 'one of the fiercest factors in her make-up was her inborn dislike of authority', a trait that he ascribed to her experience of 'her aristocratic father and the suffering that her mother, a beautiful Jewess, had had to submit to'.[13] Now, irrespective of her distinguished record, Christine's evident lack of respect for authority, rules and procedures would count heavily against her.

London had informed Christine that her services were no longer required even before the formal end of the war, in April 1945. Early memos show a complete lack of concern, or even comprehension, about her situation. 'She is no longer wanted . . .' one personnel officer wrote. 'Unless we have any likely job in the offing I suggest it would be a simpler matter to arrange for her to resign her commission and to go back to that civilian life from whence she came.'[14] Others were anxious only about the potential security risk of Christine continuing to carry a WAAF identity card or, perhaps more reasonably, not respecting the restrictions of the Official Secrets Act. However, Christine still had a number of friends in 'the firm', as SOE had always been known to insiders, and a temporary job in Cairo. In addition, SOE now agreed to keep her on half pay until the end of 1945 to give her 'every chance to arrange her affairs'.[15] She decided to take the money as a lump sum, in order to reduce her dealings with the finance department. 'They really are quite impossible', she told Gubbins. 'Wing Commander Venner refused to pay me London allowances, danger pay, and parachute pay, simply because I was not a man!'[16] Beyond these arrangements, Perkins told her that if she had any plans of her own, all help would be put at her disposal. He was rather at a loss as to what else to suggest for the sole female former agent of his section, for whom he felt so responsible. 'I know how you hate letter-writing,' he told her, 'but please answer this.'[17]

Unknown to Christine, there were quite a lot of people – 'other chaps' as Perkins's secretary, Vera Long, referred to them – who viewed her as, 'for want of a better word, "scatty"', and were quite looking forward to dropping her.[18] Not long later Xan Fielding

gently let her know that many people in SOE did not consider that they owed her anything for the simple reason that when she was in Hungary and Poland she was working not for them, but for the Poles. 'Perhaps he does not know that I was sent by George Taylor to Poland through Hungary in 1939', Christine rightly remonstrated in a letter to Gubbins. 'But it is all very hard on me if this story is believed as I have got into so much trouble with the Poles because I worked for the firm!'[19]

Christine was already at a professional disadvantage alongside her former colleagues. She had outstanding ability and experience, and her 'exceptional language skills' had been praised by Stawell among others in SOE.[20] Yet in a March 1945 list of Polish-speaking officers who might be offered post-war positions, the languages, availability and SOE's 'obligations' towards the men, including Andrzej, were all specified, while against Christine's name there were just three words: 'no employment here'.[21] In peacetime, the qualities still so highly valued in the male agents were no longer recognized in her, and she had few of the skills traditionally sought in women. Bemoaning her unchanged attitude towards secretarial work, officials began to record that 'it appears that there is little more we can do to help her'.[22] Christine's 'English is not perfect . . .' they noted, 'she cannot type, has no experience whatever of office work and is altogether not a very easy person to employ'.[23] Andrzej had a similar CV, but none of this seemed to stand in the way of his landing a post in the Allied-run military government of Germany, and later being posted to the British Intelligence Corps. Unintentionally rubbing salt into her wound, at the end of official letters informing Christine, for instance, of the termination of her commission with the Air Council, she started to receive cheery notes such as 'Hope you are being a good girl!'[24] Eventually she visited Gubbins, hoping that she would at least be treated with some respect and possibly be considered for an active commission of her own, but when she left his office she was unusually quiet. 'He just wants me in bed', she told Francis and, while she refused to elaborate, she was obviously furious.[25]

Christine considered an office job only once. Learning that

Patrick Howarth had been posted as Press Attaché to the British Embassy in Warsaw, now operating from the first floor of a former railway hotel on the outskirts of the devastated city, she sent him a telegram asking for work. Howarth was delighted to help and won the Ambassador's backing, but the Foreign Office would not countenance employing a foreign national in one of their embassies. She then applied to BOAC, the British Overseas Airways Corporation, reasoning that a stewardess was 'some sort of conducting officer', but again her nationality proved a stumbling block.[26] It was evident that whatever work she sought, she was not going to get far until she had secured full British citizenship.

As a temporary British passport holder who had spent the war risking her life in the paid service of the British government, Christine believed she would be entitled to ongoing British citizenship if she needed it. She had raised the issue with Perkins while in London in September 1944, and he had agreed that 'this would seem a very suitable recompense' for her services.[27] Both of them were shocked therefore, when word came back that Christine should apply to the Home Office through a solicitor. 'This does not reflect the spirit with which we have built up SOE and obtained the loyalty of those working for us', Perkins stormed, but the matter was dropped when Christine's 'Folkestone' mission to Poland was given the green light.[28]

Now, stuck in post-war Cairo, knowing that 'my chances of ever going back to Poland are very small', Christine raised the question again, specifying only that 'I want to keep the name Granville that I have made for myself, and of which I am rather proud'.[29] But the naturalization papers that, as Xan Fielding put it, 'from the moral point of view . . . should have been delivered to her immediately on demand' were now obstructed by a combination of prejudice and bureaucracy.[30] Internal memos began to refer to Christine as 'this girl' and to her application as a 'headache'.[31] 'I know nothing about her', one official wrote. 'I think she only assumed this name for her commissioning as they would not commission a Polish subject.'[32] Christine was not only an unconventional woman, but a Pole, and the implication seemed to be that

her application need not be taken seriously. In June 1945 it was decided that 'her naturalisation ... is absolutely out of the question'.[33] Because she had not resided in England for five years 'as required by paragraph 12', she was told that she did not qualify for 'immediate naturalisation' and should 'apply for special instructions'.[34] There was simply no precedent for someone like Christine and, despite SOE friends pressing for her to be given 'preferential treatment', by November it had become 'obvious' that her application might 'remain pending for [a] long time'.[35]

Part of the problem was that SOE had been officially disbanded in January 1946. Both Ernest Bevin, the Labour Foreign Secretary, and Dwight Eisenhower, about to be appointed Chief of Staff to the US Army, had sent Gubbins appreciative letters about SOE's contribution to the victory. But when Lord Selborne, the former head of SOE, argued that they had built up a worldwide communications network that could serve as a valuable intelligence tool in the years ahead, Clement Attlee responded that he had no wish to preside over a British Comintern, and insisted that they were closed down with immediate effect. This meant that although a small nucleus of expertise was maintained through a merger with the Secret Intelligence Service, not only was there no obvious role for Christine, but most of her friends had been dismissed too. Even Gubbins was soon informed that there was no further appointment for him. 'SOE's brilliant bloody-minded CD had been dismissed like a redundant doorman', Leo Marks commented, while Gubbins's number two, Peter Wilkinson, added bitterly that 'at this time Major Generals were two a penny'.[36] Over the following year, many SOE papers were deliberately burnt and a fire gutted the top floor of Baker Street, destroying yet more records. Editing, arson or accident, these bonfires were perhaps 'a fitting finale' to the SOE story, a story that had begun five years earlier with Churchill's order to set Europe ablaze.[37]

Refusing to be filed and forgotten, Christine applied for British citizenship through the standard, public process, proposing to settle in Kenya or another British colony should her application be successful. Her forms, dated December 1945, must have been

among the more exciting ones in the Home Office in-trays. 'I have no nationality . . .' Christine submitted her reason for making the application. 'My Polish papers were taken from me by the Gestapo in Hungary when I was in the service of the British Crown.' And when it came to the standard question about 'any previous convictions', she jotted down, as if routine, 'Sentenced to death by German military court on charge of sabotage against the Reich, 1940 Poland, 1941 Hungary'.[38]

Yet even with Perkins as her faithful and distinguished referee, nothing happened. Two months later Christine called in the support of a few bigger names. Lord Selborne cited her 'outstanding services' and 'heroic bravery' directly to the Home Secretary, before boldly stating that Christine's desire to become British 'would be a fitting tribute to her gallant and devoted service'.[39] But it now turned out that Christine's service to Britain was irrelevant, because she was not a man. 'A married woman is disbarred, under the present law, from obtaining naturalisation independently from her husband . . .' a rubber-stamping official explained.[40] Without evidence of Jerzy Gizycki's death or a valid dissolution of his and Christine's marriage, the Home Office simply saw 'no point in considering whether she could be regarded as eligible in other respects'.[41] Over six million Poles had died during the war, there were few official records, and Christine was in any case disbarred from returning to Poland because of her service for the Allies, but she was now told that to be eligible for British citizenship proof of her marital status was more important than her war record. It was a low moment for Home Office policymakers.

Sick of British red tape, Christine flew to France in July 1946, to join Francis in being honoured by de Gaulle's government. Both had been awarded the Croix de Guerre, Christine's with one star, and the Order of Vercors, a combatant's medal showing the Vercors chamois, which she claimed to 'value even more'.[42]* For a few days

* Cammaerts was awarded the British DSO, French Chevalier (later Officier) of the Légion d'Honneur, and Croix de Guerre, and the Medal of Freedom and Silver Star of the USA.

they attended memorial events, visited friends and talked and thought of the past rather than the future. A photograph shows Christine in a white summer dress, smiling beneath her sunglasses, a scarf tied loosely over her hair, and her hands, as usual, in her pockets, as she walks with local families beside a memorial to the Vercors heroes. The burnt-out skeletons of the German gliders that had descended onto the plateau two years earlier would later be brought down to rest beside the memorial park, along with upended rows of the rusting metal containers that Christine had once helped to collect from the fields to supply the resistants with arms and ammunition.

Francis had also struggled to find a satisfying post-war role. Despite having only spent ten months of his civilian life outside of the UK, after what was referred to as a 'regrettable interview' the Foreign Office had rejected his application to become a press officer for France, ostensibly because his father was Belgian.[43] This and his subsequent failure to be accepted for other jobs for which he was eminently suited caused speculation that his early pacifism might have 'caused adverse traces against his name in the central register'.[44] However, like Andrzej, Francis had eventually been found a post in the military government of Germany. He and Christine now went to Paris to book flights out to Germany together. Walking through the city Christine saw Dorothy Wakely, the Signals Planning Officer she had worked with in Algiers and who, like many of the ops staff at Massingham, was now employed at the British Embassy in Paris. Catching her arm, Christine asked if she might be able to pull any strings at the Embassy to get her some work. 'She clearly desperately needed a job', Wakely realized, but she knew that Christine was regarded 'as a loose cannon, and was not to be redeployed'.[45] Wakely stood there feeling very unhappy at not being able to help, but when she later checked at the Embassy 'they were vehement that in no way would they offer her employment'.[46] There was clearly a black mark against Christine's name at the 'central register' too.

Andrzej had spent the last months of the war attached to teams in Germany, seeking out Gestapo agents and interrogating hun-

dreds of SS personnel, work he undertook 'with great enthusiasm and loyalty'.[47] Cushioning his transition to civilian life, he was then awarded the MBE (Military Division), and given a government role with the Control Commission, enforcing measures against the black market. At the same time, and possibly not unconnected to his official work, he gradually succeeded in building up a number of business interests relating to his love of cars, themselves now a valuable commodity, while maintaining his links with military intelligence. Christine joined him in Bonn in late July, at once feeling at home in his company and enjoying driving around in his new, convertible, Opel.* But she was unable to accept his decision to make his new home in the country that had destroyed Poland. Instead she tried to persuade Andrzej to consider moving to Kenya, and getting some land outside Nairobi. Never a farmer at heart, and not a sun-worshipper like Christine, he could hardly have been less struck with the idea.

Andrzej drove Christine to Berlin, where they visited the consulate department of the Polish Military Mission, hoping to secure her legal independence from Jerzy. On 1 August 1946, Christine emerged with legal permission to contract a marriage with one 'Stanley Kennedy'.[48] As divorces were not granted under Polish law, the new Polish Republic was issuing certificates authorizing plaintiffs to contract another marriage in lieu of divorce papers. To qualify Christine had had to secure the support of three of her former lovers: her husband, Jerzy Gizycki, who confirmed his agreement from Canada, Francis who served as a witness, and Andrzej acting as the proposed third party. This was particularly generous of Andrzej, considering the number of times he had unsuccessfully proposed to Christine for more honest reasons. Perhaps this was partly why he distanced himself from the certificate, choosing to use an anglicized version of his middle name, Stanisław, and avoiding listing his Polish family name, Kowerski, in

* As, for reasons unknown, Britain had refused her a travel permit for Germany, Christine travelled anyhow and then asked Nina Tamplin, who was working in Berlin, to get her a permit. See Masson (1975), p. xxx.

the papers at all, though it was probably not unusual to be discreet in such matters. Nevertheless, the pair of them did spend a week celebrating Christine's freedom at the Palace Hotel in Brussels, drinking wine and eating butter and seafood which could not be had easily elsewhere. They then returned to London to expedite their separate naturalization processes, Andrzej's sponsored by the Control Commission, Christine submitting her new legal certificate.

'Apparently your divorce certificate has given the Home Office such a shock that they have not yet sufficiently recovered to tell us what they think of it', Perkins wrote to Christine in September.[49] She was finally granted British naturalization in November 1946, the certificate coming through the next month. Given the amount of effort that had gone into attaining it, the document was a curious work of fiction. Christine's date of birth was, of course, the usual seven years shy of the truth, but now, despite Jerzy's acquiescence in the process, she was also listed as a widow. From now on, whenever she was asked, she would explain that her husband had died fighting the Germans. Perhaps, to her, he had. The following year, Andrzej was also naturalized, taking the name Andrew Stanisław Kowerski-Kennedy.

It was with a mixture of relief and renewed hope that Christine now applied for a position with the International Refugee Organisation at the fledgling United Nations in Geneva, only to be rejected with the comment that 'you're not British at all. You're just a foreigner with a British passport.'[50] Christine's new passport declared her to be a 'British Subject by Naturalisation', and listed certificate and reference numbers that, Andrzej said, made her 'feel like a convict'.[51] Refusing to accept what she saw as second-class citizenship, Christine took the issue up with Sir Owen O'Malley and Aidan Crawley, now a Labour MP. As a result, the Home Office changed the bearer's status on all naturalized citizens' passports to 'Citizen of Great Britain and the Colonies'. Christine had won another battle, but she had had enough of British bureaucracy and headed back to Cairo. There she took a job as a switchboard operator and, living quietly, began to shun social functions and avoid anyone who wanted to talk to her about her war record.

It was at this point that Christine learned that she was to be honoured with an OBE as well as her George Medal, this time 'as a British subject'.[52] 'I don't want it', she responded. 'I told them time and again I didn't want it.'[53] Having had to fight all the way for the one prize she valued, the security of British citizenship, she was reluctant to be patronized by inappropriate honours now. Perkins had told her that her George Medal related to her work undertaken as a WAAF officer. 'It is quite clear that there is some mistake or misunderstanding . . .' Christine replied irritably. 'During my period in the WAAF I spent all my time sitting in the Imperiale in Bari, waiting for operations that never came off.'[54] Receiving honours for a cancelled mission, she argued reasonably, 'would only bring discredit to me and to any decoration that might be proposed for me'.[55] But what really insulted Christine was the level of the honour. In an increasingly heated exchange of letters, Perkins thanked Christine for her 'heart-throb', and set out to be as frank in response. 'In the first place', he wrote, 'you have not been decorated for sipping dry martinis in the bar of the Imperiale'.[56] The 'much coveted George Medal . . . an extremely good decoration' had been awarded for her work in France. Other recognition had been delayed pending her naturalization to avoid unnecessary explanations to the new Polish government, he wrote, which would inevitably make any possibility of her eventual return home even more precarious. 'I can well imagine . . .' he continued tactlessly, 'your feminine absence of understanding for such matters'.[57]

Christine was incensed. 'If you saw [the men whose lives I saved] on 17 August 1944 at eight in the evening, you would bet that they valued their lives a little higher than the equivalent of an MC,' she stormed, 'which, after all, is offered almost automatically to anybody who ever jumped anywhere . . . Goodbye and thank you again, Christine'.[58] It was perhaps a good thing that it was this letter that Christine posted, and not her first draft which had further complained, 'It does seem to me rather extraordinary that Mrs Sansom has been given the George Cross for not giving away the names of people she was working with and yet it is proposed to give me the George Medal for saving people's lives half an hour before they

were due to be shot . . .'[59] She had a point, but she had already said more than enough to put Perkins's back up. 'You should be more discerning in determining between your friends who are trying to help you, and those to whom the name Christine Granville means just another case to be dealt with in their "in-bin"', he warned her.[60] They were both getting fed up with this protracted correspondence, and Christine finally got down to the root cause of much of her anger. 'I am rather tired, after six years of more or less active service with the firm', she wrote bitterly, 'of being treated as a helpless little girl.'[61]

Christine's OBE (Civil Division), 'for special services during military operations', was formally announced in May 1947.[62] Congratulations poured in from her friends around the world, including Aidan Crawley, Alfred Gardyne de Chastelain, George Taylor and Colin Gubbins, who reported on all the people asking after her at the Special Forces Club he had helped to set up in Knightsbridge, in London. Even Perkins sent his 'humble congratulations', and gave her a quick round-up of the press coverage in Britain, Egypt and Poland. 'The Daily Mail is an easy winner in referring to you as a Beauty Queen!' he wrote. 'With all due respect to yourself and your charm, I must say I did not look upon you in that light, but perhaps my eyes were too full of your good work for the job as such to have any space left to notice your ravishing female beauty!'[63]

Other friends did, however, feel that Christine had been rather short-changed. 'Her pay-off and decorations were not over-generous for one who had risked her life many times to save the Allied cause', Laura Foskett wrote.[64] But it was only Francis, who had been invited to put forward a list of people who deserved recognition and later described the way the government handled the whole question of honours as 'unspeakably crass', who understood how upset Christine was by both the level and civil status of her awards.[65] Francis had not only proposed Christine for the military DSO, but argued that 'for her work in France alone' she deserved 'the highest possible honour and the immediate gift of British citizenship'.[66] 'Christine dear!' he now wrote, 'it must be worse for you than going to the dentist . . . The George Medal is a disgraceful

insult!'[67] Over a year later he was still trying to placate her, telling her it was 'among the worst examples of injustice in a hopeless mess that has been made of decorations as a whole . . . a sickening and disgusting business'.[68]

Thoroughly disappointed, Christine looked for fresh horizons. 'I want to start a new life, open and free and normal', she wrote to Sir Owen O'Malley, now the British Ambassador in Lisbon.[69] Aidan Crawley canvassed jobs for her in London, and John Roper, who had been posted to Greece, found her work in Athens. But then Michael Dunford, her former Cairo lover, wrote telling her that he had decided to settle in Nairobi, where he was working for the British Council. Remembering the dreams of African sunshine, horses and freedom that she had once shared with Jerzy, Christine wrote back, to Michael's astonishment, saying that she would join him there. She arrived in Nairobi a few weeks later, and although she took rooms of her own at the New Stanley Hotel, from where she could watch the green and cream national buses on the main road out of town, the two of them were quickly an item again.

The New Stanley had been a social cornerstone for settlers in Nairobi for over forty years, watering many of the thousands of white émigrés who had arrived with the encouragement of the British government after the First World War, and later becoming famous when Ernest Hemingway propped up the bar in the 1930s. Now Kenya was once again a fashionable destination for European migrants, and Christine soon found herself at the centre of a large Polish émigré community, as well as being welcomed by Michael's British friends. Among the Poles was Christopher Czyzewski, who had known Christine and her Lwów cousins when they were young, and had introduced her to his wife, Anna, in Cairo. The two women had got on well, Christine agreeing to act as godmother for her friends' son when he was born in 1945, and they now developed a closer friendship.

As Czyzewski had been seconded to Nairobi from the Cairo-based Polish General Staff, his family lived in army quarters just outside the city. Of their many regular guests, Christine was the only one who bothered to spend any time with their children. She

was particularly fond of eight-year-old Suzanna, who she entertained with invented stories about a cat, and once gave a small watercolour of a mother cat feeding her kittens. Another time she invited Suzanna, with her mother, for tea at the New Stanley, plying her with cakes until she was sick. Michael was also good with children, once taking Suzanna to meet Tyrone Power when he briefly visited Kenya. Everyone seemed to think that Christine, slight, attractive but perhaps a little fragile in her simple, well-cut clothes, and the terribly nice, pipe-smoking Michael, tall and fair beside her, made a wonderful couple. It was obvious that Michael adored her, and together they would go out riding, drag hunting and shooting, sometimes bagging antelopes for their meat. In the evenings they joined in the endless round of parties or spent quieter nights together at the cinema and the city's many bars.

But Christine was never entirely divorced from Europe and her past. Christopher Czyzewski was involved with resettling or repatriating the Polish refugees arriving in Kenya, and Christine would join in the heated discussions about the ethics of returning Poles to Communist Poland. Like many others, she also helped organize food parcels to be sent home. She had had no more news of her brother, and could only hope that he and his family were living quietly somewhere, unaffected by the press attention she had recently received for her decorations. The Polish émigrés all felt that their country had been betrayed by Churchill at Yalta and, given her direct service for the British, Christine was particularly bitter about it. She started losing weight, and sometimes suffered from bad dreams and stomach pains that her friends believed were brought on by stress. With this fresh and sympathetic audience, however, Christine began to bring out her war stories again, including tales that she had once slept with a man on a rescue mission, and had stabbed another. 'I hate guns, so noisy', she told Anna Czyzewska when she asked about the knife on her mantelpiece, the only 'ornament' on display in her room. 'This weapon is swift and deadly, and I have made good use of it on many occasions.'[70] But even her new friends realized that 'she just told you what she wanted you to know' as she reconstructed her own

history, including many stories about her 'extremely rich' first husband, but never a mention of cuckolded Jerzy.[71]

To distract her, Michael took Christine out of town as much as possible. Soon after she arrived they had travelled to the Belgian Congo, but it was the open spaces of Kenya that really caught her imagination. Nairobi was surrounded by game parks where they could see herds of impala crossing the road in single file, leaping over the tarmac, and sometimes baboons, or hippos wallowing in the shady water of tree-lined rivers, and occasionally lions with their cubs. Further out, the slopes around Kilimanjaro provided some of the most beautiful farmland in the world, where sisal, alfalfa, sweetcorn, avocados, citrus fruits, pineapple and mangoes were harvested. Christine was entranced and cautiously started to dream of a new future. She applied for permission to live and work in Kenya, and while waiting wrote letters to friends sketching out plans to 'start something of my own', perhaps a dairy farm or 'a tea shop at a crossroads'; anything that would give her 'the feeling of belonging to something or somewhere'.[72] Then perhaps, she wrote to Sir Owen, he and Kate could stay with her 'for ever and ever and *we all will be happy!!!*'[73] But a few weeks later the Colonial authorities, drowning in residency applications, turned hers down.

With immaculate timing, Christine now received an envelope from the High Commissioner's office, containing a gilt-edged invitation to a ceremony at which her George Medal and OBE were to be presented to her by the Governor of Kenya, Sir Philip Mitchell. 'Bloody bastards', she spat.[74] In what Michael called 'typical Christine fashion', she quickly made it known that she was not about to accept honours from the king's representative in Kenya when His Majesty's Government regarded her as an unsuitable resident.[75] It was only when, to avoid an embarrassing incident, she was granted permission to stay, that she agreed to accept the awards. Engraved around the rim of the George Medal were the words 'Madame Christina Gizycka', but the OBE on its civil ribbon, 'For God and the Empire', was for the British Christine Granville.[76] She was also presented with the War Medal 1939–1945, crowned stars for service in Africa, Italy, France and Germany, and

the 1939–1945 Star. Along with the Croix de Guerre, with one star, the Vercors Combatants' Medal, and her British parachutist's cloth wings, it made an impressive collection. To these Christine would add the commemorative gorget in the shape of a shield, depicting the Polish eagle protecting a Madonna and child – the Musketeers' badge that she and Father Laski and others had once held in secret. The design was remarkably similar to the token she had been given as a child visiting Częstochowa with her father. As a British agent, Christine was never honoured by Poland, either by the Polish government-in-exile or the Communist regime in her homeland, but perhaps she felt she carried something just as precious with her in this little Polish talisman, a reminder that she had always fought for the free Poland of her youth.

Michael now took a job heading the new Kenya Tourist Travel Association, and Christine correspondingly applied for a job as a ground stewardess with Kenyan Civil Aviation. During another unfortunate interview, however, despite her residency permit she was asked why she was travelling on a British passport, and why she did not therefore return to her own country. Kenya was awash with Polish refugees seeking work and Christine was seen as just another immigrant, second-class again. Infuriated, she returned to the offices with a lawyer the following day, and asked her interviewer to repeat his statements, but inside she was sick of such battles.

Too proud to stay somewhere she felt so unwelcome, Christine travelled back to London, meeting Andrzej, who flew over from Germany to join her, Aidan Crawley and his wife, the war correspondent Virginia Cowles, and other friends. Life had already moved on for most of them; they were settling down in steady jobs and busy with their growing families. Even Francis's wife, Nan, was pregnant again. Crawley could see that Christine was immediately 'stifled by an ordinary climate of living', especially in the grey autumn of dismal post-war London, where Poles were no more welcome than they were in Kenya, and where life seemed to be held together by ration books and food queues.[77] Feeling no more at home in Britain than Kenya, and missing the warmth, good food

and wide horizons of Africa, Christine begged Andrzej to join her there, and returned to Nairobi.

Andrzej, however, had no wish to leave his many friends and new plans for his own future. The idea of 'boiling my brains in the sun' didn't appeal to him in the least, he said, and besides he was sure that if he held out Christine would finally come back to live among her friends in Europe.[78] Feeling slighted, Christine threw herself back into life with Michael Dunford, travelling extensively in the Middle East with him that autumn. By the end of the year she was trying to persuade her cousin Jan to come out, settle, and lend her some roots. But while fond of Christine, Jan felt that any suggestion of hers should be treated judiciously and, busy trying to make ends meet and support his family in London, he never even managed to visit her. He was right to be cautious. Christine was enjoying a temptingly easy life with Michael, but she was not satisfied. 'She pined for action . . .' Anna Czyzewska realized, 'for the ancient parapets of Europe, and for Andrew'.[79] In 1948 Michael and Christine visited Cyprus, where they spent some of their happiest weeks together and he bought land to build a holiday house, but Christine was always glad to get back to Nairobi, where she could catch up with her friends and the post bringing news from Europe.

Henry Threlfall, with whom she had waited interminably in Bari to be dropped into Poland, was in Beirut, and invited her to join him there, as he felt so 'sad and lonely'.[80] Aidan Crawley had secured her an interview through the WAAF if she was interested in returning to London. Andrzej was 'flourishing' and still 'fulminating against officials of all kinds', Crawley told her. 'I suspect he loves you as much, and as little, as ever.'[81] A more recriminatory letter arrived from Sir Owen. 'Providence's intention was, I am sure, and is, that you should not lose touch with Kate and me as long as any of us three are alive', Sir Owen tried to tick her off without seeing her off. 'You have always gone against Providence, and have left my letters unanswered . . . I do not ask much of you, but I do ask this, that you should remember me at least once a year

and send me a postcard or the shortest of letters.'[82] Although not
an overt love letter, the strength of Sir Owen's feelings for Christine
was clear. She dutifully replied, saying she would love to sit at his
feet, in front of a big fire, and hear all his news, but meanwhile
asked after his happiness, before rather pointedly asking how Kate
had been, and specifically 'whom did she pick up as a flirtation?
Did she again get engaged to some smart Guards officer?'[83]

Francis also wrote regularly. He had now been appointed as
the first director of UNESCO's Central Bureau for Educational
Visits and Exchanges, with Vera Atkins as his deputy. His third
child, another daughter, had been born in February, in Brussels,
and, showing the measure of Nan's generosity as much as Francis's
admiration, she had been called Christine.*

Despite hating letter writing, Christine was also constantly in
touch with Andrzej, trying to tempt him out with stories of great
sun-washed valleys, open roads, the help ex-servicemen received
with the purchase of land, and the time they all spent watching
the cricket. Andrzej was unmoved. Farming had never appealed to
him, and the thought of a life built around sowing, reaping and
'ticking off days until there was Saturday again, and he could roll
down to Nairobi and get hopelessly drunk in a hotel lounge with
some war-pal' kept his resolve firm.[84] Come to Germany, he
wrote back, where the country was being reconstructed and full of
opportunities. But Christine could no more contemplate a life
in Germany than Andrzej could imagine living in Kenya. They had
reached an impasse.

The summer of 1948 stretched on and Christine drifted through
it without much of a plan. 'Where in the wide world are you?' Sir
Owen wrote. 'Is your restless spirit at peace or war with itself? And
have you got a husband or a lover?'[85] Sir Owen had finally retired
to his ancestral home in Ireland, where he had a horse, five cows, a
small sailing boat named *Christina* and a rather strained relationship
with his wife. 'No two lives could be more different than yours and

* A year later Francis and Nan's son was born, and they named him Paul, after
Francis's friend, the French resistance leader Paul Hérault.

mine, but we are linked together,' Sir Owen wrote romantically, 'and so I send you my love from afar; and it will go over mountains and lakes and swan-haunted shores, over the sea, over sunny comfortable England, perhaps over the deserts of Africa and reach for somewhere, some time, and perhaps you will think that enduring affection deserves a response'.[86] She did not, at least not immediately.

That autumn Christine received a telegram telling her that Andrzej had been involved in a serious car crash in Bonn. Given his love of fast cars, it had been an accident waiting to happen for some years. Days later he was still unconscious, and being held on the hospital critical list. Christine took the next available flight out. She never returned to Kenya. Anna Czyzewska was furious with her for not marrying Michael, who was left cursing himself for knowing all along that she could never be tamed. She had a sort of 'esprit de contradiction' he once said, and seemed to enjoy the chase more than the catch, be it for a medal, a passport or a relationship.[87] It was true that Christine certainly always wanted the recognition that she felt was due to her, yet afforded her little satisfaction when it came. Michael's love was heart-felt, but very civil, and although Christine had sheltered in it gratefully during the early years of the peace, momentarily allowing herself to dream of a future among the landscapes and animals of Africa, ultimately she was more interested in action. Desperate for freedom, Christine had treated Andrzej badly, but she still knew that the bond between them was deeper than any fleeting romance. As loyal as she was patriotic, when the need came she made sure she was there for him, hoping that there might even be further battles they could fight together.

16: DEEP WATER

Andrzej was down, but not out. When he finally opened his eyes Christine was there, glowering at him from the end of his bed. Delighted though he was to see her, Christine was no ministering angel. She kept him company at the clinic, laughing at his refusal ever to slow down and his almost complete set of broken limbs, and living by necessity at his expense. But when he was discharged and able to stand on his own, she made it clear that she would not be staying in Germany for very much longer. They agreed that although Christine would make a go of life in London and Andrzej would continue living in Bonn, they would find a way to meet regularly.

Back in London by default in early 1949, Christine met up with her Lwów cousins. Jan and Andrzej Skarbek had arrived in Italy in 1945, where they had joined the Polish II Corps under British command. Their father had been appointed minister for defence in the Polish government-in-exile in London and Jan had served as a junior adjutant to General Anders, and as a result in 1946 the whole family was evacuated to England. The brothers were in their early twenties and spoke no English when they arrived, but Jan took a series of manual jobs to put Andrzej through medical school. The next year Andrzej married an attractive, horse-loving, Irish woman, and moved to a flat in Lexham Gardens, in Kensington. Christine now took a room in a hotel on the same street. The Shelbourne comprised two town houses knocked together by the Polish Relief Society to provide cheap accommodation, mainly for émigrés. The cook was another reduced Polish aristocrat, Countess Przezdziecka, whose Polish teaching qualifications were not recognized in Britain, and who had landed the job after buying some second-hand cook-

books and experimenting. She and Christine would soon become firm friends.

Christine stowed her few clothes and possessions at the Shelbourne: her uniforms from the WAAF and the FANYs; a couple of books including a biography of a Siamese cat called, amusingly, O'Malley; her unloved medals and a few pieces of good jewellery, mostly presents from Andrzej; her standard-issue commando knife in its metal-tipped leather sheath, and her heavy wireless radio transmitter that no one in SOE had remembered to recall.[1] Then she walked across the road to warm her hands round a cup of hot lemon tea in her cousin's kitchen, the conversation slipping from Polish to English as it switched from the war to showjumping.

Christine soon tracked down another cousin now in London, Stanisław Skarbek, whom she had not seen since before the war. Stanisław thought that Christine 'seemed to have lost a little of her brilliance', but 'even so, she was more *alive* than most people'.[2] One evening the various cousins all got together for rather an intense reunion, raising many toasts to absent family including Jan and Andrzej's mother, who now lived near Bletchley; their tough Skarbek aunt in Nice who had served briefly with the Polish government-in-exile when it was based in France; and Christine's older brother Andrzej, still in Poland. This Andrzej Skarbek had joined the resistance and survived the conflict as a prisoner-of-war, almost certainly under an assumed identity. Christine had sent him a parcel in 1945, but she had no idea if it had arrived. She did not expect to hear from him – she was a prominent émigré and a former British agent. Andrzej would have been wise to keep his distance. But after being liberated from the camp, Andrzej enjoyed only a few years of freedom before – unknown to Christine – he was arrested and imprisoned by Poland's new Communist leadership.

Those relatives who had to be presumed dead were also now toasted in London. When prompted, Christine added Jerzy to the list, adding only that they had been divorced for some time. Christine's mother, Stefania, was also quietly remembered. Although many Poles applied to trace their families after the war, there is no record in the archives of the Polish Red Cross that

either Christine or her brother ever searched for their mother. Christine had long believed Stefania dead and, according to Stanisław Skarbek, 'any mention of her upset her terribly'. He had no doubt that 'Christine had loved her mother deeply'.[3] Although she was drawn to her relatives, and happy to spend time with them, Christine was clearly deeply unsettled, refusing to talk about what had happened since they had last met, or what the future might hold. There were people to whom she could tell her tales and act a part, enjoying the admiration or shock she could so easily provoke, but with her surviving family, the past was not just a series of stories, and it was not to be despoiled.

Christine also reached out to the wider Polish émigré community in London. About 150,000 stranded Poles had settled in the city, mostly in or around Kensington, working in low-paid jobs through the week, attending mass at Brompton Oratory on Sundays, and otherwise congregating in the restaurant and bars of the patriotic Klub Białego Orła, the White Eagle Club, in Knightsbridge. It was here that ministers of the no longer recognized Polish government-in-exile would meet to plan campaigns against the Communist regime in Poland, and former officers would dissect every detail of the war and, when in their cups, rail against the perfidy of their 'allies'. In August 1949, the 'Polish Association of Former Soviet Political Prisoners' was founded, partly to demand an investigation into the massacre of the tens of thousands of Polish officers at Katyn. Among their supporters was General Anders, a regular at the White Eagle, where he would discuss politics or play bridge upstairs while his wife danced the mazurka at the parties held in the ballroom below. Another refuge was Ognisko, the Polish Hearth Club on Exhibition Road, which was established just after the war to provide a home away from home, with Polish music and theatre, and which, despite its rather grand exterior, in common with a number of homes at the time, could not afford to carpet the upstairs rooms. Christine made a bee-line for both, and also made a note of the addresses of the Polish Air Force Association and other officers' clubs.

Given that many of the members of these clubs had previously

belonged to the Polish 6th Bureau, Christine expected a mixed reception. Even among exiles she was still an outsider – the half-Jewish daughter of the once-landed gentry, and a double divorcee with a reputation as, at best, a flirt. Wladimir Ledóchowski's wife, whose father was a well-known Polish author and diplomat, met Christine several times in the years immediately after the war, and later described her as 'nothing special', which was about as dismissive as she could get.[4] Perhaps most damning of all, however, was the fact that Christine was still widely considered as suspect for having worked with the British secret services rather than directly for the official Polish underground.

When Christine told her war stories she enjoyed winning her audience over through a combination of flourish and apparent frankness. By now her anecdotes were well honed, 'every sentence', wrote the author Stanisław 'Cat' Mackiewicz, one of the White Eagle regulars, 'glazed in extraordinary adventure'.[5] Furthermore she never dodged the difficult issues, once refusing to deny that a relative had been executed by the Home Army as a traitor, and another time detailing the 'swift and deadly' use to which she had put her commando knife.* But when Christine recounted once losing her nerve after the Nazis 'shot dead a whole village of the world's most innocent peasants' in reprisals for sabotage work with which she was involved, Stanisław Mackiewicz was probably not alone in thinking, 'Miss Krysia . . . did you not pay a huge price in blood everywhere so that the British could make war, using the hands of others?'[6]†

Former agents though, were more sympathetic. Jan Marusarz, the Olympic skier who had once guided Christine across the snow-covered Tatras into occupied Poland, was now working at the Club as a general factotum, and would loudly welcome her whenever she arrived. Later he gave her a silver bracelet studded with turquoises

* Christine's distant relative Countess Maria Grocholska was connected to Rudolf Schelich, a functionary at the pre-war German Embassy in Warsaw who later served as a Nazi intelligence agent. See Roman Buczek, *The Musketeers* (1985), p. 41.

† Stanisław Mackiewicz would serve as prime minister of the unrecognized Polish government-in-exile between 1954 and 1955.

which he had made for her himself. Other regulars at the White Eagle included the former Musketeers Michal 'Lis' Gradowski, and Teresa Łubienska, who had survived not only Pawiak prison, but incarceration in both Auschwitz and Ravensbrück concentration camps.* Gradowski introduced Christine to Józef Kasparek, who also had experience of covert operations, and with whom he now ran a small business from the basement of the club. Christine took a shine to Kasparek, and learning they were distantly related took to playfully calling him 'cousin' and inviting him to join her for lunch upstairs. There she entertained him with elaborate stories, once claiming to have visited Britain before the war and, through family connections, met and married an Irish aristocrat named Granville. But however unreliable her stories, and whatever the opinion of some politicians and intellectuals, the old Polish intelligence hands at the club always asked after her, Kasparek remembered proudly, and soon she was dubbed 'a queen of the European underground' by an organization honouring the achievements of Poles in the resistance.[7]

Christine soon found that many other old Polish friends were also in London, including the journalist Florian Sokolow, and Richard Truszkowski, with whom she had worked in Cairo, and whose young daughter she now shocked when she visited by sitting cross-legged at Truszkowski's feet in front of the fire, a very bohemian and unladylike thing to do, prompting a diary entry describing her as 'a horrible lady'.[8] Andrzej's cousin, Ludwig Popiel, who had smuggled the anti-tank rifle out of Poland, was also in town, working as a builder and decorator after a hare-brained scheme to buy hashish in Lebanon and sell it in Cairo for a profit had failed to make his fortune. Zofia Tarnowska, her brother Stas, and her new husband, Bill Stanley Moss, who had both been involved in Ludwig's scheme, were there too. When they did not feel up to the formal surroundings of the big clubs they would meet for pirogi and beetroot soup, or tea and chocolate éclairs, at

* After arriving in London, Łubienska devoted herself to fighting for rights and compensation for former Polish prisoners-of-war.

Daquise, the cosy Polish café beside South Kensington tube station. Sometimes they would go on to the Pheasantry on the King's Road, where the rooms were full of smoke, laughter and people dancing and 'drinking to destruction' as Maryś Tyszjiewicz, who would later marry Christine's cousin, Jan Skarbek, put it.[9]*

They were all at a bit of a loose end, but Christine perhaps most of all. Andrzej was working and building up savings in Germany. Moss was writing *Ill Met by Moonlight* and, a jobbing journalist, he was also starting to consider the possibilities of turning Christine's stories into something that could be published. She let him interview her, along with a reporter from the *Daily Express* purportedly examining the lives of Polish émigrés, and had fun with them both. 'As soon as I was old enough my father taught me to use a rifle, though in later years I preferred a hand grenade', the *Express* later quoted her. 'I could kill fifteen men with one hand grenade . . . later I carried a machine gun and grenades and killed many people'.[10] Spicing the drama with tragedy, she added that her former husband, Jerzy Gizycki, had been killed in action. She must have decided he was unlikely to see the *Daily Express* in Canada. But the paper did not run the piece straight away and Moss was busy completing his own memoir. Zofia was pregnant with their first child and they needed the publisher's advance.† Their daughter was born in July 1949 and Christine visited the new family in Bayswater a few days later. When Zofia said that they had not yet settled on a name, Christine told her to 'name her for me', because Christine was the 'lucky name' that had got her through the war unscathed.[11] Zofia loved the idea, but little Christine Isabelle Tarnowska Moss soon refused to answer to anything other than 'Pussy Cat'.[12]

* One evening Ludwig Popiel took Maryś out dancing, was too broke to pay the bill, dropped her home, and then shinned up the drainpipe to claim a kiss before he left. As Maryś was sleeping on her mother's bedroom floor she acquiesced to keep the peace, only to have him climb back up moments later, having forgotten his hat.

† Not expecting to get much more use from her Cairo evening dresses, Zofia sent them to Andrzej's niece in Warsaw, where it was impossible to buy clothes, but where there was little call for ball dresses.

Émigré Poles in Britain had every reason to seek talismans that might bring good fortune. Clement Attlee had agreed that demobilized troops and their families could stay in the country, but he still hoped that many of them would return voluntarily to Poland, where the Communist regime was introducing land reforms, nationalization and reconstruction. In this he caught the British public mood. 'Poles go home' was increasingly found scrawled across walls in Britain's cities, insults were shouted in the streets, and former aristocrats and decorated servicemen were reduced, as they saw it, to working as barmen, bottle-washers and jobbing decorators.[13] Even the former head of the Polish 6th Bureau, Jósef Smolenski, ended up washing dishes for TWA in Hounslow.[14]* He, like many, felt deeply humiliated. 'How odd it is that one is not afraid of death at war, yet one is frightened of such a life . . .' one Polish colonel wrote. 'Friends and colleagues . . . when my hour comes how will you greet me, a labourer from an English laundry?'[15] 'How the English treat us Poles!' Christine stormed to Józef Kasparek in the bar of the White Eagle, but she also knew that she needed to find a job. 'You think I'm set up for life', she sighed. 'I'm not.'[16]

Christine's compatriots could do little to help her find work, but British friends, like Francis Cammaerts, Harold Perkins and Aidan Crawley, rallied round. An agency had been set up to help former SOE people into employment, but after offering Christine a number of secretarial roles, it gave up the attempt to place her. Christine still 'could not bear to work in an office', she told her friends at the Shelbourne, 'she wanted to live'.[17] The difficulty, Francis believed, was that 'no one really took the trouble to find the kind of job she would have done very well'.[18] Christine told Francis that she wanted to work with people, but other than that she could only specify what she hoped to avoid. There were to be no long training courses, and 'she definitely did not want to become involved in administration'.[19] He suggested a job vetting hotels for

* Smolenski's brother in Poland was then arrested on the pretext that Smolenski was working for the Americans.

a travel agency, but there was not a lot going in that line. She held on to the hope that there might be more intelligence work, and kept a note of both Lord Vansittart and Freddy Voigt's addresses at the back of her diary, but there was nothing for her there either, and Sir Owen was unable to find anything in the diplomatic world. Some weeks later Kate O'Malley turned up in London, returning from a job at the British Embassy in Rome with a new surname and baby to match. Christine duly visited, cooed, and never went back. It seemed that all the women from Christine's recent past had now embraced motherhood. Christine embarked on a series of uninspiring, low-paid and short-lived jobs instead.

Calling on her Cairo switchboard experience, her first position was as a telephone operator at India House, the home of the Indian High Commission. A friend, Izabela Muszkowska, worked in the restaurant there and the pair of them would meet to gossip through their lunch hours, Christine joking about their reduced circumstances and 'laughing like mad' at any story that saw them through the day.[20] Their pay packets helped to keep up their spirits too, and Christine was soon able to enjoy buying a dressing gown and decent leather shoes, and having her hair done in Alfonse Ltd in Piccadilly, who billed themselves as 'Court Hairdressers'.[21] For a few short weeks she was happy living in the moment, as the two women had a tacit agreement not to talk about the past or future. Christine was therefore shocked when Iza broke the news that she too was pregnant. 'Oh my God! What have you done!' she cried.[22] It was not just that Iza and her husband were only just managing to cover their rent and food bills on two salaries; she was losing yet another friend to family life.

Although she had none of her own, Christine was not without sympathy for individual children. In Nairobi she had sometimes sought out the company of her friends' daughter, and in Cairo she had made a point of visiting the lonely five-year-old daughter of a colleague, who was boarding in a Catholic school. She even took a distant interest in the baby daughter of her cousin Andrzej Skarbek and his wife, once commissioning a copy of the Skarbek family crest, worked in leather by Polish artisans in London, to hang above

her cot. But she rarely chose to hold a baby, and when Iza gave up her job to care for her child, Christine stayed in touch by phone but never visited.

Without Iza, Christine did not last long at India House. Her next jobs were more sociable, but still left her aching with boredom and frustration. She took a position selling frocks at Harrods, where she quickly made friends with another salesgirl, retelling her most outlandish war stories, and gossiping about their supervisors: 'ladies with bosoms and backsides so symmetrically arranged about their waists', she once commented, that 'putting them upside-down wouldn't perceptibly change the general aspect'.[23] A similar blunt honesty with clients quickly made her unemployable. 'The customers found me too rude', she admitted.[24] A role running the linen room of a Paddington Hotel, where 'make do and mend' was the order of the day, lasted little longer; a position as a hat-check girl less still. Sometimes she did not even get past the interviews. A friend introduced her to the manager of a chain of hotels. Told that only married women need apply, she asked whether the same rule applied to men. On hearing that it did not, she smiled, and asked for a list of his unmarried staff, telling him 'I'll marry one of them.' 'I was thrown out', she reported with more pride than contrition.[25]

Finally she found a job as a waitress at the Marynka, a small Polish café on the Brompton Road in Knightsbridge, where her sense of humour, marital status and accent were irrelevant. Here she served strong dark coffee to all ranks of the demobilized Polish military, former civil servants, and ex-ministers. Most bore a grudge against the British government, and would sit muttering infamies or tapping their papers and exclaiming in delight, 'Serves them right, the bastards' at the worst domestic news.[26] Many, however, recognizing Christine, would gallantly spring to their feet to kiss her hand before placing their orders. Soon wartime friends, colleagues from SOE, parachutists who had met her in Egypt and Palestine, and FANYs and agents from Italy would all drop by to chat with her, inviting her out for lunch at Ognisko, dinner at the Special Forces Club or dancing at the White Eagle.

Christine was coping, but as the war retreated and life returned

to normal for so many, she found she was far from happy with her safer, smaller, civilian life. She missed the excitement of her special-agent years, and was constantly drawn to conflict, change or any argument to get her blood up. 'She found post-war Britain a drab place', Patrick Howarth realized, and Vera Atkins, now working with Francis, saw that 'she was quite unable to adapt to boring day-to-day routine . . . she lived for action and adventure'.[27] Even Francis recognized, with some pain, that Christine 'was a deeply unhappy and unsettled woman'.[28] One afternoon she was hit by a car at Hyde Park Corner. More shaken than seriously injured, she was perhaps hurt most by the rumours that now began to circulate about her state of mind. Andrzej's loyal old friend, Stas Tarnowski, saw the worst in her: a woman drinking too much and, he guessed, taking painkillers and sleeping pills. His new young wife, Ada, also thought Christine was 'very unhappy, always sad and bitter'.[29] Yet other friends, such as Iza Muszkowska, remembered her as 'always laughing and joking . . . healthy, straight, noble and energetic', and her friends at the Shelbourne Hotel thought she was lively, out-going, and no more sad than any other politically aware Polish émigré at the time.[30] She was often to be found at the heart of a party, telling her stories and always surrounded by men 'like bodyguards'.[31] But Bill Stanley Moss would later say that he never heard her talking about herself, and felt she dodged his questions with 'a self-effacing smile', and only accepted social invitations if she knew there would be no other guests. 'She used to raise an imperceptible barrier against deep personal relations with anyone', he later claimed.[32]

London depressed Christine. She could not bear the thought of spending the rest of her life as a spectator, doomed for ever to stand offstage with only a growing sense of containment, boredom and isolation in place of purposeful activity. She had not entirely given up her hopes of moving to Africa, and still sometimes daydreamed about the acres she would manage while following stories about Kenya in the British press. When she could afford it, she satisfied her need for action and freedom by travelling, mainly to see Andrzej in Bonn or Lucerne, where she indulged in the good food that was

hard to come by in austerity Britain, and visits to a beauty salon. At one point she picked up a pretty silver-covered Elizabeth Arden notebook, inside which an admirer pencilled in imperfect German, 'Christiana: Mein liebling, ich leiber ich'.* Whoever the author was, Christine kept the page in, while tearing out those around it. She would also visit friends in Paris or stay in Nice, close to her aunt who was now, despite being in her eighties, actively promoting the welfare of Poles in the south of France. She even considered taking a local job in an estate agents there, and Andrzej thought that had she had enough money she might have bought herself an old farmhouse in the hills, with no electricity, and never enough furniture, but 'a family of stray dogs, cats and birds', and 'for the rest of her life she would have lain in the sun'.[33]

But Christine refused to settle, even when the opportunity was handed to her on a plate. Some time after the war a firm of chartered accountants notified her that a colonel with whom she had enjoyed a romance in Cairo before he was killed on active service had left her a London house in his will.† Christine reportedly renounced the gift without even checking the address, or stating her reasons. And when Livia 'Pussi' Deakin, with whom she had once sat gossiping round the Gezira Club pool, asked why she did not simply marry Andrzej, warning her that she was not getting any younger and he might not wait for ever, Christine laughed it off, saying that her only plans were to go travelling and send back 'sackfuls of pretty postcards'.[34] She was already looking for work that involved travel. A distant cousin called Hanka Nicolle, the sister of a Polish journalist Christine had known before the war, had a job as a stewardess on a passenger liner taking Polish émigrés to Argentina, and bringing back excellent meat.‡ Christine met her for lunch when she was on shore leave in London, but the thought of changing sheets and cleaning bathrooms put her off the idea of

* The handwriting is not her own, and the initials below the message are undecipherable. Polish Institute and Sikorski Museum, Christine Granville papers (1949–50)

† Probably Colonel Cookham.

‡ Hanka Nicolle was the sister of the diplomat, journalist and author Tadeusz Breza.

signing up as a cabin steward. In January 1950 Francis gave her a glowing reference for a job with a travel agency, and in March, Aidan Crawley's lobbying finally led to an offer of work, as a secretary, but in the Air Attaché's office in Paris. By then, however, another, more exciting, opportunity had come up.

In early 1950 Christine heard again from George Michailov, the Serbian pilot with whom she had had a brief fling in Cairo. Having settled in Australia, Michailov had joined forces with a well-connected Australian pilot called Norman Hamilton to set up an ambitious network of car dealerships across the continent. In Britain it was all but impossible to buy a new car, as almost everything produced was being shipped to the USA to help pay off the British war debt, but Christine immediately thought of Andrzej. Andrzej was still living in Germany and had now swapped his interest in Opels for an obsession with Porsche, who had brought out their first branded sports car two years earlier. Discussions began about the possibility of a car dealership joint venture, with Andrzej responsible for supply and Michailov and his partner running the sales side in Australia. Christine and Andrzej spent the next few months developing motor contacts in Britain and Germany, among other coups winning the rights for Porsche agencies in Australia. Andrzej was in heaven. That summer they drove through France together, ostensibly for work but also taking in a tour of Christine's old haunts, meeting Sylviane Rey and the other friends who still knew her as 'Miss Pauline', and ending up at the annual commemoration ceremony at Vercors. By the end of the trip, Andrzej felt that their relationship was back on track and they returned to London in high spirits.

Michailov and Hamilton, who had travelled over to London, were duly entertained at the White Eagle. They discussed the finer details of the joint venture, and registered samples of their signatures for a joint business bank account. A few days later they returned to Australia with the promise of some serious investment to back the Australian side of the start-up. 'Please immediately transfer by telegram all money to national bank Australia in Sydney . . .' Andrzej received a telegram a few days later, 'love

George Michailov'.[35] Andrzej knew a lot about cars, and plenty about German tax and export duties, but much less about business. 'He didn't love to work', his niece said tactfully, he 'preferred to enjoy life, read history books, and talk about how to change the world'.[36] But the world was already changing. A few months later the deepening recession in Australia completely knocked the bottom out of the market for expensive European cars, Michailov and Hamilton fell out, and Andrzej's investment appeared to be completely irrecoverable. Both he and Christine were now once again penniless. Christine, who had brokered the partnership partly as a way of squaring her debt to Andrzej, was mortified. But without the means to get to Australia there were few avenues they could pursue either to make good their investment or to decide whether to make a claim against their former partners.

It was now that Christine learned that her brother had died in hospital in Poland the previous June. Andrzej Skarbek had been released from Wronki prison with a lung condition, almost certainly tuberculosis either contracted in custody or exacerbated by the conditions there. He died soon after and was buried beside his father in the Skarbek family plot in Warsaw's famous Powązki Cemetery. Although they had not seen each other since 1939, and had not managed to re-establish contact after the war, Christine was deeply affected by the news of her brother's death. She would never know that he had kept a photograph of her among his few family possessions all his life.[37]*

Christine and Andrzej spent the next few weeks in Germany.† By the mid-autumn of 1950, with no further word from Michailov, she had decided to look for work as a stewardess on a shipping line

* Andrzej Skarbek's first wife, Irena, lived until 1982, and their daughter Teresa, Christine's goddaughter, until 2002. Their family photos were passed to Teresa's son, Andrzej Christian, born in 1956. Both Irena and Teresa were buried in the Skarbek family plot in Powązki Cemetery. It is not known what happened to Andrzej's second wife, Alexandra.

† At least once that summer Christine underwent some radium treatment in Bonn, but unfortunately there is no record of whether this was for a benign condition, often treated with radiation in the 1950s, or for something more serious.

with routes to Australia, so she could both earn a wage and hopefully pin him – and Hamilton – down. The tedious process of job-seeking followed. In the new year she applied to the Merchant Navy for work as a stewardess with the New Zealand Shipping Company, only to be rejected in March. She then resubmitted her application for a job as an air stewardess with BOAC, directly lobbying Whitney Straight, the deputy chairman, who had served as a pilot in the Battle of Britain and crossed paths with Christine in Cairo in 1943. However, she was now forty-three, eight years above the company's age requirement for air stewardesses, and her application was rejected, but by then it didn't matter. In late April she had been taken on by the Shaw Savill Line as a stewardess, ironically for the New Zealand Shipping Company's new luxury ocean liner, the *Ruahine*.

On 1 May 1951 Christine travelled up to Glasgow to join the crew of the *Ruahine* in advance of her maiden voyage. She was an impressive ship. Over 580 feet long and weighing nearly 18,000 tons, she had the capacity to carry over 300 passengers serviced by 200 staff. The passengers had the run of four decks, including a sports deck with a small pool surrounded by red and white striped deckchairs, a promenade deck with lounge, library and reading room, a gently curving smoking room with the all-important bar, and a 'verandah lounge' boasting a dance-floor that overlooked the pool. The last time that Christine had been on a liner, she was in first-class, heading to South Africa with Jerzy in 1939. Now, ten years later, she was on the staff, up at six in the morning to take charge of second-class passengers' cabins on deck D, and in a uniform unlike any she had worn before. The shipping company stipulated light blue cotton dresses with a crisp flared skirt of the length 'as usual in leading hospitals', a nurse's white apron with bands crossed over the shoulders and a white 'Sister Dora Cap'.[38] She looked more like a staff nurse than a stewardess, and very little like any previous incarnation of Christine Granville.

Christine arrived at the Glasgow docks with her new Merchant Seaman's card and record book in her pocket, and her uniform and other personal effects in a heavy, square, shipping trunk. Leaning

over the ship's railings, 'neat, tidy, well dressed in a rather spivvish way', was a steward called Dennis George Muldowney, who had been working on passenger liners for the last two years.[39] Dennis, who always had an eye for the ladies and was known to brag about his conquests, watched Christine struggling, ran a hand through his Brylcreemed hair and headed down to help. As usual she did not demur, but neither did she expect much of a friendship with this vain working-class man from Wigan. Dennis, however, was rather struck with his down-on-her-luck Polish aristocrat.

A week later, the Ruahine was in London's Victoria Dock, with all staff fully outfitted, trained and ready to take on passengers for New Zealand via the Lesser Antilles, through the Panama Canal and on to Tahiti before docking in Wellington. As there were a few days before they set sail, Andrzej flew out from Germany to see Christine before she left. She told him that she was not happy with the atmosphere on the Ruahine and, disappointingly, that they would not be stopping at Australia on this maiden voyage. However, it was a start. A few days later Andrzej drove her down to Southampton Docks and saw her off.

The Ruahine would be at sea for four months; discipline was strict and appearances mattered. One of the requirements was that while on duty staff were expected to wear any decorations they had been awarded during the war. Christine's impressive line of ribbons, enough to flatter a general, made her an immediate favourite with the passengers, and an obvious target for resentment among the crew. Naturally proud, speaking heavily accented English, and decorated to the nines, she was soon the victim of a campaign of abuse for being a foreigner, a woman and a suspected liar, which made her life a complete misery. The only person to stand up for her was the steward who had helped her at Glasgow Docks, Dennis Muldowney. Things got worse when several groups of passengers, Polish émigrés hoping to make a fresh start abroad, gained a reputation for drunkenness and disorder. Complaints about their behaviour led to xenophobic gossip in the staff rooms, with even the Captain himself loudly expressing his dislike for foreigners. Eventually Christine could no longer let the moaning about spend-

ing taxpayers' money to ship émigrés overseas – 'in luxury' – go unchallenged.*[40] Having not minced her words she stormed out of the staff mess, followed only by Dennis, who lent her his shoulder, and then gave a piece of his mind to the rest of the crew. Things improved slightly, but Christine was still ostracized. It was to be a much more difficult voyage than she had anticipated. A week later Christine sent her first letter to Andrzej, mentioning only that 'the other stewards are not very friendly, except one'.[41] After that she wrote two or three times from every port of call, almost every letter repeating how unhappy she was.

Dennis Muldowney liked a pretty face, but he also recognized pride, frustration and loneliness. The son of a Lancashire woman and her Irish Catholic husband, he had grown up in a household in conflict. His parents were both hard drinkers and as a child he was often left outside pubs to wait for them, sometimes being abused by other adults, only to watch them fighting violently when they were thrown out. His sister Lillian died in infancy, and some years later he gained three half-siblings but never felt particularly close to them. Leaving school at fourteen, he tried to improve himself through reading, but became obsessed with his appearance, working as a hairdresser and then in a range of service jobs before marrying and having a son in 1940. His wife divorced him seven years later, citing cruelty and the excessive 'sexual demands' he made upon her.[42] He later confessed to having an unusually high libido. He had worked as a fireman and fire service dispatch rider during the war, hazardous work during the Blitz but, as he was all too aware, never in the front line. After his divorce, he joined the Merchant Navy as a steward. It was work he enjoyed, and he soon relaxed into the routine of life on board, replacing his rather earnest Errol Flynn look with a clean shave and easy smile. With plenty of experience under his belt, he now taught Christine how to balance multiple tea trays, strip a bed in seconds, and manage her relationships on board ship, and when his own chores were done he would often head

* Free-passage schemes had been set up to the Antipodes for ex-servicemen, with the first 200 families leaving in November 1946.

down to deck D to give her a hand. Christine gratefully accepted his help, becoming increasingly attracted to this blunt man who was so different to her previous, officer-class, admirers.

Two months later, the *Ruahine* was heading back to London. The ship was almost empty on the return journey, and Christine passed much of the time sunning herself on deck, as often as not with Muldowney beside her. According to him they were already lovers. She was, he said, 'the only woman who would meet his constant sexual demands'.[43] But they were something more as well. Christine, Muldowney claimed, was 'neurotic', torn between determination and depression, and at times obsessed with death to such a degree that in Panama they made a suicide pact, which in the event came to nothing.[44] Muldowney was clearly under her spell, recognizing the grief and bitterness under the web of stories, but so besotted with her, and so damaged himself, that he was unable to offer any constructive support. If Christine was sinking, Muldowney would loyally sink with her. In better days, she might have dismissed him as just another lame dog, but during the months on board ship, shunned by the rest of the crew, Christine had no one else to turn to. Instead she focused the full beam of her personality on Muldowney, and he became convinced that she was in love with him, and unable to live without him. Whether from real feeling, or the lack of it, Christine did nothing to counter this impression. By the time they arrived back at Plymouth, in mid-September 1951, she had decided that it was time to repay all Muldowney's kindnesses to her, starting with a lift to London in Andrzej's car.

Perhaps unexpectedly, the 'cheerful though often wistful' Christine, as one passenger described her, had turned out to be an excellent stewardess, caring for the deck D inhabitants as they struggled with sea-sickness, and giving them consistently good-humoured attention, as several letters of thanks testify.[45] These letters also reveal how obviously painful much of the passage had been for her. 'I hope your future voyages will be good ones', one woman wrote just before they docked. 'As a passenger I have not found this ship a "happy" one – the atmosphere is definitely against that.'[46] 'You were always so willing and obliging and cheery

in spite of the many difficulties and trials you had', wrote another. 'Wishing you all good luck and a happier ship.'[47] But Christine had no wish for a happier ship. As soon as she got to London she solicited her British friends to help get her any other line of work. Aidan Crawley, now MP for North Bucks, recommended her as 'a woman of great integrity and distinction ... capable of filling any administrative or other post with great ability'.[48] Patrick Howarth pointed out that she was 'widely travelled' and 'a most accomplished linguist', well able 'to establish happy relations with people of the most varied backgrounds'.[49] But it was Francis who went overboard. 'I cannot speak too highly of her abilities as a serving officer or as a human being', he wrote in a reference that Christine had copied many times. 'Her ability, which is quite exceptional, should make her of the greatest value to any employer who wishes to use her services...' It is impossible, he finished, 'to cover all the qualities of so outstanding a personality'.[50] That the reference had been written by a lover was all too obvious, and Francis later admitted that he had to tone it down. But even that version had little effect.

Once in London Christine had checked back into her old room at the Shelbourne Hotel, booking another down the corridor for Muldowney. Two days later he moved into the Merchant Navy Welfare Club a short walk away at Lancaster Gate, the other side of Kensington Gardens. According to the hotel records, however, he was back for at least one night, discreetly booking a separate room on 17 October, when Christine was also in residence. There seems little doubt that their relationship was more than platonic. When Christine had first got back, Countess Przezdziecka, the cook, noticed how tired she looked and asked her if it wasn't very hard for her, as a young woman, to work as a cabin steward. Christine just laughed, saying 'No, no, no, I have a young man, he always steps in.'[51] The Countess disapproved, telling Christine that it was dangerous to get the man's hopes up, especially as he was clearly not a suitable partner. Christine paid no need, so the Countess repeated her anxieties – and the accompanying lecture – to her teenage daughter, Teresa. Teresa, however, knew that Christine

had risked her life for their country during the war, had heard the stories of her rescuing men in Poland and France, and believed her to be 'a great hero, very beautiful, tall and slim ... and very capable'.[52] She was certain that Christine could take care of herself.

Andrzej, meanwhile, was only too happy to show Muldowney his gratitude for standing up for Christine throughout the voyage. Thanking him 'heartily' for 'being so decent' he introduced him to their London circle.[53] Christine asked her friends to be kind to her colleague, explaining that he had stood by her, but also warning them that he was 'very sensitive'. Muldowney was given a warm welcome, regularly invited out for lunch, drinks and to the cinema, and Ludwig Popiel even gave him a petrol lighter as a token of friendship. Soon Muldowney was spending most afternoons among 'the dispossessed aristocrats and aging generals' at the White Eagle, waiting for some of Christine's circle to come over.[54] He even started to learn Polish.

But although Muldowney was pleasant and polite, he was as intimidated as he was impressed. Clearly out of his depth, he would sit nervously on the edge of his chair, hesitant in conversation and ashamed of his war record and job as a steward.[55] Patrick Howarth remembered having tea with Christine and Muldowney at the White Eagle, but after a few abortive attempts to strike up a conversation Howarth simply forgot all about him, admitting that 'he never made the slightest impression on me'.[56] Andrzej, meanwhile, gave Muldowney every chance to make his mark, but soon described him as having 'a sort of face over the surface of which words seemed to hover for a while, as though in search of an orifice to sink in'.[57] Soon Andrzej had reached the slightly worrying conclusion that what Muldowney really wanted to do was to stay silent, and 'curl up on a mat, on the threshold of Christine's bedroom'.[58] Muldowney was 'a curious little creature', Christine's Zakopane friend remembered. 'It was obvious that he had a frightful inferiority complex. We used to wonder why he was with her. He did not come from her milieu, and he was definitely not her type. Christine always had a wide choice of stunning men, so why did she waste her time with a goblin like Muldowney?'[59]

Back among friends, Christine began to wonder the same thing. Andrzej was now with her whenever possible, much better company, and clearly still deeply in love with her. For some time he had been pressing Christine to sit for a portrait by the society artist Aniela Pawlikowska, who was in London exhibiting in the Polish clubs. Christine finally agreed, and Pawlikowska made an initial sepia pastel sketch showing Christine with her dark hair set high on her head, looking much more aristocratic, and slightly more nervous, than she does in any photograph. She then sat for a formal oil painting, with the same hairstyle and slight look of hesitancy, but this time in profile as she leans on the arm of a chair, her long fingers clearly displaying her Skarbek signet ring; it is a portrait of a lady, not a ship's steward, but above all it is a portrait of a defiantly proud woman.*

In mid-November Christine joined Hanka Nicolle on the *New Australia*, sailing this time to Australia from Southampton. Muldowney was serving on a different ship. During her shore leave, three weeks later, Christine visited Michailov and Hamilton, but she could neither revive the business plan nor extract Andrzej's investment from them. The night before they sailed for Britain Christine wired Andrzej, telling him to write off his capital.† Despite this disappointing result, the voyage itself had been much happier, and on the homeward journey she and Hanka decided to sign up for another trip on the same ship a few weeks later. The *New Australia* slipped back into Southampton on 20 January 1952. Muldowney was there, waiting to meet them, which surprised Hanka as she knew that Christine had neither wanted nor encouraged him to come. The three of them caught the train to Waterloo, Christine becoming increasingly irritated until she abruptly told Muldowney

* Aniela (Lela) Pawlikowska (1901–80) later also sketched Maryś Tarnowska and Jan Skarbek on the eve of her wedding, and Zofia Tarnowska Moss's daughters with their cousins and aunt Ada Lubomirska, although this was not to mark any particular occasion.

† Instead he started legal action. By March 1952 Andrzej was pursuing £30,000 in damages to his personal reputation and business position in Germany, in addition to repayment of his investment.

to leave her alone, at which point he backed down, apologizing and saying that he hadn't meant to offend.

Christine had only just over a fortnight before she and Hanka were due back on the *New Australia*. Although still tolerated, Muldowney's constant presence was now regarded as 'tiresome' by Christine and all her friends. Francis called him 'a pathetic bore', 'intolerably clinging', and Andrzej thought him 'unbelievably thick-skinned . . . a dangerous simpleton' with 'a mass of obsessions and neurosis' who jumped whenever Andrzej clicked his fingers, as he habitually did, mistaking the noise for hammers pounding in his head.[60] Aware that his welcome had cooled, Muldowney became moody and resentful, but he could not leave Christine alone. He was 'violently in love with her', Kate O'Malley wrote, and Andrzej noticed that he had started pathetically following her around 'like a dingo dog, trotting at Christine's heels', sometimes even pacing the streets outside her friends' houses when she visited them or simply waiting for her to turn up at the Shelbourne or White Eagle.[61] One evening, during dinner with John Roper, Christine told him that Muldowney was starting to frighten her and, fearing that they might not see each other again, when they parted she said an impromptu prayer for Roper and his young family.

Soon Christine admitted that she was thoroughly tired of the 'obstinate and terrifying' Muldowney.[62] Telling Francis and Andrzej that they had to shake him off, she started avoiding the White Eagle, considered putting out a story that she had sailed on another ship, and asked the Shaw Savill Line not to assign her to ships on which he would be serving. Andrzej now worried about the effect that a blunt rejection might have on Muldowney, warning Christine that 'not only is he madly in love with you, but *mad*'.[63] Knowing that Muldowney was due to sail for South Africa, Andrzej persuaded her to keep the peace a little longer. As a result, Muldowney joined them at the cinema on his last evening in London. It was a mistake.

Christine had always told him, Muldowney later claimed, that she had known Andrzej since childhood, and that it was a purely platonic friendship. 'In fact he had had a leg shot off', he said, 'and

was impotent – no good sexually'.[64] If this was Christine's story, it would not have been the first time that she had used it. However, something about the way that she and Andrzej behaved towards each other that evening made Muldowney start to have his doubts. 'As a result I got upset', he admitted. 'I thought she had been playing the fool with me and kidding me all the time.'[65] After the cinema, Christine and Andrzej walked Muldowney to his ship at Albert Dock. Delighted to see the back of him, Christine kissed him goodbye in the traditional Polish way, and flippantly promised to write at every port. She later told Andrzej that she had no intention of writing at all, thinking that this would be the best way to finish what was now an unwanted friendship. 'He bores me so, he's such a nuisance', she told Andrzej, but when Andrzej remonstrated that it would be both hurtful and possibly provocative to cut Muldowney out altogether, she agreed to drop him a last short note.[66]

A few days later, at the start of February 1952, Christine and Hanka rejoined the *New Australia*. They were away until mid-April. This time Andrzej came to meet Christine on her return to Southampton docks. Learning that he had only a week in London before flying to Switzerland, Christine decided to go with him. At the end of a note to Hanka, letting her know her plans, she added a PS: 'Not a trace of Dennis, what luck'.[67] But Muldowney sailed back into London the next day. He had not received any letters from Christine, and he had had plenty of time to brood over her. Now he found her last note to him, hoping that he had had a pleasant trip, and letting him know that she was leaving the Merchant Navy and going to the Continent. She wished him all the best.

Irritating and slightly worrying though he was, Muldowney was the last thing on Christine's mind that week. Earlier in April a select committee of the US Congress had arrived in London to take the testimony of witnesses to the Soviet massacre of Polish officers at Katyn. Thirty Polish witnesses were heard during the course of four days, after which a mass meeting was held to commemorate the twelfth anniversary of the massacre. Although not a witness

herself, Christine could hardly have missed the speculation sur-
rounding the interviews. The Soviets had killed her brother as
surely as they had killed the officers at Katyn, and it was probably
not coincidence that she and Andrzej booked their flights to Swit-
zerland for just after the remembrance meeting. Returning to the
Shelbourne the night before they were to leave, Christine went
ahead while Andrzej parked the car. Before he had time to lock it,
Muldowney came rushing down the hotel steps. Andrzej called out
a greeting, but he stormed past. Christine was in the lobby, shaking
with anger that Muldowney had reproached her, in a 'very rude'
and threatening way, for not writing from her ship and for avoiding
him since her return.[68] She had told him, bluntly, that she did not
want to see, or be pestered by, him any more. She then told the
porters not to let him into the hotel again and, if he ever enquired
about her, to tell him that she was not there.

The next day Christine and Andrzej left for a week in Switzer-
land. As the Pawlikowska portrait had not yet arrived, she gave the
pastel sketch to Andrzej as a promise of things to come. Andrzej
later told his niece that he had given Christine an open proposal,
that they marry and live somewhere in Europe on condition that
she would be faithful to him. Christine had yet to make a commit-
ment when she received a telegram from the Union Castle Line
shipping company, offering her work on the *Winchester Castle* sailing
from Southampton to South Africa at the end of the month. She
decided to accept the job, with its useful salary, after which she
and Andrzej would hole up together for a while in Brussels or
Liège and plan the future.

With Christine in Switzerland, Hanka bore the brunt of Mul-
downey's frustration in London. Unknown to either of them, he
had left his job on the ships to take work as a resident porter at the
Reform Club on Pall Mall, for what he called 'pin money', purely
so as to be closer to her. Now she was not to be found at her
regular haunts, Muldowney started repeatedly phoning Hanka,
asking to meet, and when Hanka said she had no wish to discuss
Christine with him, he swore that he had no feelings for her before
asking whether she had met someone else.

Christine wisely stayed with Andrzej until the last moment, returning to London only on 28 April, two days before she was due to join the *Winchester Castle*. Coming back from a restaurant the following evening, she had a sudden surge of anxiety and phoned Ludwig Popiel, asking him to meet her at High Street Kensington. As they walked back to the Shelbourne together Christine told her old friend how frightened she was of Muldowney, and how he had been 'molesting' her, following her wherever she went and watching her hotel.[69] Ludwig was sceptical and told her she was exaggerating, but Christine was convinced that Muldowney would be 'prowling around', and when they reached the hotel, at about 11 p.m., they saw him there, waiting.[70] After a few pleasantries Muldowney said he wanted to speak to Christine alone. She refused, giving the classic 'I have no secrets from anyone' line, although all of them knew this was patently not true.[71] When pressed she said that she had now repaid his kindness, she did not mean to be rude but he was behaving oddly, and she insisted that she no longer wanted to see him and that he should leave. Ludwig watched the distraught man struggle to control himself, and was struck by what he called 'a strange look in his eyes'.[72] Finally Muldowney mumbled that he knew he was not good enough for Christine and her friends, agreed to go and, shoving his hands deep into his raincoat pockets, he stalked off down the street.

17: BRUTAL END

Christine had never had a strategic approach to life. Since child-hood, her most defining characteristic had been an intense desire for freedom: freedom from authority, to roam and ride and live, as wealthy men did, a life of action and adventure. Jobs, marriage, and the polite rules of society were unacceptable constraints, quickly making her, as SOE's Vera Atkins astutely recognized, 'a loner and a law unto herself'.[1] When Germany invaded and occupied Poland in 1939, Christine suddenly found herself perfectly placed to fight. Duty and pleasure at last went hand-in-hand as she pitted her wits, courage and charm against absolute, imposed authority. Christine was an opportunist, whose greatest opportunity came with the war, but Poland's defeat had left her not only without a home, but without a role. It was, as Paddy Leigh Fermor wrote, 'out of restlessness, independence and need, and at a loss suddenly with nobody to rescue', that she 'sailed away from her rather thoughtless adopted country with a temporary job as a transatlantic stewardess'.[2] But by 1952 Christine knew that while working on the ships felt in some ways like helping to run another escape route, she herself remained trapped. The shore leave was not enough to compensate for the long weeks spent cleaning bathrooms and serving as a personal maid. And then there was Muldowney, a black cloud, waiting for her every time she sailed back into London. She needed a strategy. Andrzej was her 'one lasting attachment', as Atkins put it, and Christine began to wonder whether he might not, after all, be her best chance of some kind of freedom.[3]

The day after Christine sent Muldowney packing from the Shelbourne, in April 1952, Hanka saw her off at Waterloo station, on her way to join the *Winchester Castle* at Southampton for a six-

week round trip to South Africa. As the ship was run by a different line she felt there was no chance of Muldowney being signed up to the voyage and little likelihood of him knowing she was sailing. A few days later Hanka spotted him walking past her house in Hammersmith, and in early May he booked a room at the Shelbourne under an assumed name. Christine's ship had sailed, but she knew Muldowney would be waiting for her. At her last port of call on the return passage, Christine called her friend Livia Deakin to ask if she might stay for a few nights when she got back. 'I am very tired', she said. 'I don't want any food, I just want to sleep.'⁴ The *Winchester Castle* arrived on schedule on Friday 13 June, but instead of heading to her friend's, Christine met Ludwig for coffee at the Marynka café. Working on the ships over the last year had not brought the results she had hoped for, she told him. She had signed up to one more voyage on the *Winchester Castle*; after that, she said, she was quitting. She then booked the first available flight, for that Sunday, to spend the week before her last voyage with Andrzej in Belgium.

Christine sorted through her things the next day. Still unable to part with them, she stowed her heavy SOE wireless radio and commando knife at the bottom of her ship's trunk, and laid some clothes on top. Her uniforms and linen went to one side, to be labelled before they were stored. The Shelbourne had agreed to keep them for her until she was ready to collect them. The Pawlikowska portrait had arrived, and she left it leaning against her trunk, ready to go with her. Looking at it again, she pulled out the outfit in which she had been painted: a soft, black, short-sleeved jumper, pearls, and her favourite scarlet silk scarf with a repeating pattern of foxes' heads. Wearing the clothes to hand over the portrait would enhance the symbolic nature of the gift. Andrzej told his niece that he and Christine were getting married. It had been a difficult decision for them both but, he said, 'we finally decided that we wanted to be together forever'.⁵

The next morning, Sunday 15 June, brought both good and bad news. Christine's flight to Belgium had been cancelled due to engine failure, but Muldowney had reportedly been locked up following a

brawl the night before. Having telegrammed Andrzej to let him know she would be a day late, Christine killed time meeting friends for coffee and lunch. That afternoon she washed her hair and, everything else packed, she put on the good clothes she had laid out to travel in before meeting Ludwig at the Polish Air Force Club in Earls Court. After supper with a couple of friends at the Marynka, Ludwig left her at South Kensington tube and she walked back to the Shelbourne alone.*

It was a quarter past ten when Christine got back. Muldowney was waiting for her. At the cinema earlier that evening he had happened to meet a fellow seaman just off the *Winchester Castle*, who told him there had been a Polish stewardess on board 'always running after the stewards' on the ship, and telling stories about him being in some trouble on the *Ruahine* the year before.[6] Muldowney was incensed. He returned to the Reform Club, collected a wooden-handled, double-edged sheath knife, and walked round the park to Kensington. An hour later he watched Christine arrive and let herself in. After a moment's hesitation, he steeled himself to follow.

While Muldowney stood on the street, his fingers checking the knife in its sheath down the back of his trousers, Christine was inside, carrying a bottle of marking ink and a pen. She had borrowed them earlier that day to label her linen before putting it in storage, and was just returning them to the hotel housekeeper before going to bed. As she went upstairs, Muldowney stormed

* There are conflicting reports of this evening. Sonya Masters claimed to have been at the supper party, and to have seen a man staring through the café windows, prompting Christine to respond rather stylishly that 'when I was twelve or thirteen my father gave me a rifle and took me wolf-hunting. We had plenty of wild wolves in Poland in those days. I got lost and was attacked by a hungry wolf pack of perhaps ten to twelve beasts. I took my rifle and shot and killed them – all of them. Since that day I have not been afraid of men or wolves.' Popiel, however, claimed that he had not walked Christine home because he understood Muldowney was safely in police custody. Later Stanisław Mackiewicz claimed to have walked her home, kissing her hand goodnight as he turned down her offer to come in. 'No doubt, if that night I had accepted Krystyna's invitation to visit her at her hotel, I would have been the first to be stabbed in the stomach', he selfishly concluded. See Mackiewicz, *Two Ladies Die After Talking to Me* (1972).

though the lobby and shouted up to her, demanding the return of his letters. The hotel porter came out, waited a moment to see whether Christine wanted Muldowney to be thrown out, judged not, and disappeared again. Christine sighed, came back down the stairs, and told Muldowney that she could not return his letters as she had burned them. She was off to the Continent, she said, and would be gone for two years. She then repeated that she did not want anything more to do with him. For her the very phrase had become tedious. She was bored by Muldowney. Bored by his persistence, his lack of self-respect, and his lack of understanding. Bored with trying to shake him off. Bored, and contemptuous.

Muldowney lunged at her, pinning her against the wall, his face just inches from hers. She was not engaging with him. The porter heard her scream 'get him off me'. Muldowney raised his right arm and thrust the knife deep into her chest in a single, powerful movement. The five-and-a-half-inch blade penetrated her red silk scarf, her soft black jumper, and her heart. Instinctively she moved one hand up towards the blow, but she was dead from shock and haemorrhage within seconds.

Hearing Christine's scream, the porter ran back into the hall, where he saw her and Muldowney against the wall at the foot of the stairs. Thinking Muldowney was forcing himself on her, the porter pulled him off and slammed him to the floor. Unsupported, Christine, too, slipped to the floor, the right side of her face falling against the Victorian tiles, her legs drawn up towards her waist. At first Muldowney did not know if he had killed her, and kept demanding to see her.* The porter told him there was nothing to look at, but realizing the truth, Muldowney uttered his only words of remorse, 'Oh no, Christine', before adding, 'I did it because I loved her.'[7]

A second porter and the cook arrived moments later and, thinking that Christine had fainted, they propped her up in a sitting position. As soon as they let go she slumped back down the wall. The housekeeper was next at the scene, and lifted Christine's head

* He later told the police that he thought he had stabbed her in the shoulder.

to try to revive her with a drink, but the water 'ran down from her mouth'.[8] She 'seemed to have no life in her' the second porter commented flatly.[9] None of them noticed the knife. A minute later the hotel manager came in. Seeing the porter repeatedly 'banging [Muldowney] on the stairs', he pulled the two men apart.[10] He then turned to Christine, saw the knife, instinctively pulled it out and in the same movement dropped it to the floor. It was 'bloodstained to the hilt'.[11]

Although he had struggled with the porter, Muldowney made no attempt to leave. Ten minutes later the first police officers arrived. Sitting Muldowney in an armchair in the hotel lounge, they told him 'the lady' was dead, and asked what had happened. Muldowney told them that he had killed her, but that she had driven him to it. At around midnight, one of the officers noticed him trying to pour something into his mouth behind the unlikely cover of a coloured silk handkerchief. Knocking his hand away a bottle of aspirin powder went flying, spilling its contents across his clothes, the chair and the floor around. The officer then examined Muldowney's mouth and finding some powder adhering to his dentures, removed the lot.* It was a quarter past twelve when Chief Superintendent George Jennings arrived at the Shelbourne. By then a doctor had already been at the site for over an hour, and had estimated Christine's time of death to be 10.30 or 10.40 that evening. Muldowney was now so eager to make a full confession that he could not wait for his police caution, later giving the inspectors some cause for concern as the case approached court. His statement ended: 'I killed her. Let's get away from here and get it over quickly.'[12]

Just before two that morning, a police photographer arrived and took five remarkably clear photographs of the crime scene. In life Christine had never been camera shy, yet most pictures of her are blurred and grainy. Her identity photos are clearer, but the teenage beauty queen in her fur, and the no-nonsense FANY in someone

* Complete sets of dentures, or false teeth, were still common at this time, sported by Winston Churchill amongst others.

else's uniform buttons, both present an image more than a person. Only these police photographs expose Christine in absolute clarity and intimate detail, from the soft dark hair on the back of her wrists, and her upper lip, and the moles on her neck and face, to the fillings in her teeth as her mouth rests open. But they are photographs of a dead body; the camera had not caught Christine at all.

Among the papers in Christine's room, the police found a plane ticket for a 10.15 flight that coming morning, and her seaman's papers, which gave her next-of-kin as Andrew Kennedy, Alexander Strasse, Bonn. Jennings sent him a telegram. Somehow Andrzej managed to get to London later that day. As the official next-of-kin he was shown Christine's Skarbek signet ring, which he recognized at once.* Later that afternoon he managed to give a brief statement. He had known 'Mrs Granville' since childhood, he told the inspectors, and they had 'always been on very friendly terms'.[13] Apart from providing contact details for her Skarbek cousins, he added little more. Both shock, and his training in surviving interrogation, had kicked in. He would not add unnecessary comment. Christine was dead, yet Andrzej still felt a lifetime's unrequited need to protect her.

On the evening of Friday 20 June 1952, Kate O'Malley was among the friends who paid their last respects to Christine. 'She looked eighteen', Kate wrote to her father afterwards, her skin unlined, and just the faintest trace of grey in her thick hair.[14] Looking at her old friend, Kate opened her purse and took out the medal of the Madonna of Częstochowa that she had carried with her ever since Christine had given it to her when fleeing Budapest. Now she quietly slipped it into Christine's hands, to be buried with her. Andrzej was the last to say farewell, giving Christine a final salute as he left the room.

Christine was buried the following day, less than a week after

* Christine's cousin, Andrzej Skarbek, identified her body on 17 June 1952. When he came out he was surrounded by press photographers and journalists, all anxious for a story.

she died, under a scattering of Polish soil in the Roman Catholic cemetery at Kensal Green in London. Her medals were carried in the cortege on a velvet cushion, and the Polish national anthem, *Marsz, Marsz, Dabrowski* (Poland Is Not Yet Lost), was sung as the coffin was lowered into the ground. Although a bright day, a fierce wind shook the wreaths of red and white carnations and whipped at the coats and hats of the mourners. It even helped to blow down the freshly planted metal cross bearing Christine's Polish name, which slipped in the newly cut earth and fell into the grave, sending Andrzej rushing forward to right it again.* Two hundred mourners had come to pay their last respects, including many of Christine's friends and colleagues from the services, from Colin Gubbins to former FANYs. Among them were many of her closest friends and allies. Francis, who confessed to being usually 'very little aware of what people call pain, tragic suffering and so on', had broken down completely at the news of her death.[15] Disappearing for three days, he had left Nan alone to deal with the mass of press people who camped on their doorstep. The Polish émigré community was also out in force, with Teresa Łubienska representing the Musketeers, and forty veterans of the French Resistance had travelled over from south-eastern France. A more unexpected guest among the mourners was Stanisław Kopanski, who came to quietly represent the Polish government-in-exile.†

'To the many who knew and served with "Christine", as she was known throughout Special Forces, her untimely death has come as a terrible shock', Gubbins wrote for the *Times*. 'Happy only in

* Four years later this would be replaced by a 10-foot-high wooden cross carved from a Zakopane pine, and set in a headstone engraved 'Krystyna Skarbek-Granville, GM, OBE, Croix de Guerre avec palmes, Poland 1.5.15 – London 15.6.52', alongside the 'W' symbol from the Skarbek coat of arms. The cross holds a shield bearing the Polish White Eagle protecting the Madonna of Częstochowa.

† The few missing names included Christine's former husband, Jerzy Gizycki, still in Canada, and Wladimir Ledóchowski, who was working in remote southern Africa. 'Is it possible for two lives as intertwined as were yours and mine, to disentangle to such an extent that the most important decision – when to die – could be taken unilaterally?' he later wondered. See Ledóchowski, 'Christine Skarbek-Granville: A Biographical Story', p. 3.

'action', she was bravely facing life in exile 'in her own independent way' when she died – a great woman of 'spirit and courage'.[16] The War Office, Patrick Howarth, John Roper and others all also released statements. 'She was certainly one of the finest members of the service', Francis told the *Daily Mirror*, 'a magnificent person'.[17]

Perhaps appropriately, Christine's death certificate also tells a set of stories. Only the cause of death, 'stab wound to the chest', is truly accurate. The name 'Christine Granville' was her adopted name, of which she had come to feel so proud, and her age '37 years' came with it, but neither corresponds with the name and date of her birth, forty-four years earlier, in Warsaw. But perhaps most misleading is her stated 'occupation': 'the former wife of George Gizycki, a journalist from whom she obtained a divorce'.[18] Never was a memorial less appropriate. Christine was a wife, twice, and might have been again, and she was a lover many more times than that, but she was never defined by her relationship to a man. Christine loved passionately. She loved men and sex, adrenalin and adventure, her family and her country; she loved life, and the freedom to live it to the full. When that freedom was denied her by law or convention, she defied expectations by breaking the rules or simply changing her faith, age, name or story. When it was threatened by invasion, occupation and terrorism, she fought back with a passion, patriotism, determination and courage unsurpassed by any other special agent in the Second World War.

War, subverting the disciplinary structures of peacetime, in many respects liberated Christine. Her achievements are extraordinary. She was the first woman to work in the field as a special agent for the British, starting just weeks after Britain's declaration of war, and two years before SOE officially recruited women, and indeed before it was even established. She was Britain's longest-serving female agent, undertaking missions in numerous theatres of the war throughout the conflict, including undercover operations in two different occupied countries where an agent's life expectancy was little more than a few months. She delivered some of the first intelligence to reach Britain showing German preparations for the invasion of the Soviet Union, weeks before Churchill accepted this

possibility. With Andrzej, she helped to 'exfiltrate' hundreds of Polish and international servicemen from POW camps in Hungary back to the frontline, including many of the pilots who flew in the Battle of Britain. With Francis, she supported preparations for the Allied invasion of southern France, including the subversion of a strategic enemy garrison, and the rescue of key resistance leaders at huge risk to her own life. The list of Polish, French and British officers whose lives she saved makes an impressive roll-call on its own: Andrzej Kowerski extracted with her from a Budapest jail; Wladimir Ledóchowski, from arrest in Poland; Francis Cammaerts, Xan Fielding and Christian Sorensen, from execution in France; and Max Waem, their would-be executioner, from retribution days later.

It has been suggested that Christine's great tragedy was not to have been killed in action, but perhaps the real tragedy was that she was denied the chance to discover what she might have been in a post-war world. Although, like many former special agents, at first Christine found the harness imposed by peace intolerable, it is unlikely she would have let this defeat her. It was what Paddy Leigh Fermor once called 'her fatal gift of inspiring love' that would finally lead to her death.[19] Laura Foskett went even further, commenting: 'one cannot help feeling that her early death was somehow inevitable and the manner of it in keeping with the many dramas of her life'.[20] But such a neat synopsis is reductive, and responsibility for a murder cannot be ascribed to its victim, however much they once chose to live life on the edge.

Christine did not live, or love, as most people do. She lived boundlessly, as generous as she could be cruel, prepared to give her life at any moment for a worthy cause, but rarely sparing a thought for the many casualties that fell in her wake. Dennis Muldowney, the last of her 'lame dogs', made a full confession and declined to submit any pleas in mitigation. He was hanged at Pentonville prison on a rainy morning in September 1952. Obsessed with Christine to the end, his last statement as he left his cell was, 'to kill is the final possession'. But Muldowney was wrong. He had never possessed Christine; the resistance burning within her was too great. No one

ever really possessed her. Not her parents. Not her two husbands, though Gizycki had a good shot at it. Not her many lovers. Nor even her closest ally in life, Andrzej Kowerski. If anything she was possessed by her drive to free Poland. Christine's defining passion was for liberty: in love, in politics, and in life in its widest sense.

Epilogue: the Afterlife of Christine Granville

For a once renowned woman who loved telling tales of dodging bullets, wielding grenades and subverting dogs trained to kill, Christine's story is, surprisingly, little known today. The reasons are both personal and political. In 1952, when sensational headlines blazed across the British papers, 'Kindness Led to Murder', 'Stabbed Heroine told her Story', 'Drama of Quiet Countess who was British Secret Agent' and 'Heroine Dared Me Three Times to Kill Her' among them, a coterie of men who adored Christine, led by Andrzej Kowerski, collectively agreed to protect her reputation, and in many cases their own, by refusing to be publicly drawn into commenting about her.[1]

It was in the traumatic days immediately after Christine's murder that Andrzej began a campaign that would sustain him throughout the police investigation and Muldowney trial. After all her years in active service, in some of the most dangerous theatres of the war, Andrzej had lost the woman he loved, pointlessly. Such a meaningless death did not befit Christine. Andrzej had not been able to save her life, but he was damned if Muldowney would also destroy her reputation: that, at least, was something he could defend.

Two weeks later Andrzej telephoned Chief Superintendent Jennings to raise his concerns about 'possible aspersions of immorality' that might surface during the murder investigation or the publicity surrounding Muldowney's trial.[2] He was worried that as Muldowney was pleading guilty, there would be no cross-examination and no opportunity to refute publicly Muldowney's claims that he had had an affair with Christine. In a second statement to the police, Andrzej made clear that while in London Christine was 'constantly' in the company of her Polish friends, emphasizing that

'I do not think Muldowney had the chance of seeing her alone'.[3] He now roped in Christine's friends to help press this point. Behind the scenes Aidan Crawley agreed to do his 'utmost to see that her name is not sullied' and wrote to the Director of Public Prosecutions.[4] Ultimately the court would be sympathetic, the director making clear that he 'would be glad if Counsel would take any opportunity which might present itself to re-establish the good name of Christine Granville'.[5] In the event the press widely reported the statement prepared by 'certain relatives and friends' of Christine, making it clear in court that 'there is not one particle of truth in the allegations contained in those statements by Muldowney that he was on terms of intimacy with Miss Granville and that he was in fact carrying on a love affair with her'.[6] Perhaps Andrzej even believed this.

Whatever the truth behind their relationship, Muldowney had killed Christine, a decorated war heroine, in an appalling act of premeditated murder, and the papers' sympathies were entirely with her. Most focused on presenting rather fantastical stories of her heroism alongside large photographs of the Polish beauty queen turned British agent. According to the *Mail* Christine had 'saved hundreds of lives', and the *Evening Standard* not only had her and Andrzej escaping into Polish woods under gunfire, but also reported that Christine had married an English agent who later failed to return from a mission.[7] It was the *Express* – 'that sewer' as Kate O'Malley called it – whose reporter had met Christine a few years earlier, that had the most fun though.[8] Presenting Christine as raised among 'warfare, Cossacks, bandits and wolves', they reported that she had killed 'many people' in the war, and returned to London 'in clothes that were practically sackcloth'.[9] And if this was not sensational enough, the Polish journalist Karol Zbyszewski later claimed to have seen 'a strip cartoon about Countess Skarbek and her fight with the German in a Spanish local paper', and in France Daniel Huillier, the young man who had briefly fought beside Christine and Francis in the Vercors, even read a report that Christine's body had been found 'floating in the water in the London docks'.[10]

Seeing Christine's life so wildly reported across the papers was too much for Andrzej to bear. Aidan Crawley's wife, the journalist Virginia Cowles, had known Christine in London and was now commissioned to write a biography with Andrzej's blessing, but pulled out when she decided there was not enough material. Bill Stanley Moss was a close friend and was, by 1952, also a well-established author and journalist. Andrzej thought the solution might be for Moss to write something definitive on Christine and, with the help of her friends, 'make the book as valuable and dignified as possible', after which any independent requests for interviews could be politely refused.[11] In 1952 *Picture Post* published a series of four illustrated articles on Christine by Moss.[12] At the same time Andrzej pulled together his 'Panel to Protect the Memory of Christine Granville', comprised of Francis Cammaerts, John Roper, Patrick Howarth and Michal Gradowski. As Francis later explained it, knowing that the world's media would 'fantasize quite wrongly' about the nature of Christine's life and death, they 'made a pact' that her name should not be sullied, and succeeded in stopping several press reports and two books.[13] The first book was Moss's. Despite spending some years researching Christine, both at Andrzej's flat in Bonn, 'a transit camp' as Moss described it, and touring the scenes of Christine's service in France, when Moss completed his manuscript Andrzej was not impressed.[14] 'It was not a hagiography', Moss's daughter Christine Isabelle later commented, 'but Christine was no saint.'[15]

Twenty years later Wladimir Ledóchowski's manuscript, also researched with help from Andrzej, was also rejected by the panel. The essential problem, Wladimir's son Jan later wrote, was that Wladimir 'saw Christine as a kind of train that had stopped at numerous railway stations in her life, marked from "Charles Gottlich" at the beginning to "Dennis" at the end, and she had simply stopped at the station called "Andrew" more frequently than the others'. Andrzej, by contrast, 'saw a planetary system: Christine and he coupled at the centre with satellites with names like "George" and "Wladimir" orbiting round them'.[16] While it is

doubtful that Christine subscribed to either view, it is clear that these were incompatible perspectives.

Just two years later, however, an approved biography of Christine was published. The author, Madeleine Masson, was herself a resistance worker in France during the war, and had met Christine briefly when she was working as a stewardess in 1952. Masson remembered that initially she found it extremely hard to research the book as, she said, there were 'twelve men who all loved Christine, not physically, who banded together to make sure that no-one wrote rubbish about her'.[17] She was then hindered further by the reticence of officers like Peter Wilkinson, who when approached for information sent 'a rather chilly reply' which played down Christine's official role, describing her early work for Section D as 'uncoordinated efforts . . . encouraged by the British government' but 'strictly a private enterprise'.[18] Eventually, fearing Christine's story might be permanently lost, Andrzej decided to give his guiding support to the Masson book, essentially taking over the narrative drive himself. Despite the pleading of some of the women who knew Christine, such as SOE's Vera Atkins, who told Masson not to 'diminish her by whitewashing her faults. She was no plaster saint', the book presented a thoroughly scrubbed version of its subject.[19] There is much here 'that is interesting and admirable', Francis Cammaerts wrote in his foreword, but 'much more still remains hidden and unknown'.[20] 'It was not the real Christine', Zofia Tarnowska Moss felt sadly, 'just the version Andrew wanted told'.[21]

Andrzej had been trying to protect Christine's reputation for over twenty years but, ironically, he succeeded only in creating an intriguing void that was inevitably filled with growing numbers of rumours and conspiracy theories. First among these was that Christine had been assassinated. In 1952 it was rumoured that the Soviet NKVD were sending executioners all over the world to liquidate people who knew too much. As Christine had worked as a British special agent with knowledge of the Polish anti-Communist underground, Scotland Yard conducted a criminal investigation into the

possibility that her murder had in fact been a political assassination. Sir Percy Sillitoe, chief of MI5, studied the reports prepared by Special Branch, but concluded there was no evidence that either Communists or Nazis had been behind the murder. MI5 and Scotland Yard concluded it was a crime of passion, with Jennings recording that 'there is no suggestion whatsoever that the crime is in any way connected with her former activities as a Secret Agent'.[22]

But the stories persisted. For some the idea that such a brilliant agent could have let a plodding stalker surprise her with a knife seemed curious. For others, Muldowney seemed to be an obvious blunt instrument who would have needed little further encouragement by the NKVD, or any other agency, to turn his already murderous thoughts into action. 'Too many agents have been liquidated by foreign secret services in the same manner', the former agent Kurt Singer wrote in 1953, before asking whether her death was arranged by Soviet Poland, Trotsky's killers or another 'Kremlin gang'.[23] Four years later the debate was reignited by the brutal stabbing of Christine's friend and fellow former-Musketeer, Teresa Łubienska, by then campaigning for former political prisoners from German prisons and concentration camps.* Łubienska died in hospital the evening she had been attacked at Gloucester Road underground station. Her killer was never apprehended, but although her murder may have been political, it is just as likely to have been the failed mugging of a woman who put up greater resistance than expected.†

For conspiracy theorists, however, the field had been thrown open. Some suggested that Christine had simply known too much about the death of Sikorski in 1943, warning Patrick Howarth or

* Teresa Łubienska was fatally stabbed on 24 May 1957, on the eastbound platform of the Piccadilly Line at Gloucester Road underground station. General Anders awarded her the posthumous Golden Cross of Merit with swords. See Jonathan Oates, *Unsolved London Murders: The 1940s and 1950s* (2009).

† For some former SOE officers and agents, the fear of retribution was very real. Peter Wilkinson reportedly never joined the Special Forces Club, as he was concerned not to associate with anyone who might know people he had helped to send to their death.

even Churchill himself about the general's impending 'assassination'. Others recognized that she had a dynamic sense of service and believed that, like Andrzej, she maintained her connections with British intelligence during the post-war years. Perhaps, it was suggested, her role as a ship's steward was a cover to enable her to collect information about the political and economic situation in her ships' ports of call, especially where Polish émigrés were settling, or gossip from the captain's table. There is nothing to support this in any of the recently opened files, however, and although in 1944 and 1945 there had been some discussion about maintaining links with key Poles known to SOE, as 'in the event of war against Russia they would be of inestimable value to us', Christine was unlikely to have been selected for inclusion.[24] The British knew the NKVD already had her details, because they had handed them over, and she was generally just too well known, especially after her decoration. Furthermore, after Zionist extremists blew up the King David Hotel in Jerusalem in 1946, killing over ninety people, there was increasing concern about Zionist terrorism and, fearing divided loyalties, MI5 stopped recruiting from the Jewish community altogether. Christine's mother was Jewish, and Christine was known to have close links with the Sokolow family.[25] It seems extremely unlikely that the British would have re-employed an angry, exiled, female, Jewish, Pole whom they had so often considered a liability and had thrown off so casually a few years earlier.

Other rumours focused on Christine's romantic life. Ironically, given the number of secret lovers she had taken, entirely new candidates began to be linked to her name, most notably the former naval intelligence officer Ian Fleming, now famous as the creator of James Bond. According to Fleming's biographer, Donald McCormick, the two had been introduced through a mutual friend, the journalist Ted Howe, who had first met Christine in Hungary in 1940, and knew Fleming as his commissioning editor at the Kemsley newspaper group. McCormick has Howe meeting Christine again in Cairo in 1947, where he gives her Fleming's address as a possible employer.[26] After lunch with Christine in Charlotte Street

in London, McCormick claims Fleming reported back enthusiastically to Howe, eulogizing that 'she literally shines with all the qualities and splendours of a fictitious character. How rarely one finds such types'.[27]

The dates fit, and Howe certainly knew both Fleming and Christine. Indeed he is one of several mutual friends who might have introduced them, including Aidan Crawley, Paddy Leigh Fermor and Colin Gubbins. Furthermore, Fleming was Christine's type, upper-class, tall, fair and blue-eyed, and Christine is a perfect match for Fleming's ideal woman as described by another biographer, Andrew Lycett: 'thirtyish, Jewish, a companion who wouldn't need education in the arts of love'.[28] She is also a good match for Vesper Lynd, the first 'Bond-girl', a dark and enigmatic European agent, perpetually caught between sunbathing and action, who serves as Bond's love interest in the first 007 outing, the 1952 *Casino Royale*. Lynd was 'very beautiful ... very beautiful indeed', with black hair, 'cut square and low on the nape of her neck, framing her face to below the clear and beautiful line of her jaw ... her skin was lightly suntanned and bore no traces of make-up except on her mouth ... On the fourth finger of her right hand she wore a broad topaz ring'.[29] A wireless expert who speaks French like a native and is in love with a Pole, she manages to combine being 'full of consideration without compromising her arrogant spirit', and believes in 'doing everything fully, getting the most out of everything one does'.[30] Fleming teasingly referred to his Bond books as 'autobiography' and took many of his characters' names and natures from the people he knew, reportedly including Colin Gubbins and Vera Atkins, so the idea of his using Christine and her childhood nickname 'little star' – given as 'Vesper', the evening star – is appealing.[31] 'Can I borrow it?' Bond asks Vesper of her name at an early meeting, in the sort of in-joke that Fleming liked to play.[32]

But if Christine was immortalized as the carelessly beautiful double agent Vesper Lynd, Fleming is more likely to have been inspired by the stories he heard than the woman in person. In later interviews and writing he would sometimes refer to Christine as being a 'dark haired beauty' or having 'a fabulous record in war-

time espionage', but he never claimed to have met her, even in passing.[33] The name 'Vesper', meanwhile, came from an evening cocktail once served to Fleming at a mansion in Jamaica.[34] In fact the only known source for the much-quoted story of Christine's affair with Fleming is McCormick, who claims to have seen the letter from Fleming praising Christine, and his supporting witness, an Olga Bialoguski (*sic*), who testified to McCormick that she was the sole person Christine confided in, and who is also untraceable.* McCormick had already written a history of the British Secret Service, and a 'Spyclopaedia', both of which mention Christine without reference to Fleming.[35] It seems that the opportunity to bring them together finally proved irresistible.†

Whether or not Vesper Lynd was partly inspired by stories of Christine, memories of the real woman did live on. As well as the two known unpublished biographies by people who knew her, and Masson's official version, there is a Polish novel by Maria Nurowska, whose father had known Christine in Poland.‡ Xan Fielding and Patrick Howarth also dedicated their own war memoirs to Christine's memory, and Howarth even immortalized her in verse.[36] More poignantly, not only Christine's brother, but also Francis and Nan Cammaerts, Bill and Zofia Tarnowska Moss, and Jan and Maryś Skarbek all named their daughters 'Christine', as too did Gwendolin Lees, a FANY Christine had known in Cairo; Wladimir's son, Jan Ledóchowski; and even, most surprisingly, Dennis Muldowney's half-brother, Jack Muldowney, who gave the name to his daughter, born in 1953, even though there had never been a Christine in their family before.

* The name Olga Bialoguski is incorrect. Polish men's names of this type end in '-ski', women's names end in '-ska', suggesting that McCormick invented this name. However, he also references Sir Owen O'Malley as O'Reilly, so the mistake may have been genuine.

† For a more thorough examination of Donald McCormick, see Jeremy Duns, 'Licence to Hoax', jeremyduns.blogspot.com (2011).

‡ Maria Nurowska, *Miłośnica* (1999). Nurowska's father, Stanisław Rudziejewski, was the Polish soldier whose odorous feet and Virtuti Militari had drawn the attention of Jerzy Skarbek at the Warsaw opera between the wars, and who later helped Christine in occupied Poland.

Only Jerzy Gizycki tried to leave the memory of Christine behind, choosing not to attend her funeral, and staying in Canada until the mid-1950s. Ever a controversial character, after alienating the Canadian Polish community he settled in Oaxaca, Mexico, where he ended his days writing books on chess, cinematography and Chopin, godson of Christine's illustrious forebear. Christine's cousins, Jan and Andrzej Skarbek, both settled in Britain. Jan married Maryś Tyszjiewicz and they had four children. Andrzej and his wife Shelagh also had four children, and after qualifying Andrzej became a pioneering psychotherapist who helped to develop psychotherapy services in the NHS. He later married the writer Marjorie Wallace, who went on to found the mental health charity SANE.

Wladimir Ledóchowski settled in South Africa, where he worked as an engineer, journalist and author, criticizing apartheid and reporting on the progress of the Communist regime in Poland. Keeping his word to Andrzej, however, he never published anything on Christine. He became involved in the anti-apartheid movement and through this, Wladimir and his wife formed a strong friendship with the author Nadine Gordimer, who later remembered his 'fine dialectical mind and bright spirit', and suggested that 'he died, perhaps, from an overdose of avidity for life'.[37]

Francis Cammaerts lived to be a very distinguished old man. By 1948 he had become the first director of the Central Bureau for Educational Visits and Exchanges, a UNESCO body set up to support the post-war enthusiasm for cultural exchanges and international bridge-building. Later he became a member of the Committee for World Peace, and worked in education in Britain, Kenya and Botswana. Although he loved his family he also craved independence and finally settled in southern France, where he died, aged ninety, his life celebrated by the whole village. He was, according to his nephew, the writer Michael Morpurgo, 'a much honoured and much loved man'.[38]

Andrzej Kowerski-Kennedy lived in Germany, but kept a flat in London. 'For the most part he spends his time travelling about the Continent in fast cars, of which he has two, staying with friends, of

whom he has legion, or in small hotels, of which he seems to know one especially good one in any town, village or hamlet in which he happens to find himself', Bill Moss wrote in 1956.[39] Andrzej maintained his love of fast cars throughout his life and was still proudly driving a blisteringly fast red Ferrari in 1975.* Although he never married, and always kept the Aniela Pawlikowska pastel sketch of Christine on his bedroom wall, he found love again, sharing his life with Angela von Koelichen, to whose sons he also became close. Always laughing and joking, he was dearly loved by all the young people who knew him, including his niece Maria, to whom he gave Christine's few pieces of dress jewellery including the gold and ivory bracelet he had once bought her. Christine's family signet ring, however, he gave to her cousin, Jan's daughter Elizabeth, as she was considered the wildest of the next generation of Skarbek girls. Bill and Zofia Tarnowska Moss's daughter, Christine Isabelle, also adored Andrzej, whom she remembered always arriving in a Porsche full of presents. When, aged six, she asked why he had a wooden leg, he told her he was a pirate, and when she looked at his 'twinkly, twinkly eyes and wonderfully bristly moustache' and told him she wanted to marry him, he told her to eat more porridge so she would grow up quickly.[40] He rarely talked about the Christine she was named after and whom he had once hoped to marry. Andrzej died of cancer in Munich in December 1988. He was seventy-eight. In accordance with his last wishes, his ashes were flown to London and interred with Christine. A memorial plaque was added to the foot of her grave: 'a humble and faithful position' some have commented, but also a deeply romantic gesture.[41]

It is not known whether Andrzej ever saw the finished Aniela Pawlikowska oil portrait of Christine. In 1971 the Shelbourne Hotel

* Andrzej liked to tell a story that in 1960 he was stopped and breathalysed while driving home across the British controlled-zone of Germany after downing a bottle of whisky. At the station the police noticed that his car had American number-plates, and seeing that his name was Kennedy, they let him off, assuming he was celebrating his family's election victory that night in the USA. In another story, in London Zofia Tarnowska once swung open the door of his Porsche without looking, only to have it ripped off by an oncoming car. She was so upset that Andrzej felt compelled to buy her some perfume to restore her good spirits.

came under new Polish management who cleared out twenty years' worth of junk from the storerooms. Among the finds was Christine's heavy shipping trunk, still unlocked and full of clothes and papers, her SOE wireless set and standard-issue commando knife. Leaning against it, lost for twenty years, was the finished portrait.*

* The portrait, wireless, knife and some papers were donated to the Polish Institute and Sikorski Museum in London, where the painting is now on display above the stairs.

My Search for Christine Granville: a note on sources

Researching the life of a secret agent entails inherent difficulties. Christine herself kept few records; I have seen only eleven letters actually written in her own hand, and one of these was just a note scrawled on the squared paper used for coding radio messages. Many official and unofficial papers relating to her have been destroyed by accident or on purpose, while others may remain unreleased. Those papers that are available are often contradictory. Letters are notoriously unreliable, and reports and interrogations often had a hidden agenda during and after the war. Even when first-hand testimony is available, Christine herself was not above telling a good story, and sometimes a very blunt lie, from her use of a commando knife to her date of birth, so it is sometimes hard to discriminate between fact and fiction. I am not the first to struggle with these problems. There have been three previously published biographies of Christine, and two unpublished. Of these, two are self-proclaimed 'fictional-biographies', although they are both based on first-hand accounts.

The first biography of Christine was written by Bill Stanley Moss, her friend and a fellow former SOE agent. When he started work on it, Moss was already well known as the author of *Ill Met By Moonlight*, an account of his and Paddy Leigh Fermor's successful mission to kidnap the German general Heinrich Kreipe on Crete during the war, and there was talk of turning Christine's story into a screenplay for a film to star Winston Churchill's actress-daughter, Sarah, in the title role. However, Christine's soul-mate and posthumous protector, Andrzej Kowerski, rejected the manuscript. The whereabouts of Moss's draft is now unknown, but his daughter, Christine Isabelle (named after Christine), invited me to see his

notes, full of humour and opinion, along with his collection of papers relating to Christine, including some unlikely love letters, Andrzej Kowerski's Polish passport and Christine's false French identity papers.

Count Wladimir Ledóchowski, another war hero and one of Christine's Polish lovers, started his account of Christine twenty years later. The unfinished manuscript presents a very lyrical and critically admiring picture of Christine, and was also rejected by Andrzej. Ledóchowski's son, Jan, kindly gave me a copy of the manuscript among other papers (and lent me his Warsaw flat during my research, outside which I was held up by the Gestapo during a Polish film shoot one afternoon). Although subtitled 'A Biographical Story', it is clear that Ledóchowski undertook thorough research, both on location and through interviews with people now deceased.

The first published biography was Madeleine Masson's *Christine: A Search for Christine Granville*, which came out in 1975. Masson had met Christine on a passenger ship in 1952, just before she was killed. Twenty years later her biography was mainly informed by Andrzej Kowerski, and the circle of male friends who had known Christine during the war and stayed in touch with each other after her death. The resulting book is invaluable for presenting Andrzej's perspective on Christine. Unfortunately he wished to present her in what he considered a good, rather than necessarily true, light.

Some years later came the Polish author Maria Nurowska's novel, *Miłośnica*. Although often dismissed as pure fiction, the book was informed by three primary sources: interviews with some of Christine's London friends; Wladimir Ledóchowski's manuscript; and the recollections of the author's father, who knew Christine before and during the war. Maria met me in Zakopane to disentangle fact from fiction, and told me how struck she had been with the overlap between Ledóchowski's account and her father's own memories.

A final publication, *Krystyna Skarbek: Agent with Many Faces*, by Colonel Jan Larecki, a former intelligence officer with the post-war Communist government in Poland, is a helpful facts-and-stats

account of Christine's life with a few new theories of its own. Colonel Larecki agreed to meet me, in Warsaw, to discuss stories and sources. It is not often in life that I have had my hand kissed by a chain-smoking, espresso-drinking, former Communist spy, and afterwards I had to think hard about just how charmed I had been.

It is still sometimes suggested that there is another published portrait of Christine, found in Ian Fleming's first Bond outing, the 1952 *Casino Royale*. The story that Christine and Fleming had an affair is appealing. She was certainly his type, and his descriptions of the dark and enigmatic Eastern European agent, perpetually caught between sunbathing and action, fit Christine well. But although Fleming and Christine had several mutual friends, and he talked about her after her death had made her momentarily famous, there is no reliable evidence that the two ever actually met. A more evidence-based, if still fictionalized, account of Christine appears in Kate O'Malley and her mother Ann Bridge's novel, *A Place to Stand*, based on their wartime exploits in Budapest.

The National Archive in Britain has many files on Christine, her colleagues and operations, which have been released over the last few years, and the Freedom of Information Act enabled me to access some more. Other documents are available in the Imperial War Museum, which also claims to have her gun; the Special Forces Club, which has her picture of a Madonna; and the Polish Institute and Sikorski Museum, which has the only known oil portrait of Christine, as well as her wireless radio, commando knife, medals and a few documents including her 1949 pocket diary. The Liddell Hart Archive at King's College London contains papers relating to Christine's work in France and Italy. There is considerable contextual information in the Polish Underground Movement Study Trust in London, the National Institute for Remembrance, and the Central Military Archive both in Warsaw, and the Vercors museums in France. Many more private archives yielded further nuggets of information, as did a fabulous range of secondary-source British, Polish, French and American books, translated by good friends in all these countries, including Maciek and Iwona Helfer, Jan Ledóchowski, Christopher Kasparek and Albertine Sharples.

However, it was the people who knew Christine and her friends, and their children, who provided me with the most vivid source of new stories and information. At an annual memorial ceremony in France I met resistance veterans who had fought alongside Christine in the Vercors. In Poland Maria Pienkowska, Andrzej Kowerski's niece, showed me his medals and let me try on Christine's coral necklace and the beautiful gold and ivory bracelet that Andrzej had once bought her. Sadly my hand was too large to fit through her wooden bangle – she must have been very slight. I also explored her childhood home in Trzepnica, central Poland, now covered in creepers, its beautiful stucco ceilings collapsing, and met the Roman Catholic parish priest who showed me the record of her baptism, but strongly advised me not to continue with the book. One evening over cherry vodka, after a long afternoon in the Polish National Institute of Remembrance, my Polish friend and translator Maciek Helfer and I realized that a few years after my mother had watched the sky turn red over London, where my grandfather was on voluntary night fireman duty during the Blitz, his grandmother had sat watching the sky burn over Warsaw during the Rising. My husband's grandfather, meanwhile, had died fighting with the Germans at Stalingrad.

Back in Britain, Polish networks led me to Mieczysława Wazacz, who kindly shared her 2010 film on Christine, *No Ordinary Countess*, for which she had interviewed many of Christine's friends. This in turn brought me to Nicholas Gibbs, a man with a great knowledge of public school, and secret agent, networks, which he generously talked through with me for several hours, all the while a small green parrot nuzzling his neck. A Second World War author and collector in Spain, Ian Sayer, who had known Andrzej Kowerski in the 1970s, tried to help me to trace his papers, unseen for nearly forty years. I was sent Christine's school reports, her first marriage certificate, the press coverage of the 1930 Polish national beauty contest in which she had been honoured as a Star of Beauty, and her second husband Jerzy Gizycki's unpublished memoirs. Count Andrzej and Countess Maryś Skarbek, Christine's cousins, invited me to lunch and to look through family photograph albums. The children of her

friends and colleagues in Budapest, Cairo, London and Nairobi pulled out letters, photos and unpublished autobiographies, and dusted off anecdotes, which they shared both over sandwiches and over the internet.

Requests made through the Special Forces Club, FANY newsletters, and an SOE Yahoo group, brought me reminiscences of wartime Cairo, dates with Christine, and illicit photographs taken of secret buildings. I met British FANYs who had worked alongside her in Cairo and Algiers, and Polish women who had known and worried about her in post-war London. I drank a glass of wine with Katharine Whitehorn, dear friend to Francis Cammaerts's wife Nan, and had lunch with Zbigniew Mieczkowski, who had served in the Polish armoured regiments, and had lunched with Christine in the same restaurant, on the day that she was killed. SOE historians including Martyn Cox and Jeff Bines allowed me to hear recorded interviews with other officers and agents who remembered Christine. The O'Malley family generously shared a collection of letters written by Christine and Andrzej to Kate O'Malley, along with Kate's account of Christine's work in Budapest and funeral in London. A note on a family genealogy website even led to my being contacted by Steven Muldowney, the nephew of the man who murdered Christine in 1952, who shared his own family's story.

But there were also numerous times when I arrived too late. Christine's brother's papers have been thrown away, stacks of letters and boxes of photos have been lost, their existence confirmed only in memories. And there are now very few people left who knew Christine personally. As time erodes the human coastline we are lucky that many of those who did know Christine wrote their own memoirs or agreed to be interviewed by the Imperial War Museum for their sound archive, for Mieczysława Wazacz's 2010 documentary on Christine, or for other film projects such as Martyn Cox's *Our Secret War*, and Channel Four's *The Real Charlotte Grays*. But it was when I saw the most focused set of photographs of Christine, which slipped from a manila envelope in the Home Office folders in the archive at Kew, that I felt she had ultimately evaded me. These were the crime scene photographs, so sharp that they

revealed every detail, from the single drop of blood on her fingers to the fillings in her teeth, and yet ironically what they showed most clearly was that she had already left.

There are still secrets surrounding Christine, as is perhaps right: a buffer to keep her from the real world in which she always inhabited the margins. But I hope that this book presents a more balanced picture of a remarkable woman who can only truly be seen in the context of her country, although it often excluded her, and her times, although she was in many ways ahead of them. I also hope that it at least catches the fierce independence, and slight vulnerability, of the woman who loved and was loved by so many, and the courageous and fiercely patriotic Pole whose greatest tragedy was perhaps that she would not live to see her country free again.

CLARE MULLEY
April 2012

Christine Granville never had children. For a woman who seemingly had every opportunity, it is intriguing to consider why not. Certainly by chance or design she managed to have a cheerfully active sex life throughout the war and afterwards, when contraception was not reliably available, without any issue. This was a notable achievement. 'There is nothing wrong about young couples sharing beds – especially in war time', Christine's second husband, Jerzy Gizycki, wrote, supporting the idea that there were rather more relaxed rules around romance during wartime.[2] The results, however, were predictable. Jerzy noted that during just the months that he was in Cairo, over twenty nurses had to be evacuated to England because they were pregnant, and they had better access to contraceptives than most. This raises the question of whether Christine's lack of children was a positive choice, that perhaps her lifelong passion for travel and adventure precluded any desire she might have had to have children, or conversely whether she already knew that she could not have children and this to some extent informed her outlook on life.

Christine's cousin, Andrzej Skarbek, told me that it was 'not in her nature to have children; she did not have maternal feelings. She was drawn to people of her own age and generation, but not so much to children'.[3] It is certainly true that Christine enjoyed her freedom, showed little interest in babies, and rarely visited friends after they had started a family. However, it is hardly unusual to find a friend's baby dull or difficult, especially when you have none yourself. The most interest she seems to have shown in a very young child was when she commissioned a version of the Skarbek

family coat of arms, worked in leather by Polish artisans, to hang above the cot of a Skarbek baby, and this feels more like a desire to pass on pride in the family than a wish to cheer the child. Even the young children of some of her friends, such as Richard Truszkowski's daughter Diana, who met her several times, felt that 'Christine didn't like children, she didn't approve of them', and even that she 'preferred dogs to children'.[4]

And yet sometimes Christine went out of her way to spend time, and form relationships, with fairly young children, often going against the grain of expected behaviour to do so. In Cairo she visited the lonely daughter of an officer whose wife had died and who was, as a result, boarding at a Catholic school, a background not unlike Christine's. Furthermore Anna Czyzewska's daughter Suzanna, whom she befriended in Nairobi, remembered that Christine was 'very sweet with children', and the only one of her parents' many house-guests who would seek her out, tell her stories and bring small gifts.[5] Christine's interest in children might be described, then, as ambiguous or episodic, but she was certainly not opposed to them on principle, or unable to empathize with individual children. The only conclusion that can be safely drawn from all of which is that she was not disposed to talk about her feelings regarding children with her younger, male cousin, who had four children of his own.

Other people during my research suggested that Christine was not so much unwilling, as unable, to have children. One theory was that she had had a secret abortion in pre-war Poland that prevented her from getting pregnant later. If so, the secrecy was maintained: there is no evidence to support this theory. Others suggested that it is common for women enduring great stress, such as when conducting covert operations during a war, to stop having periods altogether. However, Christine's special operations colleague John Anstey reported that when she was facing imminent departure from Algiers 'we had the awful dilemma when at a certain time of the month, her physical condition and the moon coincided', leading them to postpone her drop to her great frustration.[6] This would imply that Christine was not entirely free from her monthly cycle.

When Dennis Muldowney was in prison, having confessed to killing Christine, he underwent medical assessment to determine whether he was fit to stand trial. During this process, he asked one of the doctors whether a woman could have eight abortions. Explaining his interest, he said that 'sexual intercourse took place often' between himself and Christine, 'and at no time were contraceptive precautions taken' because she had reassured him that after eight abortions she knew that she would not become pregnant.[7] Although he had had a son from his marriage, Muldowney was wondering, he said, who was sterile, Christine or himself. The Polish word '*poronienie*' translates as both abortion and miscarriage. Given Christine's imperfect English, it is possible that she had meant a series of miscarriages, after which she firmly believed she could not carry a child. If this is true, it might have contributed to her rather more carefree attitude to sex than usual for her times, and perhaps also to her desire to keep her freedom rather than marry and fail to raise the expected family.

After her death, Christine's autopsy revealed that while otherwise healthy, she had suffered from a fibroid uterus; that is she had a muscular layer of benign tumours in her uterus, sometimes caused by high levels of oestrogen. There is a correlation between this condition and reproductive problems such as infertility, miscarriage and early-onset labour, although a delay in having children can also contribute to cause these fibroids. It is possible, then, that although she may not have been aware of her condition, Christine did indeed suffer from a series of early miscarriages and, finding the silver lining, felt more able to take risks with her relationships than she might otherwise have done.

Christine's reactions to the pregnancies of her friends were only recorded twice. When her post-war London colleague, Izabela Muszkowska, told her she was pregnant with her first child, Christine exclaimed with alarm, 'Oh my God, what have you done to yourself?!'[8] Her immediate thought was for her friend's wellbeing. But when Zofia Tarnowska Moss told her of her first daughter's birth, Christine asked only that the child might be called 'Christine', the 'lucky name' that had got her through the war unscathed.[9] For

whatever reason, Christine perhaps knew that she would never pass on her name herself. If so, she would have been pleased to know that the Skarbeks are still proud of their family name, and Christine Isabelle Cole, née Moss, still thinks of her namesake with great admiration.

Appendix II: She 'murdered me' Muldowney said: a note on Dennis Muldowney[1]

Dennis Muldowney murdered Christine Granville in a premeditated act of appalling brutality. He confessed to his crime, declined to submit any pleas in mitigation, and was sentenced to death after a trial that was reported to have lasted less than three minutes. Once it had been found that Muldowney was not acting as an assassin on behalf of any shadowy political organization, little further consideration had been given to his motives or to any possible mitigating circumstances. As a result the fascinating profile of Muldowney that had been built up by prison doctors, and through his own communications with the prison staff and his siblings, was largely disregarded.

In the weeks after Christine's murder, Brixton prison's principal medical officer decided that Muldowney was an 'unreliable informant who seeks to dramatize his life', but 'not feeble-minded', and so fit to stand trial.[2] This was an accurate assessment. Muldowney had sought to dramatize his life by his very association with Christine, and it was right that his statements should be treated with caution, but not that they should be disregarded entirely. Muldowney was quickly proved a liar, however, when he gave his date of birth as 1910, three years shy of his actual birth year of 1907. He had believed himself eight years older than Christine, had vainly presented himself as just five years older, but had, in reality, been less than a year her senior. What made this significant was that Muldowney's lie about his age, unlike Christine's, was discovered, casting further doubt over all his statements.

There is little doubt that Muldowney was given short shrift by the prison service, the medics, the courts, and the press covering

the story. Throughout his case records his name is repeatedly misspelled, and other details are incorrect, suggesting little concern for accuracy. His statements about his damaged childhood, the neglect and abuse he had suffered for years, were dismissed, an officer noting only that he came 'from a respectable working-class family'.[3] Emotive judgements about his character were recorded as fact. He is 'a nasty minded exhibitionist' Brixton prison's medical officer wrote to his Pentonville counterpart a week before the trial.[4] Prison staff discussed the press coverage of his case with other inmates in his presence and, in court, after consistent lobbying by Andrzej and others, once Muldowney had left the dock a statement was read out directly rejecting his claim that he and Christine had once been intimate. With no defence to report, the press focused on Muldowney's appearance, his 'casual smirk' in the dock, and his hands, 'thrust deeply in the pockets of his fawn raincoat', as if his mac were an indication not only of guilt, but of possible perversion.[5] He was also frequently presented as short, 'undersized' or 'a goblin', reflecting the popular view of him as a degenerate, although at five foot nine he was well above average male height at the time.

Despite having ruthlessly murdered a woman, Muldowney was shocked to find himself demonized. 'I've still got some constitutional rights you know', he stormed to his two half-brothers, Frank and Jack, and his half-sister Marie, when the papers published a private photograph of him.[6] These were rights that he had denied Christine, but they *were* rights, and it is questionable as to whether they had been fully respected.

There was almost certainly some truth in Muldowney's claims about the nature of his relationship with Christine. She was 'the only woman who would meet his constant sexual demands', he told prison doctors, and they had lived 'as man and wife'.[7] But she was also 'very sadistic and had had many different lovers', deliberately making him 'her slave' before breaking his heart.[8] Furthermore he claimed that Christine had dared him to kill her on three separate occasions, and that 'it was she who put the idea into my head'.[9] Perhaps in a sense this too was true, and the weight of surviving the

war, the daily grind of life in exile and the monotony and boredom that had replaced the thrill of resistance work had tempted Christine to flirt with danger again, risking only a life that had lost much of its value. In Muldowney's letter to Frank, Jack and Marie he wrote that neither Christine nor he had looked forward to getting older. 'Age – not for me! . . . The present cannot be avoided! The future can!' he wrote, cheering his sentences with numerous exclamation marks, before adding: 'A morbid philosophy? Much the same as Christine's.'[10] They had loved each other, Muldowney said, but she was 'a withering middle-aged woman', and well aware that she was 'getting a little rough around the edges'.[11] 'Christine, literally and metaphorically, asked for what she got!' he ended. 'I am sorry, but that's the *truth*!'[12]

If so, Christine would not have been the first former agent to sometimes consider ways to end her life. Francis Cammaerts later admitted that ten of his close friends from the war committed suicide, some straight after the conflict, some thirty years later.[13] But while Christine and Muldowney may well have once discussed death during a low moment on the *Ruahine*, she was essentially a fighter; it does not seem in character for her to have seriously considered a pointless end, and while she might later have taunted him or dared him to do his worst, it is unlikely that she expected him to pull the deed off. As usual, Christine had moved on, and in her mind another lover had been consigned to the past. Muldowney however, constructing his own fantasy, seemed to believe that he had remained loyal to Christine's wishes. 'We made certain arrangements', he told his siblings, which had to remain 'secret', but he was convinced that 'if she were around she would back me, I am sure of that!'[14]

Muldowney was clearly deluded, an emotionally damaged individual, obsessive, poorly treated by Christine perhaps, and unable to cope with rejection. In fact he claimed that both he and Christine 'were a couple of "Nuts" by rational standards', but he proudly said that he refused to hide 'behind a cloak of insanity'.[15] It should not have been his choice. Muldowney's sad childhood history, the

nature of his relationship with Christine, and his mental health, are not relevant to his guilt, but rightly or wrongly, they might have had significance for his sentencing.

After the Second World War there was a rise in violent crime in Britain, much of it against women by their returning menfolk. In 1945 and 1946 a series of murders of wives by their husbands hit the headlines. With domestic violence still largely seen as a private matter, and adultery regarded as serious provocation, those cases that reached court were generally presented as crimes of passion, requiring a degree of sympathy and resulting in some extremely light sentencing. In several murder cases where the wife had been unfaithful, the defendant was acquitted completely.* Over the next few years a series of popular books and films centred, not entirely unsympathetically, on war heroes emasculated by a post-war world and striking back at the women around them.† Muldowney knew he was not a returning hero, but that this was Christine's role did not emasculate him any less. As a regular cinema-goer, to some extent he may have conceived of his plan as within the bounds of recognized behaviour, if not of acceptability, and the fact was that violence against women was generally seen as more acceptable.

In this climate, had the jury had a fuller picture of events, and Muldowney's own mental state, it is possible that they might have felt compelled to request some leniency in sentencing. As it was, Christine was presented as both a Countess and a 'brilliant wartime Secret Services agent' who had been decorated for saving the lives of other heroes.[16] Muldowney was 'a lowly-born man from Wigan', with no distinguished war-record, an 'unreliable informant' and 'fantasist' according to prison doctors, and a self-confessed killer.[17]

* In 1945 Private Reginald Keymer walked free from a cheering Nottingham Court room despite admitting strangling his pregnant wife in a local maternity hospital. A year later Frederick Booth strangled his unfaithful spouse in a jealous rage, only to be acquitted after just seven minutes' deliberation. See Alan Allport, *Demobbed: Coming Home After the Second World War* (2009), p. 95.

† See for example the films *They Made Me A Fugitive* (1947) and *The Flamingo Affair* (1948); the books Raymond English, *The Pursuit of Purpose* (1947) and Elizabeth Taylor, *A Wreath of Roses* (1949). See also Alan Allport, *Demobbed*, pp. 162–74.

He was not Christine's husband, and there seemed little to reason to believe his claim that they had had an intimate relationship. In any case Muldowney did not press the point. 'I owed her some', he wrote to his family. 'That is why "they" only knew that which I, "intended".'[18] The jury made no recommendation for mercy, and after the trial the Secretary of State was unable to find sufficient grounds to overturn the death sentence.

Muldowney had no wish to live in any case. His life, he said, offered no interest for him now that Christine, 'with whom he was still very much in love', was dead.[19] On the night before his last hearing he tore strips from his prison bed-sheets, trying unsuccessfully to make a rope of his own. When sentence was passed and he heard that he would be 'taken from this place to a lawful prison, and thence to a place of execution, and there suffer death by hanging, and may the Lord have mercy on your soul', he only commented 'He will', in what the papers noted was a 'self-assured voice'.[20] Only the *Mail* commented, rather more humanely, that Muldowney had 'tried to live up to Christine's standards. He insisted on pleading guilty, knowing the consequences'.[21] 'And so he will hang, and uselessly, wastefully, bang go two lives', Christine's friend Kate O'Malley wrote reflectively to her parents. 'I suppose we must pray also for his poor benighted soul.'[22]

Dennis George Muldowney was executed by hanging at Pentonville prison at nine o'clock on the rainy morning of Tuesday 30 September 1952. After the post-mortem the prison authorities recorded that 'the execution was carried out in a humane manner' and 'death must certainly have been instantaneous'.[23] With the sentence carried out, Andrzej Kowerski and Christine's other friends might now try to move forward in their own lives, although Andrzej would never get over his loss. It was not the end of the story for the Muldowney family either.

Muldowney's son, John, turned twelve while his father was in prison. He had not seen his father for some years, and his mother had already remarried by 1952. After the trial she told the papers that she hoped her son would never know who his father was.[24] This was probably as Muldowney would have wished. 'Try hard

to forget that I ever existed', he had written to his siblings from prison, but the press stories denied them any such choice.[25] The eldest brother moved to Preston the following year, the second to Manchester. Neither of them trusted the government, police or authorities after the case, and would never use their family name outside the home unless they had to. When they did, they found their construction business was refused government contracts without clear reasons being given. Their sister emigrated to New Zealand. None of them ever mentioned their notorious elder brother, and they would deny they were related to him 'even when confronted with evidence'.[26] And yet, although there was no history of the name in the family, the eldest named his daughter, born in 1953, Christine.

Notes

Epigraphs

1 Aidan Crawley, *Escape from Germany, 1939–45: Methods of Escape Used by RAF Airmen During WWII* (1956, 2001), p. 2.
2 Winston Churchill, 'My Spy Story', *Thoughts and Adventures* (1932), p. vi.

Preface

1 Pienkowska papers, Andrzej Kowerski/Wladimir Ledóchowski (1973).
2 Jan Ledóchowski, 'Christine Granville'; also Jan Ledóchowski, 'Who was she?', p. 6.
3 Wladimir Ledóchowski, 'Christine Skarbek-Granville', pp. 5–6.
4 Ibid., p. 6.
5 Ibid., p. 5.
6 Jan Ledóchowski, 'Christine Granville', p. 1.
7 Mieczysława Wazacz, *Tydzien Polski* (*Polish Week*), (26.2.2005).
8 Jan Ledóchowski, 'Christine Granville', p. 22.
9 *Picture Post*, [Bill] Stanley Moss, 'Christine the Brave' (13.9.1952 – 4.10.1952).
10 Cole/Moss papers, Wladimir Ledóchowski letter to Bill Stanley Moss (13.0.1953).
11 Pienkowska papers, Andrzej Kowerski/Wladimir Ledóchowski (1973).
12 Wazacz, *No Ordinary Countess*.
13 Pienkowska papers, Andrzej Kowerski-Kennedy/Barbara Pienkowska (24 January, *c.* 1974).

1: BORDERLANDS

1 *Daily Express*, 'Stabbed Heroine Told Her Story' (17.6.1952).
2 Bęczkowice parish archive, Krystyna Skarbek's baptism certificate (November 1913).

3 Masson, *Christine: SOE Agent*, p. 4.
4 Kasparek, 'Krystyna Skarbek': Re-viewing Britain's legendary Polish agent', *The Polish Review*, XLIX, no. 3 (2004), p. 946.
5 Zamoyski, *Chopin*, p. 20.
6 Stefania was described by Maria Nurowska, from photographs now lost.
7 Unattributed press cutting (12.12.1898), quoted in Wladimir Ledóchowski, 'Christine Skarbek-Granville', p. 12.
8 *Alphabetical list of the landowners in the Kingdom of Poland* (1909), p. 110.
9 Royal Castle Warsaw archive, Szymon Konarski to Wladimir Ledóchowski (1960).
10 Wladimir Ledóchowski, 'Christine Skarbek-Granville', p. 8.
11 Ibid., p. 8.
12 Ibid., p. 10.
13 Wazacz, *No Ordinary Countess*, Janina Nowotna interview.
14 Zamoyski, *Poland*, p. 298.
15 Stanisław Rudziejewski was the father of the Polish novelist Maria Nurowska, who wrote a fictional account of Christine's life in her novel *Miłośnica*.
16 Tarnowski, *The Last Mazurka*, pp. 59–60.
17 Conversation with Zbigniew Mieczkowski (April 2011).
18 Maria Nurowska, interview (June 2011).
19 Ibid.
20 Wazacz, *No Ordinary Countess*, Francis Cammaerts interview.
21 *Kurjer Warszawski*, notice of Jerzy Skarbek's death (12.12.1930), p. 12.

2: TWO WEDDINGS AND A WAR

1 Mieczkowski, *Horizons*, p. 38.
2 Gombrowicz, *Polish Memories*, p. 81.
3 Breza, *Nelly*, p. 350.
4 Gombrowicz, *Polish Memories*, p. 179–80.
5 Register record, wedding Gustav Alexander Gettlich/Maria Krystyna Janina Skarbek (21.4.1930).
6 Wilnow, now Vilnius in Lithuania.
7 Wladimir Ledóchowski, 'Christine Skarbek-Granville', p. 27.
8 Fiedler, *The Women of My Youth*, p. 52.
9 Gizycki, 'Winding Trail', p. 174.
10 Ibid., p. 352.
11 Ibid., pp. 351, 352.
12 Claude Dansey, Britain's unofficial and independent spy-master, was in Rome at the same time. See Read and Fisher, *Colonel Z*, pp. 165–70.
13 Gizycki, 'Winding Trail', p. 386.
14 Wladimir Ledóchowski, 'Christine Skarbek-Granville', p. 32.

15 Tadeusz Stachowski, 'This would make a great movie!', in *Polish Week* (16.12.2000).
16 Gizycki, 'Winding Trail', p. 110.
17 Howarth, *Undercover*. The Archie Mayo film *Svengali*, starring John Barrymore, had been released in 1931.
18 Gizycki, 'Winding Trail', p. 386.
19 Masson, *Christine: SOE Agent*, p. 291.
20 Cole/Moss papers, Patrick Howarth correspondence with Bill Stanley Moss (12 March, year unknown).
21 Mieczkowski, *Horizons*, p. 49.
22 Gizycki, 'Winding Trail', p. 389.
23 IWM, Gubbins papers: 'Gubbins, Poland – The Final Curtain, 1939'.
24 Carton de Wiart, *Happy Odyssey*, p. 156.
25 Davies, *God's Playground*, vol. 2, p. 435.
26 Gizycki, 'Winding Trail', p. 390.
27 Moorhouse, *Killing Hitler*, p. 89.

3: HUNGARIAN EMBRACES

1 TNA, HS9/612, 'C/H Madame Marchand. MP. 4827' ('Madame Marchand' and '4827' are both Christine Granville, C/H is George Taylor, MP is Harold Perkins.).
2 TNA, HS9/588/2, 'Statement by "X"' (23.2.1941) ('X' is Granville, misfiled in Jerzy Gizycki's file.).
3 Francis Cammaerts quoted in Jenkins, *A Pacifist*, p. 169.
4 Gizycki, 'Winding Trail', p. 395.
5 Karbowska, *Getting to know Mackiewicz*, p. 273.
6 Gizycki, 'Winding Trail', p. 394.
7 Masson, *Christine: SOE Agent*, p. xxi.
8 TNA, HS9/612/C425259, 'To D/H from M/103, Fryday' (7.12.1939).
9 Sweet-Escott, *Baker Street Irregular*, p. 27.
10 Read and Fisher, *Colonel Z*, p. 168.
11 Gizycki, 'Winding Trail', p. 394.
12 Nicholson (ed.), *Nicholson Diaries and Letters*, pp. 256–7.
13 Granville's 1949 pocket diary, The Polish Institute and Sikorski Museum, London.
14 Conversation with M. R. D. Foot (March 2011); also Tony Wheeler, 'Taylor, George Francis, 1903–1979', *The Australian Dictionary of National Biography*, online edition (accessed May 2011).
15 Howarth, *Undercover*, p. 67.
16 TNA, HS9/612, 'To D/H from M/103, Fryday' (7.12.1939).
17 TNA, HS9/588/2, 'Statement by "X"' (23.2.1941).
18 TNA, HS9/612, 'Notes on Madam G' (7.12.1939).
19 Ibid., 'Mme Marchand' (20.12.1939).

20 Ibid.,'C/H Madame Marchand. MP. 4827'.
21 Gizycki, 'Winding Trail', p. 395.
22 TNA, HS7/162, SOE histories, Hungary, 'Hungarian Section History compiled by Major GI Klauber'.
23 Józef Kasparek, 'Poland's 1938 Covert Operations in Ruthenia', *East European Quarterly*, vol. XXIII, no. 3 (1989), p. 370. See also Józef Kasparek, *The Carpathian Bridge: a Covert Polish Intelligence Operation* (1992).
24 TNA, HS7/162, SOE histories, Hungary: 'Hungarian Section History compiled by Major GI Klauber'.
25 TNA, HS9/588/2, 'Statement by "X"', (23.2.1941).
26 Carton de Wiart, *Happy Odyssey*, p. 157.
27 Foot, *SOE: An Outline History*, p. 8.
28 Wilkinson, *Foreign Fields*, p. 72.
29 Ibid., pp. 72, 75.
30 Ibid., p. 75.
31 Bailey, *Forgotten Voices*, p. 3.
32 Wilkinson, *Foreign Fields*, p. 83.
33 Patrick Leigh Fermor, 'The One-Legged Parachutist: Send for a Blacksmith!', the *Spectator* (1.1.1989); Maria Pienkowska interview (June 2011); conversation with Maryś Skarbek, née Tarnowska, childhood neighbour and friend of Andrzej Kowerski (April 2011).
34 Patrick Leigh Fermor, 'The One-Legged Parachutist: Send for a Blacksmith!', the *Spectator* (1.1.1989).
35 Wladimir Ledóchowski, 'Christine Skarbek-Granville', p. 41.
36 Wazacz, *No Ordinary Countess*, Barbara Kowerska Pienkowska interview.
37 Masson, *Christine: SOE Agent*, p. 44.
38 Ibid., p. 44.
39 Andrzej Kowerski-Kennedy quoted ibid., p. 44.
40 Masson, *Christine: SOE Agent*, p. 45.
41 This bridge was later bombed in the Russo-German battle for Budapest in 1944.
42 Andrzej Kowerski-Kennedy quoted in Masson, *Christine: SOE Agent*, p. 48.
43 Ibid.
44 Ibid., p. 51.
45 TNA, HS9/612, '"Madame Marchand" (Madame Gizycka)' (11.3.1940).
46 Ibid., 'From DH11 for DHM' (11.3.1940).
47 Ibid., 'From DH11 for DHM' (11.3.1940).
48 Bailey, *Forgotten Voices*, p. 11.
49 TNA, HS9/612, 'Madame Marchand and Freedom Station' (22.4.1940).
50 Bailey, *Forgotten Voices*, p. 11.

51 TNA, HS9/612, '"Madame Marchand" (Madame Gizycka)' (11.3.1940).
52 Wilkinson, *Foreign Fields*, p. 90; also Wladimir Ledóchowski, 'Christine Skarbek-Granville', p. 99.
53 Wilkinson, *Foreign Fields*, p. 90.
54 TNA, HS9/612, 'Madame Marchand' (11.3.1940).
55 TNA, HS9/588/2, 'Statement by "X"' (23.2.1941).
56 TNA, HS9/612, '"Madame Marchand" (Madame Gizycka)' (11.3.1940).

4: POLISH RESISTANCE

1 Bill Stanley Moss, 'Christine the Brave', *Picture Post*, vol. 56, no. 11 (13.9.1952), p. 14.
2 TNA, HS9/588/2, 'Statement by "X"' (23.2.1941).
3 Musson, *Christine: SOE Agent*, p. 52.
4 Wladimir Ledóchowski, 'Christine Skarbek-Granville', p. 55.
5 Ibid., p. 56.
6 TNA, HS9/612, 'Draft citation for Krystyna Gizycka (Christine Granville)' (nd).
7 Ibid.
8 Henryk Szymanski, Bęczkowice parish priest, Poland.
9 Wladimir Ledóchowski, *The Diary*, p. 110.
10 Davies, *God's Playground*, vol. 2, p. 435.
11 Terry Charman, 'Hugh Dalton, Poland and SOE', in Seaman (ed.), *Special Operations Executive*, p. 66.
12 Moorhouse, *Killing Hitler*, p. 93.
13 Ibid., p. 94; also Davies, *Rising '44*, p. 87.
14 Moorhouse, *Killing Hitler*, p. 102.
15 See Adam Zamoyski, 'The Underground Factory: Poland in 1939–45', *History Today* (1974).
16 Ibid.
17 See Zamoyski, *Poland*.
18 Wladimir Ledóchowski, *The Diary*, p. 109.
19 IWM, Gubbins Papers (4.1.1950), Peter Wilkinson talk entitled 'Gubbins: A Resistance Leader' (28.4.1990).
20 See Howarth, *Undercover*, p. 58, and Moorhouse, *Killing Hitler*, p. 97.
21 Stirling, Nałęcz, Dubiki (eds), *Intelligence Co-operation*, p. 185.
22 Leski, *A Checkered Life*, p. 107; also Howarth, *Undercover*, p. 68.
23 Leski, *A Checkered Life*, chapter 1.
24 See Buczek, *The Musketeers*.
25 Stirling, Nałęcz, Dubiki (eds), *Intelligence Co-operation*, p. 185.
26 *The Polish Dictionary of National Biography*, vol. 18 (1973), p. 472.
27 Leski, *A Checkered Life*, p. 106.

28 See Buczek, *The Musketeers*; also Masson, *Christine: SOE Agent*, p. 59.
29 Leski, *A Checkered Life*, p. 106.
30 TNA, HS9/612, 'Draft citation for Krystyna Gizycka (Christine Granville)' (nd).
31 TNA, HS9/588/2, 'Statement by "X"' (23.2.1941) (X is Christine).
32 TNA, HS9/612, 'DH11 to DH1 and DHM', British Section D internal report (14.4.1940). DH11 was Hubert Harrison in Budapest.
33 Ibid.
34 Ibid.
35 Wladimir Ledóchowski, 'Christine Skarbek-Granville', pp. 76–7.
36 TNA, HS9/612, 'DH11 to DH1 and DHM', British Section D internal report (14.4.1940).
37 Christopher Kasparek, 'Krystyna Skarbek: Re-viewing Britain's legendary Polish agent', *The Polish Review*, XLIX, no. 3 (2004), pp. 945–53.
38 TNA, HS9/612, 'DH11 to DH1 and DHM', British Section D internal report (14.4.1940).
39 Gordimer, 'Vladimir Ledóchowski'.
40 Wladimir Ledóchowski, 'Christine Skarbek-Granville', pp. 104–5.
41 Wladimir Ledóchowski, *The Diary*, p. 112; also Wladimir Ledóchowski, 'Christine Skarbek-Granville', p. 80.
42 Wladimir Ledóchowski, 'Christine Skarbek-Granville', p. 83.
43 Jan Ledóchowski, 'Christine Granville', p. 6.
44 Wladimir Ledóchowski, *The Diary*, p. 117.
45 Wladimir Ledóchowski, 'Christine Skarbek-Granville', p. 86.
46 Wladimir Ledóchowski, *The Diary*, pp. 118–20.
47 Ibid.
48 Wladimir Ledóchowski, 'Christine Skarbek-Granville', p. 93.
49 Wladimir Ledóchowski, *The Diary*, pp. 118–20, and Wladimir Ledóchowski, 'Christine Skarbek-Granville', p. 94.
50 Wladimir Ledóchowski, 'Christine Skarbek-Granville', p. 94.

5: A STRING OF ARRESTS

1 Wladimir Ledóchowski, 'Christine Skarbek-Granville', p. 98.
2 Ibid., p. 100.
3 Wladimir Ledóchowski, *The Diary*, p. 129.
4 Wladimir Ledóchowski, 'Christine Skarbek-Granville', p. 50.
5 Wladimir Ledóchowski, *The Diary*, p. 132.
6 Ibid., p. 132.
7 TNA, HS9/612, Letter Jerzy Gizycki to Section D (5.4.1940).
8 Ibid., Letter from Section D to Jerzy Gizycki (12.4.1940).
9 Ibid., Letter Jerzy Gizycki to Section D (21.5.1940).
10 O'Malley papers, Kate O'Malley, 'Harrison's agent, Mme Gizycka'.

11 TNA, HS9/588/2, 'Statement by "X"' (23.2.1941).
12 Ibid.
13 TNA, PREM 3/351/3, 1940 Poland, General 1, 'To PM, 14 November 1940', from Dalton.
14 Andrzej Kowerski-Kennedy quoted in Masson, *Christine: SOE Agent*, p. 63.
15 Christopher Kasparek, 'Krystyna Skarbek: Re-viewing Britain's legendary Polish agent', *The Polish Review*, XLIX, no. 3 (2004), pp. 945–53.
16 Bill Stanley Moss, 'What Makes a First-Class Secret Agent', unknown newspaper (*c.*1952).
17 Wladimir Ledóchowski, 'Christine Skarbek-Granville', p. 119.
18 Wladimir Ledóchowski, *The Diary*, p. 135.
19 IWM Sound Archive, 8682, Basil Risbridger Davidson.
20 Ibid.
21 Wladimir Ledóchowski, *The Diary*, pp. 133, 140.
22 Wladimir Ledóchowski, 'Christine Skarbek-Granville', p. 113.
23 Ibid., p. 114.
24 Ibid., p. 115.
25 Wladimir Ledóchowski, *The Diary*, p. 143, also Wladimir Ledóchowski, 'Christine Skarbek-Granville', p. 117.
26 TNA, HS9/612, Jerzy Gizycki, in Paris, to X3 (6.6.1940).
27 Ibid., Draft Citation for Kristina Gizycka (Christine Granville) (nd, *c.*1944/5).
28 Wladimir Ledóchowski, *The Diary*, p. 145.
29 Wladimir Ledóchowski, 'Christine Skarbek Granville', p. 122.
30 Wladimir Ledóchowski, *The Diary*, p. 150.
31 They were following the Poprad–Muszyna line through Slovakia to Nowy Sacz in Poland. See Wladimir Ledóchowski, 'Christine Skarbek-Granville', p. 132.
32 Wladimir Ledóchowski, *The Diary*, p. 156.
33 Wladimir Ledóchowski, 'Christine Skarbek-Granville', p. 138.
34 TNA, HS9/588/2, 'Statement by "X"' (23.2.1941).
35 Wladimir Ledóchowski, *The Diary*, p. 156.
36 Ibid.
37 Wladimir Ledóchowski, 'Christine Skarbek-Granville', p. 309.
38 TNA, HS9/588/2, 'Statement by "X"' (23.2.1941).
39 O'Malley, *Phantom Caravan*, p. 208.
40 Celt, *By Parachute to Warsaw*, p. 55.
41 TNA, HS9/612, Jerzy Gizycki to SOE, London (1.7.1940).
42 Ibid., Jerzy Gizycki to X3 (nd).
43 TNA, HS9/588/2, Jerzy Gizycki, 'W to AD1, 23.11.40'.
44 TNA, HS9/668, SOE personal files, Hubert Harrison, memo (30.6.1940).
45 Bridge, *A Place to Stand*, p. 149.

46 IWM Sound Archive, 8682, Basil Risbridger Davidson.
47 TNA, HS9/612, 'Extracts copied as citations' (1.12.1945) and HS9/612, 'Krystyna Gizycka (alias Christine Granville)' (1945/6); also TNA, HS9/830/3, Kowerski-Kennedy, dob 18.4.1912, 'Army form W3121: Andrew Kowerski-Kennedy recommended for MBE (Military Division) by Lt Col Philip Rea for Major General Colin McVean Gubbins (absent on duty)' (nd).
48 TNA, HS9/612, 'Extracts copied as citations' (1.12.1945).
49 Porter, *Operation Autonomous*, p. 73.
50 *Sunday Pictorial*, Ross Richards, 'Girl Spy' (19.8.1956).
51 Gizycki, 'Winding Trail', p. 415.
52 *Sunday Pictorial*, Ross Richards, 'Girl Spy' (19.8.1956).
53 Bill Stanley Moss, 'Christine the Brave', *Picture Post*, vol. 56, no. 12 (20.9.1952).
54 Wladimir Ledóchowski, 'Christine Skarbek-Granville', p. 48.
55 See Masson, *Christine: SOE Agent*, pp. 67–8.
56 TNA, HS9/612, George Taylor's records relating to 'Madame Marchand' (23.11.1940).
57 O'Malley, *Phantom Caravan*, p. 199.
58 Bridge, *Tightening String*, p. 18.
59 Davidson, *Special Operations Europe*, p. 77.
60 Ibid.
61 Bailey, *Forgotten Voices*, p. 15.
62 O'Malley, *Phantom Caravan*, p. 208.
63 TNA, HS7/162, SOE histories 113, Hungary, 'Hungarian Country Section' report compiled by Major G. I. Klauber with reference to reports by Lt Col B. R. Davidson, Lt Col Boughey, Lt Col Threlfall, Major J. G. Coates and others (nd).
64 TNA, HS9/612, 'Krystyna Gizycka (alias Christine Granville)'.
65 TNA, HS4/291, Poland 206, Sir Owen O'Malley to Harold Perkins (21.6.1944).
66 O'Malley, *Phantom Caravan*, p. 205.
67 Masson, *Christine: SOE Agent*, p. 66.
68 Bridge, *Facts and Fictions*, p. 83.
69 Wladimir Ledóchowski, 'Christine Skarbek-Granville', p. 169.
70 Bridge, *A Place to Stand*, p. 67.
71 Wazacz, *No Ordinary Countess*, Erica de Bosdari interview. De Bosdari worked at the British Legation in Budapest.
72 TNA, HS9/612, 'Krystyna Gizycka (alias Christine Granville)' (late 1945/early 1946).
73 O'Malley, *Phantom Caravan*, p. 208.
74 Masson, *Christine: SOE Agent*, p. 70.
75 TNA, HS9/588/2, 'Statement made by "X"' (23.2.1941).
76 Ibid.
77 Wladimir Ledóchowski, 'Christine Skarbek-Granville', p. 143.

78 Ibid., p. 171.
79 Bridge, *Tightening String*, p. 180.
80 TNA, HS9/588/2, 'Statement made by "X"' (23.2.1941).
81 Wazacz, *No Ordinary Countess*, interviews with Barbara Pienkowska and Jan Skarbek.
82 Celt, *By Parachute to Warsaw*, p. 59.
83 Maria Nurowska, interview (June 2011).
84 Celt, *By Parachute to Warsaw*, p. 37.
85 Domańska, *Pawiak: Gestapo Prison*, p. 195.
86 Museum of the History of Polish Jews, 'Historical Monuments, Places of Martyrdom, Pawiak', www.szetl.org.pl/en/city/warszawa/ (accessed June 2011).
87 Wladimir Ledóchowski, and at least one of Christine's post-war London friends, probably Stanisław Tarnowski, both reported a similar story of Christine's attempted rescue of her mother.
88 Wladimir Ledóchowski, 'Christine Skarbek-Granville', p. 151.
89 Maria Nurowska, *Miłośnica* (1999).
90 Howarth, *Undercover*, p. 73.
91 Daniel Farson, 'Riddle of the Woman Pimpernel', *Observer Magazine* (20.10.1974).

6: TRAVELS IN AN OPEL

1 Wladimir Ledóchowski, 'Christine Skarbek-Granville', p. 174.
2 Masson, *Christine: SOE Agent*, p. 90.
3 TNA, HS9/612, Draft citation for Kristina Gizycka (Christine Granville) (nd).
4 Andrzej Kowerski-Kennedy quoted in Masson, *Christine: SOE Agent*, p. 95.
5 TNA, HS9/588/2, 'Statement made by "X"' (23.2.1941).
6 Wladimir Ledóchowski, 'Christine Skarbek-Granville', p. 177.
7 TNA, HS9/612, Draft citation for Kristina Gizycka (Christine Granville) (nd).
8 Walker, *Poland Alone*, p. 75.
9 Wazacz, *No Ordinary Countess*, Barbara Pienkowska interview.
10 Bridge, *Tightening String*, p. 48.
11 O'Malley, *Phantom Caravan*, p. 209.
12 Ibid.
13 Bridge, *A Place to Stand*, p. 111.
14 O'Malley papers, Kate O'Malley to Sir Owen and Ann Bridge (24.6.1952).
15 O'Malley, *Phantom Caravan*, p. 209; also Wladimir Ledóchowski, 'Christine Skarbek-Granville', p. 181.
16 Wladimir Ledóchowski, 'Christine Skarbek-Granville', p. 183.

17 Daniel Farson, 'Riddle of the Woman Pimpernel', in the *Observer Magazine* (20.10.1974).
18 Bridge, *A Place to Stand*, p. 186.
19 O'Malley papers, Granville to Kate O'Malley (nd).
20 O'Malley papers, Andrzej Kowerski to Kate O'Malley (nd).
21 O'Malley, *Phantom Caravan*, p. 209.
22 Masson, *Christine: SOE Agent*, p. 103.
23 TNA, HS4/291, SOE Eastern Europe files, Poland, Sir Owen O'Malley letter to Harold Perkins (21.6.1944).
24 Wilkinson and Astley, *Gubbins and SOE*, p. 75.
25 Stafford, *Secret Agent*.
26 IWM, Gubbins papers 2/11, Gubbins lecture, 'SOE' (June 1959).
27 TNA, HS9/588/2, Jerzy Gizycki, 'Jerzy Gizycki Operations Report: D/H Norton, 4826'.
28 Crawley, *Leap Before You Look*, pp. 161–2.
29 O'Malley papers, Granville to Kate O'Malley (nd).
30 HS9/588/2, 'Statement made by "X"' (23.2.1941), Aidan Crawley's comments at the end of Christine's report.
31 Stahel, *Operation Barbarossa*, p. 35.
32 Churchill, *The Second World War*, III, p. 287.
33 TNA, HS9/830/3, Kowerski-Kennedy.
34 O'Malley papers, Granville to Kate O'Malley (nd).
35 Christine Isabelle Cole interview (May 2011).
36 O'Malley papers, Andrzej Kowerski to Kate O'Malley (nd).
37 Amery, *Approach March*, p. 186.
38 Crawley, *Leap Before You Look*, p. 154.
39 TNA, HS9/612, 'Krystyna Gizycka (Alias Christine Granville)' (late 1945/early 1946).
40 O'Malley papers, Granville to Kate O'Malley (nd).
41 O'Malley papers, Granville to Kate O'Malley (25.3.1941).
42 Howarth, *Undercover*, p. 66.
43 Gizycki, 'Winding Trail', p. 415.
44 Ibid., p. 417.
45 Ibid., p. 420.
46 Ibid., p. 421.
47 TNA, HS9/588/2, Jerzy Gizycki, 'Recommendation for award' (nd).
48 Ibid., Jerzy Gizycki, 'Filenote re Norton, from D/H13 to M/X, Istanbul, 31.5.41'.
49 Churchill, *The Second World War*, III, p. 137.
50 Bridge, *A Place to Stand*, p. 196.
51 Williams, *Parachutes, Patriots and Partisans*, p. 33.
52 TNA, HS9/588/2, Jerzy Gizycki, 'Telegram Norton, Budapest to Air Attache and DH2' (9.4.1941).
53 Ibid., Jerzy Gizycki, 'From GN Norton, For S.O.2 Head Quarters' (nd).

54 The 'exfiltration' organization was handed over to Polish Intelligence on the orders of Peter Wilkinson: see TNA, HS9/612, letter in support of 'Draft Citation for Kristina Gizycka (Christine Granville)' (1.12.45).

55 *The Times*, 'Michael Lis', obituary (16.8.1994).

56 TNA, HS9/612, Draft citation for Kristina Gizycka (Christine Granville) (nd).

57 TNA, HS9/588/2, Jerzy Gizycki, Letter written to 'My dear George [probably George Taylor], in support of Citation for Jerzy Gizycki' (1.12.1945).

58 TNA, HS4/201, SOE Poland 93, vol. 2 (October 1942 – January 1943).

59 Ibid., SOE Poland 93, vol. 1 (March 1942 – September 1943).

60 Amery, *Approach March*, p. 189.

61 Andrzej Kowerski-Kennedy quoted in Masson, *Christine: A Search*, p. xxxiv.

62 Andrzej Kowerski-Kennedy quoted in Masson, *Christine: SOE Agent*, p. 127.

63 TNA, HS3/198, SOE/MIDEAST/50, Gladwyn Jebb to C/D (9.5.1941).

64 Masson, *Christine: SOE Agent*, p. 128.

7: COLD IN CAIRO

1 TNA, HS4/198, MX to M (27.4.1941).

2 Ibid., MX to M (28.5.1941).

3 TNA, HS9/612, 'From Mid East' (30.5.1941).

4 Sweet-Escott, *Baker Street Irregular*, p. 73.

5 TNA, HS9/588/2, Jerzy Gizycki, 'Filenote from D/H13 from M/X, Cairo' (7.5.1941).

6 Stirling, Nałęcz, Dubiki (eds), *Intelligence Co-operation*, p. 323.

7 TNA, HS9/588/2, Jerzy Gizycki (30.5.1941 and 10.6.1941).

8 Ibid., Jerzy Gizycki, Yolcu Tena Yazi to de Chastelain, Istanbul (31.7.1941).

9 Amery, *Approach March*, p. 189.

10 TNA, HS9/588/2, Jerzy Gizycki, D/H13 to M/X (18.6.1941); and MX to DH/13 (2.6.1941).

11 Masson, *Christine: SOE Agent*, p. 131.

12 O'Malley papers, Granville to Kate O'Malley (14.4.1942).

13 Andrzej Kowerski-Kennedy quoted in Masson, *Christine: SOE Agent*, p. 132.

14 Masson, *Christine: SOE Agent*, p. 132.

15 IWM, Gubbins papers, 2/11, Wilkinson to Gubbins (30.10.1974); and TNA, HS9/588/2, MX to AD (23.10.1941).

16 Wilkinson, *Foreign Fields*, p. 122.

17 TNA, HS4/198, MX to M (10.6.1941).

18 Binney, *Women Who Lived for Danger*, p. 72.
19 Masson, *Christine: SOE Agent*, p. 139.
20 Larecki, *Krystyna Skarbek*, p. 157.
21 Cooper, *Cairo in the War*, p. 80.
22 Ibid., p. 26.
23 Davidson, *Special Operations Europe*, p. 108.
24 Amery, *Approach March*, p. 202.
25 O'Malley papers, Granville to Kate O'Malley (30.1.1942).
26 TNA, HS9/588/2, Jerzy Gizycki, D/H13 to M/X (18.6.1941).
27 Ibid., 'From GN Norton for SO2 HQ'.
28 Ibid.
29 Ibid.
30 O'Malley papers, Granville to Kate O'Malley (30.1.1942).
31 TNA, HS4/199, MDH to M (7.8.1941).
32 Ibid., MX/PD/201, MX to MDH (21.10.1941).
33 Cole/Moss papers, Bill Stanley Moss papers (*c.*1952).
34 Churchill, *The Second World War*, III, p. 299.
35 Binney, *Women Who Lived for Danger*, p. 72.
36 TNA, HS4/199, MDH to M (16.8.1941).
37 O'Malley papers, Granville to Kate O'Malley (30.1.1942).
38 TNA, HS9/612, 'KRYSTYNA GIZYCKA (alias Christine GRANVILLE)'.
39 TNA, HS4/199, MDH to M (31.8.1941).
40 Ibid., MDH to M (26.10.1941).
41 Ibid., MX to MDH (8.12.1941).

8: THE BEAUTIFUL SPY

1 R. P. Weston and Bert Lee, 'Olga Pulloffski, The Beautiful Spy' (1935).
2 TNA, HS4/200, MDH to MX (17.6.1942).
3 Ibid., MXI to MX (11.8.1942).
4 Ibid., MPX (25.7.1942).
5 Pope, 'Remembering Richard', p. 63.
6 Liddell Hart Centre for Military Archives, O'Regan papers, 'Surrender can be fun' leaflet (nd).
7 Pope, 'Remembering Richard', p. 63.
8 Manning, *Levant Trilogy*, p. 337.
9 Gizycki, 'Winding Trail', p. 412.
10 Masson, *Christine: A Search*, p. xxix.
11 Henryk Koaratynski, Mieczysława Wazacz interview, *Tydzien Polski* (*Polish Week*) (26.2.2005).
12 Margaret Pawley, interview (December 2010).
13 Michael Ward, email (March 2011).
14 Pope, 'Remembering Richard', p. 121.

15 Masson, *Christine: A Search*, p. xxxiv.
16 Ibid., p. xxxiii.
17 Pawley, *In Obedience*, p. 71.
18 Michael Ward, email (March 2011).
19 Manning, *Levant Trilogy*, p. 93.
20 O'Malley papers, Granville to Kate O'Malley (14.4.1942).
21 TNA, HS9/612, MX to D/HV (19.1.1942).
22 Ibid., D/HV to A/D4 (20.1.1942).
23 Ibid., D/HV to A/D4 (20.1.1942); and HS9/612, SOE 855, Gubbins to Cairo (22.1.1942).
24 TNA, HS4/201, MDH to M (24.4.1942).
25 Ibid., MPX to MX, 'ME gossip' (28.5.1942).
26 Ibid., MPX to MX (19.12.1942).
27 Cooper, *Cairo in the War*, p. 305.
28 TNA, HS9/588/2, Jerzy Gizycki, Aidan Crawley to British Legation, Sofia (30.3.1942).
29 Wladimir Ledóchowski, *The Diary*, p. 232.
30 Ibid.
31 TNA, HS4/199, MX to MDH (2.3.1942).
32 Ibid., MX to MDH (24.2.1942).
33 TNA, HS9/612, LSOE/39B to Moscow (20.4.1941).
34 Ibid., MX to MDH (28.1.1942).
35 TNA, HS4/201, MDH to M (26.5.1942).
36 TNA, HS4/200, MX to D/CE (14.9.1942); this was Richard Truszkowski.
37 Olson and Cloud, *Kościuszko Squadron*, p. 275.
38 O'Malley papers, Granville to Kate O'Malley (14.4.1942).
39 TNA, HS4/201, MDH to MX (17.6.1942); ibid., MXI to MX (19.12.1942); and TNA, HS9/612, MPX to MX (16.12.1942).
40 TNA, HS4/141, MXI to MX (1.1.1943).
41 TNA, HS4/200, MPX to MX (21.7.1942).
42 Ibid., MDH to MX (17.6.1942).
43 TNA, HS9/612, SOE999 (19.7.1942).
44 O'Malley papers, Granville to Kate O'Malley (28.8.1942).
45 TNA, HS4/201, MPX to MX (29.8.1942).
46 Ibid., MPX (25.7.1942).
47 Ibid., MPX to MX (13.8.1942).
48 Ibid., MPX to MX (26.9.1942).
49 Ibid.
50 Selwyn (ed.), *From Oasis Into Italy*, Anon, 'Ode to a Gezira Lovely', pp. 69–70.
51 Tarnowski, *The Last Mazurka*, p. 201.
52 Masson, *Christine: SOE Agent*, p. 140.
53 Patrick Howarth interview, Jeff Bines private archive (August 2001).

54 Patrick Howarth, 'Play back a Lifetime', poem first published in Masson, *Christine: SOE Agent*, p. 251.

55 Howarth, *Undercover*, p. 72.

56 TNA, HS4/201, MXI to MX (29.9.1942).

57 Ibid., MPX to MX (16.12.1942).

58 Ibid.

59 O'Malley papers, Granville to Kate O'Malley (9.4.1942).

60 Patrick Howarth, quoted in Masson, *Christine: SOE Agent*, p. 144.

61 Imperial War Museum, sound archive, 9827, Patrick Howarth.

62 Ibid.

63 Howarth, *Undercover*, p. 37.

64 Ibid., p. 73.

65 Ibid., p. 72.

66 IWM, Sound Archive, 11087, Gwendolin Lees.

67 Ibid.

68 TNA, HS4/201, MXI to MX (29.9.1942).

69 Ibid., MXI to MX (24.10.1942).

70 Howarth, *Undercover*, p. 255.

71 IWM, Sound Archive, 8685, Annette Street.

72 Margaret Pawley, interview (December 2010).

73 Howarth, *Undercover*, p. 74.

74 Marks, *Between Silk and Cyanide*, p. 108.

75 IWM 2/11, Gubbins papers, BBC speech on SOE and the use of women (4.1.1946).

76 Pawley, *In Obedience*, p. 71.

77 Wazacz, *No Ordinary Countess*, Margaret Pawley interview.

78 TNA, HS4/201, MPX to MX (26.9.1942).

79 Ibid.

80 TNA/HS4/201, MPX to MX (16.12.1942).

81 TNA, HS9/612, MPX to MX (16.12.1942).

82 TNA/HS4/201, MPX to MX (16.12.1942).

83 TNA, HS9/612, AD to DCD (15.12.1942).

84 Masson, *Christine: SOE Agent*, p. 141.

85 Escott, *Heroines of SOE F Section*, pp. 211–15; also Wladimir Ledóchowski, 'Christine Skarbek-Granville', p. 213.

86 TNA, HS9/612, Granville to Francis Brooks Richards (27.7.1944).

87 O'Malley papers, Granville to Kate O'Malley (16.9.1943).

88 TNA, HS4/141, MPX to MXI (4.5.1943).

89 Wladimir Ledóchowski, 'Christine Skarbek-Granville', pp. 197–8.

90 TNA, HS4/201, MPX to MX (16.12.1942).

91 TNA, HS4/141, MXI to MX (1.1.1943); and MXI to MX (6.2.1943).

92 Marks, *Between Silk and Cyanide*, p. 323.

93 TNA, HS4/141, MXI to MX (27.2.1943).

94 Ibid., MX to CD (20.3.1943).

95 TNA, KV2/517, DG through DDE (nd); also Vera Long interview with Jeff Bines (c.2000).
96 TNA, HS4/141, MPX (6.4.1943).
97 Ibid., MPX to MXI (3.4.1943).
98 Ibid., MXI to MX (7.4.1943).
99 Ibid.
100 TNA, HS4/141, MPX to MXI (4.5.1943).
101 Engel, *Facing a Holocaust*, p. 71.
102 Fitzgibbon, *Katyn Massacre*, p. 13.
103 Ibid., p. 222.
104 Leon Najberg, quoted in Leociak, *Text in the Face of Destruction*, p. 188.
105 Howarth, *Undercover*, p. 58.
106 IWM, sound archive, 9827, Patrick Howarth.
107 TNA, HS4/141, MXI to MP (2.7.1943).
108 TNA, FO954/19B, Minister of State Cairo to Foreign Office (3.7.1943).
109 Sebastian Chosinski, 'Daughter of Count Skarbek', *Esensja* magazine (10.12.2007).
110 IWM, 2/11 Gubbins papers, 3/2/59, letters between Gubbins and Hugh Trevor Roper (February 1969).
111 Ray Kipling, 'Lives Remembered', letter to *The Times* (15.12.2004).
112 TNA, FO/371, Death of Sikorski, draft broadcast by the prime minister.
113 TNA, HS4/141, MXI to MP (17.7.1943).

9: OUR WOMAN IN ALGIERS

1 Wilkinson and Astley, *Gubbins and SOE*, p. 181.
2 Marks, *Between Silk and Cyanide*, p. 222.
3 Wilkinson and Astley, *Gubbins and SOE*, p. 181.
4 Marks, *Between Silk and Cyanide*, p. 358.
5 Douglas Dodds-Parker, interviewed by Jeff Bines (c.2000).
6 Wilkinson and Astley, *Gubbins and SOE*, introduction.
7 Ibid., p. 155.
8 TNA, HS4/201 (29.10.1942).
9 TNA, HS4/141, MXI to MP (10.8.1943).
10 O'Malley papers, Granville to Kate O'Malley (16.9.1942).
11 IWM, Sound Archive, 13442, Richard Trevebyn Rockingham Gill.
12 O'Malley papers, Granville to Kate O'Malley (16.9.1942).
13 Patrick Leigh Fermor, 'The One-Legged Parachutist', the *Spectator* (1.1.1989).
14 Ibid.
15 O'Malley papers, Granville to Kate O'Malley (16.9.1943).

16 Patrick Leigh Fermor, 'The One-Legged Parachutist', the *Spectator* (1.1.1989).

17 Masson, *Christine: SOE Agent*, p. 148.

18 O'Malley papers, Andrzej Kowerski to Kate O'Malley (25.3.1944).

19 O'Malley papers, Granville to Kate O'Malley (16.9.1944).

20 Ibid.

21 Ibid.

22 Tarnowski, *The Last Mazurka*, p. 215.

23 Cooper, *Cairo in the War*, p. 285.

24 Tarnowski, *The Last Mazurka*, p. 221.

25 Patrick Leigh Fermor, 'The One-Legged Parachutist', the *Spectator* (1.1.1989).

26 Pope, 'Remembering Richard', p. 12; and Howarth, *Undercover*, p. 73.

27 Howarth, *Undercover*, p. 73.

28 Cole/Moss papers, Bill Stanley Moss papers (*c.*1952).

29 Ibid.

30 Ibid.

31 Patrick Leigh Fermor, 'The One-Legged Parachutist', the *Spectator* (1.1.1989).

32 Cole/Moss papers, Bill Stanley Moss papers (*c.*1952).

33 Ross Richards, 'Girl Spy', *Sunday Pictorial* (19.8.1956).

34 Cole/Moss papers, Bill Stanley Moss papers (*c.*1952).

35 Darlow Smithson/Channel Four, *The Real Charlotte Grays*, Francis Cammaerts interview.

36 Helm, *A Life in Secrets*, p. 8.

37 IWM, Gubbins papers, 2/11, 6/1-2-3, Gubbins's SOE manuals.

38 Porter, *Operation Autonomous*, p. 83.

39 Howarth, *Undercover*, p. 188.

40 IWM, Sound Archive, 8680, Maurice Buckmaster.

41 Foot, *SOE: An Outline History*, p. 82.

42 Stafford, *Secret Agent*, p. 30.

43 Wilkinson and Astley, *Gubbins and SOE*, p. 169.

44 Tarnowski, *The Last Mazurka*, p. 221.

45 IWM, Annette Street papers, 'Darling Joe, Please Go'.

46 TNA, HS4/86, MXI/SKE/559, 'Appreciation on proposed operation to prepare reception committee in Hungary' (25.3.1944).

47 Ibid.

48 Liddell Hart Centre for Military Archives, Julian Dobrinski papers, 21/6.

49 TNA, HS9/612, MXI/SKE/559, 'Appreciation on proposed operation to prepare reception committee in Hungary' (25.3.1944).

50 TNA, HS4/86, MXI/SKE/559, 'Appreciation on proposed operation to prepare reception committee in Hungary' (25.3.1944).

51 Liddell Hart Centre for Military Archives, Julian Dobrinski papers, 21/6.

52 TNA, HS4/86, MXI/SKE/559, 'Appreciation on proposed operation to prepare reception committee in Hungary' (25.3.1944).

53 Ibid.
54 Liddell Hart Centre for Military Archives, Julian Dobrinski papers, 21/6, 'Operation Kris' (22.3.1944).
55 TNA, HS9/612, MP/3048 (7.4.1944).
56 Liddell Hart Centre for Military Archives, Julian Dobrinski papers, 21/6, Cipher message (14.4.1944).
57 TNA, HS9/612, DEN/20/24 (17.4.1944).
58 Wladimir Ledóchowski, 'Christine Skarbek-Granville', p. 200.
59 Bill Stanley Moss, 'Christine the Brave', Picture Post (27.9.1952), p. 30.
60 Marks, Between Silk and Cyanide, p. 84.
61 Wilkinson and Astley, Gubbins and SOE, p. 144.
62 Dodds-Parker, Setting Europe Ablaze, p. 168.
63 Douglas Dodds-Parker, interviewed by Jeff Bines (c.2000).
64 Liddell Hart Centre for Military Archives, Patrick O'Regan papers.
65 Masson, Christine: SOE Agent, p. 166.
66 TNA, HS16, code card prepared for Christine Granville.
67 Paddy Sproule, Martyn Cox, 'Our Secret War' interviews.
68 Liddell Hart Centre for Military Archives, Patrick O'Regan papers.
69 Dorothy Wakely, Massingham Signals Planning Officer, correspondence (April 2011).
70 Sweet-Escott, Baker Street Irregular, p. 202.
71 Liddell Hart Centre for Military Archives, Patrick O'Regan papers.
72 IWM, Sound Archive, 8880, Havard Gunn.
73 Liddell Hart Centre for Military Archives, Patrick O'Regan papers.
74 Stafford, 'The Tragedy of Christine Granville'.
75 Lady Diana Duff Cooper, quoted in Masson, Christine: SOE Agent, p. 165.
76 Andrzej Kowerski-Kennedy, quoted in Masson, Christine: SOE Agent, p. 159.
77 Ibid., p. 190.
78 Ibid., p. 159.
79 Howarth, Undercover, p. 73.
80 Ibid., p. 73.
81 Andrzej Kowerski-Kennedy, quoted in Masson, Christine: SOE Agent, p. 159.
82 Ibid., p. 160.
83 Buckmaster, They Fought Alone, p. 91.
84 Maurice Buckmaster, 'All Communications Will be Cut', Chambers's Journal (1946–7, republished online by Steven Kippax, 2011), p. 23.
85 Cowburn, No Cloak, No Dagger, p. 67.
86 Masson, Christine: SOE Agent, p. 160.
87 IWM, Sound Archive, 10447, Pearl Cornioley.
88 Douglas Dodds-Parker, Head of SOE Massingham, interviewed by Jeff Bines (c.2000).
89 IWM, Sound Archives, 9970, Reel 12, Sir Brooks Richards.

90 Ibid.
91 Foot, *SOE: An Outline History*, p. 75.
92 John Anstey quote in Masson, *Christine: SOE Agent*, p. 168.
93 Binney, *Women Who Lived for Danger*, pp. 9–10.
94 Helm, *A Life in Secrets*, p. 14.

10: A FRENCH OCCUPATION

1 Jenkins, *A Pacifist*, pp. 9, 25.
2 Ibid., p. 35.
3 Ibid., p. 54.
4 TNA, HS9/258/5, 'MI5 record sheet' (13.7.1942).
5 Ibid., Francis Cammaerts 'training report' (8.12.1942); also 'Paramilitary training' (nd).
6 Marks, *Between Silk and Cyanide*, pp. 200–201.
7 TNA, HS9/258/5, Francis Cammaerts, 'Paramilitary training' (nd).
8 TNA, HS9/258, Cammaerts, 'Historical Account of Mission' (nd).
9 Jenkins, *A Pacifist*, p. 4.
10 IWM, Sound Archive, 11238, Francis Cammaerts; also Jeremy Clay, 'The Pacifist Who Led a Secret Army', *Leicester Mercury* (2005).
11 TNA, HS9/258, Cammaerts, 'Historical Account of Mission' (nd).
12 Foot, *SOE: An Outline History*, p. 10.
13 Jenkins, *A Pacifist*, p. 70.
14 Cowburn, *No Cloak, No Dagger*, introduction.
15 Marks, *Between Silk and Cyanide*, p. 9.
16 TNA, HS9/258, Cammaerts interview by Capt Howard (16–18.1.1944).
17 Escott, *Heroines of SOE F Section*, pp. 103–6.
18 Jenkins, *A Pacifist*, p. 95.
19 TNA, HS9/258/5, 'Interrogation of Roger' (21.11.1943).
20 See Helm, *A Life in Secrets*, pp. 101, 312; Jenkins, *A Pacifist*, p. 226.
21 TNA, HS9/258/5, 'Interrogation of Roger' (21.11.1943).
22 Binney, Marcus, *The Women Who Lived for Danger*, p. 22.
23 TNA, HS9/258/5, Cammaerts, 'Historical Account of Mission' (nd).
24 Buckmaster, *Specially Employed*, p. 122.
25 Bailey, *Forgotten Voices*, Francis Cammaerts, p. 204.
26 TNA, HS9/258/5, Roger Report (26.3.1944).
27 Daniel Farson, 'Riddle of the Woman Pimpernel', *Observer Magazine* (20.10.1974).
28 Mackiewicz, *Two Ladies Die*, pp. 321–5. A similar version of this story was later repeated by Andrzej to Wladimir Ledochówski.
29 Howarth, *Undercover*, p. 81.
30 Cole/Moss papers, 'Forces Françaises du Vercors, Autorisation de

Circuler sur le Plateau de Vercors', identity card 504 for Jacqueline Armand (8.7.1944).

31 Barbier, *Here, once, there was a French village*, p. 41.
32 Cookridge, *They Came From the Sky*, p. 129.
33 Wladimir Ledóchowski, 'Christine Skarbek-Granville', p. 216.
34 IWM, Sound Archive, 11238, Francis Cammaerts.
35 Masson, *Christine: SOE Agent*, p. 187.
36 Ibid., p. 190.
37 Ibid.
38 IWM, Sound Archive, 11238, Francis Cammaerts.
39 Cowburn, *No Cloak, No Dagger*, p. 133.
40 TNA, HS9/258/5, 'Interrogation of Roger' (21.11.1943).
41 Ibid.
42 IWM, Francis Cammaerts's papers, Ray Jenkins's papers.
43 IWM, Francis Cammaerts's papers, 'Conversation between M. Francis Cammaerts, DSO and Professor David Dilks at Le Pouget' (17.9.2002); also Cookridge, *They Came From the Sky*, p. 178.
44 TNA, HS9/258/5, 'Interrogation of Roger' (21.11.1943).
45 Jenkins, *A Pacifist*, p. 89.
46 TNA, HS9/258/5, interview by Capt Howard (16–18.1.1944).
47 Jenkins, *A Pacifist*, p. 168.
48 Daniel Farson, 'Riddle of the Woman Pimpernel', *Observer Magazine* (20.10.1974).
49 TNA, HS9/258/5, interview by Capt Howard (16–18.1.1944).
50 Jenkins, *A Pacifist*, p. 138.
51 TNA, HS9/258/5, 'Francis Cammaerts's Recommendation for the award of DSO' (nd).
52 Jenkins, *A Pacifist*, p. 168.
53 TNA, HS9/258/5, Cammaerts to Brooks Richards (27.7.1944).
54 TNA, HS9/612, 'To Brooks From Pauline' (19.8.1944).

11: THE BATTLE OF VERCORS

1 IWM, Gubbins papers, 4/1/4, Gubbins lecture 'SOE' (June 1959).
2 Jenkins, *A Pacifist*, p. 171.
3 Masson, *Christine: SOE Agent*, p. 192.
4 Jenkins, *A Pacifist*, p. 170.
5 Sylviane Rey quoted in Masson, *Christine: SOE Agent*, p. 191.
6 Eduoard Renn, interview, Vassieux-en-Vercors (July 2011).
7 Ibid.
8 *The Times*, 'Francis Cammaerts', obituary (6.7.2006).
9 Jenkins, *A Pacifist*, p. 119/20.
10 Stafford, *Secret Agent*, p. 129.
11 Cookridge, *They Came from the Sky*, p. 150.

12 Pearson, *Tears of Glory*, p. 37.
13 Ibid., p. 44.
14 IWM, Sound Archive, 9970, Sir Brooks Richards.
15 Ibid.
16 Jenkins, *A Pacifist*, p. 150.
17 TNA/HS9/285/5, Cammaerts, 'Historical Account of Mission'.
18 Jenkins, *A Pacifist*, p. 142.
19 IWM, Sound Archive, 11238: Francis Cammaerts.
20 TNA/H59/258/5, Cammaerts to Brooks, Richard (7.7.1944).
21 Daniel Huillier, interview, Vassieux-en-Vercors, (July 2011).
22 Masson, *Christine: SOE Agent*, pp. 192–3.
23 Jenkins, *A Pacifist*, p. 172.
24 Ibid.
25 Ibid.
26 Ibid.
27 Foot, *SOE in France*, p. 153.
28 Ibid.
29 Wilkinson and Astley, *Gubbins and SOE*, p. 194.
30 Wladimir Ledóchowski, 'Christine Skarbek-Granville', p. 236; also Binney, *Women Who Lived for Danger*, p. 85.
31 Cookridge, *They Came from the Sky*, p. 157.
32 Ibid.
33 Jenkins, *A Pacifist*, pp. 173–4.
34 IWM, Sound Archive, 9970: Sir Brooks Richards.
35 Jean-Paul le Chanois (dir.), *Au Coeur de l'Orage*.
36 Wladimir Ledóchowski, 'Christine Skarbek-Granville', p. 234.
37 Singer, *Spies and Traitors*.
38 Cookridge, *They Came from the Sky*, p. 157.
39 Binney, *Women Who Lived for Danger*, p. 86.
40 Gagnol, *The Martyrs of Vercors*, p. 13.
41 Daniel Huillier, interview, Vassieux-en-Vercors (July 2011).
42 Cookridge, *They Came from the Sky*, pp. 161–2.
43 Jean-Paul le Chanois (dir.), *Au Coeur de l'Orage* (1948).
44 TNA, HS9/258/5, SOE communications with Nan Cammaerts (24.7.1944).
45 Wladimir Ledóchowski, 'Christine Skarbek-Granville', p. 236.
46 Cookridge, *They Came from the Sky*, p. 160.
47 Ibid.

12: SWITCHING ALLEGIANCES

1 TNA, HS4/141, Lt Col Perkins to Col Protasewicz (26.6.1943).
2 Masson, *Christine: SOE Agent*, p. 188.
3 Jenkins, *A Pacifist*, p. 100.

4 Funk, *Hidden Ally*, p. 52.
5 Jenkins, *A Pacifist*, p. 169.
6 Ibid.
7 TNA, HS9/612, Cammaerts, 'Report on Christine Granville, known as Pauline' (22.10.1944).
8 Mackiewicz, *Two Ladies Die*, pp. 321–5.
9 TNA, HS9/612, Granville to Brooks Richards (27.7.1944).
10 Ibid.
11 Wladimir Ledóchowski, 'Christine Skarbek-Granville', p. 188.
12 Darlow Smithson/Channel Four, *The Real Charlotte Grays*, Francis Cammaerts interview.
13 Jenkins, *A Pacifist*, pp. 185–6; also IWM, Cammaerts papers, 'Conversation between M Francis Cammaerts, DSO, and Prof David Dilkes' (17.9.2002).
14 Mackiewicz, *Two Ladies Die*, pp. 321–5.
15 TNA, HS9/612, 'To Brooks From Pauline' (19.8.1944).
16 Liddell Hart Centre for Military Archives, O'Regan papers, annotated photograph album (nd).
17 Ibid., typed report (nd).
18 Ibid., untitled note (1.8.1944).
19 Ibid., 'Patrick's parachute drop into France' (nd).
20 Ibid., typed report (nd).
21 Ibid., 'In France' (nd).
22 TNA, HS9/612, Cammaerts, 'Report on Christine Granville, known as Pauline' (22.10.1944).
23 Liddell Hart Centre for Military Archives, O'Regan papers, untitled note (nd).
24 Ibid., 'In France' (nd).
25 Ibid., Granville to Marcellini (6.8.1944).
26 IWM, Francis Cammaerts papers, 'Francis Cammaerts draft obituary for John Roper' (nd).
27 IWM, Sound Archive, 12195, Robert William Berry Purvis.
28 TNA, IIS9/258/5, Cammaerts.
29 Liddell Hart Centre for Military Archives, O'Regan papers, 'In France' (nd).
30 Liddell Hart Centre for Military Archives, O'Regan papers.
31 TNA, HS9/612, Cammaerts, 'Report on Christine Granville, known as Pauline' (22.10.1944).
32 *The Times*, Francis Cammaerts, 'Mr Patrick O'Regan' (14.3.1961).
33 TNA, HS9/612, Granville to Brooks (27.7.1944).
34 Ibid.
35 Masson, *Christine: SOE Agent*, p. 221.
36 TNA, HS9/612, Cammaerts, 'Statement with regard to Mary Christine Granville' (20.11.1945).
37 Wladimir Ledóchowski, 'Christine Skarbek-Granville', p. 246.

38 Liddell Hart Centre for Military Archives, O'Regan papers, typed note on surrender procedure (nd).
39 Ibid., Patrick O'Regan to General Schlemmer, Commander 75 Army Corps (27 April, year unknown).
40 Funk, *Hidden Ally*, p. 184.
41 IWM, Francis Cammaerts papers, 13/2, 'Report on Christine Granville, known as Pauline' (22.10.1944).
42 Funk, *Hidden Ally*, p. 184.
43 IWM, Francis Cammaerts papers, correspondence with Arthur Funk (9.12.1983).
44 Wladimir Ledóchowski, 'Christine Skarbek-Granville', p. 247.
45 TNA, HS9/612, Cammaerts, 'Statement with regard to Mary Christine Granville' (20.11.1945).
46 Ibid., General Stawell, 'Citation in respect of Miss Mary Christine Granville' (10.12.1944).
47 Jenkins, *A Pacifist*, p. 192.

13: OPERATION LIBERTÉ

1 Pawley, *In Obedience*, p. 48.
2 Fielding, *Hide and Seek*, pp. 229–32.
3 Ibid.
4 Cookridge, *They Came from the Sky*, p. 166.
5 Fielding, *Hide and Seek*, p. 233.
6 Ibid., p. 234.
7 Ibid., p. 233.
8 Ibid.
9 Ibid., p. 234.
10 Ibid.
11 Mackiewicz, *Two Ladies Die*, pp. 321–5.
12 Fielding, *Hide and Seek*, p. 236.
13 Ibid., p. 238.
14 TNA, HS9/258/5, Cammaerts, interview by Capt Howard (16–18.1.1944).
15 Ibid.
16 Yesterday Channel, *The Secret War: Christine Granville, Polish Spy*, Francis Cammaerts interview (27.6.2011).
17 Binney, *Women Who Lived for Danger*, p. 41.
18 Jenkins, *A Pacifist*, p. 124.
19 Fielding, *Hide and Seek*, p. 240.
20 Ibid., p. 241.
21 Masson, *Christine: SOE Agent*, p. 211.
22 Fielding, *Hide and Seek*, p. 243.
23 Ibid., p. 244.

24 IWM, Sound Archive, 11238, Francis Cammaerts.
25 Ibid.
26 Ibid.
27 Fielding, *Hide and Seek*, p. 246.
28 Jenkins, *A Pacifist*, p. 124.
29 IWM, Christine Granville file, 'Union Mission report' (nd).
30 TNA, HS9/258/5, SOE communications with Nan Cammaerts (14.8.1944).
31 Liddell Hart Centre for Military Archives, O'Regan papers, O'Regan typed report (nd).
32 Jenkins, *A Pacifist*, p. 197.
33 TNA, HS9/612, 'Statement made by Miss Christine Granville' (1.11.1944).
34 Ibid.
35 IWM, Sound Archive, 11238, Francis Cammaerts.
36 Noreen Riols, interview (October 2011).
37 TNA, HS9/612, 'Statement made by Miss Christine Granville' (1.11.1944).
38 Ibid.
39 Ibid.
40 Ibid.
41 Fielding, *Hide and Seek*, p. 247.
42 Jeremy Clay, 'The Spy Who Saved Me', *Leicester Mercury* (2005).
43 Jenkins, *A Pacifist*, p. 199.
44 Fielding, *Hide and Seek*, p. 247.
45 Ibid., p. 248.
46 Jenkins, *A Pacifist*, p. 200.
47 Daniel Farson, 'Riddle of the Woman Pimpernel', *Observer Magazine* (20.10.1974); also Darlow Smithson/Channel Four, *The Real Charlotte Grays*, Francis Cammaerts interview.
48 Pawley, *In Obedience*, p. 48.
49 TNA, HS9/612, 'Statement made by Miss Christine Granville' (1.11.1944).
50 Sir Douglas Dodds-Parker, interviewed by Jeffrey Bines (c.2000).
51 Ibid.
52 O'Malley archive, Christine Granville to Sir Owen O'Malley (10.4.1947).
53 Ibid.
54 TNA, HS9/612, cover note for Cammaerts's report on Christine Granville (15.11.1944).
55 *Sunday Pictorial*, Ross Richards, 'Girl Spy' (19.8.1956).
56 TNA, HS9/612, Christine Granville, General Stawell, 'Citation in respect of Miss Mary Christine Granville' (10.12.1944).
57 TNA, HS9/258/5, Cammaerts, interview by Capt Howard (16–18.1.1944).

58 IWM, Sound Archive, 9970, Sir Brooks Richards.
59 HS9/612, Buckmaster, 'Christine' (18.9.1944).
60 Buckmaster, *They Fought Alone*, p. 232.
61 TNA, HS9/612, Cammaerts, 'Report on Christine Granville, known as Pauline' (22.10.1944).
62 IWM, Sound Archive, 11238, Francis Cammaerts.
63 Fielding, *Hide and Seek*, p. 249.
64 TNA, HS9/612, Christine Granville, General Stawell, 'Citation in respect of Miss Mary Christine Granville' (10.12.1944).
65 TNA, HS9/258/5, 'Francis Cammaerts's Recommendation for the award of DSO' (nd).
66 Bailey, *Forgotten Voices*, p. 231.
67 Fielding, *Hide and Seek*, p. 252.
68 Jenkins, *A Pacifist*, p. 204.
69 Bailey, *Forgotten Voices*, p. 212.
70 Jenkins, *A Pacifist*, p. 204.
71 Ibid., p. 206.
72 IWM, Francis Cammaerts papers, correspondence with Arthur Funk (9.12.1983).
73 Pawley, *In Obedience*, p. 48.
74 Masson, *Christine: SOE Agent*, p. 223.
75 Lyall, *Midnight Plus One*, p. 96.
76 IWM, Gubbins papers, 2/11, Gubbins 'SOE' (June, 1959).
77 Jenkins, *A Pacifist*, p. 209.
78 Ibid.
79 IWM, Francis Cammaerts papers, 3, Ray Jenkins papers (2002–5).
80 Pope, 'Remembering Richard', p. 120.
81 Ibid.
82 Daniel Huillier, interview, Vassieux-en-Vercors (July 2011).
83 Masson, *Christine: SOE Agent*, p. 222.

14: MISSION IMPOSSIBLE

 1 TNA, HS9/612, MPP/PD/879 to D/CE.g. (9.11.1944).
 2 Ibid., 'Krystina Gizycka (alias Christine Granville)' (nd).
 3 Noreen Riols, SOE Section F secretary, interview (October 2011).
 4 Buckmaster, *They Fought Alone*, p. 232.
 5 Masson, *Christine: SOE Agent*, p. xx.
 6 Noreen Riols, SOE Section F secretary, interview (October 2011).
 7 Helm, *A Life in Secrets*, p. 4.
 8 Cole/Moss papers.
 9 Masson, *Christine: SOE Agent*, p. 225.
10 Jenkins, *A Pacifist*, pp. 220–1.
11 Ibid., p. 216.

12 IWM, Gubbins papers, 4/1/4, Gubbins, 'SOE' (June, 1959).
13 Zamoyski, *Poland*, p. 328.
14 Wilkinson, *Foreign Fields*, p. 124.
15 Zamoyski, *Poland*, p. 328.
16 Walker, *Poland Alone*, p. 204.
17 Davies, *Rising '44*, p. 249.
18 Ibid.
19 IWM, Gubbins papers, 2/1, 'Talk to the Anglo-Polish Society in Connection with General Bór-Komorowski's Memorial Evening' (23.11.1966).
20 Bines, *The Polish Country Section of the SOE*, p. 200.
21 Davies, *Rising '44*, p. 264.
22 *Pravda* (6.8.1944), quoted in the Warsaw Rising Museum, Warsaw (2011).
23 IWM, Gubbins papers, 4/1/4, Gubbins lecture 'SOE' (1959).
24 Olson and Cloud, *Kościuszko Squadron*, p. 300.
25 Peszke, *The Polish Underground Army*, p. 124.
26 Ibid., pp. 124–5.
27 Walker, *Poland Alone*, p. 246.
28 Bines, *The Polish Country Section of the SOE*, p. 200.
29 Sgt Alan Bates quoted in Bailey, *Forgotten Voices*, p. 256; also Garlinski, *Poland, SOE and the Allies*, p. 192.
30 Garlinski, *Poland, SOE and the Allies*, p. 192.
31 IWM, Sound Archive, 8685, Annette Street.
32 Dodds-Parker, *Setting Europe Ablaze*, p. 182.
33 Jenkins, *A Pacifist*, p. 244.
34 Noreen Riols, SOE Section F secretary, interview (October 2011).
35 Walker, *Poland Alone*, p. 277.
36 Bines, *Operation Freston*, p. 16.
37 Ibid., p. 18.
38 TNA, HS9/612, 'Folkestone – SOE sub-mission to Polish Home Forces' (26.12.1944).
39 Ibid., addendum (26.12.1944).
40 Ibid., D/CE.G. to MPP (11.11.1944).
41 Statistics from the Warsaw Rising Museum, Warsaw (2011).
42 IWM, Gubbins papers, 2/11/8, Gubbins, 'Poland' (nd).
43 Pienkowska papers, Special Forces Club notes on speakers at Andrzej Kowerski's memorial event (1989).
44 Bines, *Operation Freston*, p. 21.
45 TNA, HS9/612, SO2 'vetting forms' (13.11.1944).
46 PUMST, correspondence Perkins/Tabor (23.11.1944).
47 TNA, HS9/612, MPP/PD/897 (14.11.1944).
48 Andrzej Kowerski-Kennedy quote in Masson, *Christine: A Search*, p. 220.
49 Duncan Stuart, official historian, Special Forces Club (December 2010).
50 Col Henry Threlfall, quoted in Bailey, *Forgotten Voices*, p. 258.

51 TNA, HS4/184, Col Threlfall's reports on Air Operations from
 Mediterranean Theatre, Memo to SOM Liaison Staff (12.1.1945).
52 TNA, HS9/612, 'Miss Granville, Christine. Financial Arrangements'
 (1.12.1944); also HS9/612 (4.12.1944).
53 Wazacz, *No Ordinary Countess*.
54 TNA, HS9/612, 'FIN/FD/10332' (25.11.1944).
55 Ibid., 'MPF/GEN/473' (2.12.1944).
56 Ibid., 'Folkestone – SOE sub-mission to Polish Home Forces'
 (26.12.1944); and ibid.,'Operation Folkestone' receipt (23.12.1944).
57 Kasparek, 'Krystyna Skarbek', unpublished manuscript (2011), p. 6.
58 Kemp, *No Colours or Crest*, p. 250.
59 Marks, *Between Silk and Cyanide*, p. 85; also Kemp, *No Colours or Crest*,
 p. 250.
60 TNA, HS9/612, MPP/PD/1021 (26.12.1944).
61 Ibid., 'Folkestone – SOE sub-mission to Polish Home Forces'
 (26.12.1944).
62 Bines, *Operation Freston*, p. 55.
63 Peter Solly-Flood quoted in Peszke, *The Polish Underground Army*,
 p. 177.
64 IWM, Gubbins papers, 2/11, Foreword to *The Silent and Unseen*.
65 Wilkinson and Astley, *Gubbins and SOE*, p. 227.
66 Stanisław Kujawinski quoted in Bailey, *Forgotten Voices*, p. 264.
67 Pawley, *In Obedience*, p. 115.
68 Tucholski, *Cichociemni 1941–1945*, p. 260; also HS7/183, SOE History
 131, Polish Section, 'List of Operators dispatched to Poland from
 Great Britain and Middle East' (nd).
69 TNA, HS4/311, L.dz.2986 (31.12.1944); see also Patrick Howarth,
 interviewed by Jeff Bines, August 2001.
70 Wladimir Ledóchowski, 'Christine Skarbek-Granville', p. 278.
71 Peter D. Stachura, 'Towards Yalta and Beyond', in Stachura (ed.), *The
 Poles in Britain 1940–2000*, p. 8.
72 TNA, HS9/612, Draft citation for Kristina Gizycka (Christine
 Granville) (nd).
73 Wladimir Ledóchowski, 'Christine Skarbek-Granville', p. 281.
74 Bines, *The Polish Country Section of the SOE*, p. 188; also TNA, HS7/
 183, 'History: Poland' (nd).
75 Celt, *By Parachute to Warsaw*, p. 20.
76 Jenkins, *A Pacifist*.
77 Wladimir Ledóchowski, 'Christine Skarbek-Granville', p. 281.
78 Binney, *Women Who Lived for Danger*, p. 104.
79 Martyn Cox, Peter Murray Lee, 'Our Secret War' interviews (nd).
80 Wladimir Ledóchowski, 'Christine Skarbek-Granville', p. 283.
81 Ibid.
82 Cole/Moss papers, correspondence between Harold Perkins and
 Christine Granville (15.3.1945); copy in TNA, HS9/612.

83 TNA, HS9/612, Granville to Perkins (25.3.1945).
84 Ibid.
85 Ibid.
86 Cole/Moss papers, Granville/Perkins (15.3.1945); copy in TNA, HS9/
 612.
87 Pope, 'Remembering Richard', p. 98.
88 TNA, HS9/612, Granville to Perkins (25.3.1945).
89 Binney, *Women Who Lived for Danger*, p. 107.
90 Ibid.
91 Fielding, *Hide and Seek*, p. 254.

15: SECOND-CLASS CITIZEN

1 Richard Usborne, 'Our Secret Service', in Howarth (ed.), *Special
 Operations*, pp. 225–6.
2 Stafford, *Secret Agent* p. 186.
3 IWM, Sound Archive, 26813, June Kerr Darton.
4 Margaret Pawley, Cairo-based FANY, and Ann Bonsor, FANY in
 Algiers, interviews (December 2010).
5 Liddell Hart Centre for Military Archives, O'Regan papers, Leonard
 Hamilton/Patrick O'Regan correspondence (27.5.1945).
6 Fielding, *Hide and Seek*, p. 254.
7 *Pittsburg Post-Gazette*, Dorothy Thompson, 'Major Questions
 Unanswered by Churchill' (2.3.1945).
8 TNA, HS9/612, 'Citation in respect of Miss Mary Christine Granville'
 (10.12.1944).
9 Wazacz, *No Ordinary Countess*.
10 *The Telegraph*, 'Pearl Cornioley', Obituary (26.2.2008).
11 TNA, HS9/612 (22.1.1945).
12 Ibid. (nd).
13 Jenkins, *A Pacifist*, p. 245.
14 TNA, HS9/612, 'F/O C. Granville, Honorary Commission, WAAF'
 (5.5.1945).
15 Ibid., 'Miss Christine Granville' (22.6.1945).
16 Cole/Moss papers, Granville to Gubbins (nd).
17 TNA, HS9/612, Perkins to Granville (15.3.1945).
18 Vera Long, Harold Perkins's secretary, interviewed by Jeff Bines
 (2000).
19 Cole/Moss papers, Granville to Gubbins (nd).
20 TNA, HS9/612, 'Citation in respect of Miss Mary Christine Granville'
 (10.12.1944).
21 Ibid., Telegram 8140 (11.3.1945).
22 Ibid. (22.11.1945).
23 Ibid. (3.12.1945).

24 Cole/Moss papers, Michael JTP to Christine Granville (27.6.1945).
25 IWM, Cammaerts papers, 'Conversation between M. Francis Cammaerts, DSO, and Professor David Dilkes at Le Pouget' (17.9.2002).
26 Cole/Moss papers, Granville to Gubbins (nd).
27 TNA, HS9/612, 'Christine Granville' (25.9.1944).
28 Ibid., 'Christine Granville' (30.9.1944).
29 Cole/Moss papers, Granville to Gubbins (nd).
30 Fielding, Hide and Seek, p. 254.
31 TNA, HS9/612, 'Miss Mary Christine Granville' (26.1.1945).
32 Ibid.
33 TNA, HS9/612, 'Christine Granville' (19.6.1944).
34 Ibid. (27.11.1945).
35 Ibid. (22.11.1945), also (17.11.1945).
36 Marks, Between Silk and Cyanide, p. 593; also Wilkinson and Astley, Gubbins and SOE, p. 237.
37 Stafford, Secret Agent, p. 236.
38 TNA, HO382/44, Gizycka Krystyna, 'Application for a certificate of naturalisation' (1.12.1945).
39 Cole/Moss papers, Lord Selborne/Home Secretary correspondence (3.1.1946).
40 Cole/Moss papers, Mr Chuter Ede/Lord Selborne correspondence (1.2.1946).
41 Cole/Moss papers, internal Home Office note (12.2.1946).
42 Cole/Moss papers, Perkins/Granville correspondence (nd).
43 TNA, HS9/258/5, File 8, AD/B to CD (9.3.1945).
44 Ibid., File 7, F to AD/E (27.3.1945).
45 Dorothy Wakely, personal letter (April 2011).
46 Ibid.
47 TNA, HS9/830/3, JS Nichols memo (29.6.1945).
48 Cole/Moss papers, 'Legal permission to Contract a Marriage' (1.8.1946).
49 Cole/Moss papers, Perkins/Granville correspondence (19.9.1946).
50 Picture Post, Bill Stanley Moss, 'Christine the Brave: Postscript' (4.10.1952), p. 31.
51 Ibid.
52 TNA, HS9/612 (nd).
53 News Chronicle, Cairo, Victor Azam, 'Shyest Secret Agent' (23.5.1947); also Picture Post, [Bill] Stanley Moss, 'Christine the Brave: Postscript' (4.10.1952), p. 31.
54 Cole/Moss, Perkins/Granville correspondence (nd).
55 Ibid.
56 Cole/Moss, Perkins/Granville correspondence (7.11.1946).
57 Ibid.
58 Ibid. (4.12.1946).

59 Ibid. (nd).
60 Ibid. (28.12.1946).
61 Ibid. (17.1.1947).
62 *The London Gazette*, Third Supplement (16.5.1947).
63 Cole/Moss papers, Perkins/Granville correspondence (21.5.1947).
64 Pope, 'Remembering Richard', p. 122.
65 Jenkins, *A Pacifist*, p. 292.
66 TNA, HS9/612, 'Report on Christine Granville, known as Pauline' (22.10.1944).
67 Cole/Moss papers, Cammaerts/Granville correspondence (17.4.1947).
68 Ibid. (12.11.1948).
69 O'Malley papers, Granville/Sir Owen correspondence (10.4.1947).
70 Masson, *Christine: SOE Agent*, p. 262.
71 Wazacz, *No Ordinary Countess*, Anna Czyzewska interview.
72 O'Malley papers, Granville/Sir Owen (10.4.1947); also Cole/Moss papers, Sir Owen/Granville (19.7.1948).
73 O'Malley papers, Granville/Sir Owen (10.4.1947).
74 Wladimir Ledóchowski, 'Christine Skarbek-Granville', p. 286.
75 Masson, *Christine: SOE Agent*, p. 239.
76 Granville's medals, mounted in their Spink and Son box, have been loaned for safe keeping to the Polish Institute and Sikorski Museum, London.
77 Masson, *Christine: SOE Agent*, p. 240.
78 Ibid., p. 241.
79 Ibid., p. 263.
80 Cole/Moss papers, Threlfall to Granville (4.4.1948).
81 Ibid., Crawley to Granville (4.12.1947).
82 Ibid., Sir Owen O'Malley to Granville (4 March, probably 1947).
83 O'Malley papers, Granville/Sir Owen (10.4.1947).
84 Wladimir Ledóchowski, 'Christine Skarbek-Granville', p. 285.
85 Cole/Moss papers, Sir Owen O'Malley to Granville (19.7.1948).
86 Ibid.
87 Wladimir Ledóchowski, 'Christine Skarbek-Granville', p. 287.

16: DEEP WATER

1 Michael Joseph, *Charles: The Story of a Friendship* (1943).
2 Masson, *Christine: SOE Agent*, p. 244.
3 Ibid.
4 Jan Ledóchowski, interview (April 2011).
5 Mackiewicz, *Two Ladies Die*, pp. 321–5.
6 Ibid.
7 Krzysztof Dubinski, 'Like Dynamite', *Beauty* magazine (nd).

8 Diana Hall, daughter of Richard Truszkowski, diary entry for 13.6.1949, private correspondence (May 2011).

9 Maryś Skarbek, interview (April 2011).

10 James Gleeson, 'Stabbed Heroine Told Her Story', *Daily Express* (17.6.1952).

11 Christine Isabelle Cole, interview (May 2011).

12 Ibid.

13 Evan McGilvary, 'General Stanisław Maczek and Post-war Britain', in Stachura (ed.), *The Poles in Britain 1940–2000*, p. 64.

14 Jeff Bines, interview (July 2011).

15 Mieczkowski, *Horizons*, p. 124.

16 Kasparek, 'Krystyna Skarbek', unpublished manuscript, p. 6.

17 Eva Hryniewicz, widow of Shelbourne Hotel manager, telephone interview (February 2011).

18 Daniel Farson, 'Riddle of the Woman Pimpernel', *Observer Magazine* (20.10.1974).

19 Masson, *Christine: SOE Agent*, p. 242.

20 Izabela Muszkowska, telephone interview (June 2011).

21 Ian Sayer private archive, cheque signed by Christine Granville (2.3.1950); also Polish Institute and Sikorski Museum, Christine Granville's appointments diary (1949).

22 Izabela Muszkowska, telephone interview (June 2011).

23 Wladimir Ledóchowski, 'Christine Skarbek-Granville', p. 290.

24 *Daily Express*, James Gleeson, 'Stabbed Heroine Told Her Story' (17.6.1952).

25 Ibid.

26 Wladimir Ledóchowski, 'Christine Skarbek-Granville', p. 292.

27 Howarth, *Undercover*, p. 84; also Masson, *Christine: SOE Agent*, p. xx.

28 Jenkins, *A Pacifist*, p. 245.

29 Ada Tarnowska, telephone interview (June 2011).

30 Izabela Muszkowska, telephone interview (June 2011).

31 Maria Nurowska, interview (June 2011).

32 Bill Stanley Moss, 'What Makes a First-Class Secret Agent', unknown publication (June 1952).

33 Andrzej Kowerski-Kennedy, quoted in Masson, *Christine: SOE Agent*, p. 237.

34 Masson, *Christine: SOE Agent*, p. 246.

35 Cole/Moss papers, telegram George Michailov to Andrzej Kowerski (nd).

36 Maria Pienkowska, interview (June 2011).

37 Jan Larecki, interview (June 2011).

38 Cole/Moss papers, Union-Castle Mail Steamship, Stewardess Uniform guidelines.

39 TNA, PRI COM 9/1634, Muldowney/Prison Commission and Home Office papers, hospital case paper (16.6.1952).

40 Wladimir Ledóchowski, 'Christine Skarbek-Granville', p. 298.
41 Arthur W. Jacobs, 'The Little Man Who Loved a Heroine', *Evening Standard* (11.9.1952).
42 TNA, PRI COM 9/1634, Muldowney/Prison Commission and Home Office papers, hospital case paper (16.6.1952); also ibid., JCM Matheson, Principal Medical officer, Brixton prison, to Dr D Hill, Maudsley Hospital (21.8.1952).
43 TNA, PRI COM 9/1634, 'Hospital case papers' (16.6.1952).
44 Ibid., Muldowney/Prison Commission and Home Office papers, hospital case paper (17.9.1952).
45 H. M. Edinburgh, letter, 'The Strange Stewardess', *Picture Post* (4.10.1952).
46 Cole/Moss papers, Mrs MacKinnon to Christine Granville (12.9.1951).
47 Ibid., letter to Christine Granville (*c*.September 1951).
48 Ibid., Aidan Crawley, MP, North Bucks, reference for Christine Granville (1.10.1951).
49 Ibid., Patrick Howarth Ministry of Local Government and Planning, reference for Christine Granville (15.10.1951).
50 Ibid., Francis Cammaerts, Central Bureau for Educational Visits and Exchanges, reference for Christine Granville (15.10.1951).
51 Teresa Robinska, daughter of Countess Przezdziecka, the Shelbourne Hotel cook, telephone interview (March 2011).
52 Ibid.
53 TNA, DPP2/2169, Director of Public Prosecutions, case papers, Muldowney, 'Statement of Witness, Andrew Kennedy' (11.7.1952).
54 Tarnowski, *The Last Mazurka*, p. 302.
55 Bill Stanley Moss, 'Christine the Brave: Postscript', *Picture Post* (4.10.1952), p. 31.
56 Masson, *Christine: SOE Agent*, p. 248.
57 Wladimir Ledóchowski, 'Christine Skarbek-Granville', p. 303.
58 Ibid.
59 Masson, *Christine: SOE Agent*, p. 249.
60 Jenkins, *A Pacifist*, p. 246; and Masson, *Christine: SOE Agent*, p. 249.
61 O'Malley papers, correspondence Kate O'Malley to Sir Owen and Ann Bridge (*c*.24.6.1952); also Masson, *Christine: SOE Agent*, p. 249.
62 Ibid, p. 251.
63 O'Malley papers, correspondence Kate O'Malley/Sir Owen and Ann Bridge (24.6.1952).
64 TNA, PRI COM 9/1634, Muldowney/Prison Commission and Home Office papers, hospital case paper (17.9.1952).
65 TNA, DPP2/2169, Director of Public Prosecutions, case papers, Muldowney, 'Statement of Witness, Dennis George Muldowney' (*c*.June 1952).
66 O'Malley papers, correspondence Kate O'Malley/Sir Owen and Ann Bridge (24.6.1952).

67 TNA, DPP2/2169, Director of Public Prosecutions, case papers, Muldowney, 'Statement of Witness, Ann (Hanka) Nicolle, Ships Stewardess' (12.8.1952).
68 Ibid., 'Statement of Witness, Andrew Kennedy' (11.7.1952).
69 Ibid., 'Statement of Witness, Ludwig Popiel (18.6.1952).
70 Ibid., 'Statement of Witness, Ludwig Popiel (18.6.1952).
71 Ibid., 'Statement of Witness, Ludwig Popiel (18.6.1952).
72 Bill Stanley Moss, 'Christine the Brave: Postscript', *Picture Post* (4.10.1952), p. 31.

17: BRUTAL END

1 Masson, *Christine: SOE Agent*, p. xx.
2 The *Spectator*, Patrick Leigh Fermor, 'The One-Legged Parachutist: Send for a Blacksmith!' (1.1.1989).
3 Masson, *Christine: SOE Agent*, p. xx.
4 Wazacz, *No Ordinary Countess*.
5 Maria Pienkowska, Andrzej Kowerski's niece, interview (June 2011).
6 TNA, PRI COM 9/1634, 'Hospital case paper' (16.6.1952).
7 TNA, DPP2/2169, Muldowney, 'Jósef Tadeusz Kojdecki' (15.6.1952).
8 Ibid., Muldowney, 'Statements of persons not called at Magistrates Court: Irena Krasuska' (16.6.1952).
9 Ibid., 'Michal Perlak' (16.7.1952).
10 Eva Hryniewicz, widow of the manager at the Shelbourne Hotel, telephone interview (February 2011).
11 TNA, DPP2/2169, Muldowney, 'G Jennings, Chief Superintendent 'F', Metropolitan Police Report, Kensington Station 'F' Division (23.6.1952).
12 Ibid.,'Central Criminal Court' (9.9.1952).
13 Ibid., 'Andrew Kennedy' (16.6.1952).
14 O'Malley papers, Kate O'Malley to Sir Owen and Ann Bridge (24.6.1952).
15 Jenkins, *A Pacifist*, p. 254.
16 IWM, Gubbins papers, 5/1–31, 'Miss C Granville, GM, OBE' (nd); also *The Times*, Colin Gubbins, 'Christine Granville' (21.6.1952).
17 *Daily Mirror*, pp. 6–7, 'Drama of Quiet Countess Who Was British Secret Service Agent' (17.6.1952).
18 General Register Office, Death certificate of Christine Granville (3.10.1952).
19 Patrick Leigh Fermor, 'The One-Legged Parachutist: Send for a Blacksmith!', the *Spectator* (1.1.1989).
20 Pope, 'Remembering Richard'.

Epilogue

1 *Daily Express*, 'Stabbed Heroine Told Her Story' (17.6.1952); 'The Ego of a Murderer' (12.9.1952); *Daily Mirror*, 'Drama of Quiet Countess who was British Secret Agent' (17.6.1952); 'Heroine dared me three times to kill her' (2.7.1952); 'The man who built his dream world around a Countess – and killed her' (19.9.1952).
2 TNA, DPP2/2169, Muldowney, 'Criminal Court Proceedings' (4.7.1952).
3 Ibid., 'Andrew Kennedy' (16.6.1952).
4 Ibid., 'Aidan Crawley to Hartley Shawcross' (7.7.1952).
5 Ibid., 'Central Criminal Court' (9.9.1952).
6 Ibid., 'Central Criminal Court' (9.9.1952).
7 *Daily Mail*, 'Kindness Led to Murder: Christine Granville's Mistake Ended in Death' (12.9.1952); *Evening Standard*, Arthur W. Jacobs, 'The Little Man Who Loved a Heroine' (11.9.1952).
8 O'Malley papers, Kate O'Malley/Sir Owen and Ann Bridge (24.6.1952).
9 *Daily Express*, 'Stabbed Heroine Told Her Story' (17.6.1952).
10 Karol Zbyszewski, 'Famous Agent' (18.10.1975); also Daniel Huillier, Vercors veteran, interview (July 2011).
11 O'Malley papers, Kate O'Malley to Sir Owen O'Malley (4.3.1953).
12 *Picture Post*, Bill Stanley Moss, 'Christine the Brave' (13.9.1952 – 4.10.1952).
13 Wazacz, *No Ordinary Countess*, Francis Cammaerts interview.
14 Moss, *Gold Is Where You Find It*, p. 17.
15 Christine Isabelle Cole, daughter of Zofia Tarnowska and Bill Stanley Moss, interview (May 2011). The whereabouts of Moss's manuscript is unknown.
16 Jan Ledóchowski, 'Christine Granville', p. 21.
17 Madeleine Masson, *Woman's Hour*, BBC Radio Four (29.12.2004).
18 IWM, Gubbins papers, 2/11, Wilkinson/Gubbins correspondence (30.10.1974); Wilkinson/Masson correspondence (30.10.1974).
19 Masson, *Christine: SOE Agent*, p. xx.
20 Masson, *Christine: A Search*, p. xvi.
21 Christine Isabelle Cole, interview (May 2011).
22 TNA, DPP2/2169, Muldowney, G. Jennings, Chief Superintendent 'F', Metropolitan Police Report, Kensington Station 'F' Division (23.6.1952).
23 Singer, *Spies and Traitors*, p. 201.
24 TNA, HS4/291, Poland 206, 'The Future of SOE Polish Section' (24.5.1945).
25 Masson, *Christine: SOE Agent*, p. 291.
26 McCormick, *17F: The Life of Ian Fleming*, p. 143.
27 Ibid., p. 141.

28 Lycett, *Ian Fleming*, p. 178.
29 Fleming, *Casino Royale*, pp. 30, 38–9.
30 Ibid., pp. 186–7, 64.
31 Macintyre, *For Your Eyes Only*, pp. 5, 63, 69.
32 Fleming, *Casino Royale*, pp. 61–2.
33 *Rogue*, US magazine, William F. Nolan, 'Personality: Ian Fleming' (February 1961), p. 80; also Fleming, *The Diamond Smugglers*, p. 54.
34 Griswold, *Ian Fleming's James Bond*, p. 60; also Macintyre, *For Your Eyes Only*, p. 78.
35 Deacon, *History of the British Secret Service*, and *Spyclopaedia*.
36 Fielding, *Hide and Seek*; Howarth, *Undercover*; Patrick Howarth, 'Play Back A Lifetime', first published in Masson, *Christine: A Search*, p. 251.
37 Gordimer, 'Vladimir Ledóchowski: Man of Two Worlds', typed manuscript (1987).
38 Michael Morpurgo quoted in Jenkins, *A Pacifist*, p. 298.
39 Moss, *Gold Is Where You Find It*, p. 17.
40 Christine Isabelle Cole, interview (May 2011).
41 Jan Ledóchowski, 'Christine Granville', p. 26.

Appendix I

1 Diana Hall interview (May 2011).
2 Gizycki, 'Winding Trail', p. 412.
3 Andrzej Skarbek, interview (May 2011).
4 Diana Hall interview (May 2011).
5 Suzanna Gaynford interview (October 2011).
6 Masson, *Christine: SOE Agent*, p. 168.
7 TNA, PRI COM 9/1634, 'Hospital case paper' (8.9.1952).
8 Izabela Muszkowska interview (June 2011).
9 Christine Isabelle Cole interview (May 2011).

Appendix II

1 TNA, PRI COM 9/1634, 'Hospital case paper' (17.6.1952).
2 Ibid., 'JCM Matheson, Principal Medical officer, Brixton prison, to Dr D Hill, Maudsley Hospital' (21.8.1952); also 'JCM Matheson, Principal Medical officer, Brixton prison, to Dr Coats, HMP Pentonville' (23.9.1952).
3 Ibid., 'JCM Matheson, Principal Medical officer, Brixton prison, to Dr D Hill, Maudsley Hospital' (21.8.1952).
4 Ibid., 'JCM Matheson, Principal Medical officer, Brixton prison, to Dr Coats, HMP Pentonville' (23.9.1952).
5 *Daily Express*, Arnold Latcham, 'The Ego of a Murderer: Everyone

knew of woman he killed – none knew him. He pursued a heroine – a hero only to himself' (12.9.1952); also *Daily Telegraph*, 'Murder Trial in Three Minutes' (12.9.1952).

6 TNA, PRI COM 9/1634, 'Dennis Muldowney, letter to Frank, Jack and Marie' (11.9.1952).

7 Ibid., 'Hospital Case Paper' (16.6.1952); also ibid., 'Hospital Case Paper' (17.9.1952).

8 Ibid., 'Hospital Case Paper' (16.6.1952); also 'JCM Matheson, Central Criminal Court report' (13.9.1952).

9 Ibid., 'Statement of Witness, DG Muldowney' (nd).

10 Ibid., 'Dennis Muldowney, letter to Frank, Jack and Marie' (11.9.1952).

11 Ibid., 'Hospital case paper' (8.9.1952); also ibid., 'Dennis Muldowney, letter to Frank, Jack and Marie' (11.9.1952).

12 Ibid., 'Dennis Muldowney, letter to Frank, Jack and Marie' (11.9.1952).

13 *Leicester Mercury*, Jeremy Clay, 'The Spy Who Saved Me' (2005).

14 TNA, PRI COM 9/1634, 'Dennis Muldowney, letter to Frank, Jack and Marie' (11.9.52); also ibid., 'Hospital case paper' (17.6.1952).

15 Ibid., 'Dennis Muldowney, letter to Frank, Jack and Marie' (11.9.1952).

16 *Daily Mail*, 'Kindness Led to Murder: Christine Granville's Mistake Ended in Death' (12.9.1952).

17 Ibid.

18 TNA, PRI COM 9/1634, 'Dennis Muldowney, letter to Frank, Jack and Marie' (11.9.1952).

19 Ibid., 'JCM Matheson, Central Criminal Court report'.

20 Ibid., Muldowney, 'Old Bailey transcript, in front of Justice Donovan' (10.9.1952); also *Daily Mirror*, 'The man who built his dream world round a Countess – and killed her' (12.9.1952).

21 *Daily Mail*, 'Kindness Led to Murder: Christine Granville's Mistake Ended in Death' (12.9.1952).

22 O'Malley papers, Kate O'Malley to Sir Owen O'Malley and Ann Bridge (24.6.1952).

23 TNA, PRI COM 9/1634, 'Pentonville Medical officer Percy Murray Coats papers', also 'Post-Mortem Examination'.

24 *Sunday Dispatch*, 'Boy does not know father is murderer' (28.9.1953).

25 TNA, PRI COM 9/1634, 'Dennis Muldowney, letter to Frank, Jack and Marie' (11.9.1952).

26 Steven Muldowney to Clare Mulley (14.6.2011).

Select Bibliography

INTERVIEWS AND CORRESPONDENCE

INTERVIEWS

Jane Bigman-Hartey, wife of Prince Marcin Lubomirski (May 2011)
Ann Bonsar, Massingham-based wireless operator (December 2010)
Julian de Bosdari, son of Erica de Bosdari, Christine's friend at the British Legation in Budapest (June 2011)
Christine Isabelle Cole, daughter of Zofia Tarnowska and Bill Stanley Moss (May 2011)
Edouard Renn, Vercors veteran (July 2011)
M. R. D. Foot, SOE official historian, friend of Francis Cammaerts (March 2011)
Suzanna Gayford, knew Christine in Kenya (October 2011)
Nicholas Gibbs, historian (April 2011)
Diana Hall, daughter of Richard Truszkowski (May 2011)
Daniel Huillier, Vercors veteran (July 2011)
Eva Hryniewicz, wife of Shelbourne Hotel manager (May 2011)
Michal Komar, Polish journalist and playwright (June 2011)
Captain Kozak, former manager of the Shelbourne Hotel (March 2011)
Colonel Jan Larecki, Christine's Polish biographer (June 2011)
Count Jan Ledóchowski, son of Count Wladimir Ledóchowski (May 2011)
Princess Renata Lubomirski, daughter of Prince Marcin Lubomirski (May 2011)
Zbigniew Mieczkowski, friend of Christine (March 2011)
Izabela Muszkowska, post-war London friend of Christine (June 2011)
Maria Nurowska, Polish novelist whose father, Stanisław Rudziejewski, knew Christine (June 2011)
Ann O'Regan, widow of Patrick O'Regan (May 2011)
Margaret Pawley, Cairo-based FANY (December 2010)
Maria Pienkowska, niece of Andrzej Kowerski (June 2011)
Noreen Riols, SOE, F Section, secretary (October 2011)
Teresa Robinska, daughter of Countess Przezdziecka, Shelbourne Hotel cook (March 2011)
Count Andrzej Skarbek, Christine's cousin (April 2011)

Countess Maryś Skarbek, widow of Christine's cousin Jan Skarbek (April 2011)
Elizabeth Skarbek (May 2011)
Matt Smolenski, son of the Head of the Polish VI Bureau (2011)
Duncan Stuart, former chairman of the Special Forces Club's Historical Sub-Committee (December 2010)
Dr Andrzej Suchcitz, Keeper of Archives, Polish Institute and Sikorski Museum (May 2011)
Henryk Szymanski, Bęczkowice parish priest, Poland (June 2011)
Ada Tarnowska, post-war friend of Christine's, Poland (June 2011)
Katharine Whitehorn, friend of Nan and Francis Cammaerts, and Sylviane Rey (May 2011)
Virginia Worlsey, daughter of Peter Wilkinson (May 2011)

Private correspondence

Joanna Cammaerts-Wey, daughter of Francis Cammaerts (June 2011)
Christopher Kasparek, son of Józef Kasparek (2011)
Princess Renata Lubomirska, daughter of Prince Marcin Lubomirski (June 2011)
Steven Muldowney, nephew of Dennis Muldowney (June 2011)
Dorothy Wakely, Massingham Signals Planning Officer (April 2011)
Michael Ward, officer who knew Christine in Cairo (March 2011)

PUBLIC ARCHIVES

The National Archives, Kew (TNA)
Records of the Board of Trade
 BT26/1186, UK incoming passenger lists (1878–1960)
 BT372/1138/116, Dennis George Muldowney, seaman's records
Records of the Central Criminal Court
 CRIM1/2252, Dennis George Muldowney (September 1952)
Records of the Director of Public Prosecutions
 DPP2/2169, case papers, Muldowney
Foreign Office
 FO/371, Death of Sikorski
 FO954/19B, Papers of Sir Anthony Eden, Secretary of State for Foreign Affairs
Home Office and Ministry of Home Security
 HO382/44, Home Office files, Gizycka, Krystyna
 HO405/30369, Home Office files, Kowerski, Andrew
Africa and Middle East files
 HS3/64, SOE North Africa
 HS3/198, SOE/MIDEAST/50

SOE Eastern Europe files
 HS4/86, SOE Hungary
 HS4/141, SOE Poland
 HS4/184, Col Threlfall's reports, Mediterranean Air Operations
 HS4/198, Middle East Org, Istanbul (Poles and Czechs)
 HS4/199, SOE Poland
 HS4/200, SOE, Eastern Europe, Poland
 HS4/201, SOE, Eastern Europe, Poland
 HS4/291, SOE Eastern Europe files, Poland
 HS4/308, Telegrams Polish 6th Bureau to Poland and Italy
 HS4/311, SOE, Eastern Europe, Poland
SOE Western Europe files
 HS6/568, SOE France
 HS6/570, Albert Floiras [Deschamps] interrogation
Histories and War Diaries
 HS7/162, SOE histories 113, Hungary
 HS7/183, SOE histories 131, Polish Section History
SOE personal files
 HS9/258/5, Francis Cammaerts
 HS9/588/2, Jerzy Gizycki
 HS9/612, Christine Granville
 HS9/630/8, Colin Gubbins
 HS9/630/6, John Michael McVean Gubbins
 HS9/668, Hubert Harrison
 HS9/830, Andrzej Kowerski-Kennedy
 HS9/1224/6, Józef Radziminski
 HS9/1253/6, Francis Brooks Richards
 HS9/1466, Henry Threlfall
SOE Playfair and Wireless Operators Codes Nominal Card Index
 HS16, Christine Granville's code card
Records of the Security Service
 KV2/517, File of Edward Szarkiewicz
Prime Minister's Office
 PREM 3/351/3, 1940 Poland, General 1
Prison Commission and Home Office
 PRI COM 9/1634, Muldowney

The Imperial War Museum, London (IWM)
Paper files
 Francis Cammaerts
 General Colin McVean Gubbins
 Krystyna Skarbek/Christine Granville
 Annette Street, including 'Long Ago and Far Away', unpublished memoir
 (c.1995)
 Henry Threlfall
 Peter Wilkinson

Sound archive
 8680, Maurice Buckmaster
 11238, Lt Col Francis Cammaerts
 10447, Pearl Cornioley
 26813, Reel 1, June Kerr Darton
 8682, Basil Risbridger Davidson
 8880, Havard Gunn
 9827, Patrick Howarth
 11087, Gwendolin Lees
 12195, Robert William Berry Purvis
 9970, Sir Francis Brooks Richards
 13442, Richard Trevebyn Rockingham Gill
 8685, Annette Street
Picture archive
 HU 57106–57120, The French Resistance in the Haute-Savoie, August
 1944

Liddell Hart Centre for Military Archives, Kings College London
 Julian Dobrinski papers
 Patrick O'Regan papers

Polish Institute and Sikorski Museum, London
 Aniela Pawlikowska portrait of Christine Granville
 Christine Granville papers, war decorations, wireless set, commando knife

Polish Underground Movement Study Trust (PUMST), London
 Musketeers file
 Krystyna Skarbek file

General Register Office, Britain
 Death certificate, Christine Granville (3.10.1952)
 Death certificate, Dennis Muldowney (1.10.1952)

Musée de la Résistance, Vassieux-en-Vercors, France
 Francis Cammaerts interview
 Vercors 1944 exhibits

All Saints' Church, parish archive, Warsaw, Poland
 Baptism record for Stefania Goldfeder (15.11.1899)
 Marriage record for Jerzy Skarbek and Stefania Goldfeder (2.12.1899)

Bęczkowice parish archive, Poland
 Krystyna Skarbek baptism record (17.11.1913, Julian calendar)

Museum of Pawiak Prison archive, Poland
 Files of former prisoners

Polish Institute of National Remembrance (IPN), Poland
 Personnel archives

Warsaw Royal Castle archive, Poland
 Szymon Konarski/Wladimir Ledóchowski correspondence (1960)
 Alphabetical list of the landowners in the Kingdom of Poland (1909)

Warsaw Uprising Museum, Poland
 Warsaw Uprising exhibits

PRIVATE ARCHIVES

Jeff Bines sound archive, Britain
 Douglas Dodds-Parker (*c.*2000)
 Patrick Howarth (August 2001)
 Vera Long, Harold Perkins's PA (*c.*2000)

Christine Isabelle Cole/Bill Stanley Moss private papers, Britain
(Intended for the Polish Institute and Sikorski Museum)
 Bill Stanley Moss private papers (*c.*1952)
 Correspondence between Francis Cammaerts, Aidan Crawley, Douglas
 Dodds-Parker, Jerzy Gizycki, Christine Granville, Colin Gubbins,
 Patrick Howarth, Andrzej Kowerski, Wladimir Ledóchowski, George
 Michailov, Bill Stanley Moss, Sir Owen O'Malley, Harold Perkins and
 Bickham Sweet-Escott.
 Christine's documents including:
 French identity card for Jacqueline Armand (8.7.1944)
 Legal permission to Contract a Marriage, Berlin (1.8.1946)
 Certificate of Naturalisation (17.12.1946)
 Job references, applications, rejection letters
 Andrzej Kowerski's passport
 Photographs of Christine Granville

The Ledóchowski family archive, Britain
 Nadine Gordimer, 'Vladimir Ledóchowski: Man of Two Worlds' (1987)
 Jan Ledóchowski, 'Who Was She? Christine and my father's unpublished
 book', unpublished manuscript (2008)
 ———, 'Christine Granville and My Father's Unpublished Book',
 unpublished manuscript (2008)
 ———, DVD, 'Discussion with Dominik Horodyñski' (2007)
 Wladimir Ledóchowski, 'Christine Skarbek-Granville: A Biographical
 Story', unpublished draft manuscript (nd) [This draft was abandoned in
 the early 1970s before finalizing and checking all the details of her life
 in France and England.]

The O'Malley family papers, Ireland
Correspondence between Christine Granville, Andrzej Kowerski, Sir
Owen and Kate O'Malley
Correspondence between Sir Owen, Kate O'Malley and Ann Bridge
Kate O'Malley notes on 'Harrison's agent, Mme Gizycka'
Jane O'Malley, 'Christina'
Photographs of Christine Granville and Andrzej Kowerski

Maria Pienkowska/Kowerski family papers, Poland
Correspondence between Andrzej Kowerski, Wladimir Ledóchowski and
Barbara Pienkowska
Andrzej Kowerski's birth certificate and war decorations
Christine Granville's jewellery

Ian Sayer private archive, Spain
Photographs of Andrzej Kowerski (1975)
Recording of Andrzej Kowerski-Kennedy and Harry Seaman, Munich
(1976)
Cheque signed by Christine Granville

The Skarbek family papers, Britain
Skarbek genealogy based on Count Jerzy Dunin-Borkowski's *Almanach
Błękitny* (*Blue Almanac*)
Family photographs

PRESS, JOURNALS, FILM, TV, RADIO

ENGLISH-LANGUAGE PRESS
Daily Express
James Gleeson, 'Stabbed Heroine Told Her Story' (17.6.1952)
'Spurned Lover Killed GM Heroine' (2.7.1952)
Daily Mail
'Beauty Queen a Secret Agent' (21.5.1947)
'Kindness Led to Murder: Christine Granville's Mistake Ended in Death'
(12.9.1952)
Daily Mirror
'Drama of Quiet Countess Who Was British Secret Service Agent'
(17.6.52)
'Heroine dared me three times to kill her' (2.7.1952)
Evening Standard
Arthur W. Jacobs, 'The Little Man Who Loved a Heroine' (11.9.1952)
The Guardian
Winston Churchill, 'Poland's and the Allies' Loss' (7.6.1943)

'Chopin's Birthplace: Centenary Plans for 1949' (27.10.1947)
'Death of Polish Countess' (11.9.1952)
'Murder of Former Secret Agent' (12.9.1952)
Annalena McAfee, 'The trouble I've seen' (16.4.2011)
The Independent
M. R. D. Foot, 'Michael Lis' obituary (18.8.1994)
Piers Plowright, 'Patrick Howarth' obituary (19.11.2004)
The Leicester Mercury
Jeremy Clay, 'The Pacifist Who Led A Secret Army' (2005)
———, 'The Spy Who Saved Me' (2005)
LIFE
'Who was Christine Granville?', pp. 43–5 (7.7.1952)
The London Gazette
Third Supplement (16.5.1947)
News Chronicle, Cairo
Victor Azam, 'Shyest Secret Agent' (23.5.1947)
Observer Magazine
Daniel Farson, 'Riddle of the Woman Pimpernel' (20.10.1974)
Picture Post
Bill Stanley Moss, 'Christine the Brave' (13.9.1952)
———, 'Christine the Brave: Fast Cars to Freedom' (20.9.1952)
———, 'Christine the Brave: The Face of a Killer' (27.9.1952)
———, 'Christine the Brave: Postscript' (4.10.1952)
H. M. Edinburgh, letter, 'The Strange Stewardess' (4.10.1952)
Rogue, US magazine
William F. Nolan, 'Personality: Ian Fleming' (February 1961)
The Spectator
Patrick Leigh Fermor, 'The One-Legged Parachutist: Send for a
 Blacksmith!' (1.1.1989)
Sunday Dispatch
'Boy does not know his father is murderer' (28.9.1952)
Sunday Pictorial
Ross Richards, 'Girl Spy' (19.8.1956)
The Telegraph
'A. Kowerski-Kennedy', obituary (14.12.1988)
'Pearl Cornioley', obituary (26.2.2008)
'Sophie Moss', obituary (3.12.2009)
'Count Andrzej Skarbek', obituary (10.1.2012)
The Times
Francis Cammaerts, 'Patrick O'Regan', obituary (14.3.1961)
'Andrew Kennedy: undercover operations in wartime Eastern Europe',
 obituary (15.12.1988)
'Michael Lis', obituary (16.8.1994)
Ray Kipling, letter, 'Lives Remembered' (15.12.2004)
'Francis Cammaerts', obituary (6.7.2006)

Unknown paper
 Bill Stanley Moss, 'What Makes a First-Class Secret Agent' (*c*.1952)

ENGLISH-LANGUAGE JOURNALS

Chambers's Journal
 Maurice Buckmaster, 'All Communications Will be Cut' (1946–7,
 republished online by Steven Kippax, 2011)
East European Quarterly
 Józef Kasparek, 'Poland's 1938 Covert Operations in Ruthenia', vol.
 XXIII, no. 3, pp. 365–73 (1989)
History Today
 Adam Zamoyski, 'The Underground Factory: Poland in 1939–45' (1974)
The Polish Review
 Christopher Kasparek, 'Krystyna Skarbek: Re-viewing Britain's legendary
 Polish agent', XLIX, no 3, pp. 945–53 (2004)
 ———, 'Letters to the Editor' L, no 2 (2005), p. 254
Reform Review, journal of the Reform Club
 Peter Hill, 'Wartime espionage heroine's murder . . . and the condemned
 man's apology to the Club' (Summer 2010)

POLISH PRESS

Beauty (Polish magazine)
 Krzysztof Dubinski, 'Like Dynamite' (nd)
Esensja magazine
 Sebastian Chosinski, 'Daughter of Count Skarbek' (10.12.2007)
Express Poranny (*Morning Express*)
 'Every Candidate: Miss Polonia 1930' (January 1930)
Kurjer Warszawski
 notice of Jerzy Skarbek's death (12.12.1930)
Newsweek Poland
 Dariusz Baliszewski, 'The Mystery of Dr Z: Who was Stefan Witkowski?'
 (no date)
Polish Week
 Tadeusz Stachowski, 'This would make a great movie!' (16.12.2000)
 ———, Mieczysława Wazacz, 'Heroes of Dangerous Adventures' (30.12.2000)
Publicystyka
 Zbigniew Cyran, 'Zakopanski Bristol – znany I nieznany' ('Bristol
 Zakopane – the known and unknown') (February 2010)
Rzeczpospolita
 Tomasz Lenczewski, '*Mariaze herbów i kont*' ('The Marriage of Coats of
 Arms and Accounts'), 22 VII (2008)
Tydzien Polski (*Polish Week*)
 Henryk Koaratynski, Mieczysława Wazacz interview (26.2.2005)
Unknown publication
 Karol Zbyszewski, 'Slawna Agentka' (Famous Agent) (18.10.1975)

BRITISH FILM/TV/RADIO

BBC Radio Four, *Women's Hour*, Madeleine Masson interview (29.12.2004)
Darlow Smithson Productions/Channel Four/Martyn Cox, *The Real Charlotte Grays* (2008), Francis Cammaerts interview
Martyn Cox/*Our Secret War* interviews, Paddy Sproule and Leslie Fernandez
RAF Film Production Unit, *Now it Can Be Told* (1946)
Mieczysława Wazacz (dir.), *No Ordinary Countess* (2010)
Yesterday Channel, *The Secret War: Christine Granville, Polish Spy*, Francis Cammaerts interview (27.6.2011)

FRENCH FILM

Association pour des Etudes sur la Résistance Intérieure, *La Résistance dans la Drôme – le Vercors* (2007)
Reymond Tonneau (dir.), *Vercors: Pays de la Liberté (Vercors: Land of Liberty)* (nd)
Jean-Paul le Chanois (dir.), *Au Coeur de l'Orage (At The Heart of the Storm)* (1948)
Laurent Lutaud (dir.), *Le Plateau Déchiré: Maquis de Vercors (The Torn Plateau)* (nd)

POLISH FILM

Andrzej Wajda, *Kanal* (1957)

MEMOIRS AND RECOLLECTIONS
(Published and unpublished)

BRITISH

Julian Amery, *Approach March: a venture in autobiography* (1973)
Ann Bridge, *Facts and Fictions* (1968)
Maurice Buckmaster, *Specially Employed: The Story of British Aid to French Patriots of the Resistance* (1952)
Sir Adrian Carton de Wiart, *Happy Odyssey: The Memoirs of Sir Adrian Carton de Wiart, VC, KBE, CB, CMG, DSO* (1950)
Marek Celt, *By Parachute to Warsaw* (1945)
Winston Churchill, *The Second World War: III, The Grand Alliance* (1956)
Ben Cowburn, *No Cloak, No Dagger: Allied Spycraft in Occupied France* (2009)
Aidan Crawley, *Leap Before You Look: A Memoir* (1988)
Basil Davidson, *Special Operations Europe: Scenes from the Anti-Nazi War* (1980)
Sefton Delmer, *Black Boomerang: An Autobiography*, vol. 2 (1962)
Douglas Dodds-Parker, *Setting Europe Ablaze: Some Account of Ungentlemanly Warfare* (1983)
Daphne Fielding, *The Nearest Way Home* (1970)
Xan Fielding, *Hide and Seek: The Story of a War-Time Agent* (1954)

Jerzy Gizycki, 'The Winding Trail', unpublished memoir (nd)
Witold Gombrowicz, *Polish Memories* (2004)
Patrick Howarth (ed.), *Special Operations* (1955)
Michael Joseph, *Charles: The Story of a Friendship* (1943)
Peter Kemp, *No Colours or Crest* (1958)
Wladimir Ledóchowski, 'Christine Skarbek-Granville: A Biographical Story', draft manuscript (nd)
———, *The Diary Abandoned in Ankara* (1990)
Leo Marks, *Between Silk and Cyanide: A Codemaker's War 1941–1945* (2000)
Zbigniew Mieczkowski, *Horizons: Reflections of a Polish Émigré* (2008)
———, 'Poland in the Battle for Freedom – World War II' (Lecture, Polish Embassy, Paris, 2008)
George Millar, *Maquis* (1946)
Nigel Nicholson (ed.), *Harold Nicholson: Diaries and Letters 1930–39* (1966)
Sir Owen O'Malley, *The Phantom Caravan* (1954)
———, *Katyn: Despatches of Sir Owen O'Malley to the British Government, etc.* (1972)
Margaret Pawley, *In Obedience to Instructions* (1999)
Laura Pope, 'Remembering Richard', unpublished memoir (2005)
Ivor Porter, *Operation Autonomous: With SOE in Wartime Romania* (1989)
Bickham Sweet-Escott, *Baker Street Irregular* (1965)
Wilfred Thesiger, *The Life of My Choice* (1987)
Lord Vansittart, *The Mist Procession: The Autobiography of Lord Vansittart* (1958)
Peter Wilkinson, *Foreign Fields: The Story of an SOE Operative* (2002)

FRENCH*

Jeanne Barbier, *Here, once, there was a French village* (2005)
L'Abbé Fernand Gagnol, *The Martyrs of Vercors* (nd)
Daniel Huillier, *Vercors: The Resistance, A teenager's memories* (2001)
Paul Jansen, *Les Photos de Macrel Jansen, Reporter au Maquis* (nd)

POLISH[†]

Tadeusz Breza, *Nelly: About Her Friends and Herself* (1983)
———, *Memories* (2002)
Regina Domańska, *Pawiak: Gestapo Prison, Chronicle 1939–1944* (1978)
Arkardy Fiedler, *The Women of My Youth* (1989)
Józef Kasparek, *The Carpathian Bridge: a Covert Polish Intelligence Operation* (1992)

* Unless otherwise stated, all French sources privately translated by Albertine Sharples.

† Unless otherwise stated, all Polish sources privately translated by Maciek and Iwona Helfer.

Kazimierz Leski, *A Checkered Life: Memoirs of a Home Army Intelligence and Counter-Intelligence Officer* (1995)
Stanisław Mackiewicz, *Two Ladies Die After Talking to Me* (1972)
Rafał Malczewski, *Navel of the World: Memories of Zakopane* (2003)
Anna Potocka, *Through Hills and Valleys . . .* (2011)

SECONDARY SOURCE PUBLICATIONS

BRITISH

Alan Allport, *Demobbed: Coming Home After the Second World War* (2009)
Christopher Andrew, *The Defence of the Realm: The Authorised History of MI5* (2009)
Roderick Bailey, *Forgotten Voices of the Secret War: An Inside History of Special Operations During the Second World War* (2008)
Jeffrey Bines, *Operation Freston: The Military Mission to Poland, 1944* (1999)
———, *The Polish Country Section of the SOE 1940–46: A British Perspective* (2008)
Marcus Binney, *The Women Who Lived for Danger: The Women Agents of SOE in the Second World War* (2002)
Maurice Buckmaster, *They Fought Alone: The Story of British Agents in France* (1958)
E. H. Cookridge, *They Came from the Sky* (1976)
Artemis Cooper, *Cairo in the War, 1939–1945* (1989)
Norman Davies, *God's Playground: A History of Poland in Two Volumes*, vol. 2, *1979 to the Present* (1981)
———, *Rising '44: The Battle for Warsaw* (2004)
Richard Deacon (Donald McCormick), *A History of the British Secret Service* (1980)
———, *Spyclopaedia: The Comprehensive Handbook of Espionage* (1988)
Jeremy Duns, 'Licence to Hoax', jeremyduns.blogspot.com (2011)
David Engel, *Facing a Holocaust: The Polish government-in-exile and the Jews, 1943–1945* (1993)
Beryl E. Escott, *Mission Improbable: A Salute to the RAF women in wartime France* (1991)
———, *Heroines of SOE F Section: Britain's Secret Women in France* (2010)
Louis Fitzgibbon, *Katyn Massacre: A Searing Indictment of the Shameful Concealment of Mass Murder* (1989)
Ian Fleming, *The Diamond Smugglers* (1965)
M. R. D. Foot, *SOE in France* (1968)
———, *SOE: An Outline History of the Special Operations Executive 1940–1946* (1999)
Arthur Layton Funk, *Hidden Ally: The French Resistance, Special Operations, and the Landings in Southern France, 1944* (1992)

Jozef Garlinski, *Poland, SOE and the Allies* (1969)

John Griswold, *Ian Fleming's James Bond: Annotations and Chronologies for Ian Fleming's Bond Stories* (2006)

Sarah Helm, *A Life in Secrets: The Story of Vera Atkins and the Lost Agents of SOE* (2008)

Patrick Howarth, *Undercover: The Women and Men of the SOE* (1990)

Ray Jenkins, *A Pacifist at War: The Life of Francis Cammaerts: The Silence of Francis Cammaerts* (2009)

Christopher Kasparek, 'Krystyna Skarbek', unpublished manuscript (2011)

Jan Leociak, *Text in the Face of Destruction: Accounts from the Warsaw Ghetto Reconsidered* (2004)

Andrew Lycett, *Ian Fleming* (1995)

Donald McCormick, *17F: The Life of Ian Fleming* (1993)

Ben Macintyre, *For Your Eyes Only: Ian Fleming and James Bond* (2008)

William J. M. Mackenzie, *The Secret History of SOE: The Special Operations Executive, 1940–1945* (2000)

Madeleine Masson, *Christine: A Search for Christine Granville* (1975)

——, *Christine: SOE Agent and Churchill's Favourite Spy* (2005)

Roger Moorhouse, *Killing Hitler: The Third Reich and the Plots Against the Führer* (2006)

William Stanley Moss, *Gold Is Where You Find It: What Happened to the Reichsbank Treasure?* (1956)

Ron Nowicki, *Warsaw: The Cabaret Years* (1992)

Jonathan Oates, *Unsolved London Murders: The 1940s and 1950s* (2009)

Lynne Olson and Stanley Cloud, *For Your Freedom and Ours: The Kościuszko Squadron: Forgotten Heroes of World War Two* (2003)

Michael Pearson, *Tears of Glory: The Betrayal of Vercors 1944* (1978)

M. A. Peszke, *The Polish Underground Army, The Western Allies, and the Failure of Strategic Unity in World War Two* (2005)

Anthony Read and David Fisher, *Colonel Z: The Secret Life of a Master of Spies* (1984)

Mark Seaman (ed.), *Special Operations Executive: A New Instrument of War* (2006)

Victor Selwyn (ed.), *From Oasis Into Italy: War Poems and Diaries from Africa and Italy, 1940–1946* (1983)

Kurt Singer, *Spies and Traitors: A Short History of Espionage* (1953)

Timothy Snyder, *Sketches from a Secret War* (2007)

Peter D. Stachura (ed.), *The Poles in Britain 1940–2000: From Betrayal to Assimilation* (2004)

David Stafford, *Secret Agent: The True Story of the Special Operations Executive* (2000)

——, *Churchill and the Secret Service* (2001)

——, 'The Tragedy of Christine Granville', unpublished book proposal (*c.*2000)

David Stahel, *Operation Barbarossa and Germany's Defeat in the East* (2009)

Teresa Stirling, Daria Nałęcz, Tadeusz Dubiki (eds), *Intelligence Co-operation Between Poland and Great Britain during World War Two: The Report of the Anglo-Polish Historical Committee*, vol. 1
Andrew Tarnowski, *The Last Mazurka: A Tale of War, Passion and Loss* (2006)
Jedrzej Tucholski, *Cichociemni 1941–1945: profiles of paratroopers* (1984)
Jonathan Walker, *Poland Alone: Britain, SOE and the Collapse of the Polish Resistance, 1944* (2010)
Peter Wilkinson and Joan Bright Astley, *Gubbins and SOE* (1997)
Heather Williams, *Parachutes, Patriots and Partisans: The Special Operations Executive and Yugoslavia, 1941–1945* (2003)
Adam Zamoyski, *Chopin: A Biography* (1981)
———, *Poland: A History* (2009)
———, *The Forgotten Few: The Polish Air Force in World War II* (2009)

Polish

Roman Buczek, *The Musketeers* (*Muszkieterowie*, 1985), translated privately by Christopher Kasparek, 2011
Jadwiga Karbowska, *Getting to know Mackiewicz* (nd)
Jan Larecki, *Krystyna Skarbek: Agent with Many Faces* (2008), translated privately by Jan Ledóchowski, 2011
The Polish Dictionary of National Biography, vol. 18 (1973)

FICTION

Ann Bridge, *A Place to Stand* (1955)
———, *The Tightening String* (1962)*
Ian Fleming, *Casino Royale* (1952)
Gavin Lyall, *Midnight Plus One* (1966)†
Olivia Manning, *The Levant Trilogy* (2003)‡
Maria Nurowska, *Miłośnica* (1999)§

* Bridge built her novels around her experiences as Sir Owen O'Malley's wife. *The Tightening String* describes the start of the war in Hungary, *A Place to Stand* is based on Christine and Andrzej's time in Hungary, and was first drafted by Bridge's daughter, Kate O'Malley.

† The fictional Ginette, Countess de Maris, in Lyall's *Midnight Plus One*, is based on Sylviane Rey.

‡ Manning used her life in Cairo during the war to inform her Levant Trilogy of novels.

§ Nurowska's Polish novel about Christine was informed by her father's memories; Wladimir Ledóchowski's unpublished manuscript; and interviews with Christine's post-war London friends.

WEBSITES

BBC WW2 People's War, 'Aniseed Balls and the Limpet Mine', A4376153
(6.7.2005) http://www.bbc.co.uk/ww2peopleswar/stories/53/
a4376153.shtml

Museum of the History of Polish Jews, 'Historical Monuments, Places of
Martyrdom, Pawiak' www.szetl.org.pl/en/city/warszawa/

SS Maritime.com, 'Ruahine: The New Zealand Shipping Company', ship's
brochure (1950s) http://www.ssmaritime.com

Picture Credits

1: Copyright © Clare Mulley. 2: Copyright © Tomasz Lenczewski. 3: By courtesy of Maryś Skarbek. 4: © *Express Poranny*. 5: Courtesy of Maria Pienkowska. 6: By courtesy of Countess Jolanta Mycielska, photograph by Mieczysława Wazacz (director) *No Ordinary Countess*, 2010. 7, 19: By courtesy of the author. 8: Special Forces Roll of Honour, www.specialforcesroh.com. 9: By courtesy of Count Jan Ledóchowski. 10, 11, 13, 17, 18, 20, 28, 33, 34: By courtesy of Christine Isabelle Cole, Bill Stanley Moss Papers. 12: © National Portrait Gallery, London. 14: By courtesy of Ivor Porter. 15: By courtesy of Michael Ward. 16: By courtesy of Diana Hall, Professor Richard Truszkowski Papers. 21: © The National Archives, ref HS16/1. 22: The Polish Institute and Sikorski Museum, London © Clare Mulley. 23: Getty Images. 24, 29: By kind permission of The Special Forces Club. 25: Marcel Jansen, *Reporter au Maquis*, Peuple Libre, 1994. 26: By permission of The Imperial War Museum, ref HU57101. 27: By permission of The Imperial War Museum, ref HU57120. 30: akg-images/ullstein bild. 31: akg-images/Electa. 32: The National Archives, ref HS9/612. 35: The National Archives, ref BT372/1138/116. 36: By courtesy of Maryś Skarbek and by kind permission of the Polish Institute and Sikorski Museum, London, photograph © Clare Mulley. 37, 38: By courtesy of Christine Isabelle Cole, Bill Stanley Moss Papers/*Picture Post*. 39: The Polish Institute and Sikorski Museum, London.

Index

THE SPY WHO LOVED

by Clare Mulley

Reading Group Gold

About the Author

- A Conversation with Clare Mulley

Behind the Book

- A Selection of Photographs

Keep on Reading

- Recommended Reading
- Reading Group Questions

A Reading Group Gold Selection

For more reading group suggestions,
visit www.readinggroupgold.com.

 ST. MARTIN'S GRIFFIN

📖 A Conversation with Clare Mulley

Could you tell us a little bit about your background, and when you decided that you wanted to lead a literary life?

If "leading a literary life" involves owning a walnut writing table and permanently ink-stained fingers then it is something I aspired to romantically as a teenager, but have sadly yet to achieve. I only started writing in my thirties, while on maternity leave from my job as a fundraiser at Save the Children. By then I think I was motivated mainly by sheer nosiness about the extraordinary woman who founded the charity at the end of the First World War. I knew she did not really like individual children (she once referred to them as "little wretches") and I was intrigued by this apparent irony. I also liked the idea of spending some of my maternity leave investigating this least maternal of children's champions, and I thought I might as well knock out an article before my own first child arrived. Seven years, several jobs, and three children later, after a long and hard labor, I delivered my first book: *The Woman Who Saved the Children: A Biography of Eglantyne Jebb, Founder of Save the Children.* Fortunately it won a prize and partly on the back of that I have been writing ever since.

When did you first learn about Christine Granville? What was it about her and her life that inspired you to write a full-length book about her?

Actually I had not heard of Krystyna Skarbek, aka Christine Granville, until my agent suggested that she might make a good next subject. I immediately rejected the idea—I wanted to find my

"Like most people who got to know Christine, I was soon fascinated by her."

own subject, and this felt rather like a blind date...
Like most people who got to know Christine, I
was soon fascinated by her. But Christine's story
appeals to me for other reasons, too. It provides
a remarkable insight into the use and abuse of
Poland during the Second World War and, I
hope, presents a more balanced view on the effec-
tiveness of female special agents. Women in the
resistance have been all too often dismissed as
courageous, and perhaps beautiful, but not really
quite up to the job. Christine's story certainly
puts the record straight.

**Can you take readers into the process of writing
The Spy Who Loved. What challenges did you
face in terms of research, for example?**

I love researching the truth—or perhaps I should
say the many truths—of someone, in the files of
public archives, or between the lines of private
letters. But researching the life of a special agent
contains inherent difficulties. Many of the papers
relating to Christine have been destroyed by acci-
dent or on purpose, and in any case agents were
trained not to leave a paper trail. When I started
my research there were only three known letters
written by Christine. I was lucky enough to find
many more in various private collections, but even
then the stories often didn't add up with what I
knew to be the facts. It turned out that Christine
loved to spin a good yarn, but even tall stories can
hold important moral or emotional truths....

In an attempt to try to distinguish fact from
fiction, emotion from deliberate disinformation,
I decided to visit the places Christine had known,
doing what Antonia Fraser calls optical research.

Reading
Group
Gold

*About the
Author*

*"Each
generation
should
revisit
the stories
from the
past."*

In Poland, I found Christine's baptism certificate
in a small parish archive. I visited her childhood
home, and talked to people she had known, or
whose parents had known her. In Warsaw I stayed
in a beautiful apartment in the reconstructed old
city, belonging to the son of one of Christine's
lovers. Walking out the door one morning I was
abruptly challenged by a Wehrmacht officer in full
uniform, toting a gun towards me. It was absolute-
ly terrifying. It turned out that I had accidentally
walked into the filming of a Polish World War II
TV drama! But even this taught me something:
I knew there must be some rational explana-
tion for this apparent time warp, and yet I found
myself frozen to the spot, almost unable to speak.
Christine, a British special agent who was herself
part-Jewish, was arrested behind Nazi lines several
times during the war but always kept her cool,
remembered her cover story, and talked herself
and sometimes her colleagues out of danger. What
extraordinary blunt courage she had!

**Do you feel you know Christine now, having told
her story?**

I do feel I have a good measure of this coura-
geous, passionate, and rather difficult woman but
I would not claim to have nailed her completely.
I don't really believe in "definitive" biographies.
Each generation should revisit the stories from the
past—biography is famously as much a mirror as
a window onto history—and everyone is open to
multiple interpretations anyhow. But that aside,
Christine was passionate above all about her free-
dom. I respect that, and would not want to dimin-
ish her by claiming to know every secret. Having
said all of which, love her or loathe her, Christine

Reading
Group
Gold

always provoked a strong response. Someone like this can't help but leave a powerful impression behind them so, yes, I feel I know what made her tick.

Are you currently working on another book? And if so, what—or who—is your subject?

Christine was always a hard act to follow, and it's no different for her biographer. However, I am delighted to have found an absolutely fascinating new subject—two extraordinary women whose intertwined stories provide another remarkable insight into the war. I am completely absorbed in it.

*About the
Author*

Christine in Syria, 1942.
Source of photo still unknown

A memorial to the women of SOE at RAF Tempsford, opened b
HRH The Prince of Wales in 2013. Christine is listed among th
honorees.

Pawel Julian Komorowski

Reading
Group
Gold

ACCUSED KILLER Muldowney (*center*) is led off by police.

Dennis Muldowney in police custody, 1952.
From the Picture Post *July 7, 1952*

Behind the
Book

Christine's cousins, Jan and Andrzej Skarbek, with friends.
Courtesy of Countess Maryś Skarbek, London

Christine in Budapest, 1940.
*Courtesy of Christine Isabelle Cole/Bill Stanley Moss private papers, Britain
(intended for the Polish Institute and Sikorski Museum)*

Mulley lays red and white flowers, the colors of Poland, on
Christine's grave at a service of thanksgiving. Kensal Green
Roman Catholic Cemetery, May 10, 2013.

Courtesy of the Republic of Poland.

Wladimir Ledóchowski, 1942.
Courtesy of Jan Ledóchowski

 # Recommended Reading

<u>Nonfiction</u>

Undercover by Patrick Howarth
Hide and Seek by Xan Fielding
Evocative SOE war memoirs from two men who
trained and served alongside Christine. Howarth
was inspired to write poetry about her, and
Fielding, whose life Christine saved, dedicated his
book "to the memory of Christine Granville."

Rising '44 by Norman Davies
Davies's masterful and deeply compassionate
account of the uprising of the people of Warsaw
against their Nazi occupiers. I imagine Christine,
then stuck in Italy, weeping over the radio reports,
and cursing to hell that she could not join the battle
and fight directly for the freedom of her homeland.

**A Life in Secrets: The Story of Vera Atkins and the
Lost Agents of SOE** by Sarah Helm
Fascinating account of the secret life of SOE
French Section coordinator Vera Atkins, and her
courageous postwar investigation into the fate
of the British female agents who went missing in
action. Vera described Christine as "very brave, very
attractive, but a loner and a law unto
herself."

Between Silk and Cyanide by Leo Marks
The brilliant memoirs of Britain's leading cryptog-
rapher who learned coding at his father's bookshop,
the famed 84 Charing Cross Road, and spent his
war with SOE where he trained Violette Szabo
among so many other brave agents. Irreverent,
funny, poignant—this is one of my favorite war
memoirs. I wish I'd met him.

She Landed by Moonlight by Carole Seymour-Jones
A new biography of Pearl Witherington, one of
the greatest female agents who, when given civil-
ian rather than military honors because she was a
woman, scorned that "there was nothing civil about
what I did." There are many other biographies of
courageous female agents worth reading by Susan
Ottaway, Shrabani Basu, and others.

Novels

A Place to Stand by Ann Bridge
Written with her daughter, Kate O'Malley, this
wonderfully evocative novel is loosely based on
Kate, Christine, and Andrzej's time together in
Budapest in 1940.

Trapeze by Simon Mawer
A well-researched tale of a British female agent
dropped into Nazi-occupied France, slightly
less romanticized than Sebastian Faulks's *Charlotte
Gray*.

The Spies of Warsaw by Alan Furst
A compelling thriller set in Poland in 1937. Could
the beautiful and courageous Anna Szarbek have
been partially inspired by Krystyna Skarbek, as
Christine was known in Warsaw at that time?

Reading Group Questions

1. First, a show of hands: Who among you ever heard of Christine Granville before reading this book?

2. What did you know about female SOE agents—either from your own studies or interests, or as portrayed in popular film/television adaptations—before reading *The Spy Who Loved*? How, if at all, did this book teach you about, or change your impression of, this particular wartime practice?

3. What literary techniques did Clare Mulley use to tell her story? Do you feel you know Christine now that you've read about her? What do you wish you could know about her beyond the world of the book?

4. The author wrote that Christine "lived boundlessly, as generous as she could be cruel." What do you think were Christine's greatest strengths, and what were her weaknesses?

5. What do you think Christine would have done with her life if the Second World War had not taken place? What do you think she would have gone on to do with the rest of her life, were it not for her untimely death?

6. Take a moment to talk about other well-known books—biographies or novels—set during the Second World War. What are some of your favorites books, and why? Who are some of the most memorable characters—real or fictional?

Reading
Group
Gold

7. Why *do* modern readers enjoy books about a particular period in history? How can Christine's story inform us about the world we live in today?

8. We are taught, as young readers, that every story has a "moral." Is there a moral to *The Spy Who Loved*? What can we learn about our lives—and ourselves—from Christine's story?

Keep
on
Reading

To learn more about Clare Mulley, her books, and special offers, visit www.ClareMulley.com or become a fan on Facebook or Twitter!

For more perfect picks and reading group guides for your book club, visit ReadingGroupGold.com.